Cristoforo Buondelmonti

DESCRIPTION OF THE AEGEAN AND OTHER ISLANDS

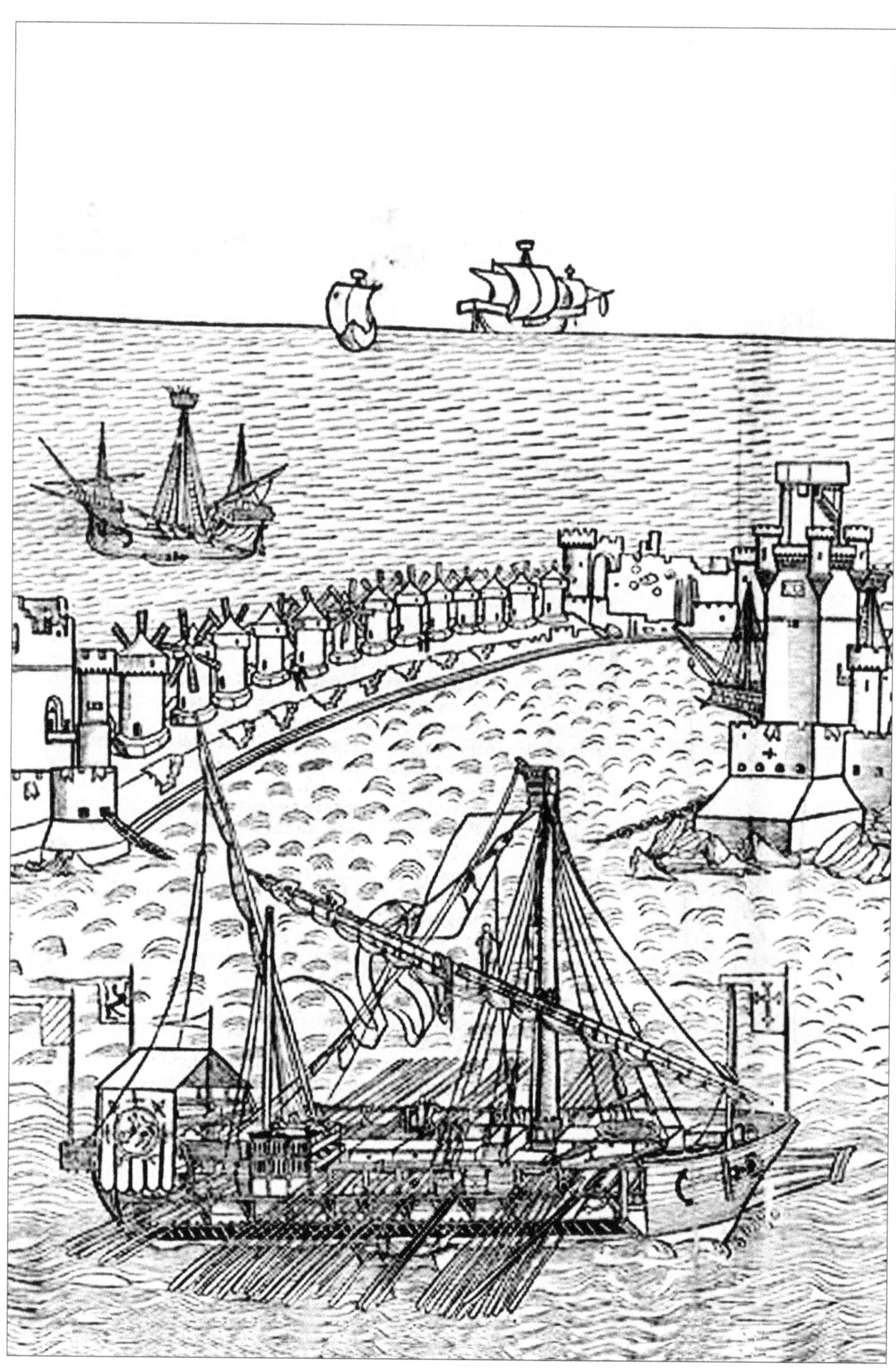

Cristoforo Buondelmonti

DESCRIPTION OF THE AEGEAN AND OTHER ISLANDS

Copied, with supplemental material,
by Henricus Martellus Germanus

A Facsimile of the Manuscript
at the James Ford Bell Library
University of Minnesota

Edited and Translated
by Evelyn Edson

ITALICA PRESS
NEW YORK
2018

ITALICA PRESS, INC.
595 Main Street, Suite 605
New York, New York 10044
inquiries@italicapress.com

Library of Congress Cataloging-in-Publication Data

Names: Buondelmonti, Cristoforo, approximately 1385-approximately 1430, author. | Germanus, Henricus Martellus, transcriber. | Edson, Evelyn, editor, translator. | James Ford Bell Library.
Title: Description of the Aegean and other islands / Cristoforo Buondelmonti ; copied by Henricus Martellus Germanus ; edited and translated by Evelyn Edson.
Other titles: Descriptio Arcipelagi et Cicladum Aliarumque Insularum. English
Description: New York : Italica Press, 2017. | Series: Italica Press historical travel series | Includes bibliographical references and index.
Identifiers: LCCN 2017021052 | ISBN 9781599103648 (hardcover : alk. paper)
Subjects: LCSH: Buondelmonti, Cristoforo, approximately 1385-approximately 1430--Travel--Aegean Islands (Greece and Turkey) | Aegean Islands (Greece and Turkey)--Description and travel--Early works to 1800 | Aegean Sea Region--Description and travel--Early works to 1800 | Aegean Islands (Greece and Turkey)--History--Sources. | Aegean Sea Region--History--Sources.
Classification: LCC DF895 .B8513 2017 | DDC 949.5/8--dc23
LC record available at https://lccn.loc.gov/2017021052

Cover illustration: The Duchy of Athens and Euboea (Negroponte). Minneapolis, MN, James Ford Bell Library, University of Minnesota, MS 1475_ fMa., fol. 37v.

For a Complete List of Titles in Historical Travel
Please visit our Website at:
http://www.italicapress.com/index004.html

CONTENTS

ILLUSTRATIONS

CONTENTS OF THE BELL MANUSCRIPT
(Between pages 18 and 19)

PREFACE

It was with great pleasure that we collaborate with Evelyn Edson and Italica Press on this wonderful volume. Our manuscript of Henricus Martellus' copy of Cristoforo Buondelmonti's *Liber insularum* is one of the most popular items in James Ford Bell Library's collection. It offers a glimpse of decoration and illumination in the medieval tradition, charming and idiosyncratic descriptions of the Aegean Islands, along with wonderful hand-colored drawings of each island. The hand is legible, even if one cannot read the Latin text, a difficulty that this volume resolves. I also would like to take this opportunity to thank the National Endowment for the Humanities for funding a project that digitized all of the maps in our book collection, among them the images you will find in this volume.

James Ford Bell once referred to rare books like this one as "bound fragments of time." In founding the James Ford Bell Library at the University of Minnesota, he and the University's regents were determined that the materials in the library would benefit everyone, both the university and the local community.

The James Ford Bell Library's focus is international trade and cross-cultural contact prior to c.1800 CE. Over the years, since our founding in 1953, we have collected a variety of materials — from rare books, both print and manuscript, to maps and archival collections — that help us to understand our deep connections to a collective past and the foundations of the globalization we are now experiencing. The Greek islands of the Aegean Sea were once the center of Western civilization, yet they did not exist in isolation. They engaged in trade with their neighbors throughout the Mediterranean Sea and beyond. Their cross-cultural experiences informed the cultural practices and beliefs that later were spread throughout the Mediterranean basin and on into Europe by the Romans and their successors. Trade brings contact, and with contact comes change, whether welcomed and embraced or rejected and scorned.

Buondelmonti was from Florence, the heart of the Italian Renaissance, and this work reflects Europe's burgeoning interest in its classical heritage. While we now have a global reach, thanks, in part, to our now digital age, there is something very personal, very intimate about holding a book in one's hands. Although experiencing the vellum-bound original is a unique experience, this volume provides a service that broadens the accessibility of the manuscript: it includes Prof. Edson's English translation. It is my hope that readers of this new English translation will appreciate this unique fifteenth-century view of the Aegean islands from a traveler's perspective and accept this as a gift from the past.

Dr. Marguerite Ragnow
Curator, James Ford Bell Library

ACKNOWLEDGEMENTS

Having now spent nearly as much time on this book as Cristoforo did on his journey, I have many scholars, librarians, and friends to thank for their intelligent assistance. First, the James Ford Bell Library at the University of Minnesota was a gracious host on several occasions where I moved in to live with their beautiful manuscript. The chief curator, Margaret Ragnow, and Margaret Borg, assistant curator, were unfailingly helpful despite their busy schedules and such library dramas as roof repair and, currently, the total moving of Special Collections. I was also indebted to the library for a short-term Bell Research Fellowship.

My debt to the scholars who preceded me include Hilary L. Turner, Claudia Barsanti, Nathalie Bouloux, Angelo Cattaneo, and the editorial team at the University of Düsseldorf. Tony Campbell was my resource for information about the mysterious and troublesome portolan charts. Chet van Duzer, whose book on the Yale Martellus will be out soon, was extremely helpful on many occasions. I also thank Bert Johnson, informed by his extensive travels in Greece and its islands, and the other members of the Washington Map Society. Manuscript librarians in Greenwich, Florence, London, Paris, Norfolk, Baltimore, Ann Arbor, Chantilly, Leiden, New Haven, and at the Library of Congress were hospitable and informative.

Two years ago I decided to follow in Buondelmonti's wake on a tour sponsored by the Archaeological Institute of America, visiting Istanbul, Crete, Rhodes, and Delos in the company of Betsy Woodard, an excellent traveling companion. Constant encouragement came from my Thursday medieval Latin reading group: David Larrick, Marvin Colker, Matt Clay, and Andrew Levisay, who are always eager to correct my grammar. As always, I owe a great debt to my family: my husband, Andy Wilson, and my fellow communards, Tom and Toots Klippstein, for their kindly interest in this seemingly interminable project. Lastly, thanks to Italica Press for publishing this book in style, with the truly worthy reproduction of the facsimile of the manuscript.

Evelyn Edson,
Scottsville, Virginia

INTRODUCTION

One of the treasures in the James Ford Bell collection at the University of Minnesota is Henricus Martellus Germanus' copy of Cristoforo Buondelmonti's *Descriptio Archipelagi et Cicladum aliarumque Insularum (Description of the Archipelago, the Cyclades, and the Other Islands)*.[1] The original work was written in 1420, and Henricus's copy dates from later in the century, perhaps 1475.[2] Buondelmonti's original book was an account of the Greek islands, illustrated with maps, beginning at Corfu, then going down the western coast of Greece and into the Aegean Sea. In his version Henricus added maps and text for five new islands. The manuscript is in magnificent shape — the writing is clear, legible humanistic script, and the maps which accompany each entry are in vivid color.

Cristoforo Buondelmonti

Buondelmonti (c.1385–c.1430), a priest and a member of a prominent Florentine family, had begun traveling in the Aegean in 1415, starting on the island of Crete. He had left home on a mission — to find Greek manuscripts for the humanist scholars in Florentine circles, among them Niccolò Niccoli. He bought two manuscripts on Crete,[3] but he also found himself captivated by the picturesque and historic islands of the Aegean world, and undertook a lengthy tour of Crete, first sailing around it, and then crossing it from east to west on horseback. He marveled and mourned at the ruins of antiquity, got briefly captured by bandits, and listened to bitter complaints against Venetian rule. He wrote up his adventures and observations and sent them to Niccolò.[4]

But this was not to be the end of his travels. Over the next dozen years, he traversed the Greek seas, going from island to island, writing up a descriptive text about each, and drawing a map. The first version of the manuscript, completed in 1420, was dedicated to the wealthy bibliophile, Cardinal Giordano Orsini, who was also interested in maps, and had an early copy of Ptolemy made for his library.

There had been other island books and lists of islands. From the Roman author Pliny, in his *Natural History,* to Isidore's *Etymologies* (c.630 CE) and on, a list of islands, sometimes

1. For a complete codicological description, see below, 12–13.

2. The Minnesota manuscript (1475 fmA) is not dated or signed. A reference to the Turkish conquest of Negroponte (Euboea) suggests that it was copied after 1470. The only work devoted to this manuscript is R.F. Hage, "The Island Book of Henricus Martellus," *The Portolan* 56 (Spring 2003): 7–23.

3. Six of seven manuscripts now in the Biblioteca Medicaea Laurenziana from Niccolò's library are thought to be those purchased by Buondelmonti. Claudia Barsanti, "Costantinopoli e l'Egeo nei primi decenni del XV secolo: La testimonianza di Cristoforo Buondelmonti," *Rivista dell'Istituto Nazionale d'Archeologia e storia dell'arte (RIASA)* 56 (2001): 83–254, esp. 102.

4. Cristoforo Buondelmonti, *Descriptio Insule Crete,* Marie-Anne van Spitael, ed. (Herakleion: Syllogos politistikes anaptyxeos Herakleiou, 1981). The original manuscript probably contained a map, but it does not survive.

with a brief descriptive tag for each, had been part of many geographical works, though none of these were accompanied by maps. In (1406) Domenico Silvestri had written *De Insulis et earum Proprietatibus,* a catalog of 900 islands from all over the world, both real and imaginary, arranged alphabetically.[5] Much of his material was from classical literature. He complained about conflicts between his sources. For example, in Cytharea, he notes that some authors say it is five miles from the Peloponnesian coast; others say fifty, a discrepancy which could have been solved easily on the spot.[6] While Buondelmonti may have been acquainted with Silvestri's work — some of the anecdotal material is identical — the approach in his book was different. First, it was about the islands of the contemporary world, islands that he had landed upon or, at least, sailed around. Second, Buondelmonti was a real traveler, not assembling his material in a library, and his islands were presented in more or less traveling, not alphabetical, order. One can follow his somewhat circuitous itinerary, although necessarily there is some backtracking. He added entries on Gallipoli, Constantinople, and Mt. Athos into his book. They were not islands, but he found them so interesting that he could not omit them.[7]

Maps were undergoing a number of changes in the fifteenth century. The introduction of Ptolemy's *Geographia* into Florence around 1400 introduced the concept of location by astronomical coordinates and showed maps divorced from theological content. Ptolemy's work was surely known to Buondelmonti, as he moved in humanist circles, but he makes only one reference to him, and does not make use of his coordinate system.[8] The sea chart, originally designed for the use of merchants and sea captains, began to have an impact on other maps, such as world maps. Ideas of measurement and direction, found in the portolans, or written sailing directions, began to be represented graphically with careful delineation of coastlines, the naming of harbors, and the indication of hazards, such as sandbars. Buondelmonti's maps, which he seems to have drawn himself, may have used nautical charts as a base, but they were larger and more detailed, and included features of the interior, whereas sea charts were limited to places on the coast. Buondelmonti's maps are a unique production, being the first stand-alone maps of most of the islands. They are a valuable record. For example, the map of Constantinople shows the city before the Turkish conquest in 1453 that caused its landscape to be irretrievably altered. Some

5. José Manuel Montesdeoca Medina, ed., *Los isolarios de la epoca del humanismo: El* De Insulis *de Domenico Silvestri* (Santa Cruz de Tenerife: Universidad de la Laguna, 2004). For an academic account, see Marica Milanese, "Il *De insulis et earum proprietatibus* di Domenico Silvestri (1385–1406)," *Geographia Antiqua* 2 (1993): 133–46.

6. #218, Cytherea.

7. Buondelmonti did not provide a general map of his travels. See the modern map by Rick Britton on pp. 16–17.

8. The reference is in the chapter on Crete, where he says that Ptolemy had indicated the site of Jupiter's tomb, f. 8v.

manuscripts, copied later, such as that in Düsseldorf,[9] show changes in the city after 1453, but in the Minnesota manuscript Henricus uses a pre-conquest version. By this time many of the great churches had already been (or were soon to be) leveled, turned into mosques, or converted to other uses.

Buondelmonti's textual descriptions did not follow a set pattern, but included many of the same materials. First, he indicated the distance and direction from the previously described island: "Crossing in our boat to the east for 100 miles" from the island of Pachiso, we come to Lefkas (fol. 3v).[10] Then he included a measurement, usually the circumference of the island, but sometimes length and width. How the island came to have its name — the beloved and sometimes fanciful etymology of the medieval world — was next, as well as various names it had been called in the past.[11] He listed any prominent features, such as mountains, springs, good harbors, and noted whether the island was well-populated or deserted, and whether it had good harbors. In many places he found the extensive ruins of the classical past, and the maps show heaps of fallen columns. Like a good Florentine of a mercantile family, he made note of any resources, from fertile fields and water supplies to special resources, such as emery on Naxos and mastic, a highly-prized resin, on Chios.

Selecting many of his stories from Ovid, he retold myths connected to specific islands, such as the concealment of the infant Jupiter on Crete and the abandonment of Ariadne and her rescue by Bacchus on Naxos. He also chose some of the most notable Greek and Roman gods and gave a detailed physical description of them as portrayed in art, complete with attributes, followed by an allegorical interpretation. For example, Minerva (Carpathia, fol. 9v) is depicted as armed, which symbolizes the wise man, who is armed with virtue. Venus and the Three Graces (Cytharea, fol. 7v) got less respectful treatment. Though Venus was depicted as a beautiful nude girl, swimming in the sea with a conch shell in her hand, the Three Graces were taken to stand for three sins: avarice, carnality and infidelity, and were categorized as three whores. Allegorical interpretations dated back at least to Cicero and were refined by Christian authors such as Fulgentius and Buondelmonti's compatriot Boccaccio.[12] The primary source for Buondelmonti's

9. Universitäts und Landesbibliothek Düsseldorf, MS G 13 (1466). The map of Constantinople can be found in Cristoforo Buondelmonti, *Liber Insularum Archipelagi,* Irmgard Siebert and Max Plassman, ed. (Wiesbaden: Reichert Verlag, 2005), II, f. 54 of the facsimile.

10. The actual distance is more like 30 miles.

11. B. Gerola points out some of the errors in his derivation of island names, some based on his knowledge of contemporary spoken Greek and assuming it to be the same as the ancient language: "Le etimologie dei nomi di luogo in Cristoforo Buondelmonti," *Atti dei Reale Istituto Veneto di Scienze, Lettere ed Arti* 92 (1932–33): 1129–74.

12. Cicero, *De natura deorum,* H. Rackham, trans. (London: Heinemann, 1933); Leslie Whitbread, ed. and trans., *Fulgentius: the Mythographer* (Columbus: Ohio State University Press, 1971); Boccaccio, *Genealogy of the Pagan Gods,* Jon Solomon, ed. and trans. I Tatti Renaissance Library 46 (Cambridge, MA: Harvard University Press, 2011).

iconography was, however, the *Ovidius Moralizatus* (c.1342), by Pierre Bersuire.[13] This is a section of a longer work, the *Reductium Morale,* a "moralization" of all the available knowledge of the time. Book xv, on Ovid, contained a prologue, circulated separately, describing the gods and their attributes. This short work was immensely popular, surviving in more than sixty manuscripts. Buondelmonti mined it for his own purposes, but, unlike Bersuire, he described each of these images as a sculpture, not a painting, connected it with a specific island, and implied that these (certainly imaginary) works of art actually existed. He did not pursue the Christian analogies as far as Bersuire had but took most of his material from the beginning of each description. See below examples, such as Cybele on Melos (fol. 14v) or Bacchus on Naxos (fol. 20r). His descriptions were briefer than Bersuire's and were embedded in a general description of each island.

The historical events that he noted were mostly from ancient Rome, taken from Livy,[14] but occasionally he referred to medieval history (Robert Guiscard, d.1085, fol. 5r), or contemporary happenings, such as the meeting of the Council of Constance, 1414–18, (Astimphalaia, fol. 13r) and the war between Venice and Genoa (1378–81) which resulted in the depopulation of Tenedos (fol. 29r). He also noted various shipwrecks, an all-too-frequent event in the stormy and rocky Aegean.

A continuing theme was the current degradation of the islands, as the Byzantine Empire was declining in power, and the Turks were extending their sway, although in his section on Gallipoli he reported that, after the travails of conquest, the Turkish government ran things in an orderly fashion (fols. 29v-30r). Elsewhere Italian families from Genoa, Naples, Florence, and Venice still ruled, conducted trade in the Aegean, and fought among themselves. Buondelmonti himself had family connections in the Ionian Islands through the Tocci and Ajacciouoli families, and in the Aegean he may have served the duke of Naxos. Pirates were rampant, and on some islands the citizens had retreated to fortified castles in the highlands in order to avoid them (e.g., Nio, fol. 21r). In other cases the island had been abandoned completely (e.g., Raclea and Chero, fol. 21r).

As a good priest, Buondelmonti was admiring of the monastic communities he visited. In the Strophades, after giving a harrowing description of the voracious Harpies, who infested them in mythical times, he commented: "Now these islands have turned from evil to good," as the monks who live there subsist on dried fish, bread and water, "that each might render his soul pure to the Almighty" (fol. 6v). He was, unusual for his day,

13. Pierre Bersuire, *Metamorphosis Ovidiana Moraliter...Explanata,* reprinted from the Paris 1509 edition and introduced by Stephen Orgel (New York: Garland Publishing, 1979). See also James Joseph Foster, "A Preliminary Text of Pierre Bersuire's *Reductorium Morale*, Book Fifteen, Prologue" (Ph.D. diss., Duke University, 1967), which has an extensive and useful introduction. Thanks to Benedetta Bessi for this reference in her "Cristoforo Buondelmonti: Greek Antiquities in Florentine Humanism," *The Historical Review* 9 (2012): 63–76, esp. 74.

14. Or from the abridgment of Livy by Lucius Annaeus Florus, *Epitome of Roman History,* Edward S. Forster, trans., Loeb Classical Library (Cambridge, MA: Harvard University Press, 1929).

accepting of the practices of the Greek Orthodox Church, perhaps in light of ongoing negotiations for church unity with Rome. He waxed quite eloquent, for example, on the virtuous lives of the monks of Mt. Athos. The infidels, or Muslims, got bad press, especially when they took on the role of pirates and sold the inhabitants into slavery, though some Christians were shown to have done the same.

He included a few personal details: when he was shipwrecked and nearly died of starvation on the island of Fourni (fol. 27r), the giant octopus he saw in Santorini (fol. 13r), the grave of his aunt, Maddalena Buondelmonti on Iacinthus (Zante, fol. 5v), his experience of good weather on Rhodes (fol. 10v). He reported on superstitions and bizarre customs where he found them, such as the many amazing cures provided by the body parts of wild asses on Antikythera (Sichilus, fols. 7v–8r). There are a few miracles, such as the monk who had his eyes torn out by an eagle and restored by St. Elias (fol. 36v). He also added entertaining or morally uplifting anecdotes, such as the dialogue between Sextus Pompey and the old woman on Cea who wished to end her life. (fol. 16r) His work was embellished with active verbs of travel: "now we cross over," "our boat now makes its way," "we descend the slope," emphasizing his personal experience and lending authenticity to his account.

Did he personally visit every one of the eighty-nine islands he describes? Probably not. Some like Polimio and St. Elias are not much more than rocks, and on small islands like these our author is understandably brief. Approaching Cytharea, he said, "It seems superfluous to me to tell how many small rocky islets there are in these parts, for we found no outstanding deed in them to relate. So we shall be silent about them..." (fol. 7v).

At least three versions of the *Descriptio* were made in his life time, but almost immediately the variations begin. The original, sent to Orsini and willed by him to the Vatican Library, is long lost, probably since the sack of Rome in 1527. The second edition, is the most common, appearing in sixty-five manuscripts, and no two are exactly the same. Copyists felt free to edit, abridge, or add new material.[15] The stemma of the maps is clearly different from that of the texts. The Düsseldorf manuscript, for example, has a text close to that of Minnesota, but the maps are different. Even the stemma for individual maps could vary from the others in the same copy.[16] As is common in medieval manuscripts,

15. The stemma of Buondelmonti manuscripts is hotly disputed. For details, see Barsanti, "Costantinopoli," 160–63; Hilary L. Turner, "Chios and Christopher Buondelmonti's *Liber Insularum*," *Deltion* 30 (1987): 47–72; Giuseppe Ragone, "Il *Liber Insularum Archipelagi* di Cristoforo Buondelmonti," in *Humanisme et culture géographique à l'époque du Concile de Constance,* Didier Marcotte, ed. (Turnhout: Brepols, 2002), 177–217, esp. 199–204; Anthony Luttrell, "The Later History of the Maussolleion," *The Maussolleion at Halikarnassos* 15.2 (1986): 189–211, including a list of known manuscripts; and Gerola, "Le etimologie."

16. The maps of Constantinople are especially variable. See Ian R. Manners, "Constructing the Image of a City: The Representation of Constantinople in Christopher Buondelmonti's *Liber Insularum Archipelagi,*" *Annals of American Geographers* 87.1 (1997): 72-102.

blank spaces were sometimes left for illustrations, which were filled in at a later date by another hand. In the case of our manuscript in Minnesota, the maps seem to have been drawn first and the text squeezed into the available space, making for variations in the size of the writing.[17]

Henricus Martellus Germanus

Henricus Martellus Germanus, who produced the Minnesota manuscript, was a German living in Florence from 1448–96, where he was employed as a house intellectual by the wealthy and powerful Martelli family.[18] His original name was Heinrich Schlüsselfelder, and he was the son of a Nürnberg businessman. He had used the name "Arrigho di Federigho," Arrigho being an Italian version of Henry, for his translations of the *Decameron* and *Flowers of Virtue* into German. Then in the 1480s he took the name of the Martelli family, and signed his name in Latin as Henricus Martellus Germanus. He did, however, continue to use Arrigho de Federigho in legal documents, including his will. He was employed first by Domenico Martelli, then, after his death in 1476, by his son, Braccio. When he made his will in 1496, he noted that he had spent forty-eight years in the service of the family.[19]

His first foray into maps, for which he later became famous, was his copy of Cristoforo Buondelmonti's *Descriptio.* He was not a mapmaker; that is, he did not go out and survey the islands himself, but reproduced them basically unaltered, though he framed them nicely and labelled the cardinal directions. Eventually he was to make four more copies of Buondelmonti's work, two copies of Ptolemy's *Geographia,* and a large wall map of the world, now at Yale University.[20] He is most famous for his world map in later editions of the *Descriptio*, which showed the African discoveries of Bartholomeo Diaz's voyage of 1489. The world map does not appear in the Minnesota manuscript, another indication of its earlier date.

Henricus Martellus Germanus stayed very close to the original Buondelmonti text he had, which was the most common one.[21] He started out with Buondelmonti's name and use of the first person in the introductory paragraph, and retained most of his personal

17. See example, fol. 8v. where the text for Crete is crowded onto the page.

18. Lorenz Böninger, *Die Deutsche Einwanderung nach Florenz im Spätmittelalter* (Leiden: Brill, 2006), chapter 7, pp. 313–48. Thanks to Angelo Cattaneo for this reference.

19. He seems to have died shortly after making his will. At least we find no further references to him.

20. Chet van Duzer, *Henricus Martellus's World Map at Yale (c. 1491): Multispectral Imaging, Sources, Influence* (Springer Verlag: forthcoming).

21. In G.R.L. Sinner's edition of Buondelmonti's work, *Librum Insularum Archipelagi* (Leipzig: G. Reimer, 1824), he uses three manuscripts in Paris, BNF, MS 4824, which he refers to as MS C, is quite close to Henricus's main text, though the prologue and conclusion are different. Sinner does not reproduce the maps or include their texts.

references. What he did leave out were most of the complimentary phrases addressed to the Cardinal Orsini, by then no longer among the living. In subsequent editions produced by Henricus he went further, dropping all references to Buondelmonti, editing the texts, and claiming authorship. He added more islands and maps to the original set, in our version five new islands: Cyprus, Sicily, Sardinia, Corsica, and Britain. In later manuscripts he would add Ireland, the Balearic Islands, Taprobana (Sri Lanka), and Cipangu (Japan), as well as a world map, maps of the Holy Land, Italy, France, Spain, and Scandinavia, and a collection of sea charts.

Buondelmonti had organized his work with an acrostic spelling out his name, his patron's name and the date, using the first letter of each section:

CRISTOFORUS BONDELMONT DE FLORENTIA PRESBITER HUNC MISIT CARDINALI IORDANO DE URSINIS MCCCCXX

[Christopher Buondelmonti, priest of Florence, sent this to Cardinal Giordano Orsini, 1420].

Henricus was apparently working with a manuscript that did not have all of the initial letters filled in, and he was forced to guess, for example, *Venio* for *devenio* (Rhodes, fol. 10r), *cum* for *dum* (Sicandros, fol. 13v), and *desumo* for *resumo* (Serphinum, fol. 15r). The maps are framed in a rectangular decorative border with the four cardinal directions, in Latin, around the rim. North is the most common orientation, except when the shape of the island (for example, Crete, fol. 9r) makes it impractical. Where there is space, there is a scroll with the island's name, its number in the sequence, and its circumference in miles.

For the descriptive text of the new islands he added to the *Descriptio*, Henricus used quotations from classical texts, such as Isidore, Pliny, and Pomponius Mela. His one modern source, Giovanni Tortelli on Cyprus,[22] is actually giving traditional information. In later editions he added other authorities, such as the newly rediscovered Strabo, and a modern source, Pius II, *Historia Rerum Ubique Gestarum* (1477), for a text to accompany his famous world map. There is no indication that Henricus traveled around the islands himself, despite the Latin verse that serves as a frontispiece in the Chantilly, Leiden, and London manuscripts:

Si vacat, ipse potes que scribimus, hospes, adire;
Tunc quoque sit, quamvis utilis iste labor
At si non facile est, patria tellure relicta,
Alba processosum per mare vela dare,
Me duce que multis ipsi lustravimus annis,
Si sapis, exiguo tempore, disce domi.

[If time allows, dear reader, you may draw near to what we write.
It may be worthwhile, but it is not easy to leave one's native soil,
And set sail through the stormy sea. With me as your guide,

22. Tortelli (1400–1466) was the first Vatican librarian. His book, *De orthographia,* gives word derivation from the Greek. For identification of the sources used by Henricus in the Leiden MS, see K.A. de Meyier, *Catalogue Codices Vossiani Latini* (Leiden: University of Leiden, 1973), 1:47–49.

Who has travelled about for many years, if you are wise
You may learn all this in a short time at home.][23]

In the new prologue to the three later manuscripts, he says that "we" have seen many of the islands described.

Despite these claims, his work shows no evidence of personal experience but instead shows off the classical learning of the humanist in relation to the islands. For example, his entry on Corsica is drawn from Pliny's *Natural History* and is a lengthy catalogue of place-names from the first century CE, most of which were no longer in use in Henricus's day. In contrast, the map that accompanies this text is very rich in contemporary place-names, few of which can be found in Pliny.

Where did Henricus get the maps he added? In one case, the detailed map (78 place-names) of Corsica, a note on an identical copy in another manuscript indicates that it was provided by Giano Fregoso, who governed the island for Genoa as duke of Corsica in the mid-fifteenth century.[24] This would explain the wealth of interior detail, which was of little interest to makers of sea charts. The average chart of Corsica would have had 12–18 names, all coastal. The provenance of the Corsica map suggests Henricus's mode of work: he was a map collector who sought out and copied the best maps he could find. Two of his maps, those of Sardinia and Britain, seem to be derived from sea charts, although the islands on the average sea chart were much smaller. For example, the island of Sardinia was 1¾ inches in length on Pietro Rosselli's sea chart of 1466 versus 9½ inches on Henricus's spacious pages.[25] There are 31 place-names on the map of Sardinia, all on the coast. Of these 14 names appear on sea charts. Similarly, the map of Britain shows mostly places on the coast, and these are in Venetian dialect, showing their derivation from an Italian sea chart and resulting in some interesting spelling, such as Huic (Isle of Wight), Artamua (Dartmouth), Dabra (Dover), and Guixalixo (Winchelsea).[26]

The intellectual community in Florence was keenly interested in geography and maps, financing a number of editions of Ptolemy after the initial manuscript arrived in town around 1400. Nicholas Germanus, another German in Florence, produced three different editions of Ptolemy in manuscript, beginning in 1460, followed by two other editions (1466–68 and 1482), which added modern maps to those made to Ptolemy's original specifications.

23. Appears on Florence, BML xxix.25, fol. 1v. and Chantilly, Musée Condé, MS 698, fol. 1v. Thanks to David Larrick for help with the translation. The framed blue panel for the verse appears in the Leiden ms, but the text is erased by water damage.

24. The manuscript is Paris, BNF, Cartes et Plans, GE FF 9351, f. 35v. See Natalie Bouloux, "L'*Insularium Illustratum* d'Henricus Martellus," *The Historical Review* 9 (2012): 77–94, esp. 91–92.

25. Minneapolis, University of Minnesota Library, MS 1466 mRo.

26. Of the 80 names on Henricus's map of Britain, 41 appear on Benincasa's chart of 1467. This chart is reproduced by Ramon Pujades i Bataller, *Les cartes portolanes: La representació medieval d'una mar solcada.* (Barcelona: Institut Cartogràfic de Catalunya, 2007).

Nicholas also added descriptive texts, a model Henricus was to follow. The third edition was to become the basis for the first printed edition of Ptolemy. Nicholas had close connections with Henricus, whom we find arranging for the marriage of Nicholas's daughter, Nanna in 1477 and, after Nicholas's death in 1480, helping to sell some globes that he had made.[27] Nicholas was a prominent figure in the mapmaking world in which Henricus moved, and the question of the nature of their collaboration is an intriguing one.

Henricus also worked closely with the map-maker Francesco Rosselli (1448– before 1527), judging by the similarity of the world maps that each produced around 1490. Francesco had begun his career as an engraver, spent some time during the years 1476–82 at the court of the learned king of Hungary, Matthias Corvinus, and returned to Florence as a cartographer. He opened a shop, where he engraved maps on copper and printed them. His world map of 1498 and Henricus's incorporate information from the 1489 voyage of Bartholomew Diaz, and show a circumnavigable Africa and an open Indian Ocean. Both retained Ptolemaic features in the east, such as the truncated peninsula of India, the enlarged island of Taprobana, and the "dragon's tail" peninsula of southeast Asia. The two seem also to have collaborated on a map of central Europe, reflecting Francesco's experience in Hungary and Henricus's knowledge of his native Germany.[28]

The two earliest copies Henricus made of Buondelmonti's work are the manuscript at the University of Minnesota and the one in the Biblioteca Medicea-Laurenziana in Florence. The latter was a working copy, with several versions of the same map and corrections to others. The Minnesota manuscript may have been copied from the one in Florence at a relatively early date, before 1480. It has only five additional islands, while the manuscript in Florence has more, including the famous world map, clearly a work in progress — one can see where Henricus has made alterations. The Florence manuscript also contains maps of the Holy Land, Ireland, Maiorca and Minorca, Taprobana (Sri Lanka) and Cimpangu (Japan), as well as sea charts of the Atlantic, Mediterranean, and the Black and Caspian Seas. Cyprus, which was described in the Minnesota manuscript, appears in Florence with a greatly expanded text.

For the new maps Henricus chose mostly excerpts from classical works that have little relationship to the maps. For example, his text for Sicily is an overheated account of the perils of the straits between Italy and Sicily, which he took from Justinus's third-century *Epitome of the Philippic History of Pompeius Trogus,* backed up by a few lines from Isidore. While this text may have warmed the heart of the humanist reader, it did little to explicate the map that followed it. In the later manuscripts he found illustrative texts in Tacitus, Julius Caesar (for France), Isidore, Pliny, and Solinus.

27. These details are from Böninger, 335–42.

28. Florio Banfi, "Two Italian Maps of the Balkan Peninsula," *Imago Mundi* 11 (1954): 17–34, explores the nature of their relationship at some length.

The other three copies Henricus made of Buondelmonti's work are to be found at London, Leiden, and the Musée de Condé in Chantilly.[29] In these manuscripts, the maps of the Greek islands remain the same, but the texts are shortened. For example, in the British Library manuscript the text on Ithaca is a mere 84 words, compared to 214 in the Minnesota manuscript. This was achieved by cutting out the story material on Ulysses. He also dropped the cumbersome circumlocution the acrostic had required, and began each section with the name of the island. He put his own name up front as the author, and took out any remaining references to Orsini, Buondelmonti's patron. He added the verse about his "sailing experience," and omitted the personal references that had been part of Buondelmonti's text: his shipwreck, the burial site of his aunt, Maddalena Buondelmonti.

The copying of Buondelmonti's text and maps seems to have been the beginning of Henricus's mapmaking career, perhaps inspired by his new patron, Braccio Martelli.[30] In Roberto Almagià's judgment, he was a good draftsman and a diligent compiler, who sought out the best cartographic sources, making corrections and improvements.[31] What had interested him about Buondelmonti was the quality of his maps, to which he made almost no changes. For the maps he added to the work, he looked for up-to-date information. Sea charts of the Atlantic, Mediterranean and Black Sea became part of his portfolio, demonstrating his interest in the new standards of geographical accuracy. He seems to have used a sea chart as a model for the additional islands, but was able to add some interior names, such as the city of Nicosia in central Cyprus.

Buondelmonti served as a model for Henricus in his novel production and use of maps, and his willingness to seek out new sources of information. As humanists, however, they followed two different tracks. Buondelmonti examined the sources of ancient Greek culture on the ground, looking at ruins and artifacts as well as the geographical setting. His original texts were a grab-bag of all sorts of information that might be of interest to a traveler — armchair or otherwise. Henricus, however, sought out the works of classical writers, regardless of their relevance to the maps. Thus their work, as combined by Henricus, is a hybrid of the traveling observer and the library denizen.

In an age of printing Henricus continued to produce luxurious manuscripts with hand-drawn and colored maps, destined to be gifts to wealthy collectors. The lavish Grande Ptolémée was dedicated to the condottiere Camillo Maria Vitelli,[32] while the island book now at the Musée Condé was destined for Cardinal Giovanni d'Aragona of Naples. When the cardinal

29. London, British Library, MS Add. 15760; Leiden, University Library, MS Voss Lat. F.23; Chantilly, Musée Condé, MS 698.

30. De la Mare lists a number of books from Braccio Martelli's library that can be identified.

31. Roberto Almagià, "I mappamondi di Enrico Martello e alcuni concetti geografici di Cristoforo Colombo," *Bibliofilia* 42 (1940): 288–311, esp. 302.

32. Florence, Biblioteca Nazionale Centrale, MS Magliabechiano XIII.16.

died in 1485, the manuscript was redirected to Claude Gouffier of Boisy, whose coat-of-arms appears on the binding, and it has remained in France ever since.[33]

Henricus was not the only one to adapt and make use of Buondelmonti's island book. The "isolario" became a popular form in the late fifteenth century,[34] beginning with Bartolommeo dalli Sonetti, who converted the text into verse and published it c.1485. In 1528 Benedetto Bordone of Venice published his *Libro,* which added islands of the Americas and Asia, as well as city plans of Venice and Tenochtitlán in Mexico, and a world map.[35] The voyage among the islands of the Aegean had been extended to encompass the wider world.

Editions

Although Buondelmonti's work was quite popular — about seventy manuscripts survive — it was not printed during the Renaissance. Perhaps this was because he was followed almost immediately by a number of imitators, who adopted his subject (the islands) and his format. The first of these, Bartolommeo dalli Sonetti, used much of Buondelmonti's material but converted the text into sonnets.[36]

The first printed edition of Buondelmonti's book was in 1824 by G.R.L. Sinner, who collated the text of three manuscripts in Paris, Bibliothèque Nationale de France (nos. 4823, 4824, 4825). He transcribed the Latin and added extensive notes. He did not include the maps or the names on the maps. These three manuscripts are based on the most common edition of Buondelmonti, similar to the one used by Henricus.[37]

In 1897 Émile Legrand published a French translation from a Greek edition, Istanbul, Topkapi Palace Library, MS Seraglio gr. 24. He also prepared a volume of notes, but unfortunately this is lost. The manuscript he was using had no maps. He included maps from an unspecified printed edition in his volume, but did not discuss place-names. As far as one can tell, without consulting the original Greek, this version is somewhat abbreviated, compared to the manuscript used by Henricus Martellus Germanus.[38]

33. Teresa D'Urso, *Enluminures italiennes chefs-d'oeuvres du Musée Condé* (Somogy: Editions d'Art, 2000), 45–46. Unfortunately the world map has been removed, probably when it was rebound in the sixteenth century.

34. George Tolias, *"Isolarii,* Fifteenth to Seventeenth Century," in *History of Cartography,* David Woodward, ed., 3 (Chicago: University of Chicago Press, 2007), 263–84.

35. *Libro di Benedetto Bordone,* Giovanni Battista de Cesare, ed. Facsimile of 1528 edition (Rome: Bulzone, 1988).

36. Printed in Venice in 1485. Dalli Sonetti is thought to be a pseudonym, but there is no agreement on the true identity of the author.

37. See note 21 above.

38. Émile Legrand, *Description de les îles de l'Archipel grecque par Christophe Buondelmonti* (Paris, 1897; repr., Amsterdam: Philo Press, 1974).

Most recently a facsimile edition has been published by a group of German scholars from a manuscript housed in Düsseldorf, Universitäts- und Landesbibliothek, MS G.13. This manuscript, from the last half of the fifteenth century, includes several other geographical and astronomical texts. Buondelmonti's work occupies folios 28–58. This edition includes a transcription, a translation into German, notes, and interpretive essays.[39]

Individual islands have been the subject of scholarly studies, but there are no other editions of the full text. The work of Henricus Martellus Germanus has attracted much attention for the beauty and excellence of his maps, but there is no modern edition of any the five manuscripts of the *Descriptio Arcipelagi* attributed to him.

The James Ford Bell Manuscript

The following description is taken verbatim from the manuscript catalog of the Bell Library.

> Minneapolis, MN. James Ford Bell Library, University of Minnesota. Ms. 1475_fMa.
> *Descriptio Arcipelagi et Cicladum Aliarorum Insularum*. Cristoforo Buondelmonti (d. c. 1431).
> Florence, Italy. XIV/3. Buondelmonti's original text (c. 1420) copied by Henricus Martellus Germanus, c. 1475. Contemporary binding, vellum over stiff boards. Parchment. 43 ff.+ 1 blank folio fore and aft. 23 x 30 cm. inches. Ornamented title page (1r.) with blank coat of arms flanked by cupids, floral border, ornamented initial.
> 19 pages, text only, 66 pages with illustrations (maps). 85 maps, some with multiple small islands. Ink (black lettering) and paint (deep blue, green, brown).
> Buondelmonti, ff. 1r–38r. Henricus Martellus Germanus, ff. 38r-43v.
> Inc, f. 1r "Cristofori Ensenii Florentini Sacerdotis Dignisssimi Descriptio Arcipelagi et Cicladum Aliarum Insularum Foelicite incipit: Cicladum Caeterarumque insularum hinc inde sparsarum enarrationis...."
> Expl., f. 38r (Buondelmonti) "Ubi etiam caput sancti georgii adoratur."
> Inc. (Henricus), f. 38r "Cyprus insula a civitate Cypro que in ea est nomen accepit...."
> Expl. f. 43v (on Scotia) "Illi nullus anguis, avis rara, apis nulla adeo et advectos inde pulveres seu lapillos siquis alibi sparserit inter alvearia examina favos deferant."
> Written by a single scribe in neat, legible humanist book hand, with a less formal hand on the maps. Each map framed with decorative scroll border, cardinal directions on scrolls, and label and number for each map. Large unornamented initials for each entry, some missing. Does not completely reproduce Buondelmonti's acrostic.

39. Cristoforo Buondelmonti, *Liber Insularum Archipelagi: Universitäts- und Landesbiliothek Düsseldorf MS. G. 13, Faksimile* and *Transkription des Exemplars, Ubersetzung und Kommentar,* Karl von Bayer, Imgard Siebert, Max Plassmann, Arne Effenberger, Fabian Rijkers, ed. and trans. 2 vols. (Wiesbaden: Reichert, 2005).

Page margins marked out with pencil. Lines per text page vary from 26 (f. 2r) to 38 (8v), the size of the script adjusted accordingly. Most pages are a combination of map and text, with one to three maps per page. Ff. 9r-14v. damaged at the top with some loss of text and map frame.
Purchased by James Ford Bell in 1953 from the Schab Gallery. The Schab records are lost, but the current proprietor recalls that the manuscript was part of a French private collection, mostly dedicated to American exploration. Gift to the James Ford Bell Library.

The Facsimile

The images of all the folios in MS 1475 that appear on the following pages are reproduced exactly as photographed for the James Ford Bell Library. They are presented at a slight reduction (generally 90%) to fit the format of this print edition. They have been aligned across each page spread by the overlapping binding thread holes that appear in the inner margins of each spread (gutter). Each folio has been numbered below, the versos on the left and the rectos on the right.

Slight differences in color and tone will often appear between the versos and the rectos — and among different groupings of folios. These are generally due both to the various parchments stocks used to create manuscript books and to the differences in each parchment surface between the exterior (hair) side and the interior (smooth) sides of the animal skin used. While the manuscript remains in wonderful condition, and the Bell Library has undertaken major restoration work, the images reproduced show the wear-and-tear associated with age: missing sections of the parchment, stains and other water damage, occasional erasures or added marks accrued over the past five centuries. Such marks highlight the unique condition of every manuscript book that has come down to us; and we hope that our presentation offers the reader some of the experience of paging through a medieval or Renaissance manuscript. A complete digital version of this manuscript will also be available through the James Ford Bell Library's UMedia Archive.

The Latin Transcription

The manuscript used by Henricus Martellus Germanus is the most common version of Buondelmonti, similar to those published by G.R.L. Sinner[40] and the academic team at the University of Düsseldorf.[41] Sinner collated three manuscripts in Paris, Bibliothèque Nationale de France, while the Düsseldorf edition uses a single manuscript of the late fifteenth century. The latter is written in an informal cursive script, in contrast with the more formal humanistic hand of the Minnesota manuscript. It also makes a number of

40. See n. 21. Hereafter referred to as "S."

41. Buondelmonti, *Liber Insularum Archipelagi*. Includes facsimile, transcription, notes, and essays. All references are to the transcription that appears in volume 2, hereafter referred to as "Dd."

infelicitious word choices, as one can see from looking at the textual comparisons in the Latin Transcription.

I have noted only substantive differences among the texts, not spelling variations (such as *ae* for *e*, and *ex* for *exs*), slight changes in word order, and the placement of the particle -que in a series. The Minnesota manuscript has very limited punctuation and no paragraphing, and I have followed that style. Sinner notes that Buondelmonti makes a number of grammatical errors, which he calls "barbarisms," such as turning fourth declension nouns into second declension, and using interchangeably the ablative or the accusative following the preposition *"in."* Some scribes correct his grammar, but not Henricus. Buondelmonti's use of contemporary Greek, assuming it to be the same as classical Greek, is sometimes a puzzle.[42]

Henricus almost entirely eliminated references to Cardinal Giordano Orsini, Buondelmonti's patron, and composed a new introduction accordingly. In later versions, he also removed all references to Buondelmonti's personal experiences. The acrostic used by Buondelmonti is present in the other manuscripts. Sinner's manuscripts include notes on the "red letters" for the date MCCCCXX in the last seven entries, indicating that "M" means 1,000, "C" one hundred, and "X" ten, or 1420. This note is missing from the Minnesota version. I have used both Sinner and Düsseldorf to fill in some gaps in the Minnesota text, as noted.

Except for the introduction, the text of the Düsseldorf manuscript is similar to the Minnesota manuscript, but the maps are different. The most significant map in the former manuscript is that of Constantinople, which is richly detailed and shows the city after the Turkish conquest, including several mosques and the burial place of the conqueror of Constantinople, Sultan Mehmet II (d. 1481), on the site of the former Church of the Apostles. The other maps in this manuscript are less detailed than those in Minnesota. Sinner makes no reference to the maps, nor does he list the place-names found on them.

Red type transcribes the labels of the manuscript. Brackets contain the information derived from each map illustration. Italics indicate my additional comments. I have marked place-names on the maps that also appear in the text with a star. There is, in many cases, quite a gap between these two categories. This is even more striking in the case of Henricus's maps (Corsica, Sardinia, Britain, etc.) that have many more place names than do their texts. But it is is also true of some of Buondelmonti's maps, such as Crete and Rhodes.

Errors occur in all manuscripts, either through the carelessness of the copyist or the failure to understand. Most common is to skip a line or a couple of words. There are a number of cases of such omissions, but also some lengthier ones, for example in the account of Chios, which seem to have been deliberately removed or perhaps were missing from the model which was used. The Minnesota manuscript, while generally in excellent condition, has been damaged at the top of folios 5 to 18. It affects the text only on folios 11 to 14. The missing text has been filled in, using the Düsseldorf manuscript.

42. Sinner, 23–24.

Other citations in the transcription refer to Pierre Bersuire (Petrus Bechorius), a fourteenth-century French churchman, who supplied the descriptions (perhaps imaginary) of the artistic renderings of the Greek gods.[43] Buondelmonti also quotes liberally from Virgil's *Aeneid*, Ovid's *Metamorphoses*, and once each from Statius's *Achilleid* and Terentius.

The place-names of the islands vary from edition to edition, and some of the smaller islands are no longer securely identifiable. The index gives the names used by Buondelmonti, the most common modern name, and some of the more common variants. The *Map of the Journey of Cristoforo Buondelmonti* by Rick Britton, on pages 16–17 below, offers a modern key to these places and their positions.

The English Translation

I have attempted to be faithful to Buondelmonti's humanist Latin while still offering a modern English text. For ease of reference the elements in the heading apparatus in the translation match those of the transcription. I have also annoted useful historical, geographical, and bibliographical information and indicated my choice of readings.

We hope that readers will use both this print edition and the high-resolution images online to deepen their understanding and enjoyment of this monument of early modern geographical and classical learning.

Abbreviations

B Pierre Bersuire, *Reductorium Morale*

BNF Bibliothèque nationale de France

C Paris, BNF, MS. 4824, in S

Dd Cristoforo Buondelmonti, *Liber Insularum Archipelagi: Universitäts- und Landesbiliothek Düsseldorf MS. G. 13, Faksimile* and *Transkription des Exemplars, Ubersetzung und Kommentar,* Karl von Bayer, Imgard Siebert, Max Plassmann, Arne Effenberger, Fabian Rijkers, ed. and trans. 2 vols. (Wiesbaden: Reichert, 2005).

MN Minneapolis, MN. James Ford Bell Library, University of Minnesota, MS 1475_ fMa.

PB James Joseph Foster, "A Preliminary Text of Pierre Bersuire's *Reductorium Morale,* Book Fifteen, Prologue." Thesis (Durham, NC: Duke University, 1967).

S G.R.L. Sinner, *Christoph Bondelmontii, Florentinii, Librum Insularum Archipelagi* (Leipzig and Berlin: G. Reimer, 1824).

43. James Joseph Foster, "A Preliminary Text of Pierre Bersuire's *Reductorium Morale,* Book Fifteen, Prologue." Thesis. Durham, NC: Duke University, 1967. Cited as "PB." Bersuire is cited as "B"

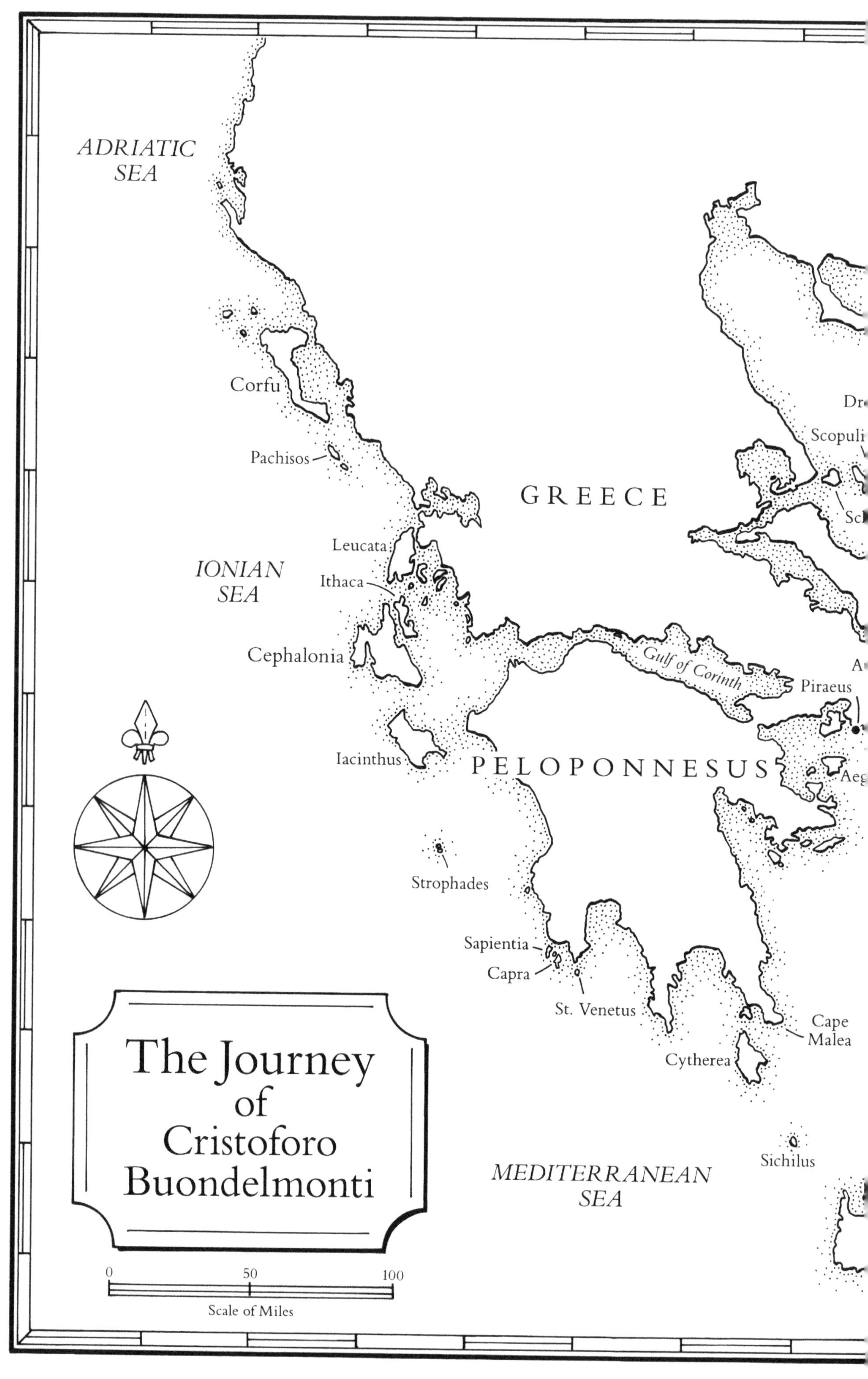

ADRIATIC SEA
Corfu
Pachisos
GREECE
Scopuli
Leucata
IONIAN SEA
Ithaca
Cephalonia
Gulf of Corinth
Piraeus
Iacinthus
PELOPONNESUS
Strophades
Sapientia
Capra
St. Venetus
Cape Malea
Cytherea
Sichilus
MEDITERRANEAN SEA
The Journey of Cristoforo Buondelmonti
0
50
100
Scale of Miles

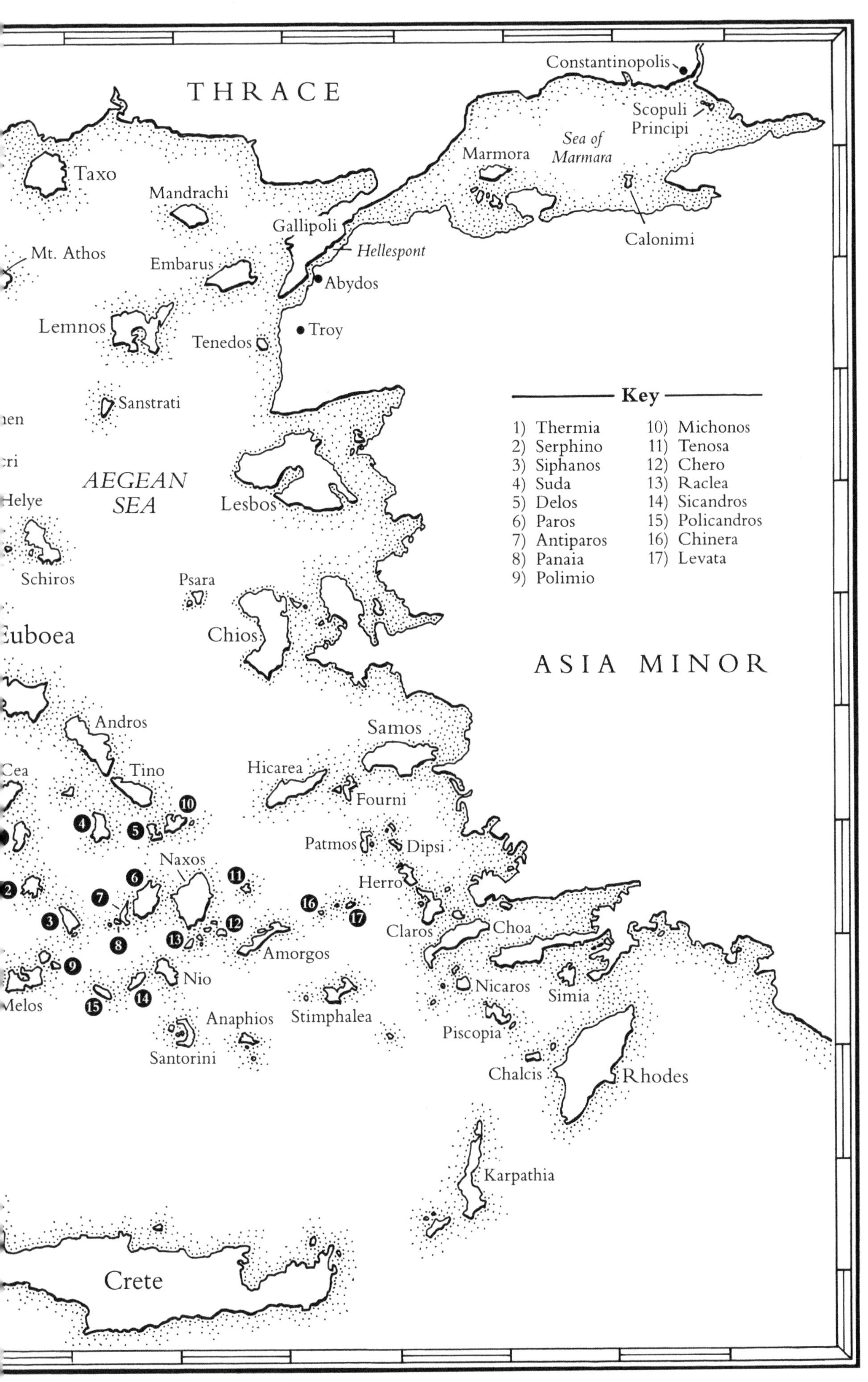

THRACE
Constantinopolis
Scopuli Principi
Sea of Marmara
Marmora
Calonimi
Taxo
Mandrachi
Gallipoli
Hellespont
Mt. Athos
Embarus
Abydos
Lemnos
Tenedos
Troy
Sanstrati
AEGEAN SEA
Lesbos
Helye
Schiros
Psara
Chios
Euboea
ASIA MINOR
Andros
Samos
Cea
Tino
Hicarea
Fourni
Patmos
Dipsi
Naxos
Herro
Claros
Choa
Amorgos
Nio
Nicaros
Simia
Melos
Anaphios
Stimphalea
Piscopia
Santorini
Chalcis
Rhodes
Karpathia
Crete
Key
1) Thermia
2) Serphino
3) Siphanos
4) Suda
5) Delos
6) Paros
7) Antiparos
8) Panaia
9) Polimio
10) Michonos
11) Tenosa
12) Chero
13) Raclea
14) Sicandros
15) Policandros
16) Chinera
17) Levata

NEC QUAERERE HONOREM NEC SPERNERE
JAMES F. BELL

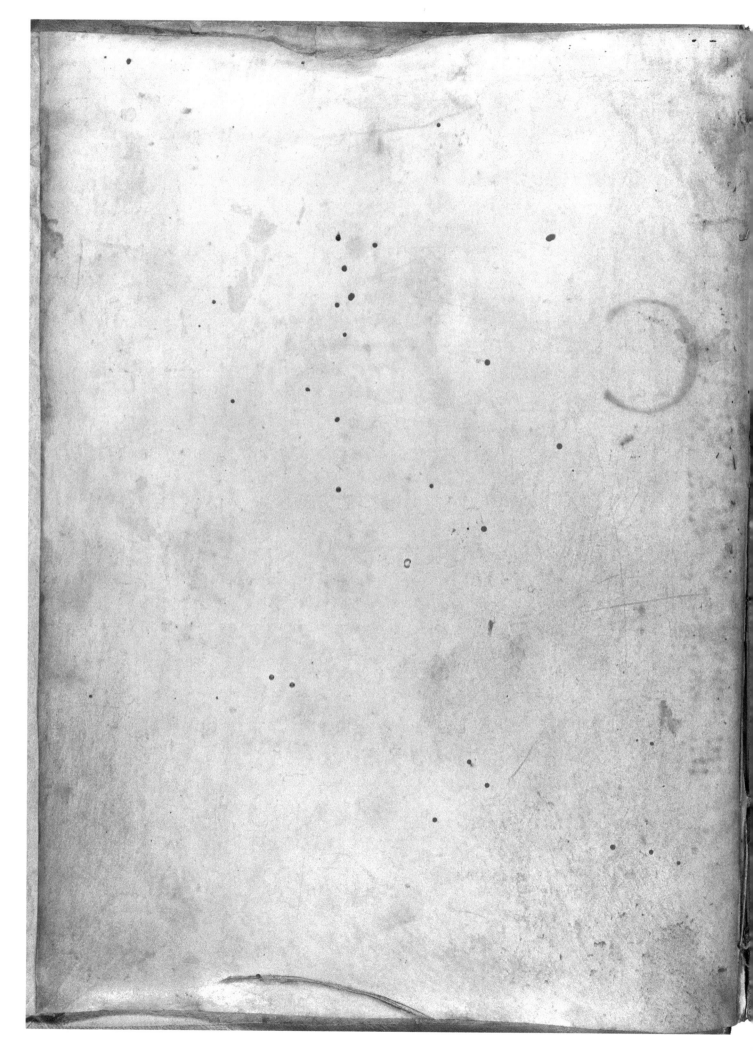

CHRISTOFORI ENSENII FLORENTINI SACERDOTIS DIGNISSIMI DESCRIPTIO ARCIPELAGI ET CICLADUM ALIARQ INSULAR FOELLICITER INCIPIT

CICLADUM CAETERARUMQ
insularum hinc inde sparsarum enarrationis
& picture libellũ aggressus non antiquos
scriptores tantum imitatus queq; ab his describũt
uerum et que hodie in illis sunt antiq; noueq;
forme necnõ ciuitates castra fontes nemora flumina maria
mõtes promõtoria portus atq; loci naturam succincte breuiterq;
recensere ac depingere constitui, quo etiã ueriora memorẽt
non que auribus percepi sed que ipse ego in sex annis pro-
prijs luminibus post multa discrimina rerum & uidi & tetigi describentur. q nõ modo legentibus gratissima erũt uerum
etiam nauigantibus utillima si didicerit q petenda queue sint et
fugienda q singula q maxima breuitate pcurram & isularum
numerum ac nomina explicabo ut facile legentibus iter pateat.
Ergo meum inceptũ a Corfu dirigatur que hodie amultis pma
grecie uersus occiduũ est appellata. Deinde Pachisos Leucata
Ithaca Chefalonũ Iacinthus Strophades Sapientia Chitarea Sequilus, Creta Carpathos Rodos Simie Charistos Delos Caria
Astimphalea Egala Sicandros Policadros Milo Siphanos Serfinos Termie Cea Andros Caloieros Tino Michone Delos

Suda Paros Antiparos Panaia Nasos Podia Raclea Chero ✝
Nio Anaphios Amurgo Chinera Levata Caloieros Choa
Calamos herro Patmos Dipsi Crusie Icarea Mandria ✝
Agatusa Formachiu Samo Furni Tenosa psara Chios
Lesbos Tenedos Galipolis Marmora Calanonimo Sco
puli Caloierorum. Constantinopolis Stilimini Embaros
Mandrachi Taxo Mons sanctus Santrati Limen Dro
mos Marri Schiati & Scopuli Sanctus Elias Schiros
Egrippos Egina Ciprus Sicilia Cursica & Sardinia ✝
Albion sive anglia Gottia Noruegia Suetia hiberniaq;

Restat nunc generales monstrare particularitates
& provincias circum circa positas cum mariũ
amplitudine & qui in hodiernum dominantur
in illis. Dicitur ergo Arcipelagum mare quasi dominus
maris. A Rhodo igitur per lineam rectam usque mal
lium promontorium nunc caput sancti angeli miliaria
cccc L. & a creta usq; tenedon. v̄. ĩ qbus totũ mare cõcludit᷑ ãcipe-

lagi. Huic asia minor adheret in qua cilicie pamphilie phri
gie. bitinieque prouincie amplicantur. Sed postquam turchi eam diu
possedere ab eis turchia nomen accepit: qui ruentes per ciuitates
sine meniis populi sub eis pacifice gubernantur. Ad occiduum
postquam mare transitur helespontum grecia statim plana amplia
tur et in omnibus usque ad andrinopolim fertilissima nimis. Et
a leua tendens uersus tessalonicam prouinciam populata satis
reperitur ubi ciuitates locaque delinquimus et ad montes deueni
mus altos: cito ad euboiam athenarumque loca pergitur ultro
quarum pars maxima turcis possidetur. Egeum uero mare
uolunt antiqui ab egeo rege et patre thesei dictum: quod ab
hellesponto incipit et multos abluens sinus usque malleum di
stenditur promontorium. Chidos enim grece latine circulus
eo quod omnes insule rotunde inter istos arcipelagi scopulos
ex cicladibus uocabantur. Peractis igitur generalibus diui
sionibus huiusmodi descriptionis ad particularitates dicta
rum insularum reuertemur ea propter ut cuncta comprehendantur
in nigro montes: in albo planities: in uiride aque pandentur
manifeste:–

INSULA hec que prius ostenditur Cercira uel Cor
cira a rege olim dicta est que Corfu nominatur. et .c.
mil. circuit. Versus autem meridiem montuosa per totum re
manet quibus montibus arbores ualanidarum fructificantur.
In amphipoli uero promontorio oppidum sancti angeli muni
tissimum erigitur: quod a longe naute prospectant. Ab orien
te uero usque Corfu et ultra ex parte trionis planities amena

& multis habitata gentibus ampliatur: & in ea olim cercira urbs
deleta cernitur torniamentis colūpnisq; ampliata. Phalarius mōs
altissimus ab ea uidetur: qui dodonam siluam in terra conspicit
firma. In qua ait Ouidius templum fuisse dodoneum maximum
ioui sacrum: in quo duas de celo columbas descendere solitas &
ueteribus insidere quercubus: & ex eis postulantibus responsa
dare. Tandem ex eis ut aiunt altera transuolauit in delphos boe-
tie ciuitatem & ibi appollinis delphici clarum fecit oraculum. Altera ad amonis iouis templum in africa transmigrauit. In radicibus aūt montis huius scopulus est: quem ad similitudinem
ulixis nauis fuisse dixere uetusti. Prope uero leucumam promo-
torium cassiopis menibus erectis etiam a pyratis olim desolata
uidetur: cuius in radicibus planities una cum infecta palude probatur. A latere uero horum meniorum ecclesia matris domini
ab hominibus uisitatur multis qui exauditi repatriantur ylares.
Ad trionem uero epirus a rege dicto altissimis incipit montibus
in quibus heleni propinqua patre troiaq; a butroto panditur
ultro. Virgilius.
Littoraq; epiri legimus portumq; subimus
Caonio & celsam butroti ascendimus arcem.
Per hanc igitur insulam Titus quintus flamminius ut securus pergeret ad romanum exercitum bellum cum Philippo macedonie
rege facturus transitum fecit;

2 v

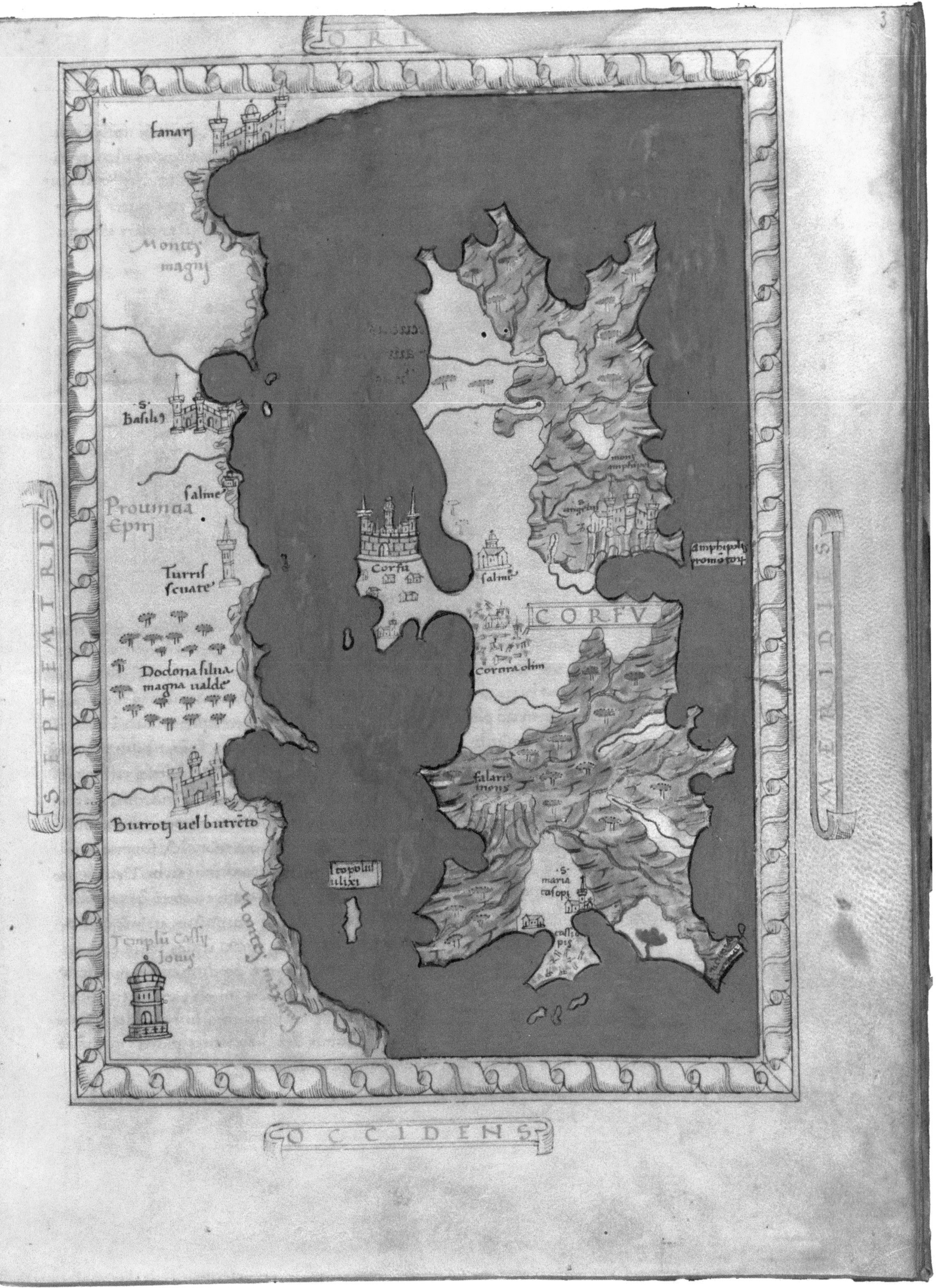
ORI
fanarj
Montes magni
S. Basilis
salme
Prouincia Epiri
Turris scuate
Dodona silua magna ualde
Butrotj uel butreto
Templu Cassij Iouis
Corfu
salmi
CORFV
Amphipolis promotori
Coriria olim
falarij monj
S. maria casopi
scopolus ulixi
SEPTEMTRIO
MERIDIES
OCCIDENS

·2·

PACHISOS OLIM ET NUC

Ambitus totius insule m p 10

Supra corciram ad orietē Pachiso est insula ·x· mil ĩ qua sine menijs nulla ē paucorum possessa hominū pp turchorū insidias: media ergo ad orietē plana remanet uineis domesticisq; arboribus fecūda & portus tutus ĩ ea includit^r: q̄ ut aiūt una cum corchira olim tenebat^r insula. Sed propter crebras tēpestates neptūni atq; eoli terra tenax q̄ inter duarū insularum medio est inuēta mare efficitur & corchira ab illa parte die ac nocte minuitur.

Transiens nr̄a ratis ad orietem p̄ cetum mil: antiqū oli leucon mōtē subimus & iā diu inter ipsū adiacētes colles mare deueniens pp fluxū refluxūq; quater idie ·Lxxx· mil insula ē effecta. Que inter umbrosas ualles fontiū irrigua efficit^r nimis: quo ĩmedio campus rurū circūdatus est: & cū armētorū multitudīe uidet^r ad orietem uō portus cōcludit^r. & si ad trionē prosequeris alterū tutiorē reperimus qui amoītib; siluisq; ac fontibus est ornatus. Cūq; nō diu procedēs fons in littore fluētissimus reperit^r: quo in loco uiatores circūstātesq; refrigerāt^r. A leua uō in radicib; mōtiū ciuitatē uetustissimā deletāq; olim uidemus: in qua tēplum apollinis erat uetustū. & in eo loco eneas discedens a troia arma dimisit abantis. Virgilius. Mox & leucate nimbosa cacumina mōtis. & formidatus nautis reperit^r appollo. Huc petimus fessi parue succedimus urbi. Deinde peractis seculis hanc octauianus cesar restaurauit deletam ciuitatē q̄ nicopolis appellabat^r ibiq; tēplum appollinis edificauit postq̄ antonium in huc locū & cleopatram deuicerat. Virgilius. hic augustus agens italos ĩ plia cesar. In cōspectu uō huius inmari turris est: a qua nō longe opidum cum ponte denotatur: ubi aer in estate infectus spirat: quibus in locis ampla pandebatur planities. Si aūt ad trionem accedens siluam & ambrachium sinū offendes: ad orietem demū insule inculte propalant^r: in quibus olim habitauere patres: nūc tādē propter insidias pyratarum ad desolationem deuenere.

Ostendimus Leucatam nūc ad Dulichias transimus que olim itacha & nūc ualdecōpare nominatur altis rupibus circūsepta que mōtuosa & ī utilis nisi inmedio exiguus planus aliquib; arborib; casisq; habetur. & circūcirca portuosa satis de oriente ad occiduum. xxx. & in latitudine. iij. mil. āpliat̃. cuius quidē duo extrema in duob; aperiunt̃ cornibus anautis innocte periculosis. Fuit. n. hic ut asserit ille eloquētissimus grecorum Vlyxes q̄ quasi ad omīa modum inuenīebat Penolopem Itaci filiam sūpsit incōiugē & ex ea Telemacum suscepit filium. Tandem rapta helena aparide ire ad troiam conatus est: & se insanum simulauit: & ueniente Palamede ad Itacā aīalia diuersi gnīs iugo cōiunxit ad aratrum & salē seminare compt9 ē. Verum palamedes astutiam uiri suspicatus capto paruulo telemaco ad explorādam ingenij sui fraudem eum aratro opposuit. Vlixes autem uiso filio cōfestim demouit aratrum: & sic cognitus in expeditionem ire coactus est. Capta deniq; troia in contione eloquentia sua arma achillis contra aiacem uicit. Postq̃ igitur a troia recessit & coactus uisitare patriam multis quippe agitatus procellis in longissimos errores ac peregrinationes decennio eiectus est. Tandem multa in itinere passus ad hanc deuenit insulam. & facto in domo sua cum procis penelopes prelio non multo post tempore uitam finiuit.

Effugimus scopulos itace laertia regna
Et terram altricem seui execramus ulixis.

4.

ITHACA OLIM NUNC VAL DI COMPARE

Habet in longitudine M. P. 30. Et latitudo M. P. 3

SEPTEMTRIO

OCCIDENS

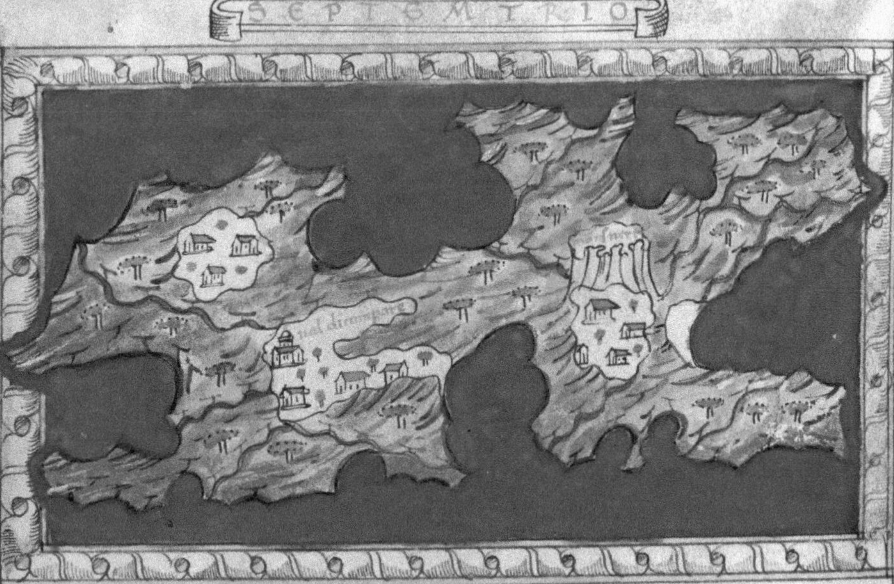

ORIENS

MERIDIES

Finis de itaca: de chephalonia incipiamus que olim chephalonum dicta & in motibus tota: chephalim grece caput latine quia apparet nautis ab austris uenientibus rotunda uel hominis caput uel q̃a a tempore troianorum usq; hodie caput dominij insularum istarum hec fuit. & titulus ducatus hu(ius) ab ea incohatur. Legi n. in antiquis cronicis Vlyxem ducem fuisse regionis huius. & a chephalonia titulum inceptabat: q̃ rotunda & in motibus aspera centum circuit mil: cuius in medio elatus mons erigit(ur): hodie leo sine flumine scaturiginibus aquarum dicitur. In quo multitudo fagorum pinorumq; per circuitum insurgunt: & quod plus est siluestria non pauca errantia sine potu nusq̃ aqua inuenientia ore aperto auram e motib(us) recipiunt in potũ estate illa. Serpentes & enim ibi & aspides inueniunt(ur): qui calorẽ sentientes hu

manum sine lesione cum eo dormiunt. Ad orientem uõ in littore francisci eccle
siam adoramus & ab eo edificatam: que in orto omĩa dulcia producebat.
Fuit etiam insula hec quasi ultima quĩa tempore belli macedonici romani ce
perunt in deditionem. Ad occiduum ergo uiscardus portus a roberto uiscar
do domino apulie dicto apparet. In qua olim pitilia ubi chilon lacedemonicus
phus aliquibus annis stetit ut ait epiphanus ciprius: & tante extitit auctori
tatis tanta uis est ut scribit cic. q nulli hominum tribuatur: cum enĩ dicit
nosce te: animam tuam intelligit: nec intellexit de membris aut statura quod
est facile. Sed intellexit ut cognitos defectus animi reformaremus & qd acti
bus nostris nosmetipsos metiamur: nec inertia sinamus corrumpi nobilitatem
nostram. Aut opinione tumefacti audacia ridicula corrumpamus. Bellisarius
denique nepos iustiniani augusti classe sua huc uenit & eam a procellis repara
uit: qui audiens italiam a gotis subiugatam pietate motus sua classe ĩ affricam
deuenit & ghotos ab ea trinachriaque expulit: deinde peruento neapolim quia
patefacte porte non fuerunt per annum in obsidione stetit: qua capta uiros
mulieres et infantulos & quos in ea repperit igni ferroque defixit. Deinde uer
sus romam deueniens ghoti fugam arripuere. Contra uõ itacam samus est
& ad meridiem portus sancti ysideri manifestatur.

Iam medio apparet fluctu nemorosa iacinthus:
Dulichiamque samos & neritos ardua saxis.

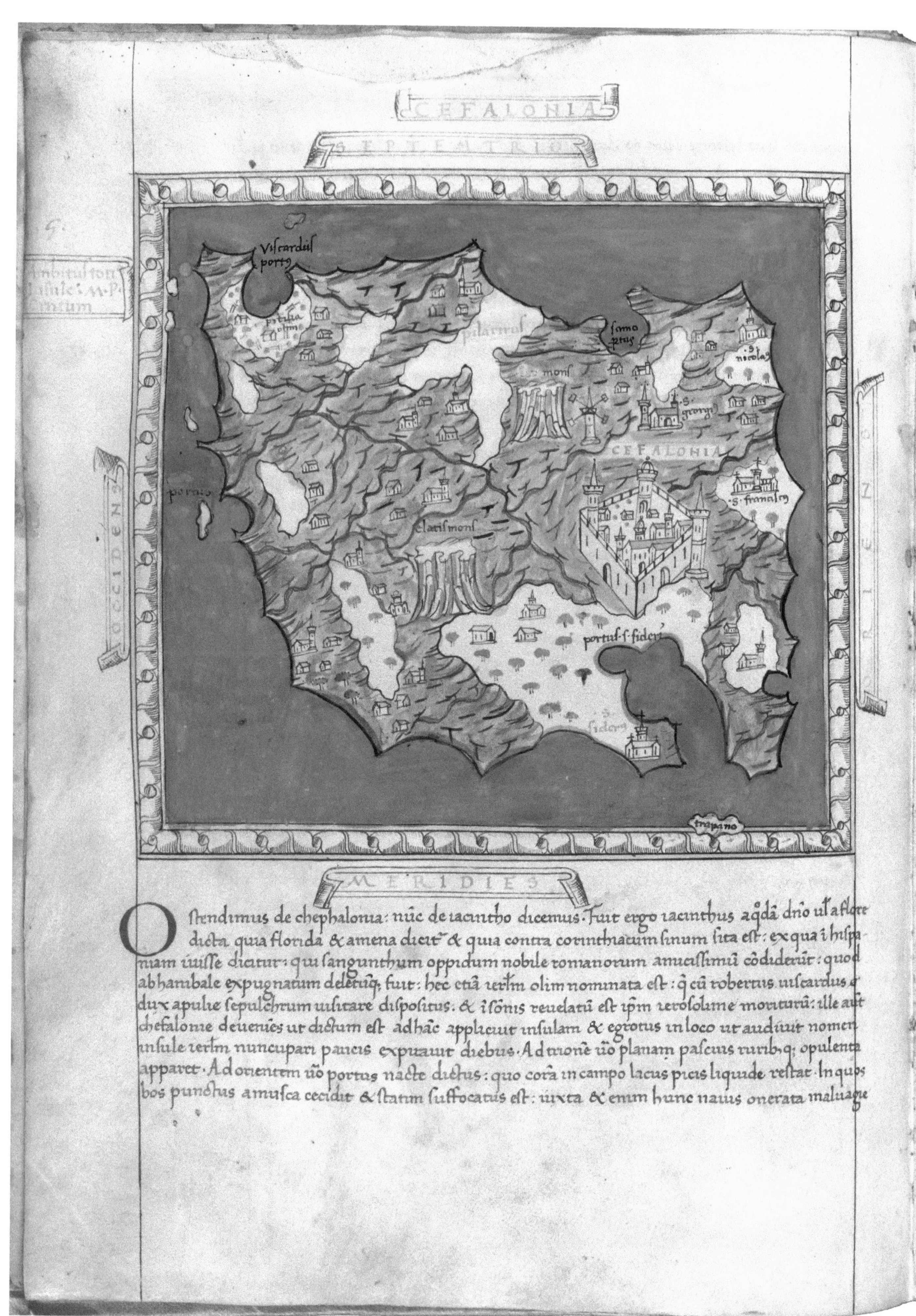

Ostendimus de chephalonia: nūc de iacintho dicemus· Fuit ergo iacinthus aq̊dā dn̄o ut a flore dicta quia florida & amena dicit᷑ & quia contra corinthiacum sinum sita est: ex qua i hispaniam iuisse dicatur: qui sanguinthum oppidum nobile romanorum amicissimū cōdiderūt: quod ab hanibale expugnatum deletuq̨ fuit: hec etiā iter̄m olim nominata est: q̄ cū robertus uiscardus dux apulie sepulchrum uisitare dispositus. & i sōnis reuelatū est ipm ierosolime moriturū: ille aūt chefalonie deueniēs ut dictum est ad hāc applicuit insulam & egrotus in loco ut audiuit nomen insule iter̄m nuncupari paucis expirauit diebus· Ad trionē uō planam pascuis iurib9q; opulenta apparet· Ad orientem uō portus nacte dictus: quo corā in campo lacus peius liquide restat· In quos bos punctus a musca cecidit & statim suffocatus est: iuxta & enim hunc nauis onerata maluagie caliginose uetis prosperis cum harena uelis tumidis ignari nauigationis sine lesione irruit & sic imobilis effecta est. Veronica et audiens nomen eius insule iterum ob deuotionem in eam ascendit & ibi ut dicitur sudarium xpi demostrans & morte saluatoris dum predicaret ad fidem deuote sunt reuersi. Ad orientem in ripa ut aiunt uena metallorum reperit & p totam meridiei plagam iter umbrosas arbores imontib; eleuatur. ubi ad occiduu uenimus. Pilosus & sci nicolai portus icludunt optimi & salinarum planus prope aperit. Ad trione denique prope mediu ciuitas insurgit. q a terremotis sepe deleta e. ibiq; ducissa mecum in progenie sepulta iac&. Ambit igit. Lx. mil. aere bono atq; placabili dilectione omniu habitatium. Virgil. Iam medio apparet fluctu nemorosa iacinthus.

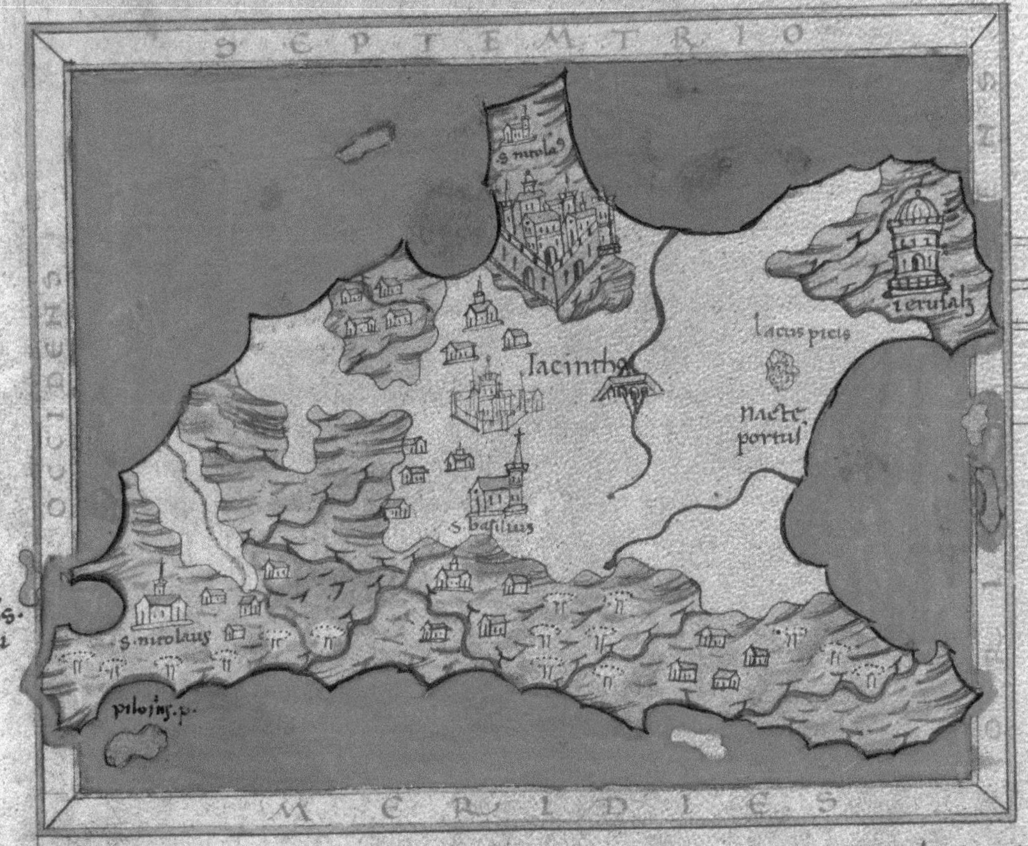

REstat nunc in hoc ionio mari ad austrum scopulos demostrare sanctissimos: q olim obsecratissimi habebant plore dicti unius mil. in circuitu deinde achinnades ab echinus piscib; in acheloo flumine propinquo. Postea strophades a strophe grece reuersio latine interptat. In ea igit fraternitas caloierorum resedit q cu piscib; & aqua asperā trahit uitā & qa semel a barbaris captiui omis uediti fuere modernj colentes ut securam uiā dei cōteplare possent turri edificauere i qua uiē uitam

getuit heremiticam : & exomi progenie plusq̃. L^a. ibi coadunati recreant̃ : hec igit
cum patria propinqua tempore phinei regis archadie & a pyratis habitate fuẽ
certũ ẽ. Qui scientes ipm̃ phineum filios suasu arpalice eorum nouerce cecasse & i
huius sceleris ultionem usq; in archadiam phineum obsederunt & admiseriã redu
xerunt : quos zetus & chalais arpalices fratres fugauerunt ipsumq; phineũ a pyr
ratis liberauere : & pyratas usq; ad istas pepulere insulas. Ergo ipsi iuuenes dixe
runt strophades hoc est reuersionem mutauere insulis. Tempore igit̃ enee q a troia
profugus petens italiam cum huc applicuisset suisq; comitib; epulantib; arpie de
archadia pulse has insulas colentes pabula aut rapiebant unguib; aut tactu fedis
simo polluebant : & ab eo ferro expulsi Celeno harum maxima dixit. Ibitis italiã
portusq; intrare licebit : Sed non ante datam cingetis menibus urbem. Q̃ uos dira
fames uestreq; iniuria cedis Ambesas subigat malis absũmere mẽsas. Ergo dicte
sunt arpie a uoracitate quia ibi pyraticum cõgeries & om̃s applicantes fedabant
auaritia & rapina. Seruatũ ex undis strophadum me littora primũ. Excipiunt stro
phades graio sic nomine dicte. Insule ionio in magno quas dira celeno. Arpieq; co
lunt alie phineia postq̃ : Clausa domus mẽsasq; metu liquere priores. Tristis haud
illis mõstrum nec seuior ulla : Pestis & ira deum stigijs sese extulit undis. Virginei
uolucrum uultus fedissima uẽtris. Proluuies uncęq; manus & pallida sep̃ ora fame.
Hunc aũt de malo in bonum he insule sũt reuerse q quãto magis olĩ procul nauiga
tes sistebant : tanto melius nũc affectuose deuotis precib; eis adherere festinãt ĩ qbus
turris cum ecc̃lia est : & caloieri horis canonicis in ea cõueniunt : ubi gũmus .i. por
uitam scõꝝ patrũ coram omnibus legẽdo declarat. Igit̃ quid sit uita istorum iudica
pater : qa certissime asperrima reputatur cũ spatium unius habeant miliarij & a
terra octingentorum stadiorum elongati. Ibi carnes neglecti sũt & cũ piscib; sepe a sole
combustis : paneq; arido & aqua uitam sustẽtare congaudent ut altissimo ĩmacu
latam quilib& suam reddere possit animam;

STROPHADES INSULE

Venio inde ad sapiētiam coram modoñese ciuitate: q̄ parua & īfructuosa apparet & dicta est sapientia ut nauis transeundo sapienter a scopulis ibi occultis se custodiat uel quia ibi mulier greca cum habitaret futura incātationibus trāseūtib; resoluebat. cuius imedio mons erigitur in quo modoñeses a longe uelū uigilant & circūstantib; innotescat. Ad orientem uō alique apparēt insule inculte & ab egis habitate: quarum minor tēpore amoracti magni turchorum. una biremi īfideliū in tēpestate noctis hic licuit. q̄ subito ecctiam inuasit. Cūq; circūsisterent & caloierum psallentem audirent porta eccłie usq̄ inuenta est. & sic usq; mane ibi remāserunt. Luce aūt facta insidias christianorum timentes donec caloiero sua dāna restitueret alitore recedere non ualuerunt. Coram ergo insulis dictis due erigūtur ciuitates. modonis prima liquoris bachi abundantissima coronis secūda a liquore dee palladis coronata: que ambe in prouincia moree consistunt & olim peloponesus dicta a pelope filio tantali ut barlaam homo bellorum & insignis plurimum qui cum apud frigias regnaret bellum habuit aduersum oenomium regem elidis atq; pise unde bellum ingens cognouit atq; ipodamia potitus est. Tandem cum apud argos regnasset a suo nomine peloponeses denominauit.

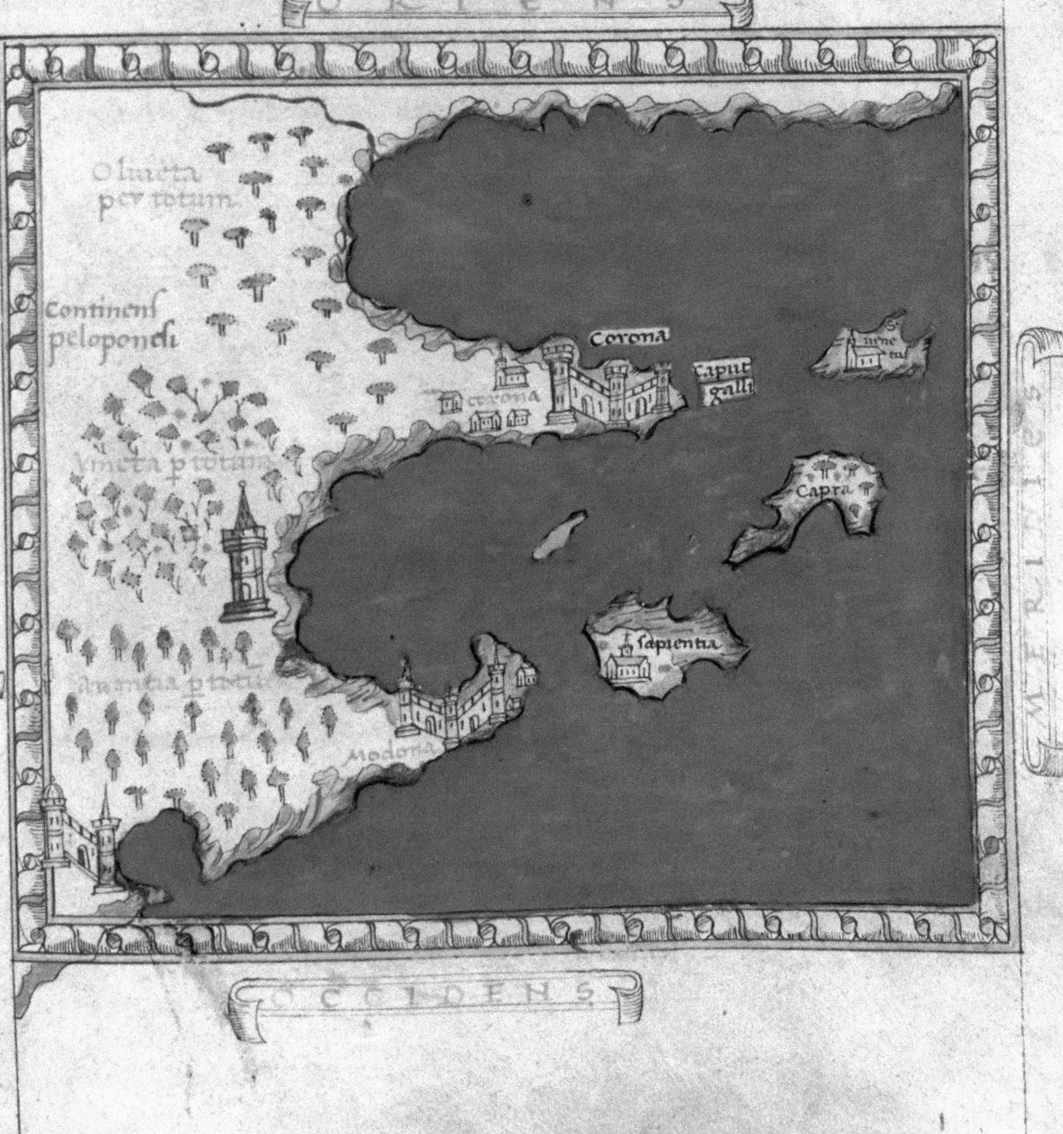

S Vp fluuium enarrare m̄ uidet̄ quot istis ī ptibus apparēt scopuli: qa extremum
nullū inuenimꝰ in eis nominare factū. Ideo de eis taceamꝰ & ad chituriā uel
cytharеam īsulā accedamꝰ: q̄ citri hodie nominatur. Vbi prima insularum ampelagi
ad occiduū cōputat̄ que quasi ꝑ totum inmōtib; īsurgit iq̄b; oppidū cutheron aperte
uidet̄: ubi uenus honorifice celebrata est ex quo & uenus & insula sūpsit noīn. Scul
pebatur .n. puella pulcherrima nuda et ī mari natans tenēs cōchā marinā: ī dextera or
nata rosis & colūbis circūuolātib; comitata. Vulcano deo ignis rustico turpissimo ī co
iugium assūpta. Ante eam tres stabant nude iuuēcule: que tres gratie uocabant̄ quarū
due facies ad ipsā̄ cōuerse erāt. Altera uō ī cōtrariū uertebat̄ cui et cupido filius suus alat̄ & cec̄
assistebat. q sagitta & arcu appollinē sagittabat ꝑꝑ qd̄ dijs turbatis ad matris gremiū puer ti
midus fugiebat. Iste planeta ē feminee cōplexiōis & ideo ī spetie puelle callida & humida & ideo
uulcano .i. igni dicit̄ maritata & ī mari īmersa qa cōuīcta calori & humori cupidinē deū amoris
peperisse .i. carnis cōcupiscētiā. Tres puelle .i. tres culpe: auaria ad lucrādū cū actu venereo: car
nalitas ad cōiugēdū actū carnalitatis. Infidelitas qa ꝑꝑ denariū diligē hominē demōstrāt. Alat̄
qa cito accedit & cōiugit̄. cec̄ qa nō curat ubi diligit. Igit̄ ex hac insula paris ꝑami filius hele
nā menelai uxorē nō īuitā rapuit: q̄ ad diē festū iux̄ mare situ templū hodie cognitū ueneris:
ubi cū alter alterū respexisset utrusq; forma opā dedit rapine. Q cū opā facto dedisset & maximū
deniq; excidiū cōsecutū est. A qua rapina ōs grecorū ꝑncipes ī desolationē troie unanimes fece
rūt cōiurationes. Cūq; illa frustra sepius repetisset sb ducatu agamēnonis cū ingēti exercitu
post decēnij ylionē ceperūt & menelao helena restituta ē. cū qua ipse tēpestate maris ipse cir
cūactus ꝑmo in egyptū delatus ē. Inde in lacedemonia sūt reuersi. Circuit itaq; .L x. mil.
in qua pauci habitāt & circūcirca scopuli uidēt̄ cū recētissima aqua scopulorꝝ draconarie dicte.

B Reue de hīc spatium breuē sichilum enumerare possumꝰ. & .x. mil. circuit ī qua
oppidum olim erat: nūc uō cum ab agrestib; sit possessa asinis nemo hominū ī ea
habitat. Itaq; si supra corium asini agrestis dormies demones nō timebis: epilēticum
curabis si de corno frontis sup se tenebit uel de ungula arsa bibet: uel anulū portabit.

Etiam fumigatione de ea facta parturientem liberat. Si de rasura petre capitis uel
maxille febricanti adbibendum pbes liber erit. Si de sanguine auricule bibes uel un
guentum facies cum suco serpentarie & oleo rosato & unge renes ante accessionē
quartane sanus remanebis. Soluentur membra contracta sicci humoris: & si cum
brudo earum carnium abluentur & femine cum brodio asine & cum adipe ungantur. Etiam incicatricibus ualet & medulla ossium interius. Semel turchi huc
uenietes nauis naufragium pertulit: hoc audientes cretici cito adinferos uiam
sibi parauere. Etiam nauis intēpeste noctis in hanc ruit insulam In qua naute
die octaua una in tabulis iam ab eis congestis natantes contra chituriam perie
runt: nisi unus illorum qui remanens in scopuli & pastus radicibꝫ arborum
atq; herbarum circa annum transeuntibus recollectus incolumis euasit.

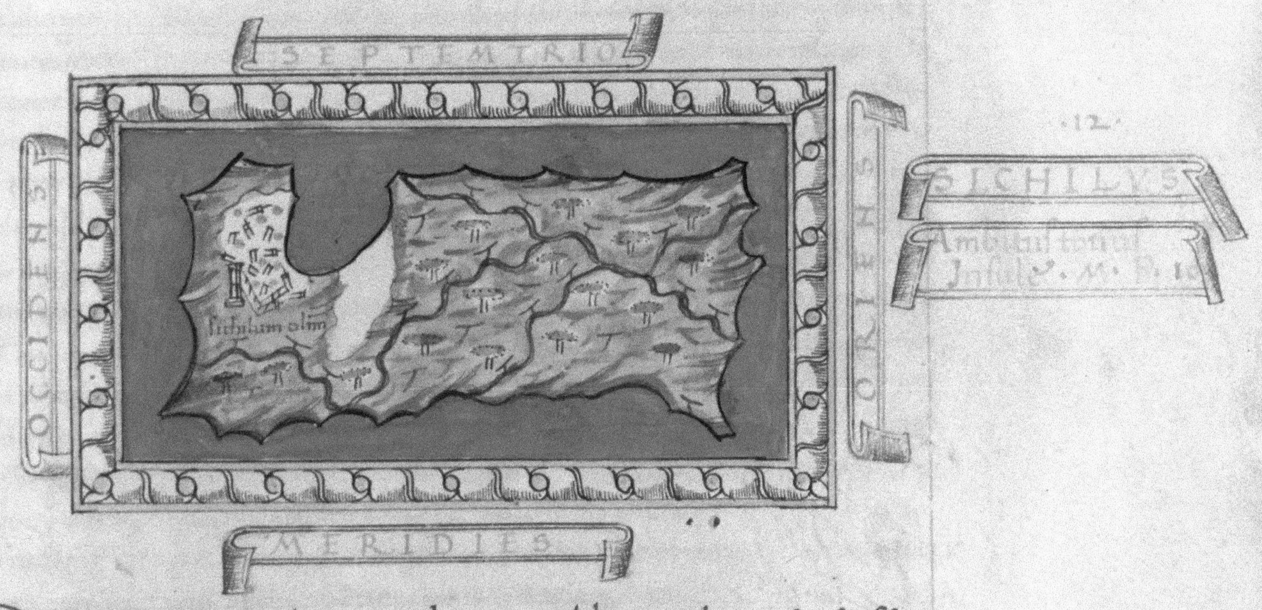

OMnia quāuis que hic narranda erunt in libro quē de creta cōposui sit pro
lixiora hic p plegentiū cōmodū succīcte ī trib; partib; īsulā clare diuidā q̄ ē ī medio
mediterranei maris posita fereq; ab oībꝫ partibꝫ mōtibꝫ circūdata & ūdiq; auētis agitata.
De oriēte ad occiduum ducēta & xxx. & ī latitudine .xxxv. distare uidet̄. ad oriētē sal
mon mons q adinsulam carpati prospectat adocciduū mons oricis eleuat̄ q admallui
respicit promōtoriū. fuit aut̄ a filio nebrot creto creta dicta: uel q̄a terra hec admo
dum terre tenacis & albe nom̄ accepit. habuit .n. cētū ciuitates quaꝝ uestigia ad sexa-
gesimū accessi numerꝫ. In qua saturnus sagax & potēs ut dixit filius urani .i. celi
& ueste .i. terre erat & ad dei similitudinē se fecit orare Ipē & .n. p̄us era signauit &
nomē ipsius apposuit. Ignaros arua colere docuit & semiā agris īponē atq; colli
gere ordinauit. Ad sui laudē aram & sacra instituit saturniaq; appellauit. Vestam
sororē suā sacro cupulauit cōnubio & ea plures susceptos filios scripsere quos aiūt os
deuorasse ne eū de regno expelleret ut inuenerat. & iouē seruatū uxoris fraude ī dā
meūdē mōtē nutriendum misit & curetis populis cōmedat̄ & inantrū mōtis yde
delatum ne aduagitū audiret tymbala & timpana pulsabat & adsonū apes mella

in os eius īferebāt· i· nutrices de lacte & melle eū nutrībāt· Hic tādē cū adoleuisset bellū
habuit cū titanis ide prēm regno expulit qa seuerus erat & carnē humanā docuit imolarē
et filios propos· Iupiter igit ex fuga patris dns creteñ factus sororē suā iunonē ī cōiugē
accepit· & glorie auidus ī multis locis ad sui nomē tēpla cōstruxere· licet multi fuint iu-
pitres· tam iste cretēsis maior omniū fuit q multa bona & utilia humane uite adīuenit.
Mortuo uō cōpus iux oppidum aulacie posuē quis dicat in celū eē deificatum· Ibi ergo
prope mōtē hodie de suo nomine dictū ī radicib; ad tonē ptolomeo demōstrāte uiā antrū manu
factū albatūq; paruo ore· xl· ī lōgitudine & iiij^or ī latitudine brachio^r repetim: cui ī capite sepulchrū iouis maxi suo epithaphio deleto cognouim: ex uō ī superficie edificia maxima admo
dū āpliabāt tēpli· Cū itaq; uersus australē plagā uergim prope mare ad oriētē ierapolis cū
ingētib; marmo^r edificijs est· Mathalia cū musaicis edificijs finicis nobilissima ruinarū
q ī tēplo grecis sculpebāt lrīs· Mūda pedē uela cap & ineta· Chissamessolis magnifica erat
ubi promōtoriū cadisti hodie spatā appropīquat: deinde chidonia: q hodie acanta amenissima habetur: in qua metellus cōtra cretā ueniēs pmo ī duob; ānis igni ferroq; īsulā
totam posuit & uindictā fecit de marco ant^o q cōflictū ī mari & a creticis rome repor
tauit: ut titus liui ad retinā uenio deinde ad canda cum hodie candia & metropolis
postq ueneti eam emere & denuo hanc edificauere: ad chersonesum uenio olim alta me-
morū deinde a dolopexopoli hodie histrinā cōcurro ī qua fōs octo molēdino^r apit & iux
sequēdo mare oppida ī sumitatib; mōtiū alia reperuit quo^r ī medio sarādapolis ciuitas
olim gigātum erat a qua sectia deriuata ē· In fine uō īsule ad oriētē Salmon mōs appel
latur omniū altissimi uicino^r· Regredior ergo usq; ad occiduū postq a salmone mōte
recedim: & p mediū insule uergēs ad dictū properam mōtē & ī sumitate hui^o lassiti cap
xviij· ī circuitu mili· ī pascuis fertilissimus habetur· Ad austrū aūt ampla elōgat planities Messarea dicta in qua circa mediū nō parua uestigia amplissime urbis gorthine
olim metropolis apparet: q minois regis pncipalior extiterat· & quātū nr̄a florētia
ī habitu manifestat: cū arce magnifica & cōductu aquarū descēdētiū· q totā deīn rigabat urbē
ī q duo ad plus milia colūpna^r marmorū & idolo^r prostrata enumeraui· Ad tonē aūt ī mōte
p miliare ore strenuo Labiritus ut aūt reperit: ī q minotaur^o a dedalo collocat^o & p Theseū frau
de fredre sororis ī eodē loco īterēptus occubuit· Ad occiduū ad x· mil· mōs famosissim^o & altissim^o
appar& ida cui ī radicib; gnosia ciuitas olī uidet· In qnq; ergo collib; sine arboib; mōs erigit iste
q^r ī medio pars sublimior ē: ubi saturni ut dr tēplū ad sui laudē stabiliuit & ibidē cānē pmo sacrificarē
īstituit. Sūt & n· de medio usq; sūmū p totū ānū niues & de Gnosia usq; ad apteriapoli xl· mil· & ī latitudīe
xx^ti· q^o ī spatio mlta erant enarāda auctoritatib; mlto^r aucto^r· Ad occiduū uō ad ūbrosā ualles de xx^ti· duob;
domib; romano^r cōstātini tēpor huc uenerē habitatū & degēte ī gētē diu renouari arma & cognomī
āntiq cognatōis usq; ī hodiernū diē tenuē & ad grecū tenuē ritū· & pmo gōtaci latine saturi qngēti nūo
mellissimi uespasiani trecēti· Ligni suttiles melle secēti· Vlasti papiniai ducēti· Cladi tamuli cētū cōsuagim
Scodili agati octīgēti· Colōni colōnēses trigita· Arculeades ursini cētū remāsē· Versus deīq; agūlū
hui^o īsule leucus eleuat mōs a q flumina hic ide descēdūt plura & ī ūbrosis ipso^r uallib; tot & tāti

cupssi pululāt & crescūt q̄ icredibile foret ad nārādū & ex eis p̄ niuesū tabule mittūt in āno. Virgil.
Creta iouis magni medio iacet insula ponto. Mons ideus ubi & gentis cunabula nostre.
Centum urbes habitant magnas ubertima regna.

SEPTEMTRIO

MERIDIES

NHARrati de creta nūc ad insulā carpathi uenio: căpos .i. grece fruct⁹ latine. &
pallene dicta a filio titanis ibi dominātē. Ab hac igit̃ pallas nomē sortita ē: ex
qua in ea fuit nutrita cum prius uocaret̃ minerua dea sapiētie & de cerebro iouis :
nata: q̄ in similitudine unius domine armate erat sculpta. Caput circūcinctū idne
& cassis cū cristalancia in dextera & in sinistra scutū cristallinū cū mōstro gorgone.
Vestes triplici colore. lux se oliua cū noctua desup. Igit̃ erat armata qa sapiens est
armatus uirtutū: scutū fortitudinis lance rectitudinis & iustitie galea sobrieta
tis & tēperātie. Iris claritatis & prudētie: oliua pietatis & prudētie: noctua humilitatis & occultātie. Triplicē uestē tres uirtutes theoricas: Cristallinū splendorem
ueritatis. Imago terribilis timō diuinus. Gorgona imago mortis uel diaboli. Crista
honoris. Fuit & enim hec pria iapeti: qui duos habuit filios epimetheū & prome
theum maximi ingenij & uehemētis studij: q de limo terre hominis formasse simulacrum dicit̃. quo dilecta minerua prometheum duxit in celū: ut siqd de cele-
stib; uellet ad sui opis pfectionem posset eligere: q de cursu solis unū ex radijs furat⁹
īn ea eius pectus animauit simulachrū. Vnde a Ioue fulminatus ī caucaso mōte liga
tus iecur uulturi pbuit pennitec cōrodēdum. In mōte uō caucaso prometheus stu
dens nām hominis a pncipio terrā eē cōsiderauit. Veniēs ad aliā nām cōphēdit aīaz
ex celo procedere cū uigorē & celestis origo furasse radiū solis .i. sua cōsolatione ad
celestia dirigens. Q uultur seu aquila iecur corrodat nil aliud est: qa uiri studētes
exteriora inficiūt & iteriora cōsumūt. Fuerē ergo hic oppida septē quoꝝ tria hodie inter mōtes habent̃: que circuit .Lxx. mil: & ad orietem olimbos ciuitas
extat cum portu tristomos scopuloq; sario. Ad occiduū ī portu theatros duo erāt
oppida in acro tiri .i. puncta uidelicet teneo & circassas ubi nūc sanctus theodorus denominatur & in cōspectu cusso insula. Ad trione uō iux mare olim :
fianti ciuitas ampliata erat: ubi nō longe quasi in medio insule mons achinata
& oros & sancti elie manifestāt ubiq;. Ad meridie uō planus estat cuius ī capite pōtus agata ampliat̃: p totam deniq; tāq̄ bruti habentur q laborantes ī pice cū
lacte sbstentant̃: Vnde semel infideles in eam uenētes & clam in nocte p insulam
lucratum dum irent Carpathi ergo uigilātes sup eos uiriliter biremē īcendere
illi uō redeuntes cōtristati nimis dimissa pda ī montib; plusq̄ cētū fame periere.

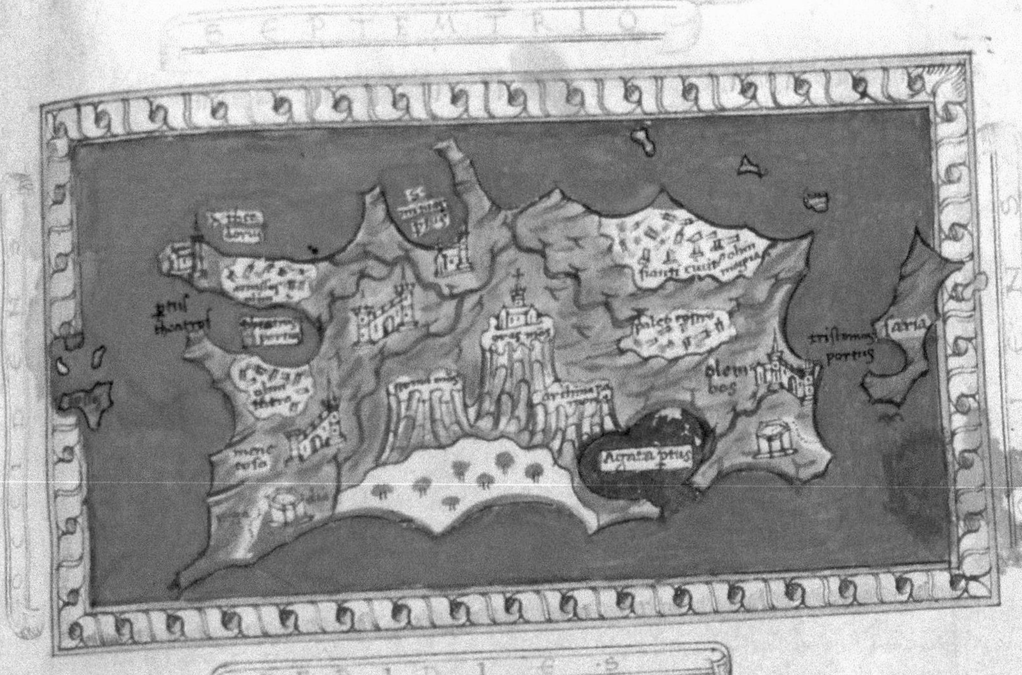

V Enio igitur ad antiq̄ssimā rhodianam ciuitatē: q̄ receptaculū dominorū
minoris asie & olim grecia q̄ nūc turchia est & mercatorum peregrinoꝝq;
ex oib; mūdi partib; huc uenientium: Dicit̄ ergo rhodo grece rosa latine quia hic
ipfectione magisq̄ in alijs rose habeantur. Vel dicit̄ rhodi a malo punico q̄ a plena ho
ipsectione ... a scō stephoro usq; ad scm̄ ioanē lepro
minū oli ita erat & admodum scuti amplabat̄ a scō stephoro usq; ad scm̄ Ioanē lepro
soꝝ & scm̄ antoniū & scm̄ gallinicū & ad p̄mū redeūdo scm̄ circūdabat. Quo i cir
cuitu turres ducēte erāt ut in cronica habet̄: quarū q̄ȝlib& cubitoꝝ q̄nquagīta
erigebat̄: quarū imedio colossum ydolum mire magnitudinis cubitoꝝ · LXX · sup
eminebat ubi uelū a longe · LXXX · mil · manifestabat̄ & cacumina totius ciuitatis
ad unū submittebat: q̄ potētissima nimis multis annis cū egiptijs p̄lui parauē · Tādē
abeis desolata remansit · Alijq; uolunt pp crebros terremotus collossū atq; turres ma
gna hominū cede funditus p̄iisse: quorū euersiones opiniones multe & diuerse pre
dicant̄: Ideo nihil audeo & rē tam antiquā ignorare. Scimus tam̄ tot eē sētētias q̄t
capita & quasi homines uolūtate potiusq̄ ratione ferre iudiciū · Reperi eq̄dē i q̄dā
greco uolumine colossum idolum eneū altitudine cubitoꝝ ut sup̄ qua i medio
pectoris speculum amplissimū mōstrabat · & ipm̄ aspiciētes naues ab egyptijs egre
dientes uideret · hic igit̄ & p insulā totam plusq̄ mille colossi sup̄ columnā iminebat
Insup & inumerabiliū opus colūpnaꝝ isignitum capitib; cerbie & p om̄s partes
hīc inde celatis signo repperimus una cum urceis cadauerum mortuoꝝ infinitis
quoꝝ uestigia usq; hodiernū p̄hibēt testimoniū. Nūc et de nouo prope sacrū āto
niū saluatoremq; in uinea quadam quingenta idola omniū manerierum i fouea

repertafuit. Huc uō ad cōpationem antique ciuitatis modica est: q̄ ad oriētē pro
spectat & inquatuor diuisa remanet. Quarum prima magister hospitalis sci Io
hannis residit. Secunda a fratribus dicti ordinis possessa est. Tertia hospitale
ipsorum uisitat. Quarta & ultima a mercatoribus una cum grecis habitata est.
que a colosso colocēsis scribit ubiq; est & enim amenissima omniū insular maris
mediterranei & . clini . circuit mil . Que iuxta mare a parte ponētis de puncta to
nis usq; ad austrum plana habet cum oppidis turribusq; ibi apparētibꝫ multis .
Quorum olim una ciuitas uasilica dicta q̄ latine imperatrix manifestat & ad
nihilum redacta . ad austrum uō prosternata oppida diu & rura plura uidēt
ubi polachia cattania eminēt fulcita rusticorum & cultiuata satis cū armētorū
multitudine . Ad oriētē uō prope salo murus īmaniū lapidum quadratum p
montes uallesq; ut aiunt inceptabat & insulam diuidebat & sic indicat dnōrū
fuisse dominiū . Lindum deniq; munitissimū uidemus in quo sacra herculi fuere
īstituta ceterorum ritu diuersa quia carnē diis sacrificabāt . Cūq; nō parua sed
magnificaq; p circuitum desolata uidemus liniamēta . Faradum fandum oppi
da petimus cum arcāgelo rure : deinde rhodum propinquamus ubi tanta est
uiriditas arborum & amenitas locorum q̄ est mirabile ad uidēdum & p̄sertī
paradisum a florentinis factum . Inmedio deniq; insule artamita mōs cū fluie
gadura patescunt : & a leua eius uirginis matris marie appollona habet mira
culis multis . Ad quintū mil . prope ciuitatē ī mōte Filerimus est oppidum & do
mina omnium gratiarum sepe uisitata adoratur a multis . Abhic igit leges
naualium habuisse uident originem . & natus appollonius q de octo ptibꝫ
orōnibꝫ laute tractans . ab eo Priscianus extraxit multa & sibi adaptauit .
Tullius deniq; perueniens in hanc urbem eloquētissimos grecor phos repe
rit & coram eis atq; populo orationem p̄clarain recitauit . Quaobrem a rho
dianis laudabilem acquisiuit laudē . Paulus et apostolus ad colocēses episto
lam mittit : colocenses enim a colosso rhodiani scribunt ubiq; . Quibus & si
pluuie sint semel in die sol apparet & iam otto annor experiētiam una cum
uarro comprobaui .

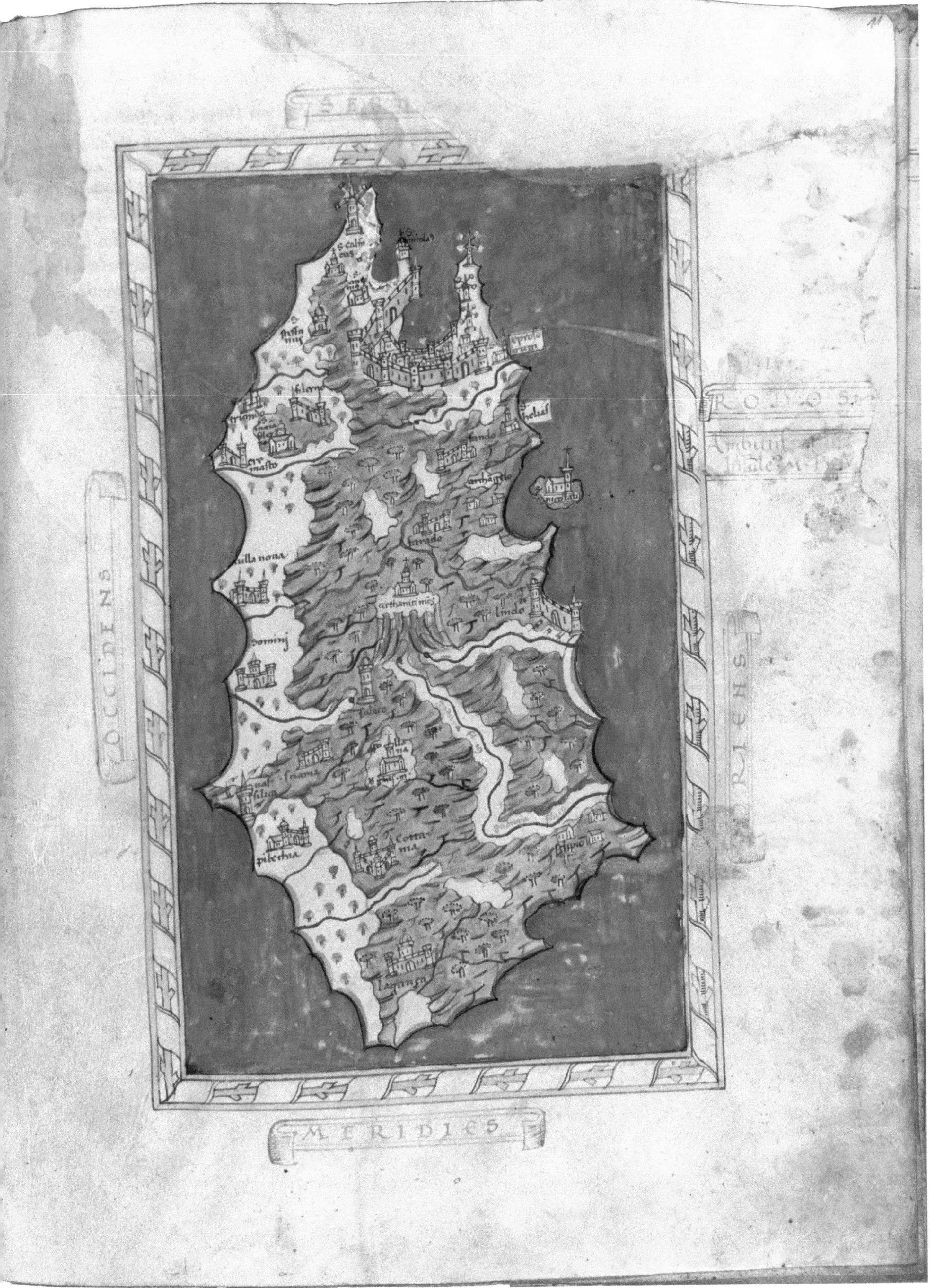
OCCIDENS
RODOS
MERIDIES

...tempore hec insula simie dicta asimeni ibi dominante ul aSi
...ece latine propinqua: qa uix minore asiam appropiquat & com
...nicanis habens uitã cum labore trahebant. Sed postq̃ a ioue maxime
prometheus iapeti filius in hãc in missus habitantibus multa demostrauit ad
uitam cõseruãdam humanam. q ualens ĩ ingenio hominẽ ex luto finxit: quod
audiens Iupiter ĩ simiã eum cõstituit & ibi uitam finiuit. Colẽtes itaq; hãc hodie
astuti nimis suis cambis inter ciuitates turchorũ rhodiorũq; uichũ studiose freque
tant. A meridiẽ deniq; scopuli adherẽt qb; crebre naues uela deponũt. Castel
lum igitur prope mare munitissimũ ẽ & i mõtib; aliud desolatũ. q̃ xxx. mil. ci
cuit. uino optimo ĩter saxa eghe abalto caprizant.

Longe no[n] nimis ab ista supradicta Caristos ol[im] nu[n]c calc[...]
g[ra]uauere & i[n]sulas briareo i[n]stituisse diuina & pauci o[mn]ib[us] i[n]colu[...]
nimis & fructuosa reman[et]: ideo mo[r]tales no[n] edificia pon[er]e curauer[un]t. In e[...]
bi[tur] quo[rum] ta[n]ta redundat copia q[uod] naues circu[m]nauiga[n]tes loca fecu[n]da[n]t. Ad orie[n]te[m] [...]
tus ampliat[ur] cui i[n] su[m]mitate oppidu[m] uetustum munitu[m]q[ue] ualde uidet[ur]: ubi nicolaus s[an]c[tu]s
extin[ct]e fatigatus reside[n]s ge[n]tib[us] illis ui[am] rectitudi[n]is demo[n]strauit: q[uo]r[um] p[re]cib[us] adeo gra[tiam] co[n]secut[us]
e[st] q[uod] secures & ad fodie[n]dum ferrame[n]ta co[n]tinue laborando i[n] istis aridis lapidosisq[ue] mo[n]tib[us]
no[n] minuere[n]t[ur]. A q[u]o te[m]pore usq[ue] i[n] hodie[r]nu[m] illesa fuha[n]t[ur]: q[uae] ad dotes filiab[us] co[m]putat canores cap[...]
ecc[les]iam ad laude[m] ip[s]i[us] ditissima[m] auri arge[n]tiq[ue] co[n]stitu[er]e qua[m] co[r]de & a[n]i[m]o gub[er]na[r]e laborat.

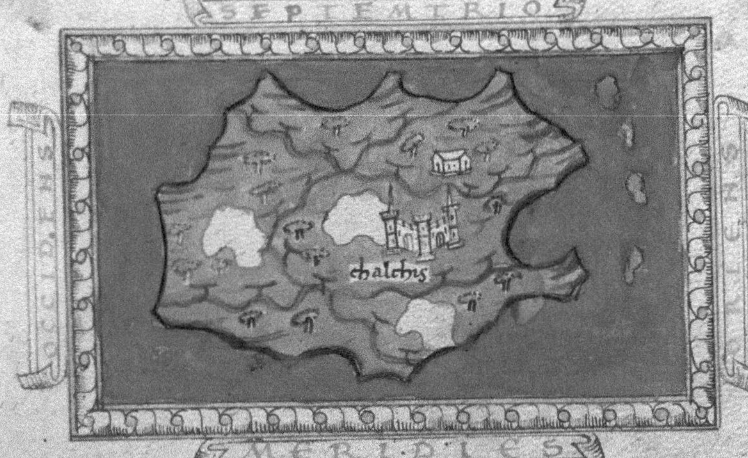

Mostrauimus de calchi: nu[n]c ad dilu[m]phanos ol[im] hodie piscopia tra[n]situ[m] parabo: diluphanos olim grece latine o[mn]ib[us] appare[n]tib[us] i[n]terp[re]tat[ur]. Piscopia grece ab epi q[uod] e[st] sup[er] & scopos speculator quasi sup[er] speculatrix: q[uia] i[n] mo[n]tib[us] ualde eleuata e[st] & a lo[n]ge cernit[ur] nimis. De
orie[n]te ad occiduu[m] elo[n]gat[ur] & XXXV circuit mil[ia]. Ad orie[n]te[m] fro[n]difluus eleuat[ur] mo[n]s: cui i[n] radicib[us]
duo exta[n]t scopuli quo[rum] un[us] ascina appellat[ur]. Ad trione[m] u[er]o oppidu[m] s[an]c[t]i stephani i[n] quo po[r]tus &
planus manifestat[ur]. Ad occiduu[m] zucharola erigit[ur] egestate plenus. In medio quoq[ue] alia duo
oppida male habitat[ur]: q[ui]b[us] potius eg[estat]e uaga[n]t[ur] q[uam] homines loca ualeat custodire.

...pte nuc ad cariã olim nuc nixaros ĩdicare ualeam cũ suo ethneo
...aribdi grece latine: nuc nixos grece ĩsula latine ĩterptat. Hic flami
niu coiul rediẽs de partib orietis & accedẽs pugnaturus cõtra gallos auguratus ẽ victo
riã obtiñe & sic factum ĩluce resoluit. Itaq; ĩsula hec sẽp beniuola romanis habita ẽ. Per hãc
ẽt trãsiẽs cleopatra cũ antonio & noletes ciues pceptis ipsoꝝ obedire totã ĩsulã deleuere
q. xviij. circuit mil. & qnq; uidẽt oppida quoꝝ duo pncipaliora Mãdrachi & paleo castra
apparẽt. Epãdenichi: nichea & argos st ĩcircuitu. Circa mediũ mõs erigit altissimũ: q ĩsuitare
psbterraneos meatus sulphureus ignis die ac nocte eructat ĩ altũ ut ĩ insula strongili apd
liparũ habet. In discẽsu uõ mõtis adiactum lapidis fons calidissimus emanat ĩuiuũ. & in
plano circa lacum profudissimũ obscuruq; aque descẽdũt. Ibiq; colẽtes quãtitatẽ maximã
sulphuris mercatorib pparãt. & qa ĩtãtũ uig & ĩtẽsitas caloris de medio usq; uerticem
nullus ẽ ausus sine sotularib accedẽ ligneis. Etiam hic tãta fecũditas ficuũ q ĩ anno
naues onerant parue. Ad trione in pede mõtis cõtigua maris cõsistit ad quã circũstãtes
dolorib oppssi accedũt & diu morati ĩ priam ĩcolumes reuertũt. & qa cõcaua ut psuit
hec insula habet sepius tot & tãti terremotus ubiq; gignũt q forẽses ob hoc pterriti lo
cũ cito maledicẽtes derelinqũt & procul accedẽ gaudet. Colẽtes uõ tale sterminium
pro nihilo reputant.

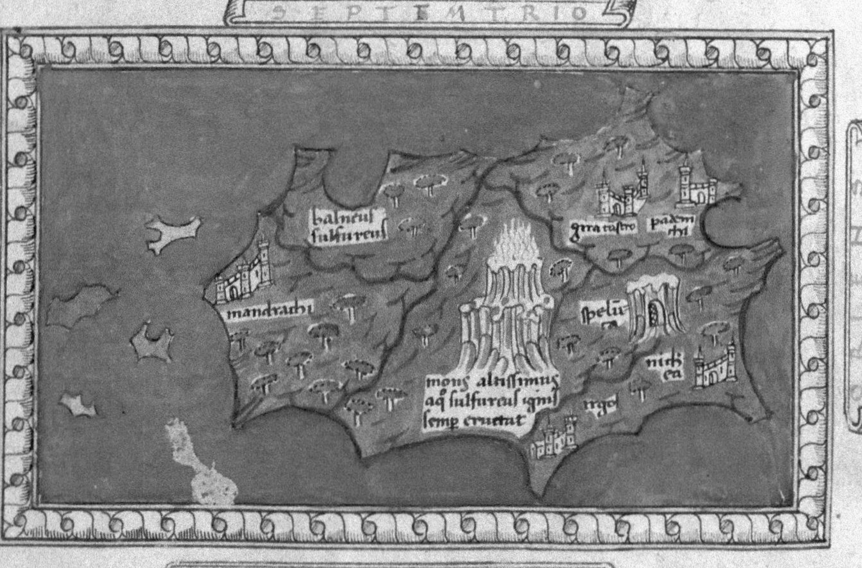

19.

...ria olim
...hisari

...sule totius
...mbitus m. p. xvii

NVHC ad stimphaleã olim hodie spelũchã meũ properabo cursum. & ut ait Plini
Astimphalea libere ciuitatis circuitus octuaginta nouẽ milia passuũ & ĩsuper
ouidius hic anaphem sibi iungit & astimphalea regna. Promissis anaphẽ regna & stimpha
lea bello cinctaq; piscosis astiphalea uadis ĩ medio aũt & tenuissima est & ĩ extremis
ampla ĩ qbus plurima castra desolata uidẽt. Ad trionẽ uathi oppidũ. Ad meridiẽ occi
duũq; ciuitas apparet Stimphalea dicta. Sũt et p insulam antiquitates multoꝝ oppi
dorum: & hic inde p circuitũ portus optimi cõcludũt & desolati iamdiu a pyratis sine
apparatu usq; ĩ hodiernũ pandũt ubiq;. Tẽpore igit morbosani turchi pueta magna classa
istas ĩsulas in totũ deluẽ pyrrate. Igit usq; ĩ hodiernũ relicta a cultorib. Solus nobilis ille
uenetus Ioañes qrinus suis iurib eã cepit tẽpore cõcilij constantie restaurare.

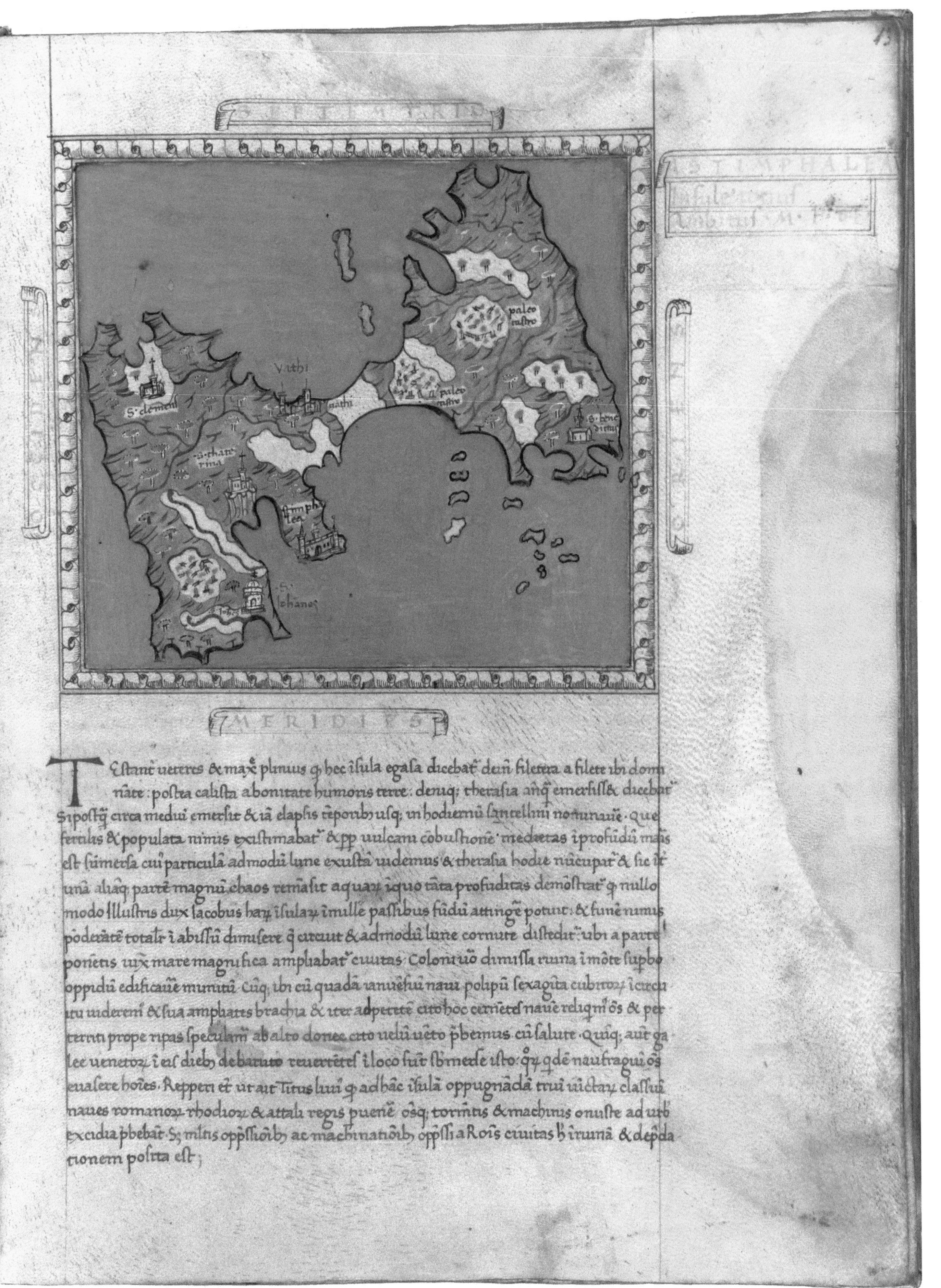

Testantur veteres & maxime plinius q hec isula egasa dicebatur. dein filetera a filete ibi dominante: postea calista abonitate humoris terre: denuq; therasia antequam emersisset & dicebatur
Si postquam circa mediu emersit & iam elapsis teporib; usq; in hodiernu Santellini nominavere. Que
fertilis & populata nimis existimabatur & pp vulcani combustione medietas i profundu maris
est summersa cui particula admodu lune exustam videmus & therasia hodie nuncupatur & sic in
una aliaq; parte magnu chaos remansit aquarum i quo tanta profunditas demonstratur q nullo
modo Illustris dux Iacobus harum isularum i mille passibus fundu attingere potuit: & funem nimis
ponderatem totaliter i abissu dimisere q circuit & admodu lune cornute distendit. ubi a parte
ponentis iux mare magnifica ampliabatur civitas. Coloni vero dimissa ruina i monte superbo
oppidu edificavere munitu. Cumq; ibi cu quadam ianuensium navi polipu sexagita cubitorum i circu
itu videremus & sua amplians brachia & iter aperiente cito hoc cernentes navem reliquimus omnes & per
territi prope ripas speculamur ab alto donec cito velud vento pervenimus cu salute. Quinq; autem ga
lee venetorum i eis dieb; debatuto revertentes i loco sunt submerse isto. quarum quidem naufragium omnes
evasere homines. Reppertum est ut ait Titus livius q ad hanc isulam oppugnandam trium victarum classium
naves romanorum rhodiorum & attali regis pervenere omnesq; tormentis & machinis onuste ad urbis
excidia prebebant. Sed multis oppressionib; ac machinationib; oppressa a Romanis civitas hec i ruinam & depreda
tionem posita est;

21 et 22

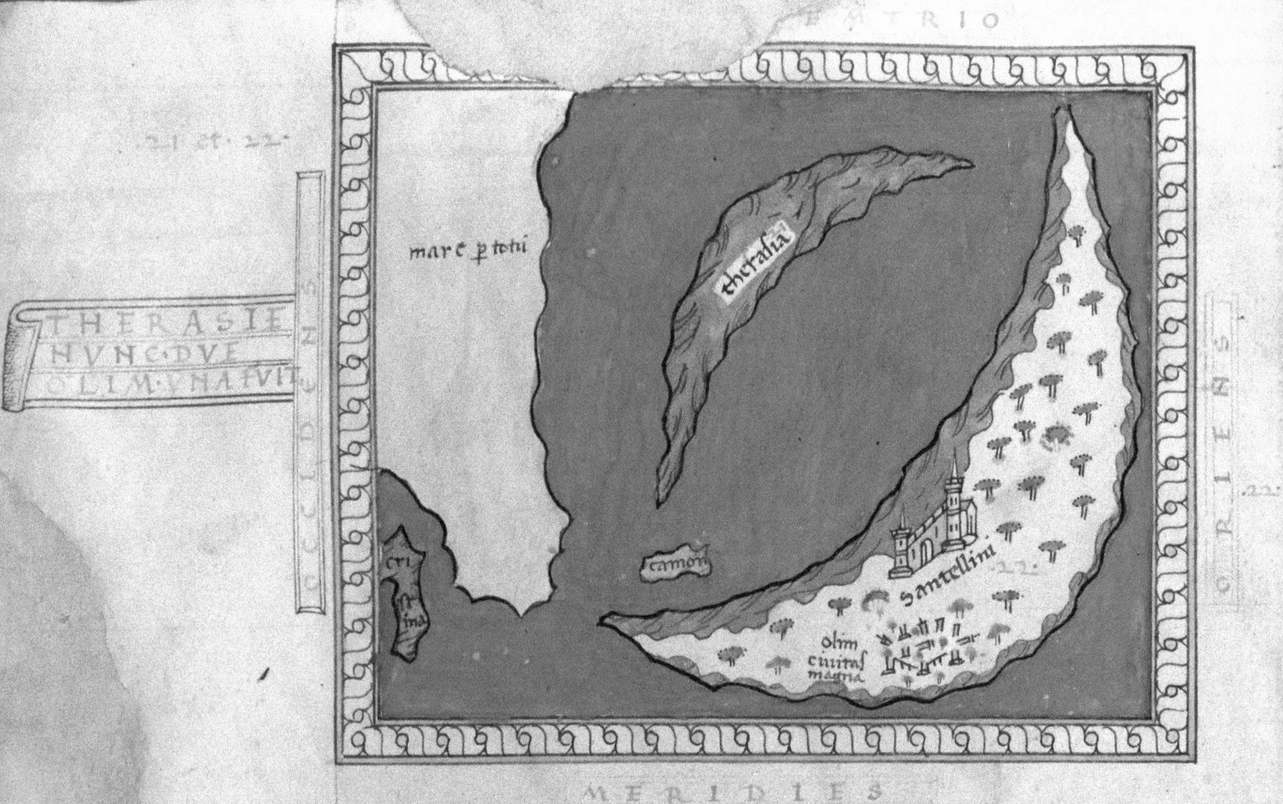

SEPTEMTRIO
THERASIE
HUNC DUE
OLIM UNA FUIT
OCCIDENS
mare ꝑ toti
therasia
camon
santellini
olim
ciuitas
magna
ORIENS
MERIDIES

22

CVM sic cernim⁹ uersus sicādrum iter arripim⁹ · & dr̄ sicādras amititudīe ficuū ibi oli fructificātium · Sica · n · grece latine ficus interꝑtat² que mōtuosa nimis a uetusto tēpore usq; nūc inculta remansit : tum propter turchorum & pyrratax insidias : tum propter ignauiam rusticorum cohaderētium & portus īcōmoditatē : inqua aselli forte ꝑ insulam relicti usq; nūc errantes ꝑ asperas ripas magno hīc inde capiūt² labore .
Volunt igit² q; in hoc loco meleus quidā uir strenuus tēpore troianorū ad exercitū grecorum duabus accessit nauibus qui adherens insule deli a longe oraculū adorauit & ꝑsequēs suum iter tempestate facta necatus est : & sic uiduate mulieres ex tūc oppidum i exterminiū declinauit · que cū i lōgissima ꝑseueraret etate ī solitudine paucox castellum ruraq; & in fine ad nihilum peruenere ;

23

OCCIDENS
SICANDROS
OLIM ET NUNC
Circuitus totius
insule m p 17
MERIDIES
sicandros
SEPTEMTRIO
ORIENS

23 in nino

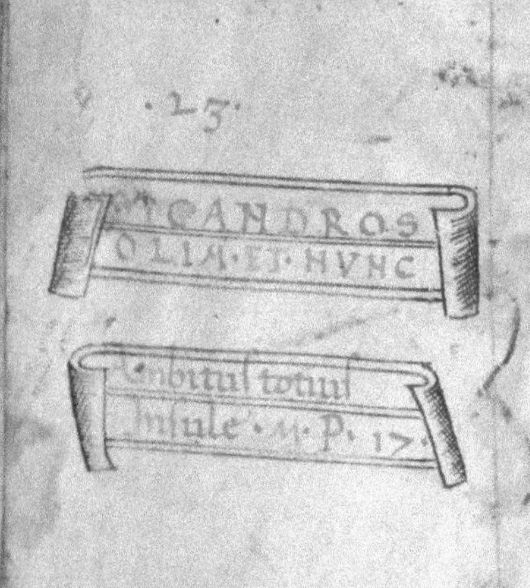

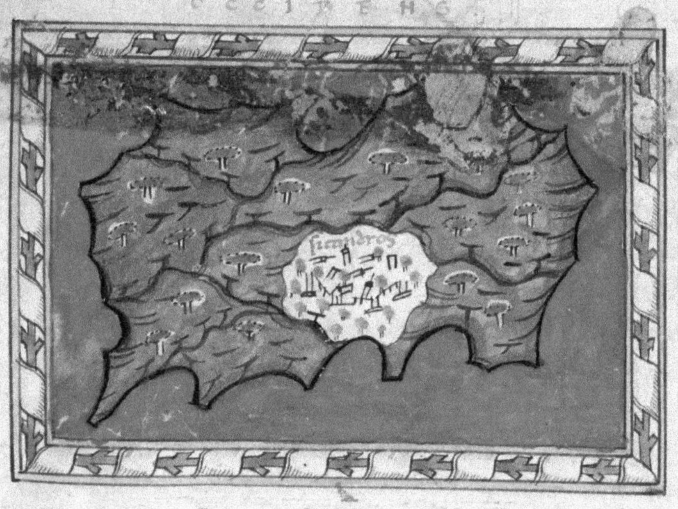

Est sequens insula policandros dicta ab herba sic nominata ad morbū caducum optima. Vel dicitur a poli ciuitas & andros homines .i. ciuitas hominū uel uirorum. Cōstat igit̃ a nomine eam habitatam fuisse cum tā seculis multis a domibus menysq; sit ad nichilum reducta. hec XX circuit mil̃ modicis arborib; uirenbusq; herbis. Euenit aūt q cum fideles eam igne suffocauerit. Cūq; recessum capere uellent uox audita est hominem innocētem & mihi propitium necauistis. ibitis nō impune transire nō lic&. cūq; hoc explicar& ensem inter culpabiles ruit & sternit improbos. Residuum uō ad patriam remeare dimisit qui deuote miraculum narrantes ad fidē christi deuenere.

Ferunt q hec insula polimio nūq̃ fuit habitata sed cū sit i aliq nemorosa loco & forme casarum patefacte homines habitasse in ea manifestatur. Sed quid i eo loco uetustum fuit ab hominibus hoc tempore ignoratur. Verū q una biremis turchorū dū hāc appeter& & ad capiendum egas accederet. Eolus boream emissus ab antro cito ratē i saxa latentia torquet & i unum miserabile uisu demissa ē. Cūq; hoc socy perciperet & in longam exclamationē erumpet in XX dierum spatio omnes animam maumeto tradidere. Circuit mil̃. XVIJ. i qua falcones quolib& āno pullos nutriūt suos.

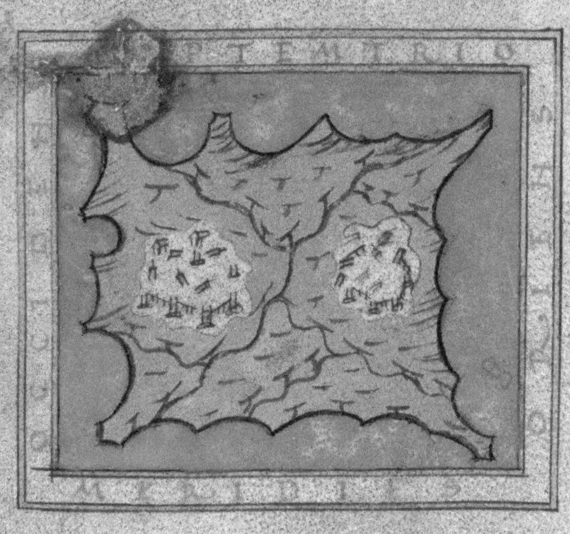

Legimus equidē multis grecoꝝ annalib; nomē huius insule discordare. &
primo Aristoteles mellidam dicit de quo nomine plinius ab abundātia mellis ī mōtib; cauer
nosis concordat. Gorgias zephiram a uento illo qui in eodem regnat loco. Calimachus mimalli
da a domina sic dicta. Eraclides simphim a sibilo quia aque descēdētes & cadentes sonitum tāq̄
sibilū emictāt. hodie u͞o milos q͞d latine molēdinū sonat q͞a p omīs cōtratas illas lapides molēdini īue
niūt & fere in alys & ideo milos merito dicta: q̄ in egeo termiāt & cōtra malleū promōtoriū eleuat
altissima. Sardus hic īuenit lapis sepe q̄ desubt niger ī medio cādidus & desup rubeus manifestat
& castū fīrētē reddit. Huc rex athenaꝝ minusteus demofōtis fr̄ & thesei de bello troiano reuertēs appli
cuit marisq; procellis ī aulta lacessitus occubuit: cui us; ī hodiernū diē honorabile sepulchrū epithaphio
sculptū cernit. Circuit h̄ mil. Lxxx. cui ī medio ad t̄onē pōt nobilissim apperit aquaꝝ medicinaliū sul
phuris existētiū ī circuitu: ī q̄ turris & plan apparꝫ domib; aliq͞b;. Ab ea u͞o parte q̄ est īter oriētē & t̄one
ciuitas eleuat munitissima: ī qua euenit mācipy capto tēpore postq̄ ciues hīc ī de ī laborib; accedētes
castellū dicte īuaserīt & dominā loci occiderīt. hoc aūt cū pceperīt circūstātes armis uirib;q; totis elap
sis diebus ī expugnabile uicerīt castrū & mācipia ad tartara descēderīt. Cybeles & n. ut reppei adorabat: q̄
sculpta ī p̄tiosis lapidib; ornata cū corona turriū & galli seq̄ntes & leones cūrū trahebāt: q̄ clauē ī manu
gestabat. Igit cybeles t̄ra d̄r ī cūru: q͞a terra ī aere pēdꝫ, ī rotis q͞a mūdus rotat & uolubilis est: leonib;
ut ostēdat materna pietas. Oīs .n. feritas materne subicit affectioi. lapidib; p̄tiosis uestita q͞a terra ē
mr̄ oīum lapidū metalloꝝq;. Galli q͞a eius sacerdotes castrati erāt q & coribātes dicebāt. Turrib; coro
nata q͞a ī terra sūt ciuitates & castra. Clauē q͞a uerno tēpore terra aperit & ī hieme claudit. Ad occidu
um oppidū erat pollonia quo corā scopuli insuleq; inculte apparēt multe & hinc inde sparse p
totum;

.26.

MELOS. OLIM
NUNC MILO
Ambitus totius
Insule M. P. 30

Ostēdi de milo nūc ad insulam sipham accedam⁹: siphanos grece surbo latine. cuiq; per eā accesseris mōtes & aridā calcabis uiā & ab egis comitata .xl. circuit mil. Ad oriētē uō ī mōte prope sarraglā ciuitas ē de nomine īsule dicta. Ad occiduū schinosi locus aperit⁹ & sinus. & ad meridiē portus cōcludit⁹ olim cū urbe deruta q̄ nūc plati iallo nominat⁹ & ī cōspectu scopulū chitriani dictū uidem⁹. In medio uō turris erigit⁹ exambeles dicta aq̄ fons usq; emanat mare. ī quo ortus omniū uirescit pomoꝝ. Pan et d̄s nē colebat⁹ ut ī sublimiori loco statua deleta demostrat. Sed postq̄ paulus & reliq apostoloꝝ uerbū diuinū p has p̄dicauē cōtratas oīa idola ruere. Igit⁹ pā cornut⁹ & rubicūd⁹ supiorē ptē mūdi īdicat ignē & etherē cū ca dijs denotam⁹. Pect⁹ stellat⁹ stelle celi. Septē calami ī ore: septē planete. Femorā ā boēs & hēbe pedes caprios āīalia denotabāt⁹. Habitāt deiq; hī pauci & misabiles q̄ꝝ nūz ps max⁹ st̄ muliēs: q̄ pp defectū uiroꝝ usq; ad senīu uitā ui castā deducūt: & q̄uis liguā ig̃rēt latinā tn̄ catholicā fidē non amictunt.

Desumo Serphinum que in montibus tota .xl. circuit mil. & dicitur a serfi grece herba que ad dolorem renum salutifera hic inuenit⁹ uel dicit⁹ a Serfino cōditore aquo assumpsit nomen. Cuiq; ad meridiem uergis portus coram scopulo quodam pan ditur ultro & citro inlatum iuxta planum oppidum eleuat⁹. Quod usq; in hodiernum a serfino conditore antiquum seruat nomen. Ibiq; circum & p abrupta uiarum eghe innumerabiles uagari cernuntur carnes quarum assate a sole diu ī cibū a colonis sūmitur laute in qua appollo celebratur in puerili forma & q̄n in senili. In capite tripodam auream in manu pharetra & sagitta cum arcu: in altera cytharam tenebat. In pedibus monstrum serpentinum tribus capitibus .s. caprino: lupino & leonino Iuxta erat laurus cum coruo uolitante. Appollo sol interp̃tatur puer in mane: uir in meridie. senex in sero quia pallet. Arcus & sagittas quia radios ad nos mittit

cythara quia mollificat sonos totius celestis melodie: tripoda propter tria beneficia. Splē
dorem calorem & interiorem uigorem quem incūctis uiuentibus operatur. Mōstrū triū
capitum. Tempus canis blandientis tempus futurum quia semper per spetiem futurorū
homini blandit̃: lupus tempus p̃teritum quod moris est lupi. capit & fugit. leo tēpus
p̃sens quod stat & fugere non dignatur. Laurus quia uirgo in estate durat. Hūc ergo p̃r
quid sit in hac insula nisi calamitas certum est cum tempus & uitam tanq̃ ad brupta-
lem p̃sequentur modum: & quod plus estat die ac nocte magno tremore ne ĩmanus per-
ueniant infidelium: tremuli annos fatigant consumere suos;

.28.

SERPHINUS
OLIM ET NUC

Ambitus m. P. 40.

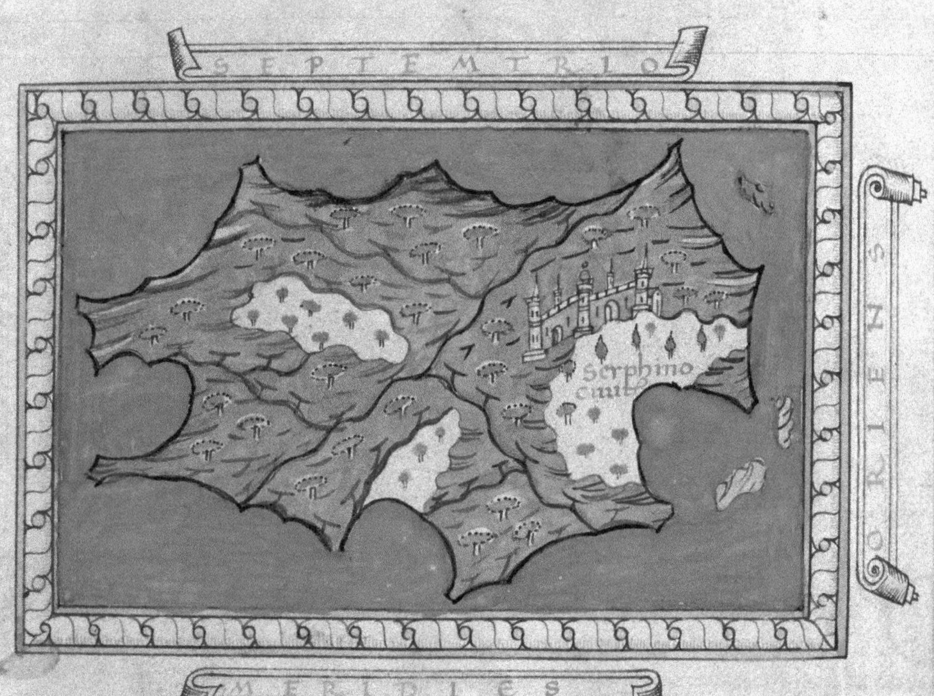

Est etiam post supradictam thermia nuncupata insula que dr̃ a thermo grece la
tine tepidum & mōtuosa ualde & xL circuit mil. Ad orientē uõ sācta elini cernitur
cernit̃ ubi planus extat quo in capite ciuitas thermia erigit̃ quā turchi ibi mācipij proditōie
in nocte captis ciuibus desolauere: sed nūc populata est. Ad occiduū aūt ĩ ecclia scī luce optimi portus ciuitas olim erat edificijs adornata. In mōte uõ quasi in medio insule turris
erigitur a qua riuulus aquarū riuat usq; salum domesticus: & ibi apocreos planus nascitur. & ad meridiem sinus & planus piscopie manifestat̃: & planus merca prope ter-
minat̃. In uino uõ blado sirico carnibusq; bene habet̃. In qua semel prope ciuitatē ĩ portu turchi forte p̃noctauerīt & due ĩtēpeste noctis eiusdem galearum cretēsium adsūt: quo mane
facto christiani irruētes in eos ad inferos omnes mandauere.

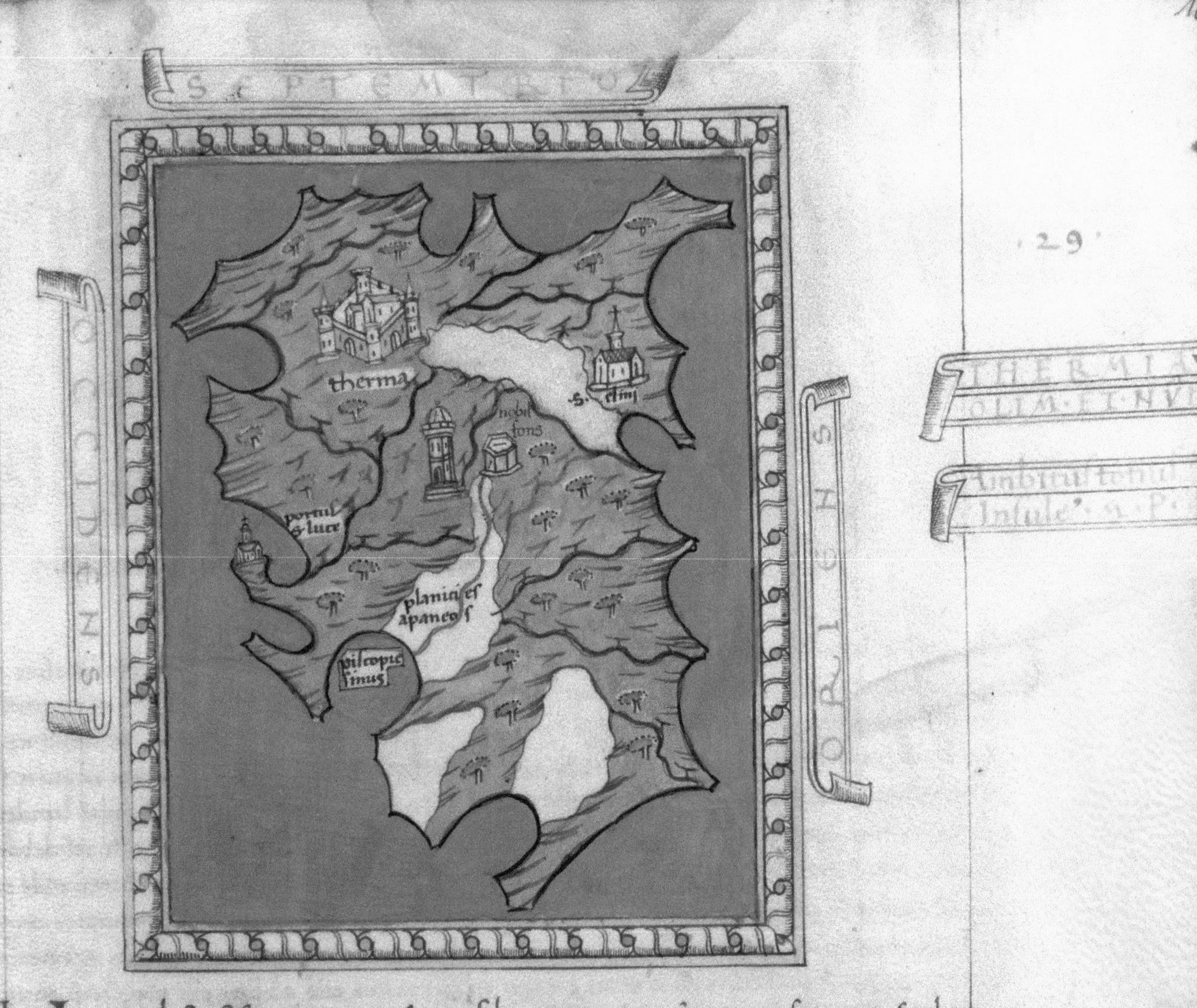

·29·

NVNC ad ceā trāseo a ceo titano & terre filio nominata: q cū extranee ferocitatis sup̄bieq;
existeret & ip̄e cū fratrib; suis una cōtra iouē insurrexert. cū pluri tēpore multo īuicem
fuisset tādē a dicto ioue ex īsulam crete sūt expulsi & hic īde facultatib; diminuti. Ea pp̄ iste
ceus maior suorū fratrū ad hanc deuenit insulam ī q latonā at asteriem uirgines pulcherrimas
genuit de quib; multa dicēdo dimitto: q mōtuosa .L. circuit mil. Ad occiduū pōtus extat & īter
ip̄m castelliq; planus habet. In quo siluestria p̄uagātes & oppidū ualide antiqū retinērē oli erat
ritū ut q senio cōfectus aut īfirmatus uitam ueneno finiret: mors eius maximis laudib; extollebatur. Cūq; sextus pompeius asiam petēs huc actus tempestatib; applicaret & audiretq; matronam quādā etate & uirtutib; ueneradā ad eā accessit & ut diutius uenenū illā nō accipet
exorabat: illa aūt lectulo cubās agnatas circūhabens sic uerbis pōpeio alloqt: Quitū & nonage-
simū annū ago & semp fortuna uultum mihi ostēdit ilarem & gremiū m̄ felicē apuit & ut sepe
fit flatu quodā subito mutate fortune calamitosū uite mee exitū posse feliciter experiri. Igitur
cū leta uita sit & ilarior mors erit & ab oīb; licētiā accipiens dijsq; uocatis cōstāter obijt & cito
sp̄s euolauit: hic et fons īuenit cui potu facuit hoīes hebetes sensu & postq ad digestionē uenerit
mēs ad p̄stinā reducit sanitatē. & qa prope hāc ad occiduū uersus tenaron pegasiq; sinū
atq; mirteū mare multi adiacēt scopuli īsuleq; inculte ideo noīa aliquar hic ponā sine narratione aliqua. Sira uel sidra: macronisso: albera: chitisos de q proculus poeta fuit: q cū Samiā
adamaret gregē multa carmina ad laudē sui nominis compilauit;

Constat hanc ĩsulam andros multis nominib⁊ pronũtiari ut phi dicũt: & primo Mirsius caurũ Calimachus antãdron: alij lagiã nonagriam idrussam a fontib⁊ multis: & Plinius pagrum nominat Andros dicta ẽ a filio annei regis: hec nobilis & pulchra satis & aquarum copiosissima apparet humane nature oĩa producẽte. In mõtib⁊ tota &. Lxxx. circuit mil. & ciuitas ad oriẽtẽ sine portu habitatur. & prope eam uõ parua insula cũ antiquo oppido apparet ad quã ꝑ põtẽ lapideum amplis edificijs accedebat. In mare prope litus turris cernitur: ĩ q̃ circũ astãtes ĩ nocte residebãt ut a pyratis salui fierẽt. Dicit̃ .n. filias annei regis aufugisse de quib⁊ ꝑ ouidiũ sic fingit̃. Bachũ eisdẽ proprietatẽ attribuisse ut quicq̃d tangerẽt in segetem uinũ oleũq; trãsformarẽt. Quo ꝑ agamenonẽ cognito cogit eas ut pascerẽt exercitũ quẽ ad troiam cõducebat. Ille aũt fugiẽtes frẽm ĩ manib⁊ agamenonis elegit eas tradere. Agamẽnon dũ uincula parabat tollẽs brachia celo a libero prẽ popos cerẽt auxiliũ in columbas uerse sunt: rei ueritas sic ẽ q̃ filie annei regis ĩ remedijs agris magnã habuerẽt solertiã adeo ut ĩ magna copia de omib⁊ habũdabãt diuites facte sũt: qua re cõpta ꝑ agamenonẽ ĩ exercitu suo oĩa abstulit eisdẽ & sic de diuitib⁊ facte paupes ad q̃stũ & uelut columbe luxuriose ad publicũ lucrũ ui uẽdi dee ueneris deuenerũt. Quid igit̃ fuerit in hac insula actũ uestiga manifestãt cũ nil aliud ĩuenit̃ nisi magna ac magnifica sculpta ꝑ totum. Insup & deũ mercuriũ fuisse uidet̃ alatũ uirgã ĩ manib⁊ circũ septã serpẽtib⁊ habentẽ galerũ ĩ capite & gallus corã eo cap̃ caninũ. Alatus q̃a stella mercurij citissime facit cursũ suũ. Sõniferã uirgã q̃a ꝓꝑ dulcedinẽ uerboꝝ homo sopit. Caninũ cap̃ q̃a ĩ eloquẽtia lattãdo .i. loquẽdo attrahit homines. In capite galerũ cũ gallo q̃a mercator sollicitus ẽ hĩc ĩgredi cũ mercãtijs & mutat ꝓpositũ ad sui cõformitatẽ. De hĩc ẽt ille Terentius poeta comicus carthaginẽsis fabulã suã incepit: q̃ hominum descripsit mores iuuenũq; senũq;. & ãdriã p̃mã suã cõmediã ĩtitulauit q̃ pãphilã p̃mo de hĩc olicẽtiũ hĩc discessisse ponit. Deniq; Crito homo senex athenas accedẽs pacẽ & gaudiũ cõclusionis fabule adaptauit. Nũc tamen hec regio ꝓꝑ crebras turchoꝝ insidias ad infimũ ẽ reducta q̃uis ad cõparationem aliarum hec melius habetur.

SEPTE

OCCIDENS

andros

ORIENS

.31.

ANDROS INSULA

Ambitus totius Insule M. P. 80

MERIDIES

Inter chion & andrũ scopulus emines caloierus dictus rupib; rapacissim⁹ solus est unde colos grece latine bonus & gherus senex .i. bonus senex. Inde caloierus iterp̃tat̃ p̃ antifrasim q̃i ualde malus & a nauigantib; minacissim⁹ oib; inuenit t̃porib;. Igit̃ hic naues trãseũtes sepe nocte sũmergũt̃ in eo. Inq̃ in eis dieb; una cannuẽsiũ nauis de pera descẽdẽs in hũc perijt scopulum. Ea pp̃ naute trãseuntes anathematizare sepe cõualescũt & digito procul indicãtes cito uelum uertũt̃ in altũ. Cũq; semel turchoȝ ratis ibi merger̃et̃ ad saltum iscopulis hominũ euẽtum est. Tertia uõ die xp̃ianoȝ puppis coram affuit eis. Que misericordia mota omnes illos semiuiuos euasit in altum. Qui post cibum cõualescẽtes i xp̃ianos irruere. & nauigantes in patriam xp̃ianos tãte euasionis causas ad cõtinuã posuẽ seruitutẽ. Hic ẽt falcones ĩ anno pullos nutriũt̃ infra ĩmeabiles ripas.

.32.

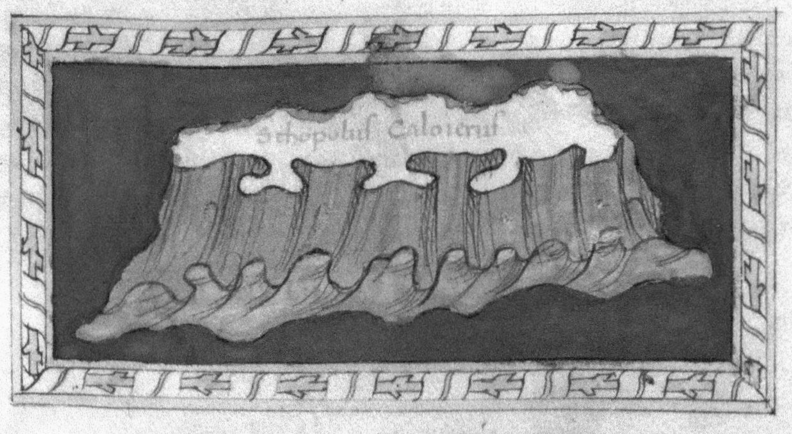

CALOIER

ARistoteles pp aquarū abundātiam idrusam hanc nominat qd latine aquatica sonat Demostenes & Eschinus fussam dicunt: hodie uō tino dictam est pp suā rotunditatē admodum tini deriuata & cōtigua andro · XL · circuit mil · q̄ ispatio duo erigūt scopuli iqua oli mulier uenefica quedā cū uider& semel hostes appropiquātes ad urbē desolandam imōtē sblimiorē ascensa ē & nuda sparsis crinib ad celū brachia extēdēs nō dū icātationē expleuerat q affricus repetinus uetus cōtra illos isgens classē imū euertit & hic pisulam pars illorum euasit maxima que potita licorib icātationū & carminum isensati remāserūt: quo iloco ad seruitutē sūt redacti & ciues effecti diuites tēpore Alexandri claruere Postea a romanis iexterminiū deuenerūt · Euenit aūt nō diu nauē ab occidēte onerātā equoꝝ huc attigisse magna maris tēpestate: q̄ inruinā omniū animātum euasione euersa est · & pisulam ferētes imaximū deuenerē numeꝝ iq̄ circa medium castrū imōte cū plano habet fertili · Ad oriētē deniq; turris sci nicolai imari eleuatur & imōte ad occiduū altera erigit munitissima · Ad trionē uō uallis amena aperit & ad meridiē oli oppidū colebatur ·

33

TINO

Ambitus totius Insule m. P. 40

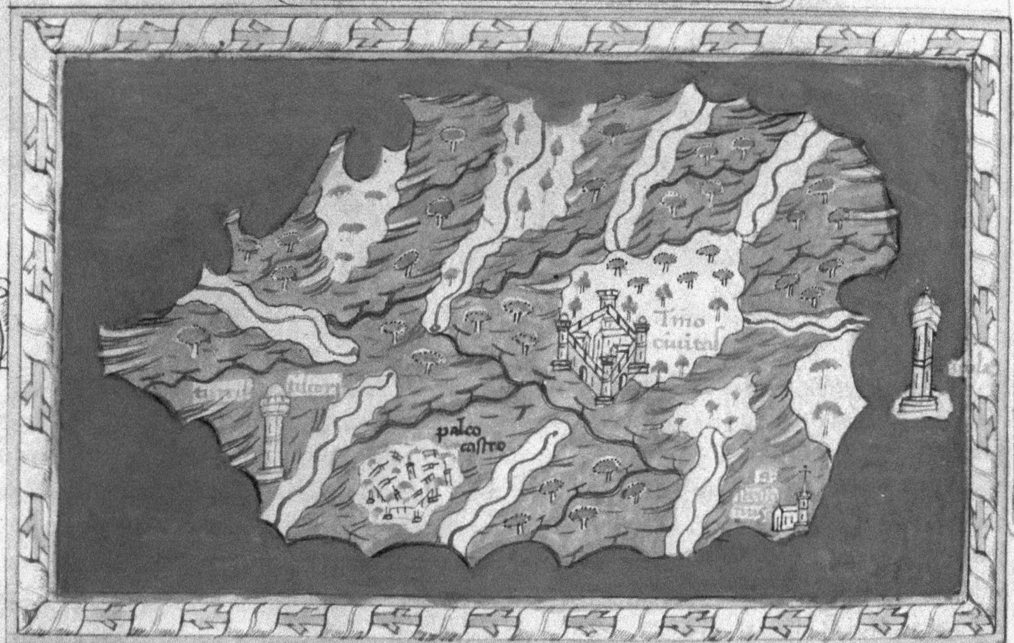

POST q̄ dixi de tino ad Michonos accedamus olim a rege dicta uel micos grece longitudo latine uel paululū qa in loco paruo habet · Fuit oli igit & splendida nimis ut per edificia testatur qa delo propinqua & peregrini ut posset plures ianno idolum uisitare hic habitaculū petebāt · Cūq; semel turchi pisulā ruerēt caloierū uirū dei adorātem iquadā iuenē speluncha · & dū strepitū faceret ut ipm caperēt spelunca ruit imū iq̄ onis pter caloierū periere: hec & enī una excicladib dicta & iegeo mari sita · XXX · circuit mil · q̄ cū portu & molo ātiqssimo ad meridiē · Stephanus Georgi Johāesq; scī habent: & scā anna ad oriētē manifestat cū pādermo portu: q̄ arida tota cum eghis multis cōprobat · Virgil · Errātem micoe celsa giaroq; reuinxit ·

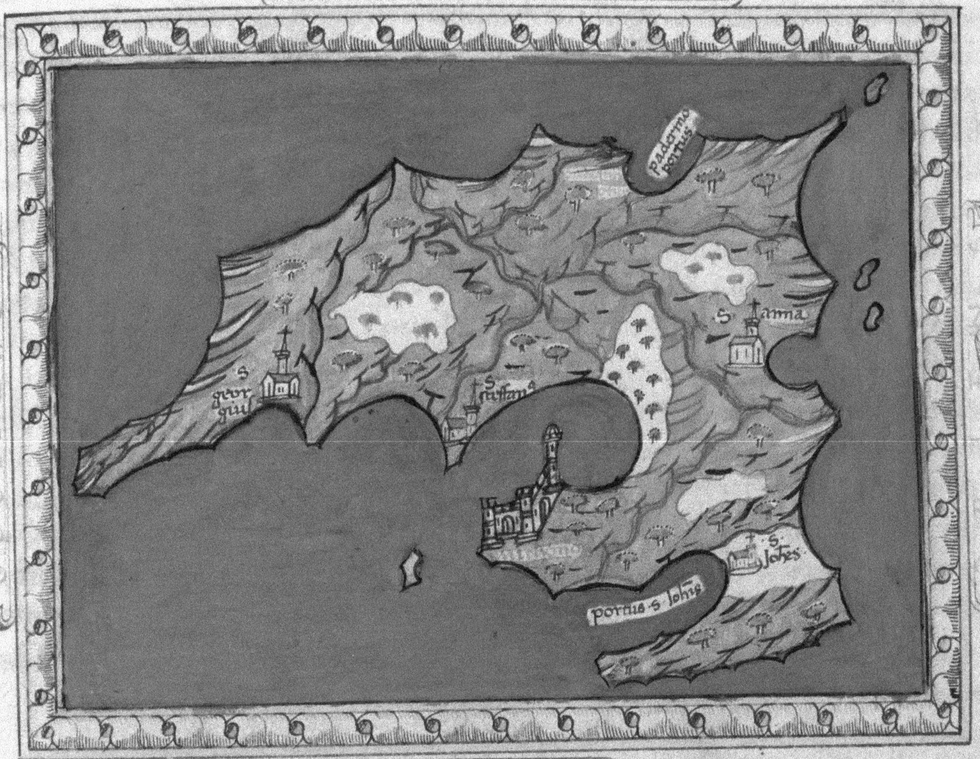

Restat nunc insulam indicare deli de qua sepe inter auctores habetur mentio & famosissi
ma in medio cicladum explendebat: quam olim mobilem uetustas asserit & multis modis
uocata fuit. Delos asteria: corona midia: lagia: cineto: purpile & nunc S diles dicta est de qua
poete taliter finxere iouem latonam ceii titanis filiam uitiasse; quo persequente ipsa cunctis
regionibus fugabatur; tandem a sorore asteria iam in insulam transmutata se littoribus applicante
edidit. Qui statim occiso phitone ultus est matris iniurias. Asserunt matri parturienti dianam
& appollinem prebuisse officium obstetricis: unde ergo dianam uirginem fingunt sub lucine nomine
eoque luci reddat infantes parturientibus inuocari. Diana omnium fere testimonio poetarum
iouis & latone fuit filia: hanc ueteres insignem uirginitate perpetua uoluere: & quoniam spreto
omnium consortio uenationibus operam dedit. Querebat in siluis cum luna in nocte feras & cum
suo frigore concupiscentias ueneres expellebat. His igitur ab ea obseruatis hanc ueteres lunam
esse crediderunt & secum lunam iniunxere & circum circa arcum sagittasque a latere posuere & ne
motum deam uocauere & circumcirca nymphas locauere tanquam ipsorum deam s. oreades: Driades: Ha
mades & Nereides que inter grecos hodie uenerantur & affirmant qualibet exercere officium suum.
Luna ergo mater est humoris habet in siluis in montibus in mari in fontibus humorem multiplicare
& in agris herbas & semina procreare: hec et proserpina dicta est. Similiter & appollo diuer
sis nominibus secundum sibi diuersas attributas potentias nominatur. Quandoque sol phebus titan
& a loco ut delius. Duo igitur numina hec huic insule mobili tunc erranti diana per noctem
i. luna prius nata est & postea natus appollo. i. dies qui solem alluminatur. Delos grece ma
nifestum latine quia post diluuium apparuit in nocte uaporibus lune estuantibus. Postea
in die sequenti radiis solaribus ea monstrantibus apparuit manifeste & ideo delos i. manife
statio cum primo ortigia uocaretur a multitudine perdicum ibi coadunatum. Ortix greco

pdix latine. Cynthius mons ibi est in quo diana nata est: & ideo aliqn cyntia dicta ē: postea dictus appollo a filio uulcani & minerue qui primus decrescat eo tempore & hora nili flumi nis qđ mirum est. In hac itaq; appollo colebat in qua de longinqs partibus dona ad eius tē plū ferebant una cum uirginib; circumstātium regionum. Cūq; enim tarquini auiculi bru ti rome regnatis filij ad hanc insulam appollinis de more sacrificaturi munerib; pexisset Ipsisq; sacrificātib; brutus qui cum eis istrionis accesserat iocabundus Scipionem q̊ aur ascēderat palam enim uenerari numen timebat ipi deo donass& eis oraculū īterrogā tib; Quisnā post tarquinum regnaturus esset rome. respōdit oraculum: q ex eis pmum matrem obscularet. Quo audito brutus qi casu aduolutus interram eā osculatus ē: ūde postea tarquini filiorum & cōsulatus cōsequutus est. Ostēdit ipsum brutum appollinē de terra comuni omnium matre intellexisse. Brutus enim fugato tarquino prim cō sul factus est. Sūt aūt insule he due cōtigue quarum minor delos ē incircuitu. uij. mil: altera decē: & de trione admeridiē elongāt ambo. Igit in delo prope oli tēplū uetustum in plano pparato colūnarum idolum uidimus quod in tanta magnitudine iac& q nullo modo nos q mille fuimus erigere potuimus argumentis rudentum galearum: sed ad suum pristinum dimisimus locum. Insup hinc inde plusq̄ mille ido lorum omni magisterio laudabili uident prosternata. Altera deniq; humilib; mō tibus cultiuata erat & p eam habitationes infinite parabant quarum porte fenestreq; uersus templum prospectabāt: quorum in medio turris erigit: in qua post desolationē templi cerimoniarūq; idolorum coloni recreabant; Virgilius.

Huc feror hec fessos tuto placidissima portu
Accipit & egressi ueneramur appollinis urbem
Templa dei saxo uenerabar structa uetusto.

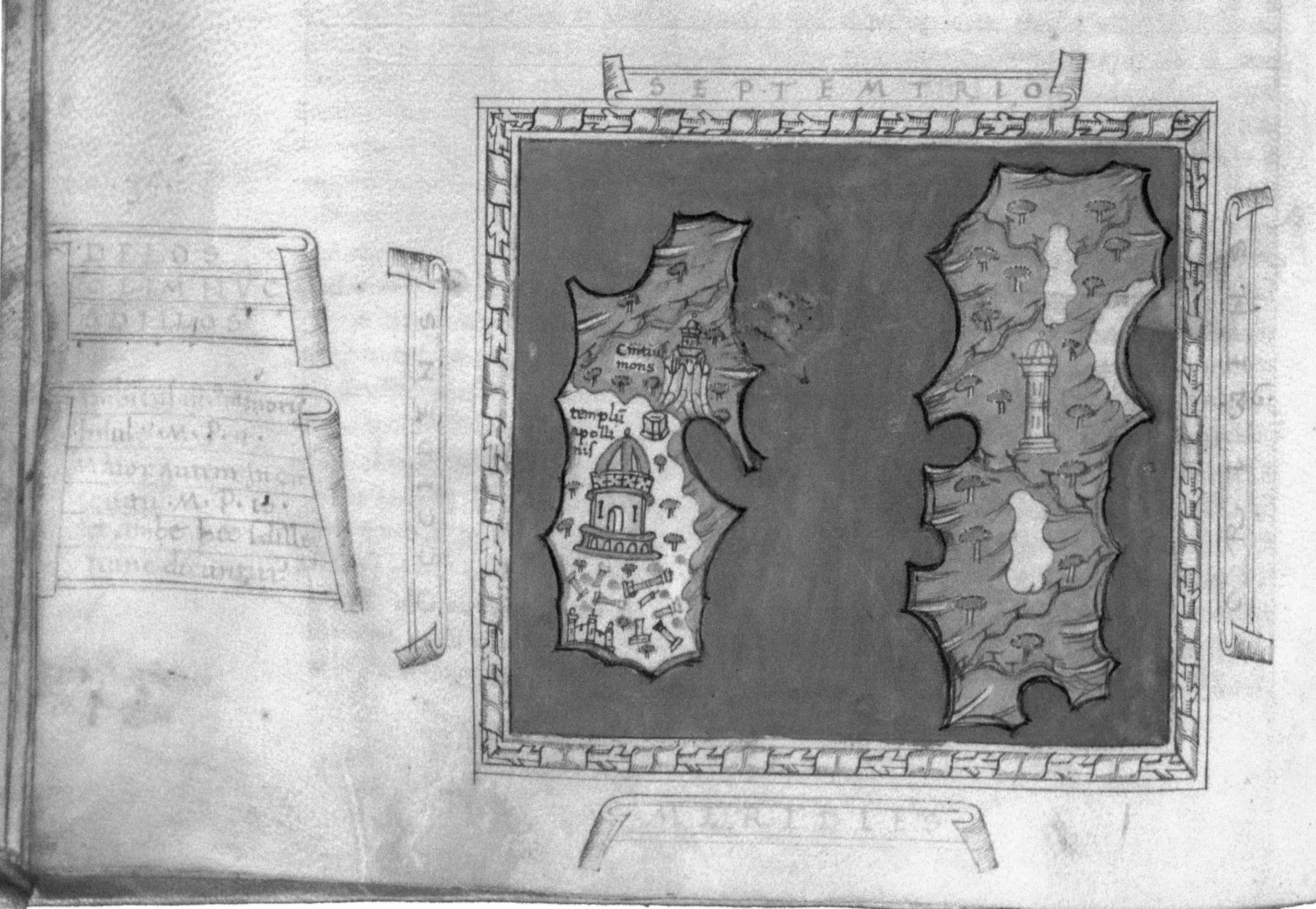

EST ad occasum suda hodie dicta ·XL· miliaria ī circuitu: q̄ olim iaro uel
ghero latine senex uel sanus interp̄tatur· In hoc itaq; scopulo dux q̄dam
calaber Sidim dictus peruenit unde magna grecia & ciuitate scillaea: quia
manib; suorum aufugerat inimicorum: & pactus nimia tēpestate iā fessi naute
pp obitū eo tēpore regis īsule huius ī coniugē reginā accepit· Postq̄ funus sui uiri
laute eo in loco finierat· Igit᷑ cum iā diu sine prole regnaret filiā procreauit quā
sudā denominauit a qua insula nomē accepit· Hunc uō ad cōparationē preteritorum tēpoꝝ nihil reputat᷑ qa ordeaceo pane currub; & egharū carnib;
uescunt᷑ maximo pirratarū timore: q̊ eoꝝ uita ī anxietate ponit᷑: q̄uis pp prolē
& affinitatē & itrinsecū amorē patrie cōtētur ī loco. Est & ut uidet᷑ ad tonē caprā
scopulus ī q̄ ut auit̄ sp̄s puagat᷑ ī mūdi: & dū naues prope trāseūt uel ī nocte calu
morant᷑ tātus strepitus & mugitus uocū erigit᷑ q̄ celum terraq; ruē uidet᷑ & uo-
cātes nomina illoꝝ uenietū altis uocib; conualescunt· Virgilius·
Errantē michoe celsa giaroq; reuinxit·

37

SVDA INSVLA

Ambitus totius
Insule ·M· P· 40·

SEquit᷑ paros albissima ualde & ex cicladib; una q̄ olī platea ab āplitudine
dicta: deinde minoa a ciuitate regis minois edificata multorū edificioꝝ.
Sed partante pluti filius q̄ie ibidē & oppidū cōstruxisse auit Insulā & oppidū
paron a suo nomine nominauit· & gignit adeo mārmō cādidissimū ut a lōge

uidentib; nix existimaret̃: & maxime carpesus mōs sublimior alijs cū scaturiginib; aquarū &
fluuiis exūdatione: que · L1 · circuit mil · Ad occiduū minoa urbs erat corā delphica īsula ĩq
colūnarū edificia supãt prata cū tēplo mārmoreo īmaculato · īsup ad radices eiusdē mōtis oppidū
uetustissimū erigit̃ īmaniū structū lapidū · Ad tonē uō cuuib; paucis paron castrū habet̃ cū molo
atq; paruo portu: q̊ iloco fōs ē ĩq̊ si albū lineū ut coriū posueris niger remanebit & ex eo molē
dina triturãt: Corā aūt naxos chefalū oppidū īmōte habet̃: cuī ascesus tāta ē difficultas q̊ ce
lū tãge uidet̃: ĩq̊ qdē ex laborioso itinere macilēte nimis & rigose anus usq; uerticē cōuale
scētes sarcinā sine sudore cōducit & ultra · Lm · annū prolē cōcipuit uitalē · Ad oriētē portus pÿ
rataṛ uidet̃ & ibi cāpus ptotū ostēdit̃ maxim̃ · Sūt igit̃ hec ex alio circūstātes īsule a turchis
oppsse nimis & īdesolatione sepe redatte & ibi habitātes cōtinuū timorē habēt ne inseruitutem redigantur;

38

Breue spatiū abhīc antiparos ē: & quis ihabilis sit ab aqlis falconib; q; nō ē derelicta: quis ue po
terit quot folie parãt̃ in anno cū lapides eo tēpore nō uideant̃ tāta est cōgeries auiū foleaq;
& pserti aliquaṛ q̊ dum i loco pdā cōducit nisi magna fame arceat̃ sola nō māducat · Duos lapi
des ptiolos masculinū femininūq; i nido suo colligit & reponit · Sine qb; ut ait plinius parere ne
quit: & achateos ad custodiēdū pullos suos a ueneno & reptiliū morsu reponit · Sed postq̄ a nido
eos expulit pdari īstruit · Quos cū uideit iā pdā capē in altū uolās ab eorū tutela se sbtrahit · & hie
mali tēpore modicam auiculam capit: quā inter pedes de nocte tenēs pp calefactionē frigēdo
nō perimit: sed orto sole illesa abire permittit ·

39

INVENI equidem ultra antedictam insulam panaiam quasi ex eadē asperitate & par
ue habitudinis a pan grece latine totum & ya sanitas: erat aūt in ea ecclesia sola nimis
in qua ut imaginat~ aliquis heremita residebat & pro suis necessarijs ad insulam pari cimba
sua navigabat. Hunc certe magna multitudo avium omnibus habitat temporibus & p
saxa nuda diebus noctibusq; transeunt ululando.

hec Insula olim heremitorium nunc deserta e[st] s[ed] aquilis et falconibus habitata

PANAIA SCOPOLUS

TUTA inter cicladarum insulas naxos habetur cum LXXX mil. circ. Plinius igit~ p̄mus
strongilem grece latine rotundā eā nomiāt. Ovidius dynisiam a fertilitate vinearū. Alij
Siciliā minorem ab abundantia rerum frugūq; q̄ ē p̄ncipalior isularum istarū in qua petra nige
rima & durissima dicta smerigdo reperit~. Coram itaq; civitate i scopulo fuit olim oppidum stron
gile dictum a quo seculis multis isula sūpsit nomen: quo coram campus vix mare vinearū am
pliat~ magnus: ideo bacho dedicata fuit: q sculptus prope oppidum puer facie muliebri nudo pec
tore capite cornuto vitibus coronato & tigribus equitādo. Puer qa hebrius tāq̄ puer sine ratione gu
bernat~. Muliebrem faciē qa icōcupiscētia mulierū p vinū in hebrijs gn̄atur. Tigrides qa furibūdi:
Nudus pp veritatē: cornutus pp auctoritatē. Sūt et̄ i ea vespes q̄ si aliquē trāsfixerit morte moriet~.
Theseus etiā filius egei regis missus cretam ut occideret~ a minotauro ipm interemit & athenas atur
pi servitio liberavit. Ariadnēq; & fedram minois filias patri surripuit & apd̄ fontē propinquum
civitati dum dormiret adrianā non merito dereliqt & phedram sibi cōiugio copulavit: & quia
i multis epistolis legi Theseū in hāc adrianam reliquisse insulā: ideo potius hic hāc pono historiam
cum intersit rectius navigationi athenarum q̄ chios. Salva tamen auctoritate Nasonis q ponit in
chio hoc fuisse factum. Post aūt recessum thesei bachus totius hui insule dux cōphendens astu
tiam & iniquam defectionem tanti iuvenis misericordia motus puellam reconciliavit & cogno
scens ipsam eē filiam regis cretensium & pasiphe in uxorem accepit. & vulcanus ei coronam
gēmis splendētibus donavit quam inter sydera collocavit: etiam cū in hac isula iuppiter
adversus titanos proficisceretur: & in litore sacrificium faceret aquila in auspitiū eius ad
volavit: quam victor bono omine acceptam sue tutele subiugavit & tempore belli troianorū
peleus hic dominabat~: erat enim tūc temporis habitata nimis & tāta multitudo virorum
mulierumq; extiterat q nihil in ea incultum videbat~. Hunc aūt p ipm bubones ululare

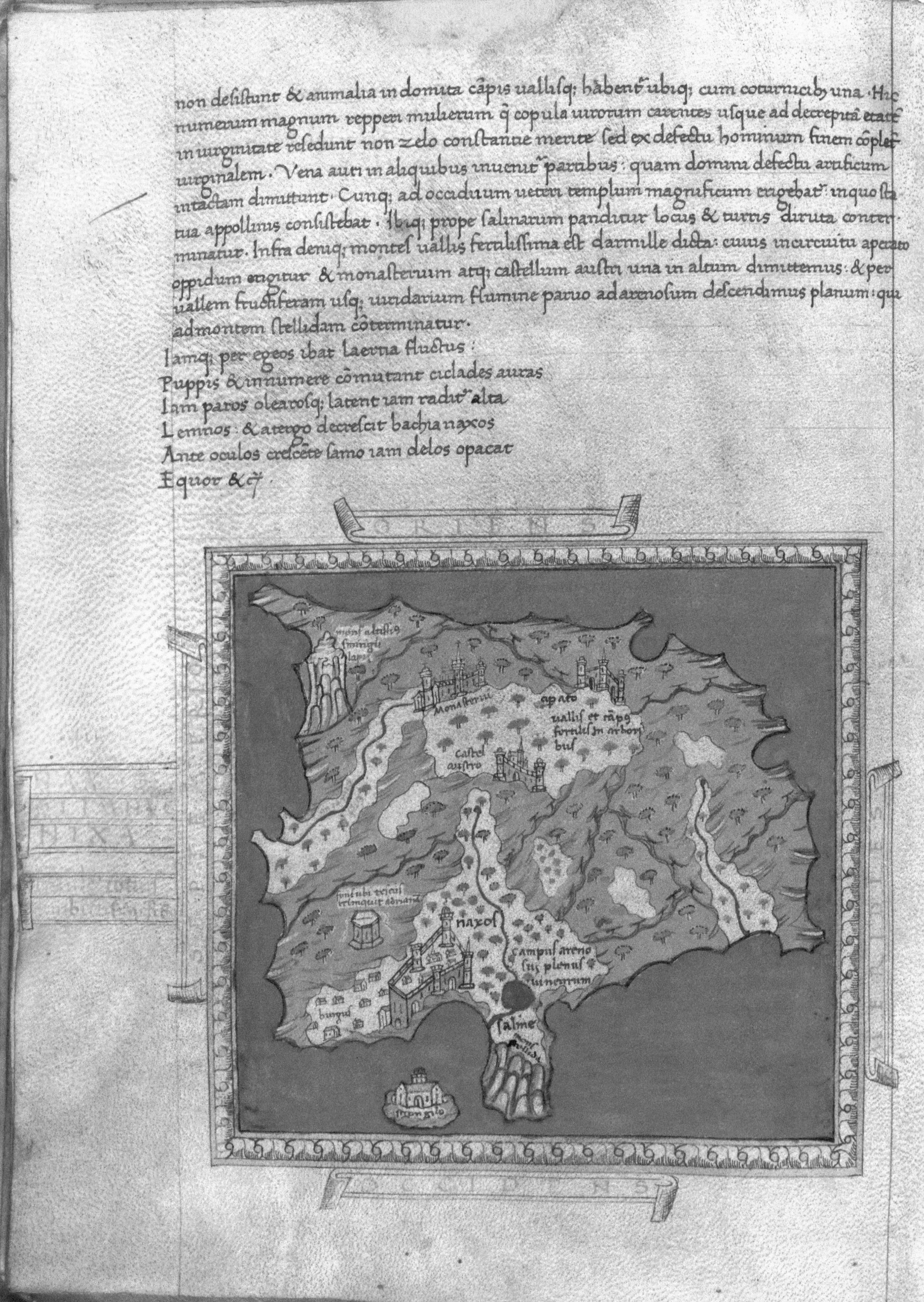

non desistunt & animalia indomita cāpis uallisq; habent ubiq; cum coturnicib; una. Hic numerum magnum repperi mulierum q̄ copula uirorum carentes usque ad decrepitā etatē in uirginitate resedunt non zelo constantie merite sed ex defectu hominum finem cōplent uirginalem. Vena auri in aliquibus inuenit partibus: quam domina defectu artificum intactam dimittunt. Cumq; ad occiduum ueteri templum magnificum erigebat in quo statua appollinis consistebat. Ibiq; prope salinarum panditur locus & turris diruta contermīnatur. Infra deniq; montes uallis fertilissima est darmille dicta: cuius in circuitu aperato oppidum erigitur & monasterium atq; castellum austri una in altum dimittemus: & per uallem fructiferam usq; uiridarium flumine paruo ad arenosum descendimus planum: qui ad montem stellidam cōterminatur.

Iamq; per egeos ibat laerria fluctus:
Puppis & innumere cōmutant ciclades auras
Iam paros olearosq; latent iam radit alta
Lemnos: & a tergo decrescit bachia naxos
Ante oculos crescēte samo iam delos opacat
Equor &c.

ERant olim ut dicit^r he ambe habitate & podia dicte: podia enim grece latine pedes quia ad figuram pedum demostrant^r: maior harum habitabilis erat cũ munito olim castello. Hũc aũt ad barbarorum insidias hanc colẽtes naxon accessere. prima. vi. Secunda. iiij. mil circuiunt.

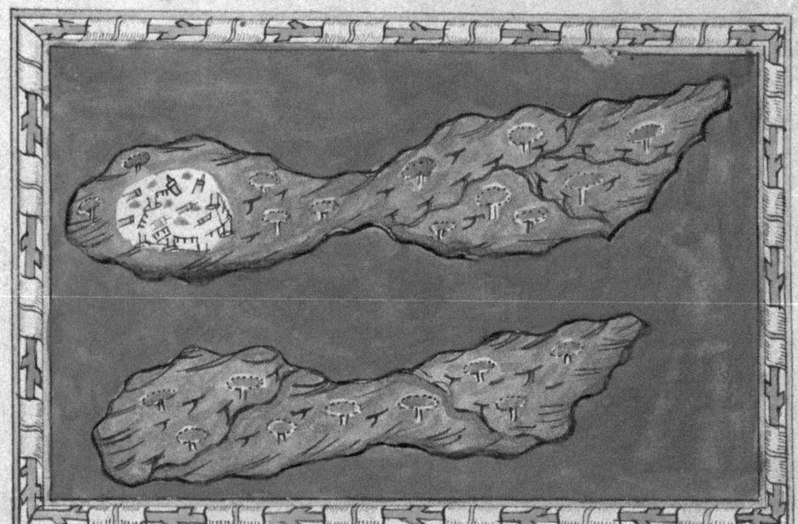

RAclea & chero due insule parue & mõtuose uidentur & inculte nimis propter turchorum insidias que olim ut aũit erant habitate q̃a uestigia in aliq̃bus partibus percipitur. In quibus multa egarum societas reperit^r que uagatur ubiq; & parue in circuitu consistunt.

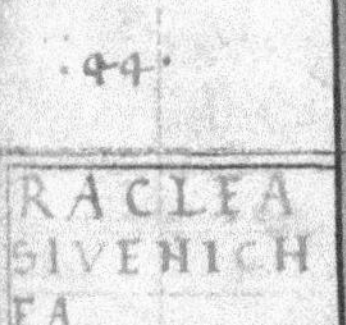

NVnc petimus portum fessi insule nio: & dicitur latine grece latine nouũ uel mos .i. naualis quia libenter in tempestate uenientes hũc portum affectuose appetere curauit. xl. circuit mil. Ad meridiem uõ oppidum sublime positum est & uallis a longe parũ cum fecundissimo campo aperitur in totum & in partes diuisus a colentibus seminatur. In sero ergo postq̃ ad occasum peruentum erit ĩ munitissimum magno labore descẽdunt castellũ: mane aũt facto uetulas ad speculandum p insulam ante aurora mittunt & dato ab eis signo porte pandunt^r in totum & sic uitam transeunt in temore. Tempore deniq; meo dũ nauis pyrratarum in portu carinam prepararet & nutu diuino aqua maris eã absorbuit que nusq̃ uisa est;

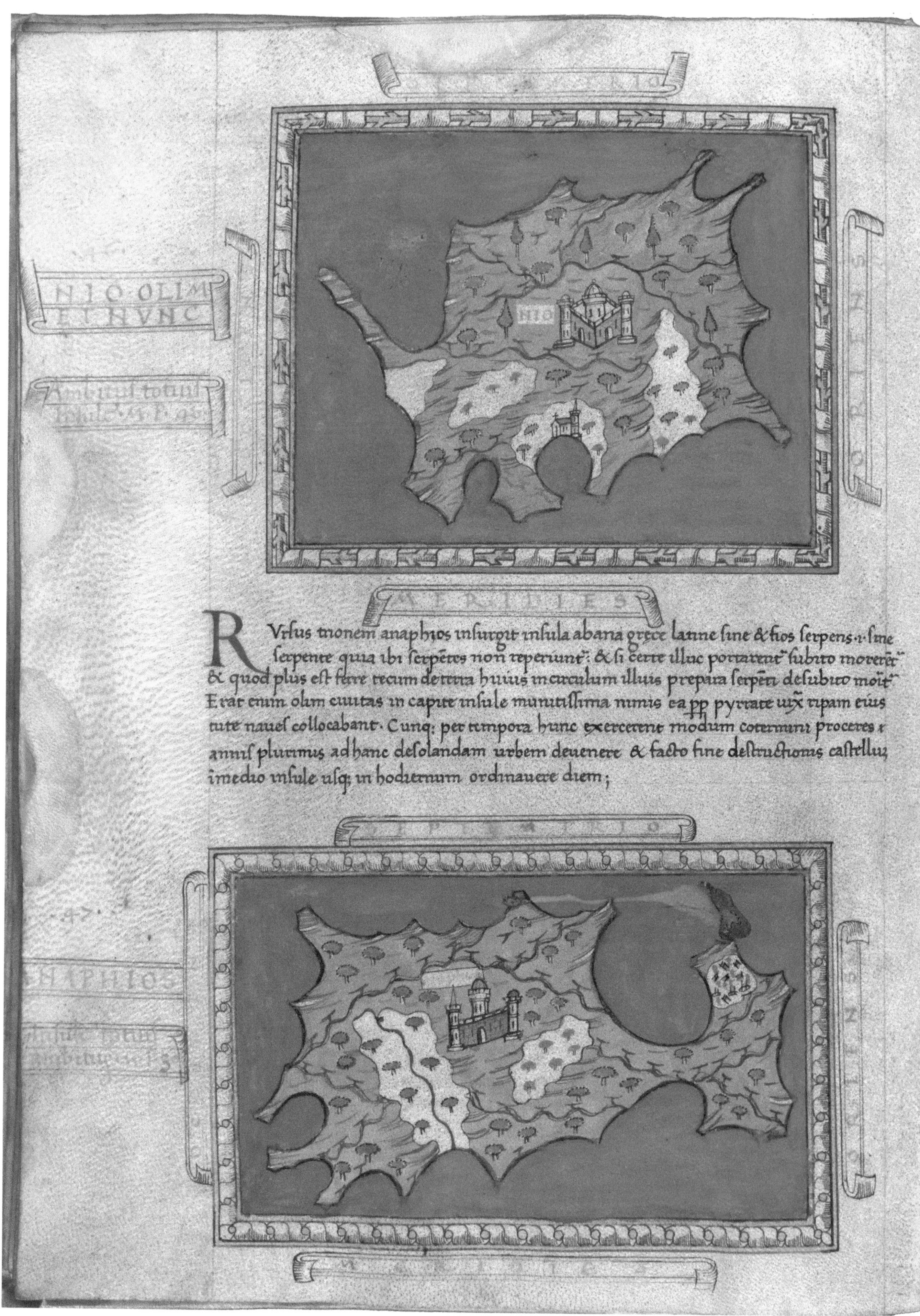

Rursus trionem anaphios insurgit insula abaria grece latine sine & fios serpens .i. sine serpente quia ibi serpetes non reperiunt. & si certe illuc portarent subito moreret & quod plus est ferre tecum de terra huius in circulum illius prepara serpeti de subito moit. Erat enim olim ciuitas in capite insule munitissima nimis ea pp pyrrate uix ripam eius tute nauel collocabant. Cunq; per tempora hunc exercerent modum coterminii proceres r annis plurimus ad hanc desolandam urbem deuenere & facto fine destructionis castellu; imedio insule usq; in hodiernum ordinauere diem;

Nonnulli olim subort hāc denominauerūt insulā & cultiuata satis · LXXX · mil · circuit
ī mōtibus tota: q̄ nūc amurgospolis dicta ē: in qua tria oppida amurgo ialli & plati ·
Ad triōnē uō tres portus uidentur: Sc̄a anna: Calos & catapla · Ad occiduum mōtes nō ita eleuātur
uelut oriētales & ideo catomerea dr̄ q̄d latine pars inferior sonat · & ad oriētē apanomerea
pars superior declaratur · Ad meridiē demq; rupes erigunt̄ terribiles & nauib; minacissime
quia uēti pcutiētes imare ī ripis redūdat · & sic scylla carybdisq; ita timescētes q̄ naues ī naufragio
sepe pereūt · & ita mirātes uiā alōge capiūt & sūmersiōis galee ibi uenetorum recordantur ·

· 48 ·

AMVRGO SIVE AMVRGOSPOLIS

Insule totius ambitus · M · P · 80

Conuicinee due sunt insule scilic& Chinera & Leuata · In quibus aiunt non
habitauere patres: nunc aūt pueniente adsolitudinem inculte remanēt propter insidias malorum hominū & sepe a circūstantibus animalia resoluce patescunt cum asinis agrestibus una ·

· 49 ·

CHINERA

· 50 ·

LEVATA

Monstrabimus nūc caloierum scopulum altissimum inmedio maris positum ubi coa īsula
ad austrum terminatur: & circūspectū ī altissimis ripis pp̄ sua eminētiam omnibus
cōuicineis insulis minat̄: in quo cacumine ecc̄lia cum plano parat̄: & eo in loco duo caloieri
adorabant secure & nauiculam rudente parato una ascēderant ut a seuis pyratis possent
eam custodire · & precibus deuotis horisq; constitutis sine timore die ac nocte ualeāt exercere & offerre libamina sacrificiaq; inmaculata · Cumq; diu misterium tale peregissent

ecce turchus indutus uestibus similibus ipsorum & ait solus in nauicula maculata uocibus
altis. Viri religiosi amore christi suscipite me miserum quia istis inscopulis dira tẽpestas
nauim nostrorum grecoꝝ impegit salo: & nemo nisi ego solus euasit: Illi misericõdia
moti ꝑ funem ascensum hospitem sinonem in altum acceptauerũt. In nocte uõ dum
intra ecc̃liam adorabant porta ab extra proditor firmauit & uocatis socijs abscõsis
iux̃ scopulum seruos xp̃i ac suplectiles ipsorum inturchiam deportauere.

COPOLVS
ALOIERO
RVM

IAmq; adinsulam deuenimus choam que latine luctus interpretatur quia propter
aeris intemperiẽ pluribus mensibus anni lugetᵘʳ atq; languetur in ea, prouincie achie
adiacens suburbana dicta est. De oriente ad occiduum. xl. mil. & plana quasi ꝑ totũ extat
Ad meridiem uõ montes cernimus sublimes inquibus oppida erant petra: cheuua atq;
pili quod hodie pipaton dicunt. Insuꝑficie uõ altioris montis Ditheus dictus munitissimum extiterat castrum: inquo hodie cisterne apparent q̃plurime. Cumq; adradices descendimus huius fontem sandion reperimus: a quo sfandanus fluuius deriuatur qui
prope cilippum oppidum olim prorumpit inmare adtrionem. Inmedio aũt uastissimorũ
camporum duo soli monticuli eriguntur: aquibus fons olim nobilissimus licastis hodie
apotomarius emanat iux̃ olim castri oppidum & molendina uiuariaq; marmorea mani
festant In quibus tanta est amenitas loci tantus diuersorum ciuium q̃ nõ solum terrenis
sed etiam dijs imortalibus placitum fore dicatur. Ad orientem inlitore arangea metropolis est cuius inmedio lacus ampliatur inestate corruptus & ab extra meriorum arãgea
multa uirescunt & ideo arangea dicta: inqua tot & tanta edificia marmorea & theatra
reppeti qd̃ est mirabile aduidendum. Extra uero castrum iux̃ lacum adtrionẽ ampla
domorum edificia ypocratis eximij medici cum fonte uisa sunt propinquo & palude
lambi dicta que inhieme ampliatur & crescit: in estate uõ desiccatur. Fuit igitᵘʳ iste
ypocrates filius sclepionis & discipulus esculapij phisici secundi & fuit de gñe esculapij
primi a quo incepit ars medicine quam ostendit & docuit filijs suis mandans eis q̃
medicinam extraneis ĩmo patres ostẽderetis uestris filijs ut artis nobilitas semper
fixa maner& in eis. & precepit q̃ inmedio habitationis insularum cycladum maneret

pp aeris temperiem uel inmontibus choe considerent in estate. Duxit igit perfectam
apud grecos medicinam. Ipsa enim medicina ut ait macrobius & ysidorus ante ypocratem siluerat p quingentos annos a tempore appollinis & asclepij qui fuerunt i-
uentores & procedendo nunc ad medium insule parui monticuli uident iceptare:
& sic altior ista planities est illius antedicte arangee. Postq ad meridiem ad antimachum oppidum cursum habemus usq; infine insule ubi chephalo paratur in altum.
Non diu est q serpens maximus apparuit deuorans armenta & territi omnes fugam
arripiebant. Tunc uir strenuus pro salute populi duellum inceptat dum inter bestias
ruere uellet: qd cum serpens hoc pcepiss& equum morsibus illico prostratum occidit.
Iuuenis aut acriter pugnans tandem uiperam interfecit. Dicitur etiam & affirmat
q filia ypocratis p insulam uiua apparet: qua loquente tecum & narrante multa i
fortunium suum infelicem comemorat rogabatq; sepe creatorem ut a tanta pena
eam dignaretur liberare. & cum plura loqueretur non longe a paternis domib;
lametabilibus uocibus in sex uel in octo annis semel cotigisse transformatione hanc
ut a multis ciuibus comprobatur. Refert et Plinius q Aristeus filius appollinis
cosilio matris relictis thebis huc uenit & i hanc habitauit insulam & sibi iugauit
eam: fuit enim ut aiut mulieres hic uiros occidisse pp eorum icostantiam: qa
semper in plijs p asiam minorem accedentes curam insule mulieribus dimittebat
Ille equatr indignate ad inorme suorum uiroru peruenere homicidium. Deinde
Iason p hanc transiens ad colchon hodie curchum accessit coram ciuitate posita &
constructa multis edificijs: que usque hodie in armenia minori coram cipro uidet.
Est denuq; hec omnium abundantissima & primo in feminarum ornamento lani-
ficij hic artem inuentam affirmant. Insup & natiuitas memorabilis philidis poete
hic fuit qui imitatus Saphon poetissam rem bachidis decantauit. Ibiq; infra ripas al-
tissimas auis duo oua peperit ex quibus ex uno auis ex altero canis nascitur. & p
capiens mater non ee cani similis illico eum occidit & fratri prebet incibu. & qa
insula hec cotigua asie minori ibi magne insurgebant ciuitates fratres sci Iohanis
ut resisterent infidelibus castellum Sancti petri hedificauere. Mcccc.

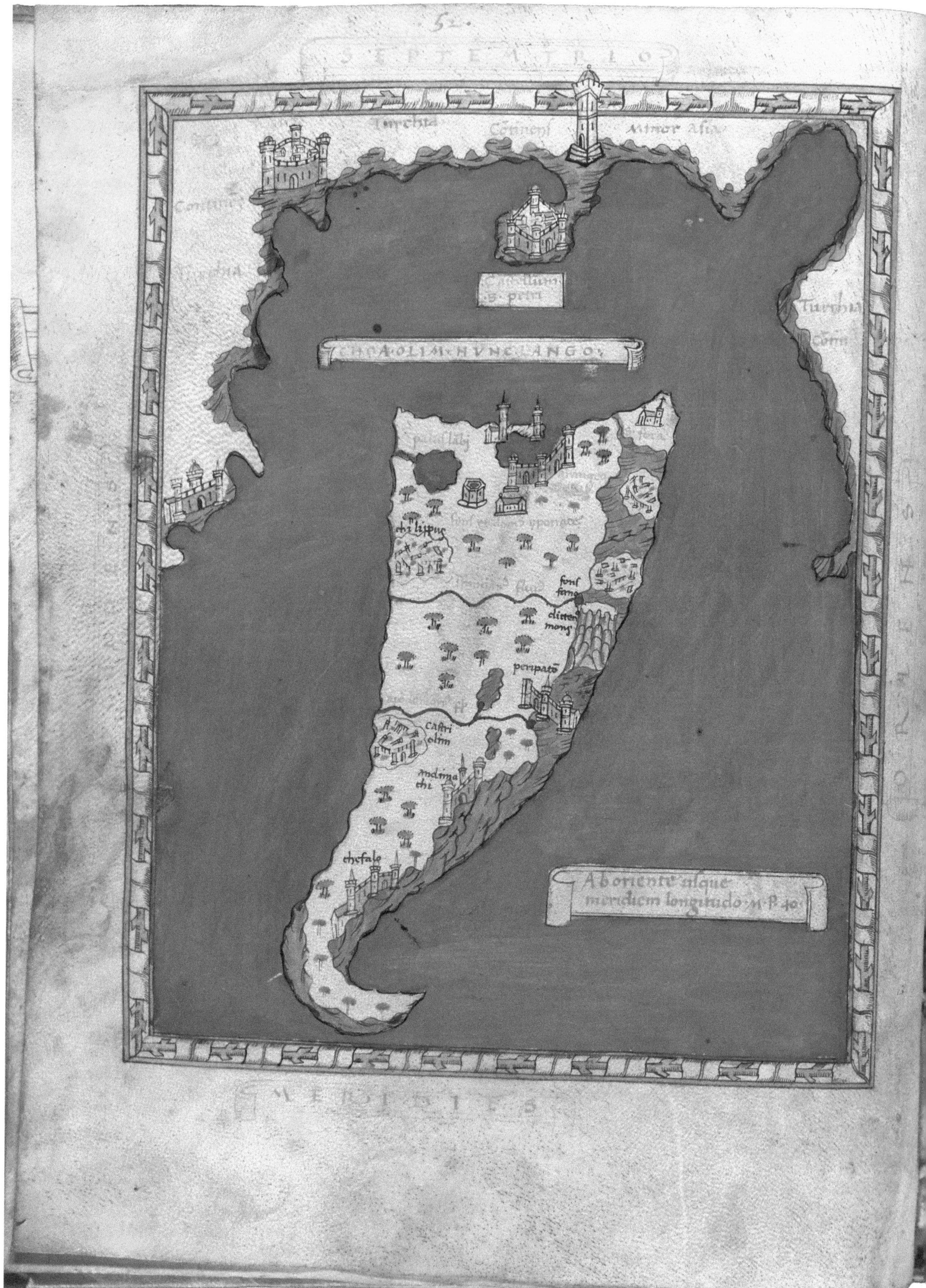
52.
SEPTENTRIO
Turchia
Comnensi
Minor Asia
Castellum S. petri
CHIA OLIM HUNC LANGO
Turchia
A oriente usque meridiem longitudo m. p. 40.
MERIDIES

Sypereminn & ī mōtibus ualde claros olim insula que hodie calamos dicta ē: Cala
mi enim grece latine arundo interpretatur: q̄ rendēs detone ad meridiē . xl . mil .
circuit & tanta est mōtiū sblimitas q siquis in altiori ascenderet & cacumine usq; chion
insulam uel ephesum urbē ut palatiam ciuitatē turchoꝝ certe uisū ꝑapet clarum
tūc cū sol inclinat ad occasum. Insitis equidē montib; ꝑ oīs saltus lanigene pecudes
tondentes odoriferas herbas incolumes accedūt sine lupoꝝ timore & flaue eghe deua-
stātes arbores ī sumitate petrarū pattizare delectāt. Ab oriēte uō oppidū ab alto ueta-
stū: quo in cōspectu īsula ꝑua elōgat: q̄ olī illustrissima usq; nūc fuisse uidet. & qs possit ī
ea tot explicare nūm antiqtatū & īdicare liniamīta marmoꝝ sparsa ꝑ totū cū nl ī ea aliud
ꝑcipere ualeam. Igit̄ ī sinu q̄dā oppidū calamos erigit̄ munitū: & ad occiduū ī sinu ꝑpe flum
falsū uathi olī ā ꝑhabat̄ ciuitā: ī q̄ edificia plura uidemꝰ. & ueniēs ad occiduū meridieq; ī radice mōtis
ut ꝑ mōtoꝝ portbs duo uidēt optimi aq̄b; magna speluch habet̄. & ī ea facūdissimꝰ nō desinit fōs
emanare & ubiq; lignū aloe crescit & salutiferū ab oībus habetur partibus;

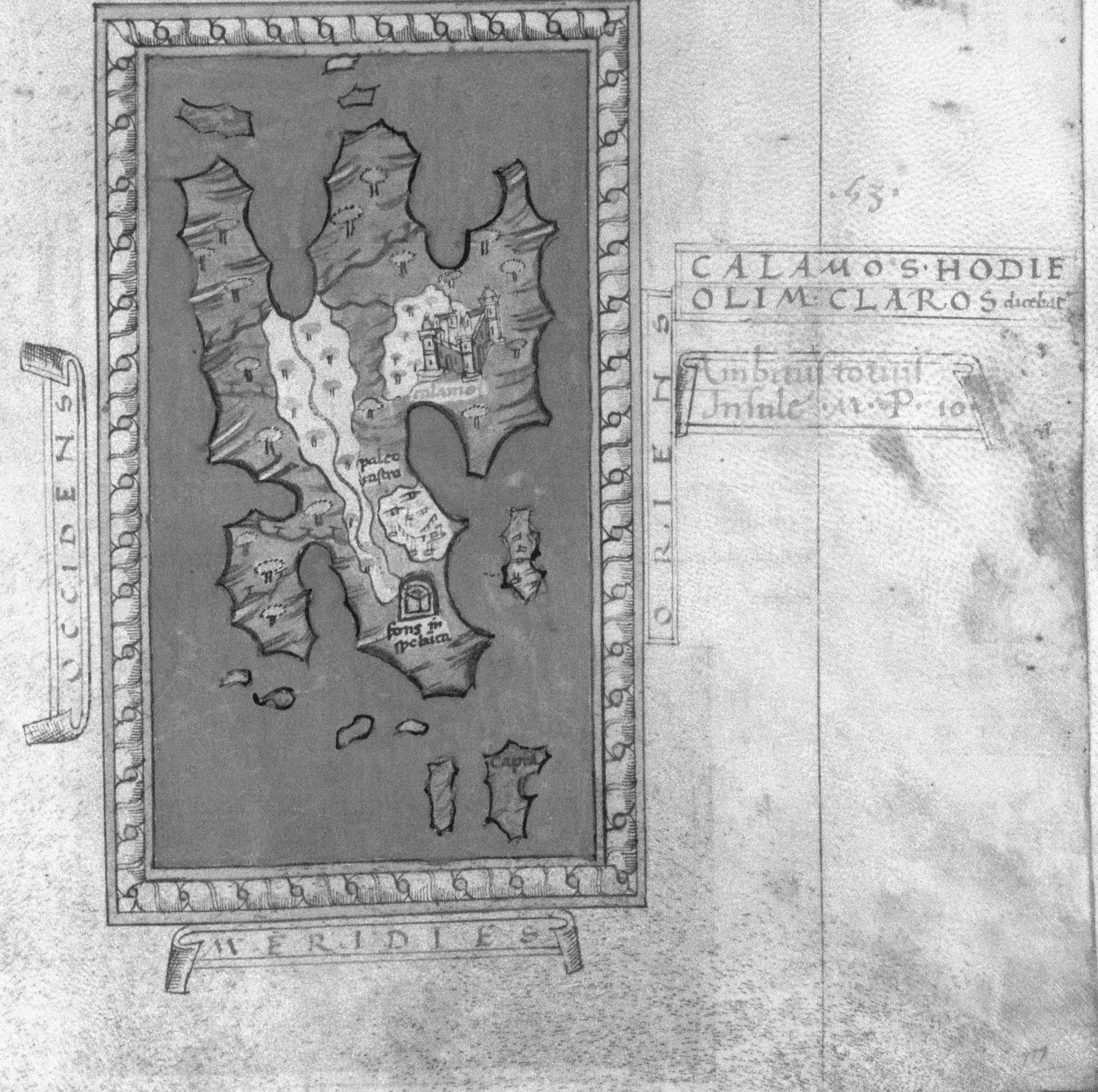

.54.

HERROS OL IA TNVNC

Insule totius Ambitus M P 18

Iuxta hāc erro mōtuosa ualde isula mamoeca estat q̄ ad oriētē castellū munitissimū habet ubi ōs coloni recreāt̄ inocte ut secure pateścat. & ad austrū lepida pōt̄ eāt ū oli ciuitas emīebat inocte & plani iradicib; ei āplat̄. Si ad occiduū pgis feradosini illico pādit̄ & oppidū pruni dictū oli cernini desolatū & sic ptotū mōtuosa uidet̄. q̄ xviij. mil circuit & ad oīa isuo gradu ipāz felicissimā noiam̄ iq̄ lignū aloe recolit̄ & mercatorib; uēdit̄ in anno;

Tractauimꝰ de herro nūc ad patmos ueniemꝰ in qua Ioānes xp̄i discipulus ad exilium tēpore Domitiani imparatoris missus est. & iportu iangulo q̄dā ipe die dnico raptus in spū magna atq; arcana de p̄sentibus futurisq; uidit conteplando. & librū apocalipseū scribēs nobis multa reuelauit. In eodē deniq; tempore mōtuo domitiano in ephesū hodie alto locō dictū Iohs magnis honoribus receptus est. Qui dū xp̄i fidem miraculis magno p̄dicaret multi ex discipulis suis ihāc isulā accessert̄ & monasteriū nō lōge a suo oracto cōstruxert̄ iq̄ q̄d usq; ihodiēnū a caloieis habitat̄: & a turchis nullā habētes molestiā sepe iturchiā recurrūt ad substētationē uite. Que mōtuosa cū humilib; collib; i ea uene metallorum reperiuntur multe;

.55.
PATMOS
Hic sanctus Iohanes stetit in exilio tpe' Domitianj Imperator

PATHMOS

Computaui de patmo: nūc ad Dipsim patriā insulā accedemꝰ: & igitᵘʳ Dipsi grece sitis latine qa sicca est & uiriditate caret. Ideo dipsi nominatᵘʳ qa arida & mōtuosa: & nūqᵃ habitauere patres ī qua sinus ab oriente uidetᵘʳ & nūc ab eqis asinisq; habitata siluestribus apparet.

66

DIPSI

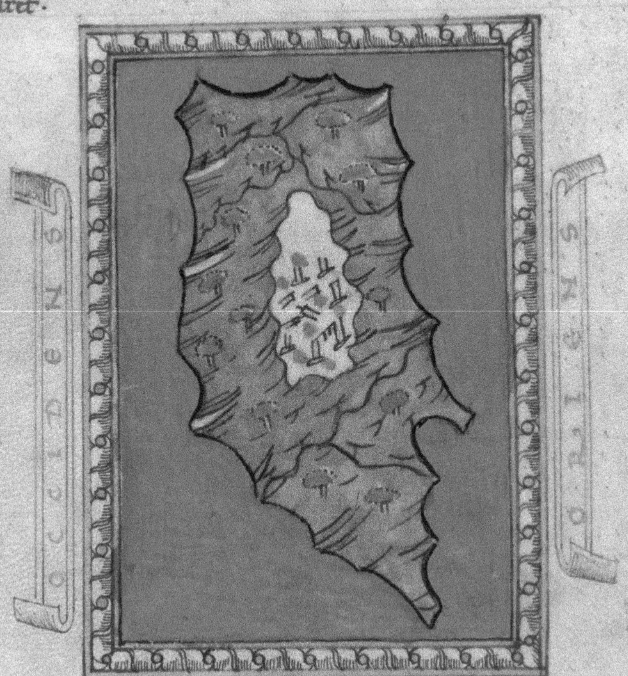

Ab alia parte huius ad occiduū crusie īsula īter icareā patmonq; humilib; mōtib; circūsepta est: cuiꝰ in circuitu aliqui scopuli apparent. & derelicta lōgo iā tēpore ab omnib; qa ī medio oppidum desolatū manifeste fuisse uidetur: nūc īdomite bestie uagari delectātᵘʳ & dr̄ crusie grece de auratē latine.

67

CRVSIE

Refert Varro qⁱ ī hac icarea insula fuit icarus cretensis & ideo icarea dicta creditur qui mox offensus fastu tyrannico relicta domo patria bruto cōsule qui reges urbe exegit italiam aduectus. Est ergo montuosa ualde & circuit milia q̄ de oriente ad occiduum in lōgitudine uelut unius ī mari reuolute nauis dorsū erigitᵘʳ & ī extremis de clinat': cuiq; naute ephesiatici maris apicem huius insule cõuictã nubibus uideret. Illico portũ procurare festinant quia signum tale addetrimetũ nauium trãseuntiũ reuertetur. Sunt & in ea inter anfractus & imeabiles ripas apes suis cauernuculis frequẽtates & ibi mel ualde nutrientes. Hic etiam album bachi liquorem illi accepto multiplicare faciunt & circũstãtibus mittũt. In cuius cacumine duo sũt oppida & ad orientẽ prope mare uidetur i mõte turris altissima q̃ fanari dicta erat in qua lumẽ olim procellosis existebat tẽporibus ut trãseũtes saluaret' q ptotã isulam non poteris portum inuenire.

·58·

HICAREA

Insule totius ambitus ·M·P· 80

·59·

MANDRIA

Tota deserta

DICITUR insula hec mandria que prope erigitur dipsi a scopulis circũdata: & q̃uis olim habitata fuerit: nunc ad solitudinem peruenit: in qua asini uoce sonora siluestres pambulant sine timore una cum equis infinitis.

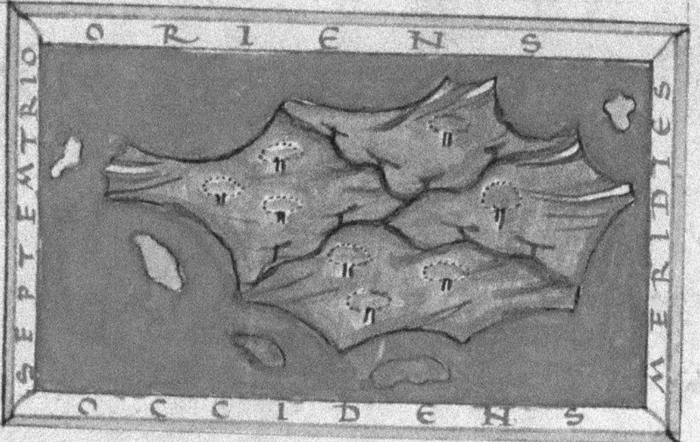

INsule due parue & nude habitãtium ad orientẽ isurgũt Agathusa & Pharmacus dicte. que coram flumine palatie diu inuẽte fuere: i quibus sepe sepius pyrate turchorum uagant' donec cõsulti quia possint uiã capere meliorẽ discedũt prima icircuitu mil. xv. Secunda. iiij. a qbus ad os palatorũ intratur & per flumen cito i urbem

peruentum est: que a palatijs olim magnificis nomen accepit: ubi lacus in hieme maximus effectus est: & tanta copia piscium anguillarumq; reperit᷑ in eo q̧ ubiq; transferuntur & biremes ab hinc per insulam deuastando sepe ī manibus fratrum sancti Ioanis
uenetorumq; deueniunt & ab eis ad infimum deducuntur.

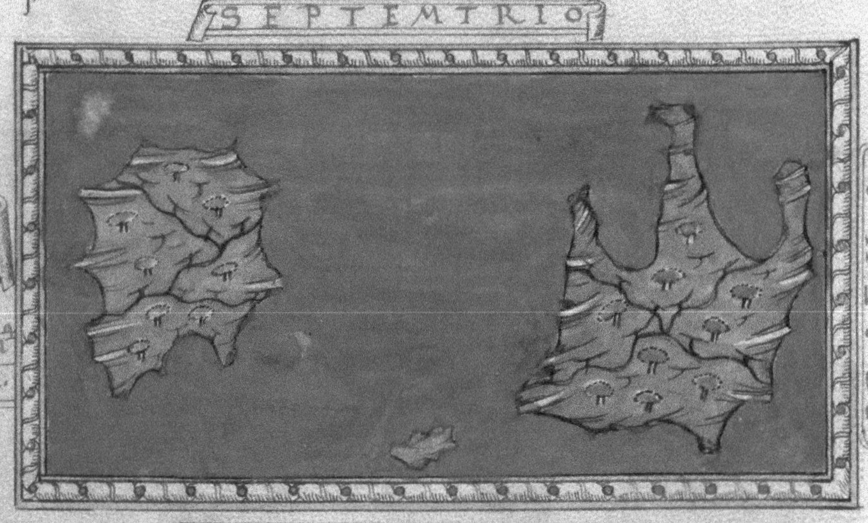

Non longe a supradictis Samo inuenit᷑ insula parū a cōtinēti distās q̄ tēpore deo-
rū gētilium existimabat᷑ ī cūctis sacrificijs sublimior. tūc cum societas maxima
philosophoꝝ regnabat in ea: q̄ circūdata altissimus mōtibꝫ · LXXX · mil · circuit · & longa
de oriente ad occiduum ex una atq; altera parte portus aquis frigidissimis emanātibus
reperimus. Ad meridiem uero in plano iux̄ mare magnifica existebat ciuitas & tāta ruina edificiorū colupnarūq; cernitur q̧ per diem impossibile foret ad nārādū & ibi iunonis
maximū āplissimus colūpnis ereptū ut dicit᷑ fuisse. qa effigies eius prope sculpta erat. Regina cū sceptro & ī capite nubes: Iris ex trāsuerso: pauones ī pedibꝫ eius lābebāt: & ideo
aues illius dicte. Iuno aer est & soror & uxor iouis · i · ignis uxor qa sub eo & ab eo ca-
lorē accipit & nutrit inferiora: soror quia prope eum est. Virgo quia de aere nihil exit
& nihil nascit᷑. Iris & nīphas qa ī aere gignit᷑: & fumi de mare ascēdētes cū aere se īmiscēt
& sic neptūn͛ nutritor iouis quia sibi alimētū aliqd̄ subministrat. De hac īsula Pythagoras
natus est phūs eximius: q babiloniā ad p discēdum siderum motus origineq; mūdi spec-
tādum profectus est: sūma sciētia cōsecutus est Polycratus ut ait Valerius seuissimus ty-
rānus ī hac fuit insula & fortunatus ī oībꝫ suis factis ad manus orotis psaꝝ uenit: q dictū
polycratum ī mote mædalēse altissimo suspēdit ī cruce. Insup hic orta sibilla quadā nomīe
phemo ex decē una q̄ postea dicta ē samia a loco. hic et paulus emilius roman͛ uicit regem pse & filiū philippi macedonīe quo ī plio · xx · hostiū milia īteremit. hic et turchi īnu-
merabiles a Tamburlano fugati euaserunt. Aiūt᷑ deniq; q̧ ī medio insule locus fructifi-

ficat pomorum & licitum est homini comedere ex eis uolens uō cum fructibus eiusdem loci ad socios remeare a uia re deuiabit. Si nihil capiet libere uia patefacta erit. Igitur p̄ insulam altissimi montes & arbores pomorum uidentur quorum unus aote alter medalens. Ad occiduum alij altiores apparent.

·62·

SAMO OLIM ET NUNC
Insule totius
Ambitus M·P·80

AD occiduum prope supradictam deserte insule furni dicuntur: q̄ nusq̄ habitate fuē & aride nimis riparum imeabiluū circūdate: iquibus sepe naues recursū capiūt: & tute a uētis sine refrigerio aquarū dulcium magno timore turchorum pyratarū uigilādo pnoctāt: quarū prima duo secūda. iij. tertia. x. quartaq; qnta. iiij.or circuit mil. Imaiori itaq; hay cum ē partib; rhodi & uersus chiū iter facerē nocte obscurissima nibosaq; nimis demisso carbaso & iportu itare credētes iscopulis uix promōtoria ruim.9 heu cecidere mari qa á ripis nauē nullo modo separe potramus. cūq; hoc cerneremus iterrā descēdim.9 oēs & sic p nibosam illā ptrāsiuim.9 noctem donec ad lucē puenit dies. Aduenietē aūt aurora nusq̄ uidim.9 nauē qa iā imū sbmerserat tota. Sed postq̄ adhāc quītū sextūq; diē sine phebo uitā trāsiuimus ad aquā q̄ fuerat icauernosis lapidibus sepe puenerām.9 ubi aliq nostrū aīām deo reddidēr. Cūq; ad septimū uenirē diem & substātiā iam herbarū nō inuenirē aduescendū i spileum declinaui gladioq; in petra nomen sculpsi meum: hic dira fame p̄sbiter Cristoforus mōtuus est. hoc aūt facto socij conualescētes nauem cōuocant trāseūtē que fuit causa nrē salutis;

63

FVRNI O[...]
DICVNT[...]

L inquimus tn̄ portus desolatasq; insulas & ad undas tenose ĩgressũ petimus leti: ubi cum
ĩ ea uenim⁹ magno labore antiquitatis interueptes anfractusq; reperim⁹: ĩquib; q̄dē pp̄ter
nimiā fluctuationē uentoꝝ ĩnocte luctātiũ tāq̄ scintille lapilli corruscāt in altũ & suauissime uo-
ces ũetoꝝ tum ĩterum infra arbusculos ĩ auribus audiētiũ ꝑcipiunt̄ ualde. q̄ mõtuosa. x. mil. circuit.

63

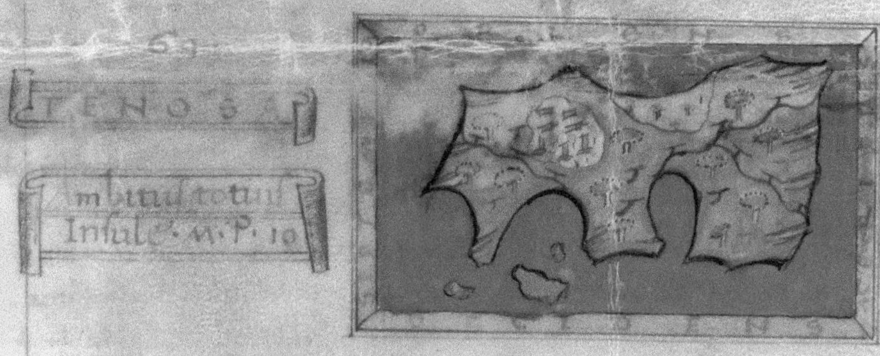

I UXTA chiũ ad occiduũ psara dicit̄ & piscator latine ĩterp̄tat̄: quo ĩspatio. xv. mil. opidũ
insurgebat: & cum ad desolationē deueniret & domestica q̄ plura dimitteret ĩdomita sui
effecta. Coram itaq; hac scopuli parant̄ & sic in ipsorũ medio portus exstat: in quo biremis turchorum semel peruenit. que & secure pp̄ insidias christianoꝝ ĩnocte ad aliam secrete partē accessit insule: & dum pnoctaret illico boreas emissam ab antro nauem sibi mergit ĩ imũ. Turchi uero
ꝑterriti p insulam ambulātes asinos egasq; una siluestres cito capiũt & carnes illarum edentes
bestiarũ coria plena uiti ordinauere: ubi ad numerũ ꝑuenerũt optatũ lignis circũpositis sup naui-
gium tale cõsedere & uersus turchiā prope ĩ miũo. xl. nõ desistũt nauigare. Cũ itaq; p triduũ tadē
prope traciā studiosius deueniẽtes nauicula sex hominũ eos ĩuasit & eos ad unum occidit.

SEPTEMTRIO

OCCIDENS

ORIENS

MERIDIES

·64·

PSARA

Insule Totius
Ambitus · M · P · 12

Insulā chion post hāc uisitamus quā Plinius Scirosior & Assanso nominauit deinde chios dcā
est: quia lingua sitica mastix latine interptatur in egeo sita mari prope minorē asiā XVIJ · mil·
passuū & cētū xx^ti^ uij^or^ mil· in circuitu eam numerauim^s^· Dicit^r^ et chios grece latine pregnās uel chion
colūpna uel chion canis inqua Ysiphiles thoantis filia patrem transmit fingēs lemniadib; ipm occidisse
In hac ē̄t i͂sula ut ait ouidius postq̄ Theseus occidit minotauꝝ & aufugiēs decreta & secū deferēs duas filia^s^
minois regis adrianā nō merito dimisit & phedrā sibi cōiugio copulauit· Protin^s^ egides rapta minoide chio
uela dedit: comitēq; suā crudelis in illo litore destituit· Deserte & multa querēti amplexus & ope liber tu-
lit utq; perenni sidere clara foret supta defronte coronā· Imisit celo tenuis uolat illa p auras· Que longa de
trione ad meridiē i duab; diuidit^r^ partib; harū p̄ma q̄ ad trionē spectat apanomerea grece dicit^r^ & latine
pars sup̄ma i͂terptat^r^· Secūda catomerea grece latine pars i͂fima declarat^r^· Prima quaū i mōtib; aspis eleu-
tur & ab arborib; pinoꝝ platanoꝝq; fulcita est Quib; fōtes emanātes p̄ rubrosas ualles flumīa frigidissima
i͂mare decurrētia molēdina triturat· Hic inde igit^r^ castra opidaq; i collib; & planis plura cernūt^r^: siuo-
lisso cū plano optimo Perparea: Scā helena: menedato Vicco: picio: & cardamile cernūt^r^ oīa circū cū scō āglo
elyaq; & olī opidū cū turre homeri dictū enumerāt^r^ i parte superiori· Quo i oppido diruto sepulchrū uatis
homeri ob nimiā antiquitatē i͂ucit^r^ deletū sed aliquo autore nūq̄ narratū repperi qd de eo certū sit ido
posteris ad ingrēdū dimittamus· Ad trionē & fōs nao uberrim^s^ extat ubi promōtoria minacissima
eleuāt^r^ i celū & nō ab ea parū portus cardamile cū plano flumineq; habet^r^ optim^s^· Deīd ad delphinū
alterū cū turre ex flumine optam^s^ p̄uenire pōtū: a q̄ ciuitas chij paucis mil cū pōtu tutissimo a ianuē-
sib; sblimat^r^· Que olī p· sup̄ mōtē expugnabilē diu tutissima uiguit· Quo i pede coronatā heremitau
laudam^s^ recte locū· Deīde ex q̄ cā dimisere ciues latia nescio & iux^a^ mare magnificā p̄parauert urbem
ude ab una alteraq; parte cāpi cū uineis ostēdūt^r^ fertilissimi omniū pomoꝝ habiti: & i͂fra mōtes nea
mone exstat· Igit^r^ a cacomerea nūc narratio nostra erit: q̄ a parte meridiei & p occiduū arbore lētisti
i humilib; collib; grumā masticis i͂solo munito coloni tēpore ueris mirifice i eadē regione p̄parant
producē laute· & qd mirū ē i apanomerea huiūmoi arbor nō inuenit^r^: Cūq; ad scm deuenio geor-
giū & i radicib; eius fontes decurrētes i unū prorūpūt & stati flumē p fertilissimū planū descendit
in mare: ubi uo ad dexterā i mōte castrū recouera recognoscim^s^ magnū· Ad calamotim plano affectam^s^
peruenire donec caput i masticis & scopolū caloieru dictū a lōge salutam^s^ recūro deīn ad pirgim
de nomine dicto p̄uenim^s^ sane & ultra ad occiduū portū late duoꝝ scopulorum & liuliménē sinū
in plano oppidū ubi procul nastasiā scām & amistre portū laudamūs a quib; cito in plano oppidoq;
cum plano & flumine manifestatur;

SEPTEMTRIO
MERIDIES
OCCIDENS
CHIOS
Cardami le porto
s. helena
castrum
S. georgi
amistae
amiste portus
Coronati
S. Johes
S. anasta sia
pigri
Castrum
Calamot

Ostendimus chion nunc Lesbos insula manifestatur & tâtum in navigijs valuit q
maris imperium diceret habere que in egeo sita mari & dicta mitilena: qa in hac
miletum solis filium patreq; pasiphis & biblidis cauniq; patrem de creta ubi venisset
profugum eoq contra minoem cognatum suum surrexerat regnasse urbemq; mileta
côstruxisse & ab eo sic dicta est. Sed postea litteris transmutatis mitilena civitas dicta
fuit quam Alceus poeta a quodam tyranno liberavit. Saphos poetissa de hac fuit îsula
& Theophrastus philosophus. Hic Pompeius in tessalia dimicaturus cû cesare suâ côiugê
deposuit. Regnavit etiam hic nicteus pater anthiope ex qua iuppiter î spetie satyri am
phionem & zetum genuit. Usq; hic castor & pollux capta helena eorum sorore î îsula
citharea paridem priami filium qui eam ceperat persequêtes & têpestate maxima nûq
côparuisse: dictum ê îmortalitatem adeptos: qd dicit in signum celeste trâsmutatos qd
hodie gemini cômemoramus. huc Paulus apostolus de syria veniens tempestate maris
vix ad terram evasit qui predicans fidem xpi anguem maximû occidit & multos cô
vertit. Sunt et p omnê circuitû plura castra quorû maior mitilena videtur: q seculis
preteritis magna potêtissimaq; civitas extiterat & p circuitû quatuor & plus mil:
hodie vo ad exiguû est reducta spatium: caloieros eqdem abhinc deo devotus ruinâ
civitatis dominiq; vidit in futurum: qui cito civibus desolationê urbis palam locut
est. Quod nô credentes dominus suiq; ac multitudo civium terremotu periere. Eveit
enim meis diebus dominum per insulam accedere & cum in quadam pnoctasset do
mo scorpio manum infixit suam. Cûq; famuli clamorem audirêt illius p scalâ ad
eum fuit ascensus & quesita restauratione doloris ita & taliter domus impleta pro
cerum famulorumq; q in ruina est eversa & dominus cum multis îsperatâ mortem
substinuerunt. Ad meridiem magnifice urbis. iiijor. colupne erigunt una cû edifi
cijs multis atq; cavernis mira industria edificatis. Ad austrum colpus Geremie de
scêdit ubi plura oppida usq; ad occiduû vident. Castel Gero Geremia: Chidonia: Cha
loni: Vasilica: Castelpetra: Castelmulgo. Ad trionê castel sci theodori: turris & c Circa
medium planus est fertilis. Ad orientê occiduûq; montes & indomita anima
lia sût una cum cipressis fagis pinetisq;. Est deniq; in circuitu portuosa & .cxxx.
circuit mil & scopuli erigunt & prope turchiam determinatur;

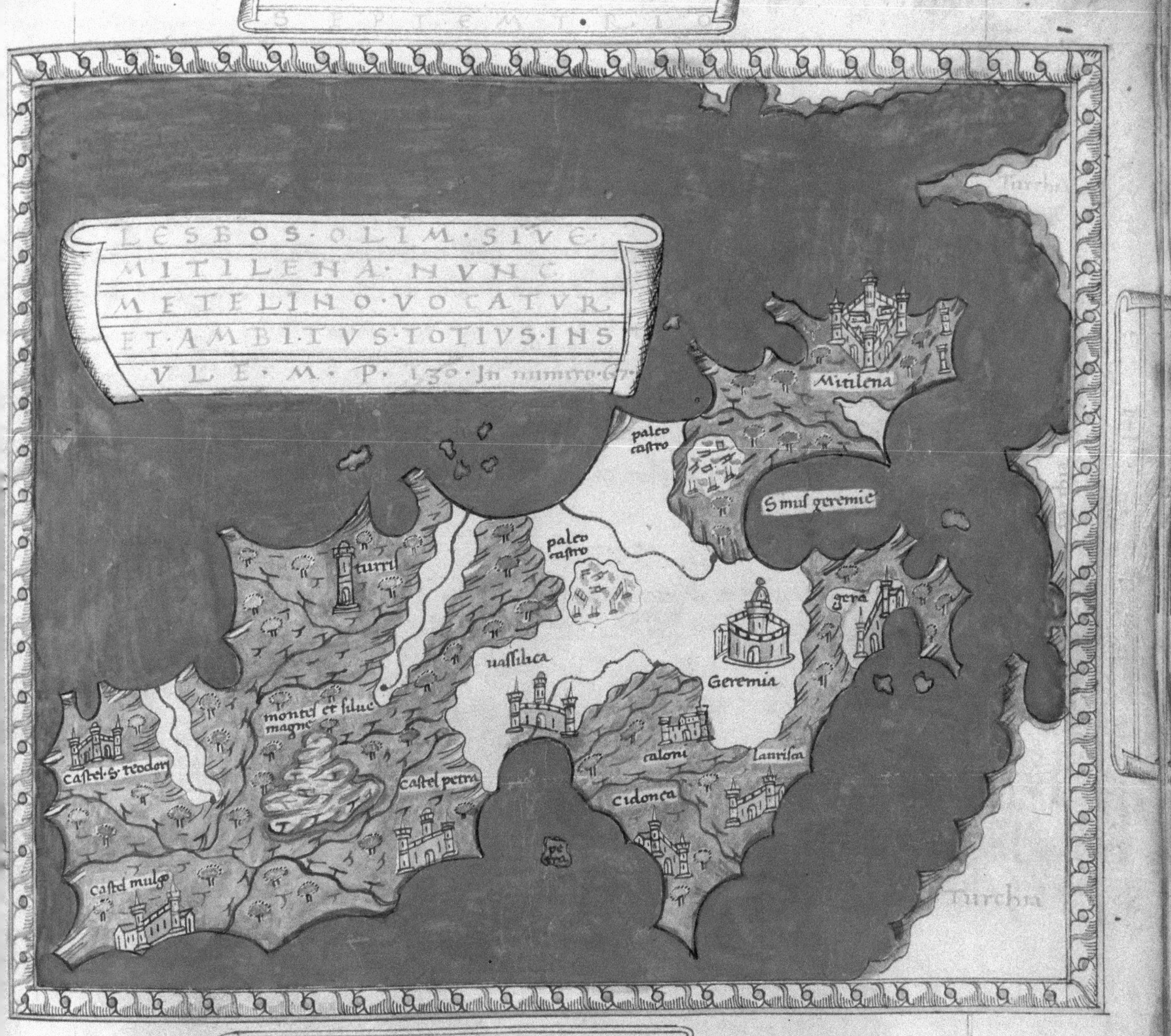

DEsũmo nũc ĩsulam tenedi que corã introitu strichi romanie uel hellesponti posita est & ĩcõspectu antiquissime troie apparata ẽ ĩegeo mari: q̃ a q̃dã iuuene sic dicto noĩa ta ẽ: q athenis ĩfamatus q̃d suã cognouisset nouercã ob uerecudiã ad hãc applicuit ĩsulã & uacuã cultorib; occupauit · Hec tẽpore Laumedõtis & priami opulẽtissima fuit & ĩ eius sinu greci parauerẽ ĩsidias troianis. a quib; troia deleta fuit: p hãc bellum atrox inter uenetos & ianuẽses tẽpore meo fuit quia quilib& ipo⁊ eã possidere uolebat: tãdẽ ex cõcordia ambarũ desolata remãsit & sic nullus in ea audet habitare · Sed postq̃ iii oĩa relicta fuere domestica multa

& animalia indomita devenere. In radicibus uõ altioris mõtis fons est q ab hora tertia noctis usq; sextam solstitio existẽte tãtũ exundat in aquis q flumẽ maximũ videt'. In aliis aũt horis nil in eo fuisse cõphẽdimus aque. Hec ẽt plana habetur & circũdata humilibus mõtib; manifestum ẽ pter unũ q ĩter alios sublimat'. In quo tria milia francoꝝ postq̃ venere classẽ turchorum corã gallipoli ĩ mari submerserũt suspẽsi sũt: qa ex oĩ gẽte ĩ favorẽ ĩfideliũ ibi erãt in classe congregati tẽpore cõcilij cõstantie. & hinc inde p planum tot vineta inculta & alia reperiũt poma q hodie transeuntibus prebeat refrigerium & sic versus nobilissimam olim aspicis troiam multa fragmẽta antiquitatis ipsius vere videbis. A leva uõ hellespontum intramus mare orestenuo in quo introitu dardanellum offẽdimus: ubi nunc & olim colũpne elevantur multe;

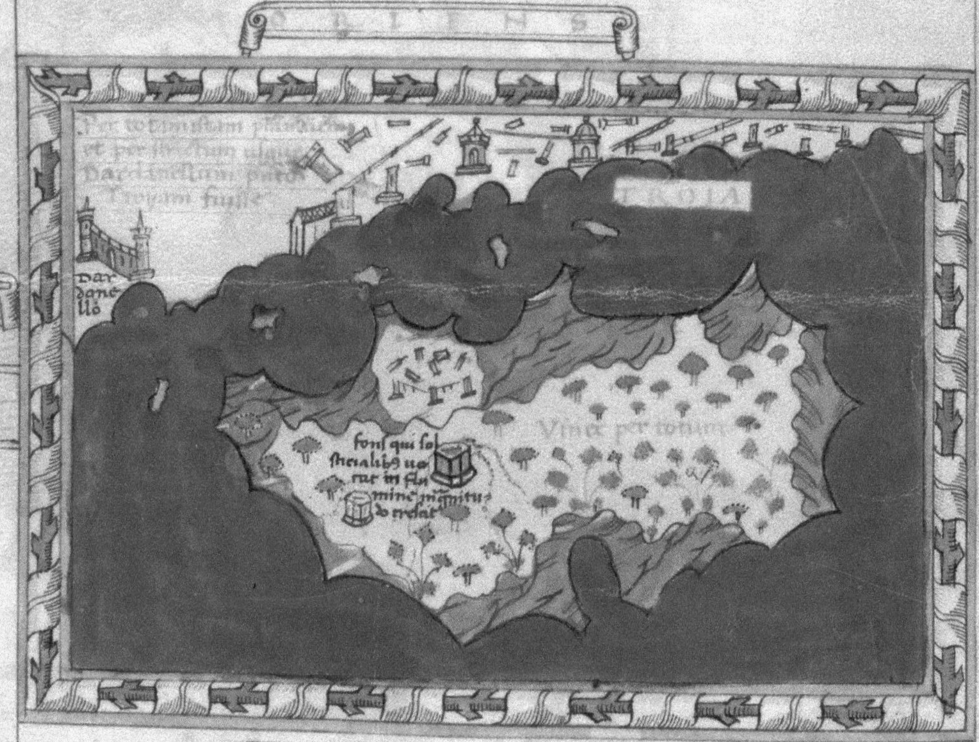

Dignum fore arbitror postq̃ hucusq; venimus urbem cõstantinopolim demostrare ut animus audientium alacer sit ad ea que dicturi sumus cũ multa miranda erunt inspecturi. Est ergo hic introitus ad hellespontum usque stenuo ore hodie strictum gallipoli dictum: & asia ab europa dirimitur: ĩ quo

primo postq̄ ad dexteram antiquam reliquimus troiam turrim aleua iuxta mare in-
ueniemus que propinquior asie fuisse memorauimus & de hinc usq; abidon oppidũ
parua extat uia. Ergo ille rex persarum Xerses in isto loco ponte s[upe]r nauibus ordinato
de asia in europiam transitum fecit. & ait demostenes decem centenis milibus militũ
elatum quatuor milium & ducentarum nauium numero terribilem exigua latẽtem
nauicula fugere coegit. Ponit etiam lucius q[uod] cum philippo rege abidenos oppugnã
re ad destructionem murorum iam uenisset & ciues ob misericordiam cũ supellectilibus
recedere uolentes. Capitaneus in castellum eos reuocauit dicens. Non pepercistis patrie
& domib[us] uestris ideo ad occasionem eritis omnes accepturi: itaq[ue] ipsi met ĩ disterminiũ
mortis irruere & domos omniaq; adignem miserere. Ultra u[er]o. xl. mil. ex parte europe munitissimum gallipolim oppidum uidemus in altum: quod sponte turchis
infidelib[us] imp[er]ator grecie tradidit & filias proprias eis copulauit. Ex qua largitione
tanta secuta est & sequitur strages christianorum q[uod] uix homo in sua etate posset nomina scripta captorum occisorumq; numerare. Igitur turchi de montibus armenie &
persieq; pauperes in hanc uenientes minorem asiam dominium ex consensu ĩpatoris
supradicti inceptauerũt. Ex quibus cito prouincia nouis linguis gentibusq; usq; in
hodiernum diem impleta est: quorum aliqui in bello fuerunt strenuissimi & memorie digniores: qui secundum ritum secte eorum laute gubernauerunt regnum & dominia multa ui abstulerunt xp[ist]ianis. Quorum unus amorathei merito diceretur. Mulier dum ferculum lactis uiro in agro portar& famulus domini nimis epulũ mulieris
cõmedit. Que conquesta cito reus coram eo conducitur & abscissus in medio lac co-
gnoscatur & iustitia coram amoracto sublimatur. Abba quidam ornamenta sanctorum
ecclieq; sue abstulit & coram amoracto magno gaudio mahometum adorauit. Monaci uero ex quo uiam didicerunt abbatis coram eodem imp[er]atore cõquesti sunt. &
Ille igitur dum astutiam atque fraudem abbatis comperit restauratis caloieris corã
eo de altissimo monte in imum delapsus est. Subulcus suo aratro uas plenum argenti adinuenit qui cito coram amoracto onerato curru accessit & monetam sibi
consignauit. Ille requisitis senioribus cuius ymago esset & neminẽ inuenirent ait
Subulco uir bone. hec ymago mea neq; meorum antecessorum fuit: quare iustum
non fore factum alienum capere & rectum alicui occupare: ergo tua ẽ Vade ĩ pace,

Cimiteriū turchoꝝ
CALIPOLI
Domus curie
ubi dantur
Juditia
Domus arma
mentuꝝ galeaꝝ
platea
Turchia
TVRCHIA
strictum
Calipolis et romoie

30v

AD orientē ī introitu mari hellespōti marmora īsula ē & · xxx · circuit mił & tota mōtuosa marmorū & arborosa zapinorum reperta est: a qua cōstātinus iustinianus & aliȷ́ imperatores innumerabilia edificia marmorū pro urbe cōstantinopoli extraxerīt & ī pōte lapideo onerabāt. Ab alio latere oppidū eleuat paucorū habitātiū ū scopuli aliq̄ p̄ualēt · Dr̄ &·n· mare hoc hellespōtū · Elles ·n· atamātis filia cū frixo frē īsidiā fugiēte nouercales aureo uecta ariete īfortunio suo ī ūdas decidit · absōta de se nom̄ dedit ūdi ppetuū ut q̄ pōtū dicebat̄ ān dicēt hellespōtū · hī igit̄ mare istud initiū ab erītheo ū aiacis sepulchrū erigit̄ ul̄ chēsonesū et ibi ī fine europe mergitur ·

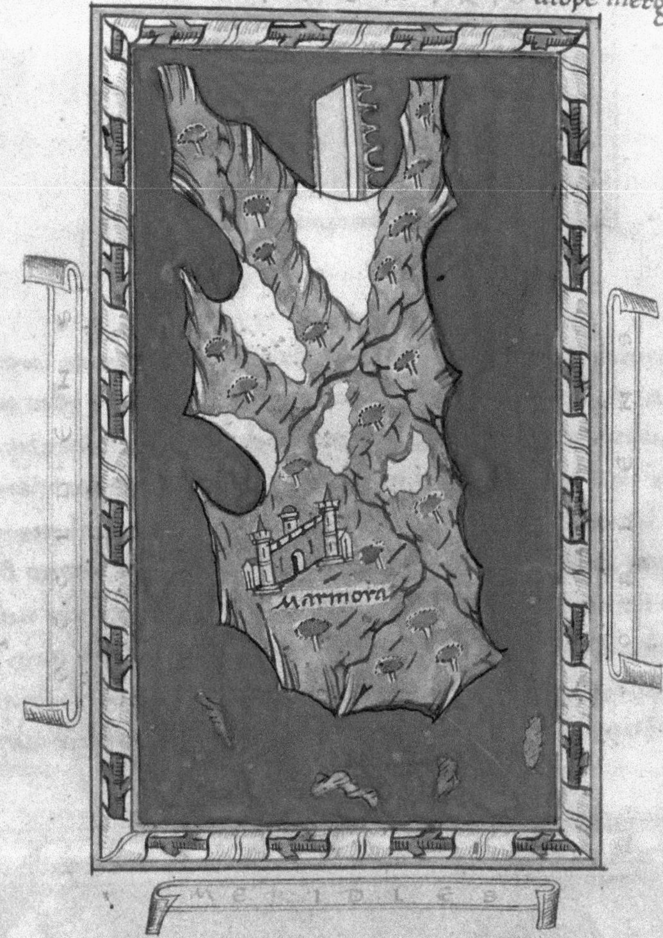

·70·

MARMORA

Insule Totius Ambitus M · P · 30

NAuigando igitur per mare supradictum & ad urbem accederemus ad dexteram colonimon insula uidetur inmontibus posita nimis & quia olim per omnem greci dominabantur tunc temporis hec erat habitata: nunc uō ad desolationem redacta & indomita animalia p eam uagantur ·

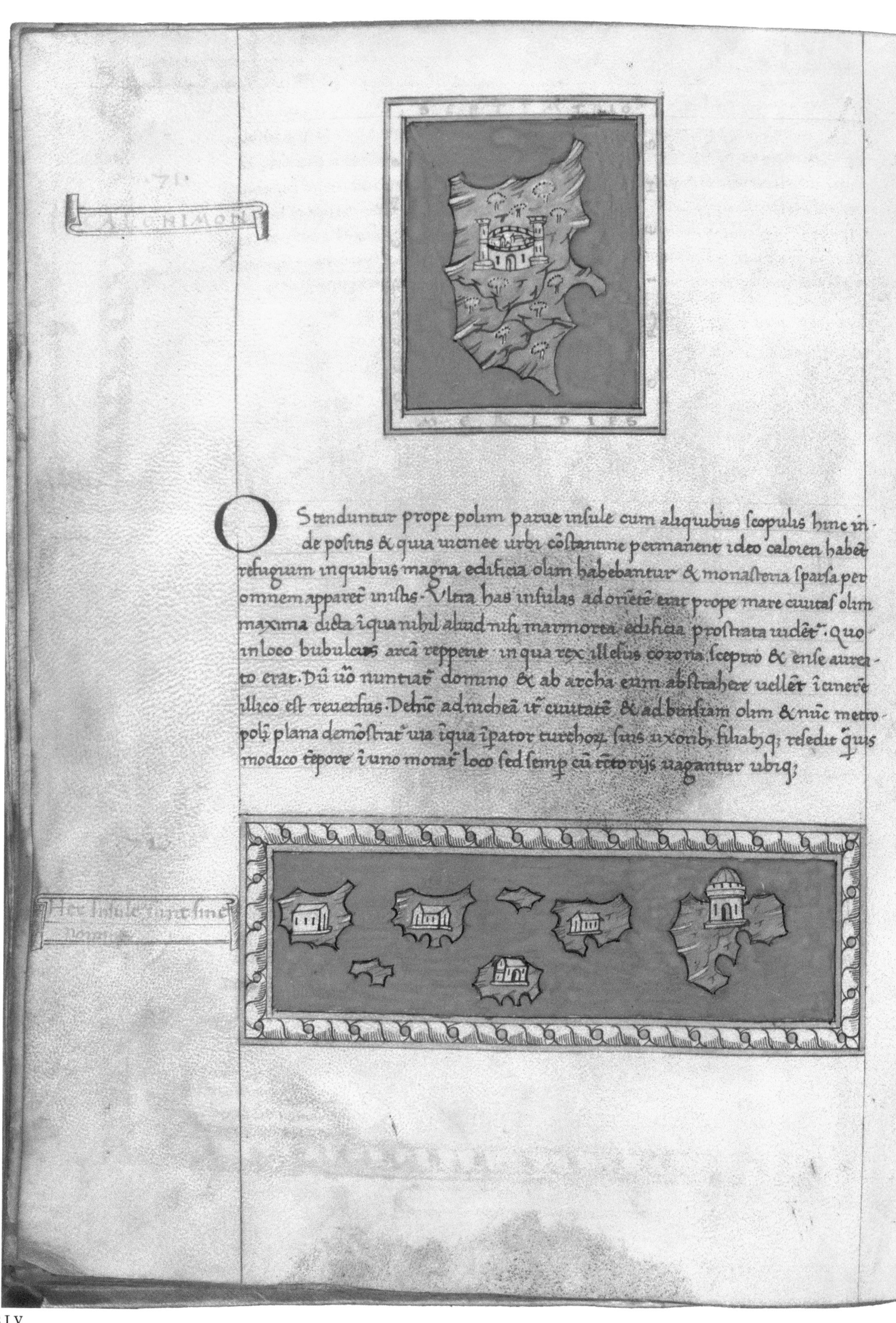

71

CALCHIMON

Ostenduntur prope polim parue insule cum aliquibus scopulis hinc inde positis & quia uicinee urbi cõstantine permanent ideo caloieri habet
refugium inquibus magna edificia olim habebantur & monasteria sparsa per
omnem apparet inuisus. Ultra has insulas ad orietẽ erat prope mare ciuitas olim
maxima dicta ĩ qua nihil aliud nisi marmorea edificia prostrata uidet̃. Quo
in loco bubulcus arcã reppe͂it in qua rex illesus corona sceptro & ense aureato erat. Dũ uõ nuntiat̃ domino & ab archa eum abstrahere uellet ĩ cinere
illico est reuersus. Dehĩc ad nicheã it̃ ciuitatẽ & ad bursiam olim & nũc metro-
polĩ plana demõstrat̃ uia ĩ qua ĩpator turchoꝝ suis uxorib; filiab;q; resedit q̃uis
modico tẽpore ĩ uno morat̃ loco sed semꝑ cũ tẽtorijs uagantur ubiq;

72

Hec insule sunt sine nomine

31v

Reuertio ad lesam nuc costātinopoli urbē & quis insula nō sit postq huc p
uenim de ea pauca ptractabimus ut ad iditum legitui pueniat. Est aut igit
a costātino dicta: que iuncta cū bisantio eā maxime āplicauit. Post aūt seculis labetib
ipatores ecctys eā ornauere & pserti Iustinianus q leges cōdidit & sanctā Sophiā
edificauit cū palatioq; prodomo. Reman& ergo triangulata & x & VIII est i circuitu
mil. Primo igit de angulo scī Dimitri usq; ad angulum Vlacherne sex mil. quo ispatio
centū & x erigūt turres. Abhic igit usq; ad crescea pōtā qnq; mil. cū muro & ānmurale
munitissimo & uallo aquar surgētiū & turres imuro altiori nonaginta sex. Dehic usq;
iterū ad scm Dimitriū mil. VII. & turres centūnonagita octo: iquib est campus ab ex
& oli portus Vlanga ubi greci. Lm rut dicit francor plane calcinee frumētato dolose ex
iuidia uel dolore occiderūt: quor ossa inumerabilia usq; i hodiernū phibet testimoniū: & propinquo huic conescali uel arsana restat: & ultra fuit sup menia āplissimū
Iustiniani palatiū cū ecctia enea dicta nobilissima musaicorumq; edificiorū atq; cū
pauimēto miro ingenio cōtexto. Ibiq; i alto & sup mare erat speculū imēsurabilis
magnitudinis circūspectū a longe nimis: & oīa edificia eius marmorea imari uidet
prosternata prope portulum ipatoris dicti: et de imēso palatio usq; sanctā Sophiā
erā p miliare uia colūnar binar p quā dominus accedebat ubi octingētor cleri
corū p circuitū dom erat & de totius insule trinacrie ut dicit fructū capiebat. Nūc
aūt sola testudo ecctie remanet intea qa omia diruta sūt & adnichilū deuenerunt
aqua usq; ad pauimētū cētū triginta quatuor brachia & a pauimēto usq; planum
fundamēti: quia tota una cisterna optima aque ampliat brachia XXII. Insuper p
ecctiam sūt de angulo ad angulum cētū XX brachia: q desup rotūda & iplano qua
trāgulata residit. Quis aūt poterit enumerare ornamēta marmorū atq; pōphiror
cū musaicis liniamētis: qa quo latere icipere uellē euanesco. Extra igit ecctiā ad me
ridiē in platea colūna septuagita cubitorū alta uidet cui in capite Iustinianus eneū
equestre habent & pomū cū leua aureū tenēs ad oriētē cū dextra minat. & iux
hāc sex colūne marmoree erepte magne uident seriatim. Vltra uō has ad meridiē
hippodromus distendit: qd latine equicursus appellat. In hoc aūt spatio nobiles
corā iustrabāt populo & duella atq; tormēta parabant. VI. LXXXX. et i lōgitudi
ne brachiorum & c XXIIII. ampliabat & sup colūnas edificatū est inquib cister
na optime aque totum supdictū cōtin& spatium. In capite uō hippodromi XXIIII or
erāt altissime colūne ubi impator cū pncipib residebat. Ab una aūt parte alte
raq; hippodromi sedilia gradatim i longitudine erāt ipsius marmorea ubi popul
sedendo ōmem ludū cōprehendebat. Per mediū deniq; dicti cursus i lōgitudine
humilis est murus: & primo uersus scām Sophiā est ecctia cū muro magnifico

inumerabiliũ fenestrarũ adornato ubi domine iuueculeq; cũ matronis suos pro-
spiciebãt dilectos ubi inp̃ncipio dicti muri sum͡ᵒ balneum erigebat͡ᵘʳ inquo ut-
nerati ponebant͡ᵘʳ. Deinde agulia xLuij. cubitoꝝ alta ex uno latere ĩquatuor
eneis taxillis in altum recta cernit͡ᵘʳ & in pede eius uersus sic sonãt. Difficilis
quõdã dñs parare seuerus. Iussus & extinctis palmam parare tyrannus. Oĩa theodosio cedũt soboliq; perenni. Ter denis sic uictus ego domitusq; dieb;. Iudice sub
prodo supas elatus ad auras. Vltra hũc lapidem tres eneos serpẽtes ex multis lapidibus agulia cõnexa. Lxuj. cubitoꝝ erigit͡ᵘʳ. Vltra deniq; ĩfine humilis muri
hui͡ᵘˢ quatuor humiles columne marmoree uident͡ᵘʳ erecte: ĩqb; imperatrix p̃emine-
bat ad festum. Fecit ergo theodosius oĩa ista & alia multa p urbẽ laudãda. Re-
periunt͡ᵘʳ ĩsup hodie ĩfinite columne quaꝝ qdẽ quinq; uidẽt͡ᵘʳ maiores. & Lx. cu.
proqualib; eleuatur inaltũ: et primo colũna iustiniani dicta: Secũda crucis: q͡ᵒ
ĩloco quatuor erecte porphiree uident͡ᵘʳ ĩquib; quid͡ᵃ eq quatuor enei aureati
politi erãt & ueneti illos uenetias apd͡ scm̃ detulere marcum colũnis remanẽ-
tib;. Tertia quartaq; colũnarũ q͡ᵉ ĩmedipolis sũt posite ĩqb; circũcirca acta im-
patoꝝ sculpta cognoscũt͡ᵘʳ. In ecctia scõꝝ aptoꝝ q̃nta cũ angelo eneo & cõstãtino genuflexo colũna ẽ: & ecctia iã diruta ãplissimaq; oĩa sepulchra ĩpatoꝝ porphirea uidẽt͡ᵘʳ
magnifica uia ĩmenso: & ibi colũna ũ͡ᵇⁱ xp̃s ligat͡ᵘˢ & flagellat͡ᵘˢ ẽ. In monasterio pãdocratora ẽ lapis ũ͡ᵇⁱ ioseph reuoluit xp̃m ĩsindone. In monasterio sci͡ Iohis depetra sũt ue-
stimẽta xp̃i & arũdo cũ spõgea lãceaq; ĩunũ seruata. Sũt deniq; p urbẽ inumera-
biles ecctie atq; cisterne mire magnitudinis & ĩdustrie fabricate & ĩruina posite uinea pro qualib; ĩea truĩ ut quatuor uegetũ uini crescat. Cisterna sci͡ Iohãis depetra
cisterna pãdepopti. Cisterna pãdocratora. Cisterna aptoꝝ. Cisterna maumethi: ĩqua
ita subtili artificio sũt ordinate colũne qd͡ ẽ ĩcredibile ad narrandũ. & alie multe
sũt scã sophia q̃ ẽ p̃ncipalior alijs & Iustiniani͡ᵘˢ in. xv. ãnis illd͡ explicauit op͡ᵘˢ. Sãctus
Gergius de magana. Scã hereni. Scs̃ Lazarus: Chirame enea petrus & paulus.
Sci xLᵗᵃ mãtiꝝ milia & sua cisterna ãplissima optime aq̃ cui͡ᵘˢ finẽ ĩueniri nequaq̃
dr͡ posse: Anastasis pente scõs. Scs̃ Iohes destudio. Scs̃ ãdreas. Vlacherna & cͣ. In q͡ᵃ
tãta copia ubiq; edificata remanẽt ipsaꝝ ecctiaꝝ & ut pulchrior altera q̃ lõgum
ẽẽt enarrare. Sũt et p ciuitatẽ pauca ĩpatores & inimici latinoꝝ q nũq̃ secretã
pacẽ cũ eis obtinebũt. & si promittẽt nõ obseruabũt. Fuit et hec urbs pulcherrima ualde & aula sapientie honestatisq;. Hũc uõ ad ignorãtiã duritiãq; ue-
tuste opinioĩs p̃ueti: pcc͡o gule adheserũt & ĩtatũ delati pp copiã p̃isciũ car-
niũq; q quarta pars ipsius ad inobiũ ĩciderũt lepre. & doctrinã Iohãis chrysostomi aliorũq; scõꝝ patrũ dimisere. Ad trionẽ p unũ miliare pera ianuẽsiũ
pulcherrima ciuitas est: q̃ p sinũ ab urbe separat͡ᵘʳ. Sũt & n. ab isto loco usq; mare
põtũ seu eusinũ. xviij. mil. Ad tonẽ ore strenuissimo cũ periculo ĩtrãtũ hodie
nauiũ. Cũ qb; postq̃ de urbe nãrauim͡ᵘˢ ad egeũ mare ad ĩsulã Stimliminin reuertẽm;

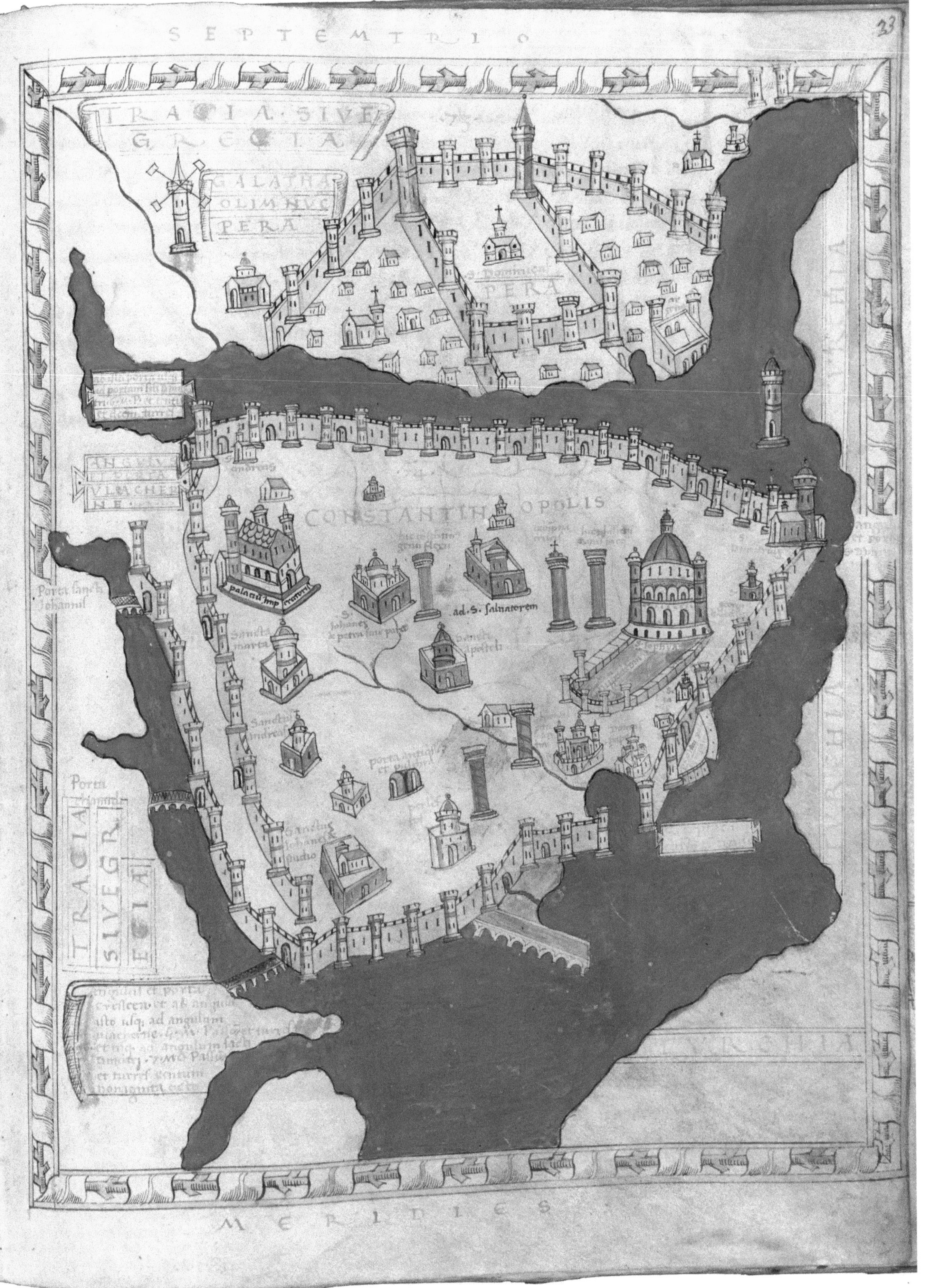
SEPTEMTRIO
TRACIA SIVE GRECIA
GALATHA OLIM NUC PERA
PERA
CONSTANTINOPOLIS
ad. S. Salvatorem
TRACIA SIVE GRECIA
TURCHIA
MERIDIES

ERAT hec ĩsula lemnos dicta: nũc ũo stalimini denominat̃ ĩ egeo mari sita &
plana tota cẽtũ circuit mil. limnia .n. greci lac̃ latine: ad quã pp eius bassitudinẽ p̱i
culosũ ẽ accedẽ: cũ ĩ ea simul & pͦtus sit optimi & plura oppida habitãt ĩ ea. Legr̃ & ĩ hac ĩsula
uenerẽ cõcubuisse cũ marte eiusq; adulteriũ solẽ uulcano suo cõiugi prodidisse: quos
ãbos uulcanus adamatinis cateris ligauit eosq; alijs dijs turpiter accubãtes ostẽdit
mulieres aũt lemniadis adulteriũ ueneris dãnãtes ipãm tãq̃ ĩdignã p̃termictẽdam
his odorẽ hircinũ misit unde oĩs mulieres ĩstigatione ueneris oĩs uiros occidert.
Sola ũo isiphile cõcubuit oeneum thoanteq; filios procreauit: Vbi aũt lemniades ysi-
philẽ seruasse   cõpetiere eã interficẽ uoluerut. Illa ũo fugiens a p̃donib; capta
licurgo regi argolico ĩ nutricẽ uẽdita est. Ex hac et ĩsula minij traxerẽ originem
unde a pelasgi expulsi a spartanis recepti sũt. Qui cũ imperium ciuitatis mutatis
uestibus uxorũ ĩ carcẽ inclinatis tectisq; capitib; ĩ signũ calamitatis relictis uxorib;
euaserẽ. Hic thias filius bachi rex fuit que abundantissima in frumẽto habetur.

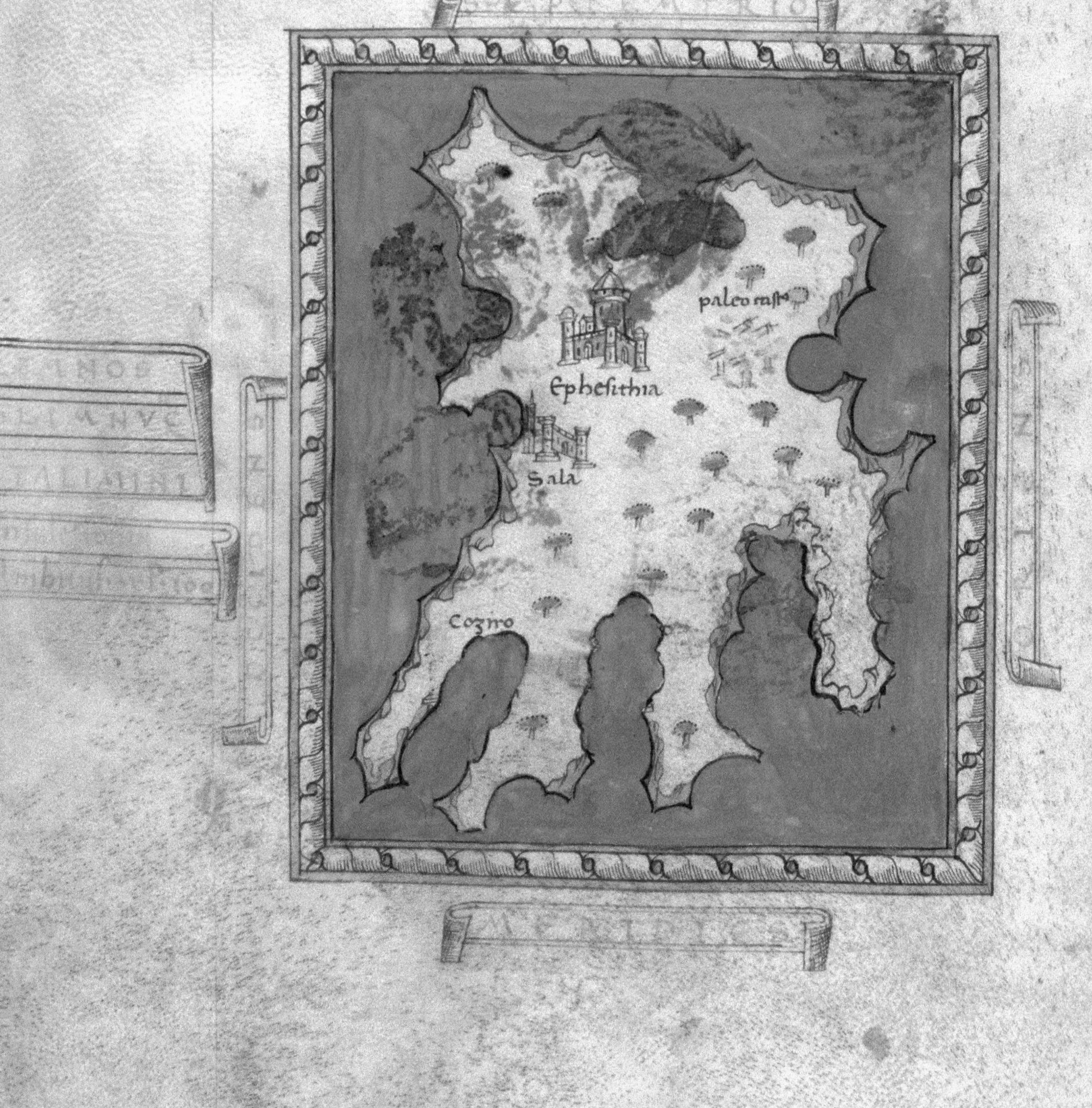

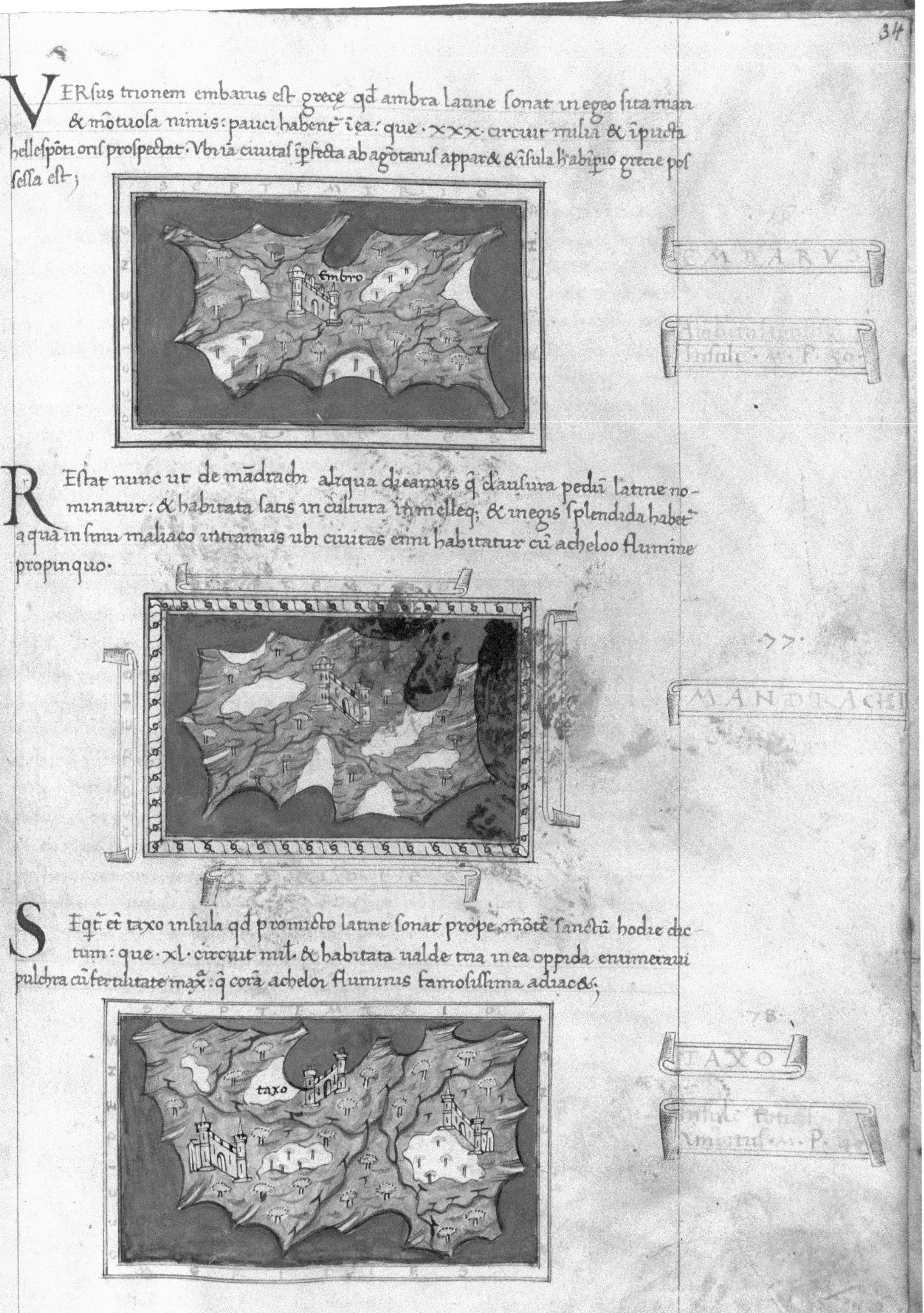
34
VERsus trionem embarus est grece qd ambra latine sonat in egeo sita mari
& mõtuosa nimis: pauci habent̃ ĩ ea: que · xxx · circuit milia & ĩ puncta
hellespõti oris prospectat · Vbi ã ciuitas ĩ pfecta ab agotanis appar& & isula h'abipio grecie pos
sessa est;
Embro
EMBARVS
REstat nunc ut de mãdrachi aliqua dicamus q̃ clausura pedũ latine no
minatur: & habitata satis in cultura itm elleq; & inegis splendida habet
aquã in sinu maliaco intramus ubi ciuitas enim habitatur cũ acheloo flumine
propinquo·
MANDRACHI
SEqt̃ et taxo insula qd promũcto latine sonat prope mõtẽ sanctũ hodie dic
tum: que · xl · circuit mil· & habitata ualde tria in ea oppida enumeraui
pulchra cũ fertilitate max: q̃ corã acheloi fluminis famosissima adiac&;
taxo
TAXO

INuenim⁹ post dictã insulã mõtẽ athos olim & q̃uis nũc sit tẽpore Xersis regis p
sarũ a cõtinẽti mõs iste diuisus erat nũc cũ terra firma cõiũctus ẽ & mõs scõs noĩat
prope salonicẽsẽ ciuitatẽ ĩ prouĩcia tracie altissim⁹ ualde & ibi propinquius cuius
ĩ sumitate acroaon oppidũ erat longior q̃ in alijs terris etas habitãtiũ extendebat:
& in circuitu mõtis ad plus · c xxiij · mil · uidet̃ habere: quo ĩ loco tot & tãta monaste
ria sũt caloierorũ scĩ Basilij: Chrysostomi · Hazãzeni & p̃teritoꝝ monacoꝝ q̃ difficile
foret ad narrandũ · Surgũt igit̃ ĩ tẽpestate noctis silẽtio postq̃ signũ p̃mũ lingee cã
panę rauca uoce dederat secũdũ grecoꝝ cõsuetudinẽ & ad ecc̃liam accedẽtes matu
tinalẽ diuinũ offitiũ: Cũq; hoc finitũ est ad suas redeũt casas & quicq̃d a suo mitit̃
priore separati cum pace cõmedũt · Sũt & aliqua horum monasteria q̃ ad comunẽ
caloieroꝝ trahũt uitam: aliqua ad aliũ asperiorẽ modũ uiuẽdi uitã ordinauere:
quia ĩ sabbato de mõte atq; solitudine oĩs ĩ cellulis redeũtes & ĩ offitio diuino die
dominico usq; meridiẽ orãtes ad refectorium accedũt: & cõpleto prãdio pars ipsoꝝ
pane leguminibusq; ĩ heremo p̃parat̃ ĩtroire. & ibi suspiciẽs celũ ac stellas tota nũc
suspirãs & p̃riam cogitãs eternã de exilij sui loco protinus adorationẽ humilẽ os
suũ cõuertit & uibrare iã sole exorto ad diurnas dei laudes proletus ore prorũpit.
Ipẽ sibi comes ipẽ sibi famulat̃ nec metuit solus ẽẽ dũ secũ est. Celũ spectare non
aurũ: terrã amat calcare & b̃ndictio cũ grãtiaꝝ actione sepe est ĩ ore suo. Scit uite
hominũ pauca sufficẽ & sũmas uerasq; diuitias nil optare. Sumũq; ĩpiũ nil timẽ
letũ agit atq; trãquillũ euũ placidas noctes occisos dies & secura cõuiuia It liber: sed &
ĩtrepidus nullas struit aut cauet ĩsidias. Angeloꝝ aula cõuiuijs odor colorq; optim⁹:
Iudex morum testisq; modestie: mẽsa pacifica: luxus ac tumultus nescia: gule domi
trix & uoluptas feda exulat & regina sobrietas regnat. Cubile castũ & quietũ:
cõscientia paradisus est p̃paratus. Multi itaq; ĩ huiusmoĩ mõte talẽ spõte eleg̃
uitã q̃ intãtũ trahit eos ad cõtẽplationẽ q̃ si materies lapidũ cõtra rueret eos
nullo modo timerent atq; caput uel oculos torquerent ad uidẽdum. Aliqui etiam
in monasterijs cum silentio tribus in ebdomoda cibum capere uicibus sũt assueti
in quibus pro quolibet cẽtum caloieros comunis uite. & in aliquibus quĩgẽtos
enumerabis. Igit̃ monasteria de decem usq; · xxx^ta^ · ulta uidet̃ uite cõmunis. Hic
aũt apes ficus oliua ĩ amenissimis uallibus uirescunt & sedentes ĩ usũ ĩ lana re
uolut. Iste canistrum uiminibus plicat & oĩs alternatim horis stabilitis deum
laudare conantur & pax in eis regnat sempiterna.

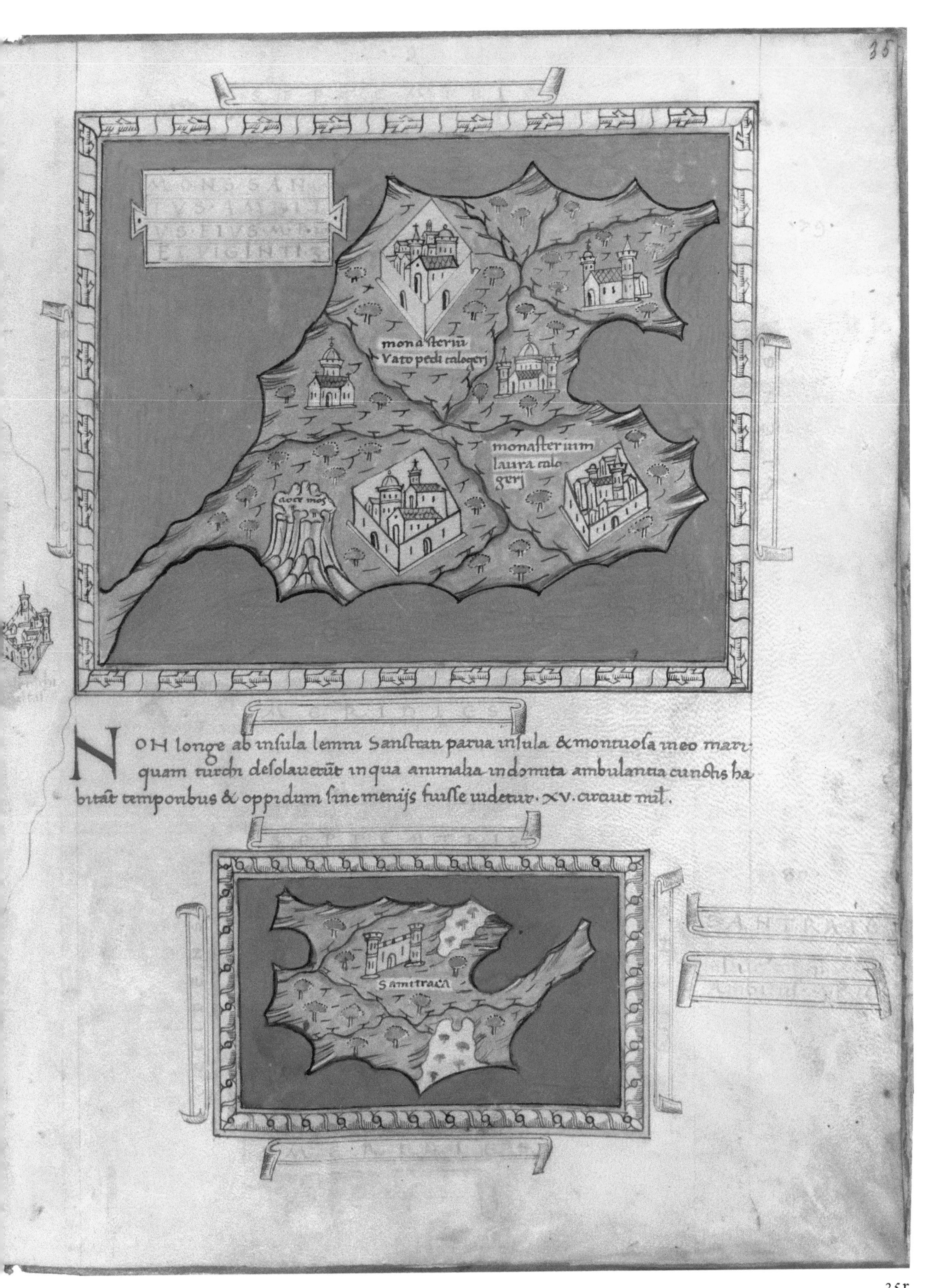

NOn longe ab insula lemni Sanstrati parua insula & montuosa ineo mari
quam turchi desolauerũt inqua animalia indomita ambulantia cunctis ha
bitãt temporibus & oppidum sine menijs fuisse uidetur. XV. circuit mil.

In hoc igit^r mari egeo limen isula imõte appar& nõ magna ualde sed pulcra olĩ extiterat que parum habitata xl · circuit mil & limẽ dicta a limite quia nauel a tessalonica
ciuitate uenietes recto tramite p istã trãsire studẽt ut nauigatio securius habeatur.

81

LIMEN

Ambitus totius Insulae M.P. 40

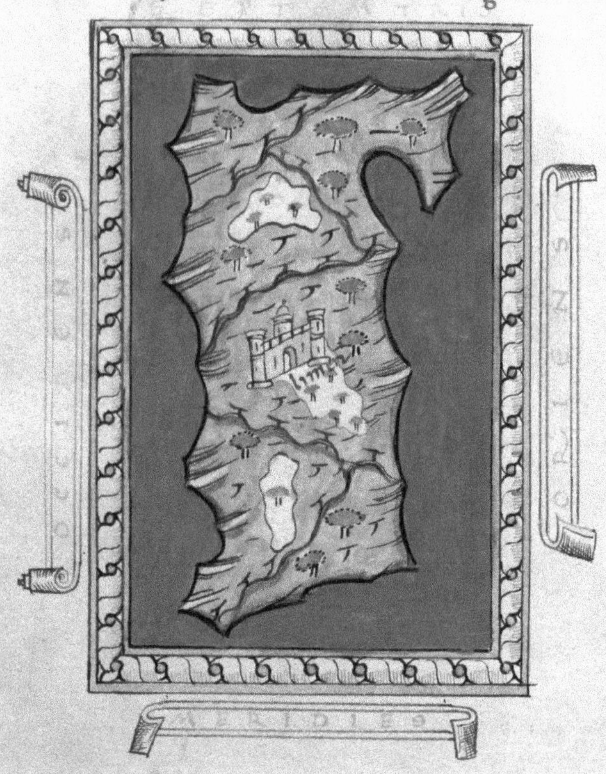

Sequit^r insula dromos dicta latine cursus: quia nauel de oriẽte ad occiduum
nauigãtes ab ista signũ capuit: & sepe ciues trãseũtibus ĩ nocte signũ demonstrant ut tutius nauiget^r. Fertilis & · xxx. circuit mil.

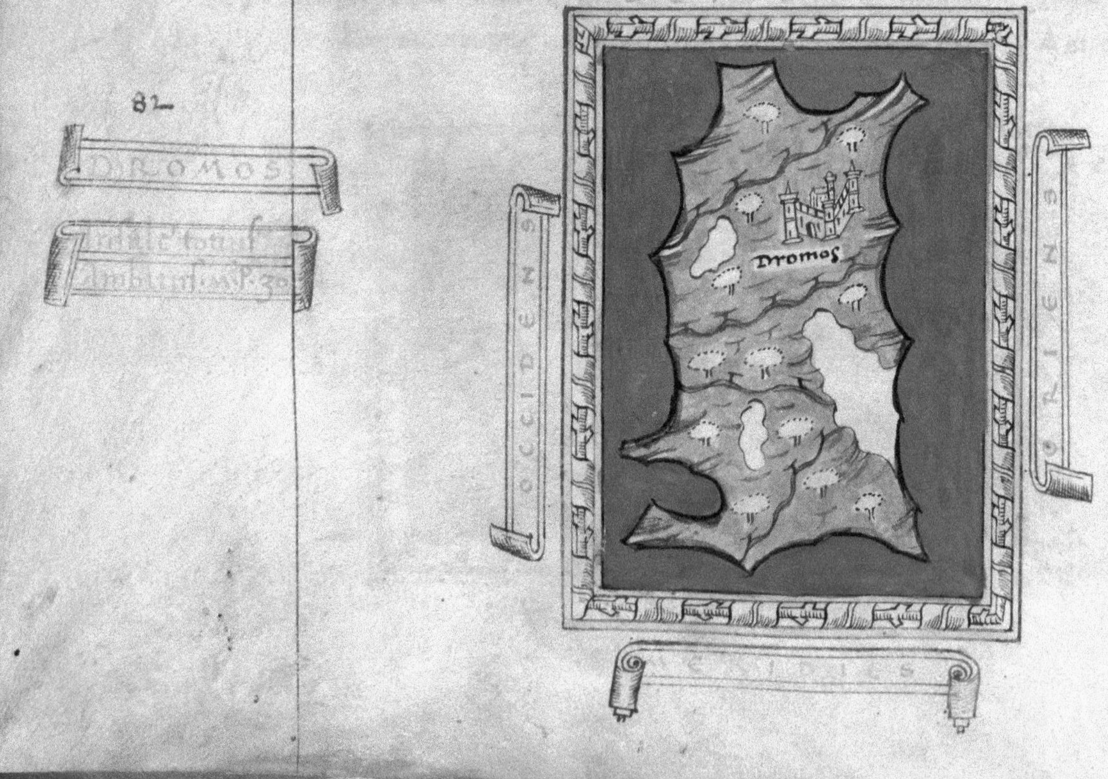

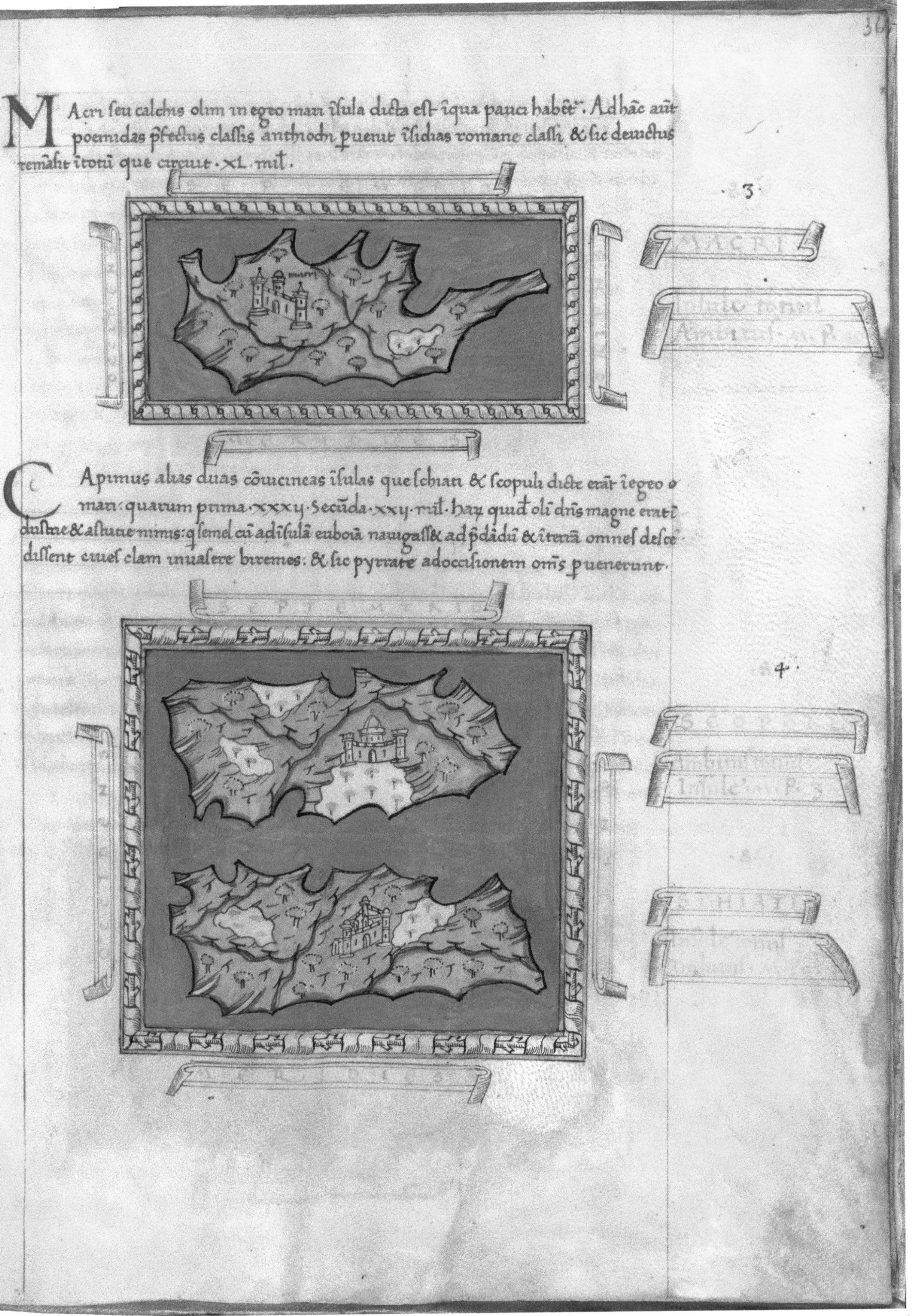

MAcri seu calchis olim in egeo mari isula dicta est iqua pauci habet. Ad hac aut poemidas pfectus classis anthiochi puenit isidias romane classi & sic deuictus remasit itotu que circuit · xl · mil ·

CApimus alias duas conuicineas isulas que schiati & scopuli dicte erat iegeo o mari: quarum prima · xxxv · secuda · xxv · mil · hay quid oli dns magne erati dustrie & astutie nimis: q semel cu ad isula euboia nauigass & ad pdadu & iterra omnes descedissent ciues clam inuasere biremes: & sic pyrrate ad occisionem omis puenerunt ·

Consurgit corã dcis isulis scopul' scs elyas dcs q sblimmo alijs ubiq; miat: i cui cacume ecclia pua isgebat: & ibi caloier' fui es deo ad solẽ dũ dormiret aqla credẽs ipm ee brutũ i eũ descẽdit & cũ rapacib; ũgulis oculos euulsit suos. Ille isnitũ dolẽs & deũ affectãter rogans ad eum elyas uenit oib; uidẽtib; socijs qui oculos suos restaurauit.

Conseqt' schiros insula: q lõga de tone ad meridiẽ de egeo mari ·LXXX· circuit mil. portuosa nimis & pegaseũ prospicit sinũ. q nemorosa satis i motib; tota. Tethis achyllis mater carpathij uatis uaticinio monita piturũ filiũ si ad bellũ iret troianum ipm achillẽ i habitu femineo i hac isula apud licomedem regẽ ascẽdit. Hicq; a Deidamia regis filia dilectus & cognitus & eã nõ iuitã clã sororibus alijs oppressit & ex ea filium habuit. Protinus aggredit' regẽ atq; ibi testib; atis hãc tibi ait, nri germanã rector achillis. Nonne uides ut torua genas equãdaq; fri: Tradimus arma humeis arcumq; animosa petebat &c. & quia nemorosa atq; aspa tot & tãta sũt animalia multaȝ generũ siluestria qd ẽ mirũ: qa pauci sũt habitatores & i circuitu magna cõsistit. Ea propt' turchi sepe eam uisitant sine habitantiũ timore. In qua quatuor erãt oppida habitata & nunc duo extant.

·87·

CORAM ducatu athenarum ad trionem Euboia olim nunc egrippum
que contigua continenti quia pons in medio elongatur cum turri munitissima sub qua tam impetus aquarum habetur bis in die quod mirabile sagitta velocissima pmeatur cum profunditate nimia. In capite pontis egripos civitas ampliatur & fertilis in partibus reputatur istis: quam naupalus possidebat & pro vindicta
filij sui palamedis qui in castris grecorum proditione occisus est Vlixis astutia:
cepit omnem greciam circuire. & regias intrare grecorum principum: & ibi suasione coniuges eorum in adulterium cum quibuscumque poterant exortabat: & sic
ad vindictam filij arbitratus est. Qui multi principes in reversione ab amatoribus uxorum suarum occisi sunt. Ultra hoc nauplus in caphareum conscendit
montem & nocte accensa face greci de troia redeuntes ad evadendam tempestatem
ad ignem in portu salubrem credentes intrare in letiferos scopulos perierunt:
& sic vindictam cepit de morte filij palamedis. In hac etiam insula Orpheus
poeta vetustissimus claruit: qui dixit esse unum deum verum & magnum
qui cuncta gubernat. & quod ante ipsum nihil sit genitum & ab ipso sint cun-
ta generata. Gorgias etiam philosophus de hac fuit insula & magister Socratis
qui in matris feretro natus dum ferebatur ad sepulchrum subito vagitus infantis
auditus est & fuit primus inventor retorice & complevit centum annos
nec unquam a suo studio opere cessavit. Fuit etiam neptunus pater naupli huius
insule dominus: que longa de oriente ad occiduum . c . mil. & . ccc . in circuitu
Ad trionem caphareus habetur mons ubi aulis insula est: in qua ephigenia agamenonis filia erat sacrificanda numini diane propter cervi mortem: & contra troianos prosperos haberent ventos. Sed miseratione numinis ephigenia sublata cervam suppositam sacrificavit. Ad meridiem civitas est posita & a longobardis usque nunc habitata: qui diu huc venere & hodie a
turchis possidetur.

Nauplius
Palamedes
Orpheus
Gorgias magister
Socratis
Aulis insula
Ephigenia

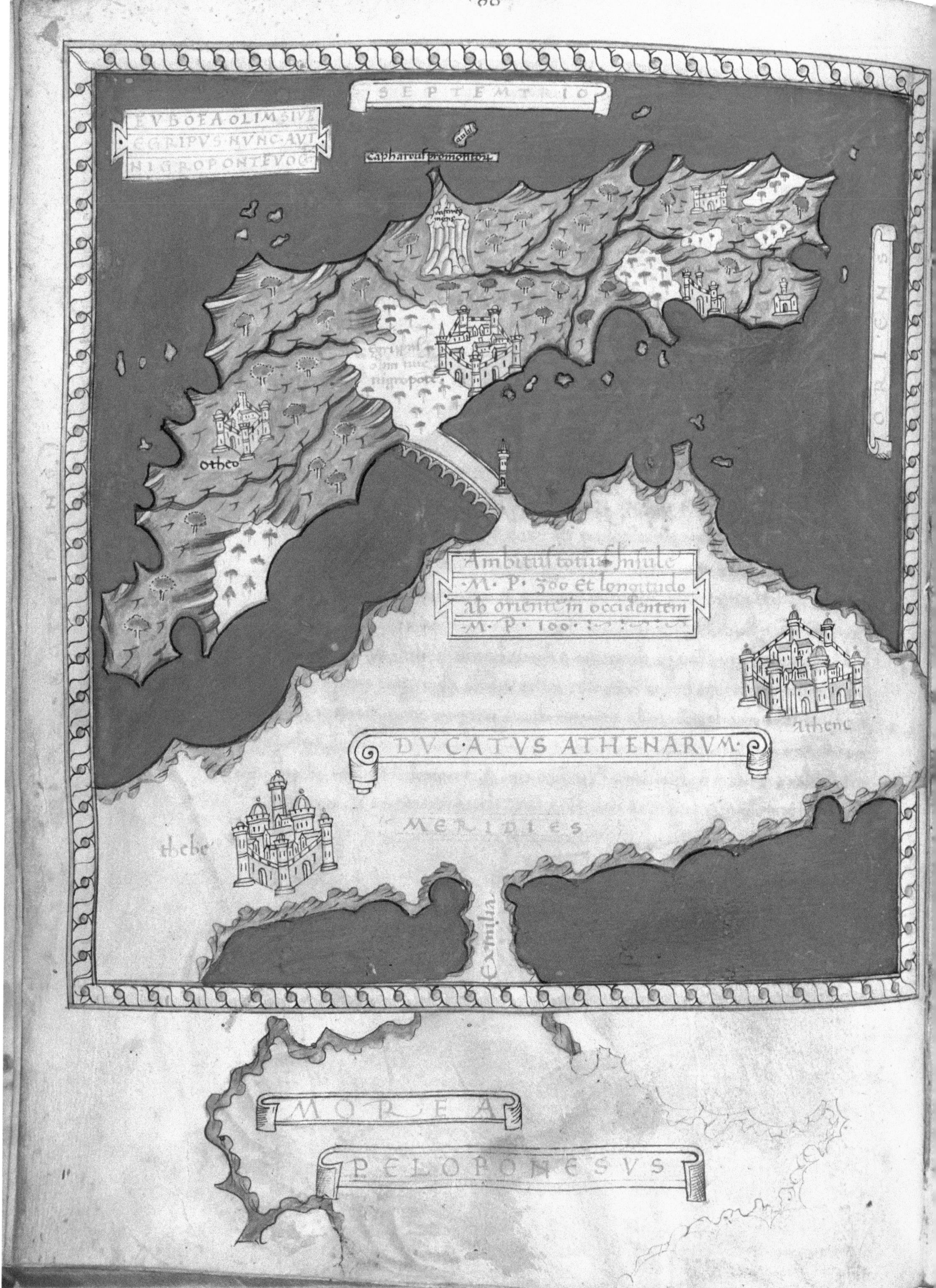
88
SEPTEMTRIO
EUBOEA OLIM SIVE
EGRIPUS NUNC AUT
NIGROPONTE VOC
Caphareus promontorium
ORIENS
otheo
Ambitus totius Insule
M· P· 300 et longitudo
ab oriente in occidentem
M· P· 100
DUCATUS ATHENARUM
athene
MERIDIES
thebe
Examilia
MOREA
PELOPONESUS

EGINA mox sequitur in conspectu athenarum parua quidē ac deserta insula: in cuius medio relliquie oppidi apparent cum parua adiacente planitie: cetera montem silue collesq; occupant: Vbi etiam caput sancti georgij adoratur.

·89·

EGINA · INSULA
VLTIMA · IN · OPA
HOSTRA · ET · ISLAD
INSVLARVM · SIVE
ARCIPELAGI · EST

Cyprus insula a Ciuitate cypro que in ea est nomen accepit, ipsa est & paphos ueneri consecrata in Carpathio mari Vicina austro famosa quondam diuitijs & maxime eris: ibi enim prima huius metalli inuentio & Vtilitas fuit. Luciflori. Aderat fatum insularum igitur & cipros recepta sine bello Insulam ueteribus diuitijs abundantem & obhoc Veneri sacram Ptholemeus regebat & diuitiarum tanta erat fama nec falso ut uictor gentium populus & donare regna cōsuetus Publio claudio tribuno duce socij uiuiq; regi confiscatione mandauerit & ille quidem ad rei famā Veneno fata precepit. Ceterum Portius cato Cyprias opes liburnis per tyberinum hostium inuexit que res latius erarium populi romani q̄ ullus triumphus impleuit. Tortellus. Cyprus insula est in Carpathio mari sita porrectaq; inter Ciliciam & Syriam inter alias orbis insulas famosissima Veterum diuitijs abundans luxui plurimum dedita ob quod Veneri sacram esse dicunt.

Isidorus

Luciflori

Tortellus

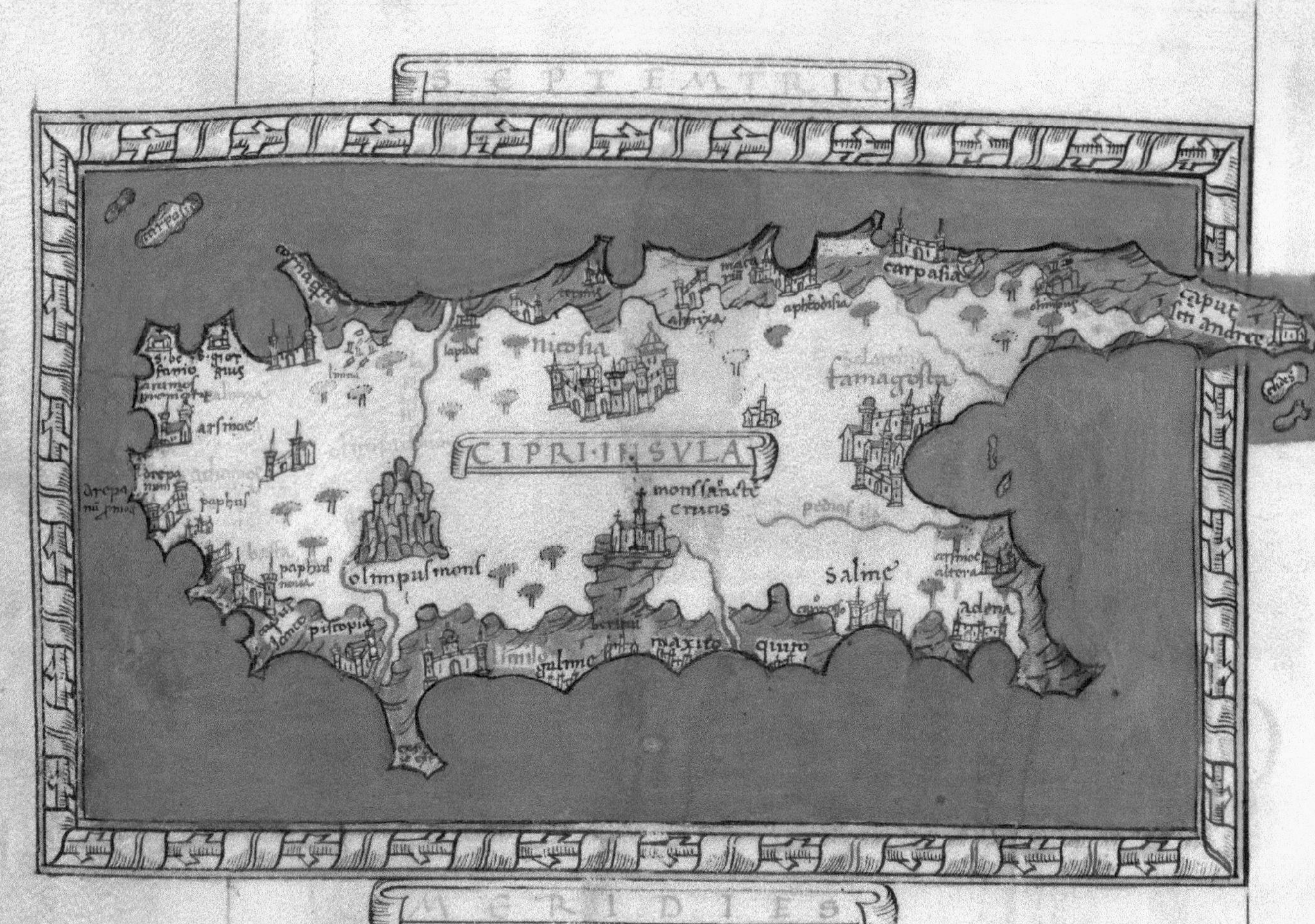

MERIDIES

IN ligustico mari est Corsica: quam greci cirnon appellauere sed tusco propior
a septẽtrione in meridiẽ proiecta longa·p·CL·m· lata maiore ex parte·L·ĩcir-
cuitu·CCC·m·XXV· abest a uadis uolaterranis·LXII·m·p· Ciuitates habet·XXXII·&
colonias marianam a mario deductã· Aleriam adictatore silla· Citra ẽ oglosa· Intra
uõ·LX·m·p·a corsica planaria a specie dicta equali freto· Ideoq; nauigijs fallax amplior urgo ac capraria quam greci aegilion dixere· Itẽ igilium & diannium: quam
artemisiam ambe contra cosanum litus & barpana menaria columbaria uenaria il-
ua cum ferri metallis· Circuitus·C·m·p· a populonio·X· a grecis etalia dicta ab
ea planasia·XXVIII· ab his ultra tiberina hostia in antiano scura mox palmaria

sinuessa aduersum formias pontia. In puteolano aūt sinu pandetoria pro
cida non ab enee nutrice: sed quia profusa ab enaria erat enarie a statione
nauium Enee homero inarime dicta grece pythicusa nō a simiarū multitu
dine ut aliqui existimauere sed a figulinis doliorum. Inter pausilipum & nea
polim megaris mox a surento VIII. m. distans. Tiberij principis arte nobiles ca
pree circuitu. XL. m. p. Leucothea extra quem cōspectum pelagus affricani attin
gens. Sardinia minus. VIII. m. p. a corsice extremis etiā eas artantibus īsulis
paruis que cuniculariae appellantur. Itemq; pintonis & fosse: a quibus fretum
ipsum taphros nominatur. Isidorus dicit. Corsice insule exordium nicole li
gures dederunt appellantes eam ex nomine ducis. Nam quedam Corsa nomine
ligus mulier: cum taurum ex grege quem prope litora regebat transnatare so
litum atq; p interuallum corpore aucto remeare uideret cupiens scire īcogni
ta sibi pabula: taurum ceteris digredientem usq; ad insulām nauigio persecu
ta est cuius ingressu insule fertilitatem cognoscentes ligures ratibus ibi pro
fecti sunt eamq; nomine mulieris auctoris & ducis appellauerunt. Hec aūt
insula grece Cyrne dicitur a cirno herculis filio habitata De qua Virgilius.
Cyrneas taxos Diuidit aūt a Sardinia. XX. miliū freto cincta ligustici equoris
sinu ad prospectum italie. Est aūt multis promontorijs angulosa gignens letis
sima pabula & lapidem quem cacociten greci uocant.

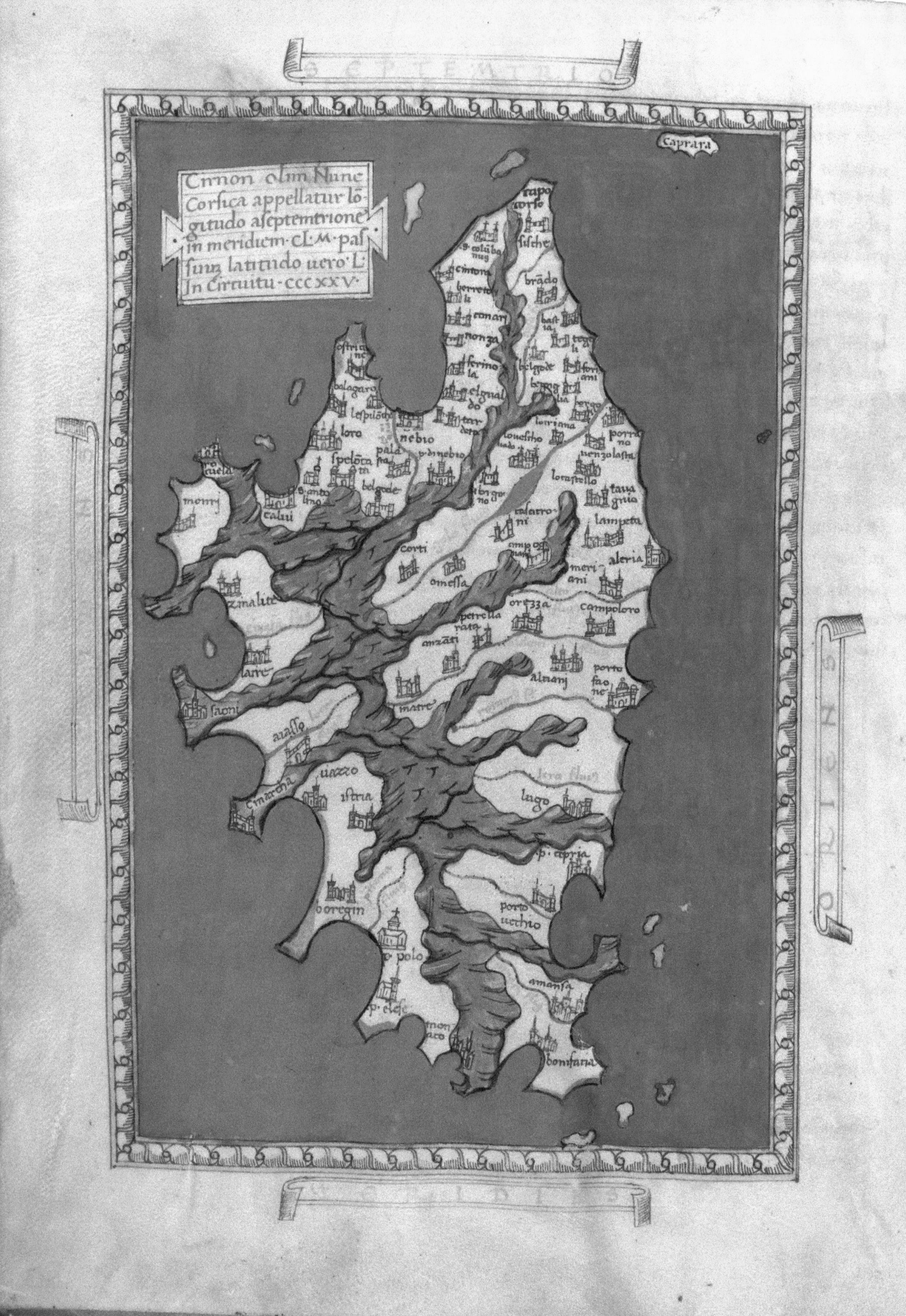

Cirnon olim Nunc
Corsica appellatur lõ
gitudo a septemtrione
in meridiem · CL · M · pas
suum latitudo uero · L ·
In Circuitu · CCCXXV ·
caprara
nebio
corti
omessa
aleria
campoloro
orezza
lampeta
lugo
bonifatia

SARDINIA ab oriente patens · CLXXXVIII · m · p · ab occidente · CL
XXV · a meridie · LXXVII · a septentrione · CXXII · circuitu · DLXV · abest
ab africa catalitaon promõtorio · CC · a gadibus · XIIIJ · Inde hab& a gorditano pro
montorio duas insulas que uocantur herculis: a sulcensi canosmiam a catalitano fi
cariam: quidam haud procul ab ea & bellitidas pontum & calode & quam uocant ba
raluta · Celeberrimi in ea populorum iliensses salari corsi oppidorum · XVIII · Sulritani
ualentini · neapolitani / nirenses / caleritani ciuium · Ro · & norenses · Colonia aũt una
que uocatur adturrim libisonis: sardiniam ipam Timeus sandaliotim appellauit ab
effigie soleę: mirsilus ichnusam a similitudine uestigij contra prestanũ sinum
leuchasia est a sirene ibi sepulta appellata: contra ueliam pontia & isatia utreq; r
uno nomine oenotrides in argumentum possesse ab oenotrijs italie contra uibonẽ
parue que uocantur ithaesie ulyxis specula · Isidorus ait · Sardis hercule procrea
tus cum magna multitudine a libia profectus Sardiniam occupauit & ex suo uoca
bulo insule nomen dedit · Hec in affrico mari facie uestigij humani in oriente q̃ in
occidente latior proeminet ferme paribus lateribus que ĩ meridiẽ & septẽtrionẽ uer
tunt · Ex quo ante comertium anauigantibus grecorum Ichnos appellata est · Terra
patet in longitudine milia CXL · In latitudine · XL · In ea neq; serpens gignit neq; lu
pus sed solifuga tantũ aĩal exiguum hominibus pnitiosum · Venenum quoq; ibi
non nascitur nisi herba p scriptores plurimos & poetas memorata a piastro similis
que hominibus rictus contrahit & quasi ridentes interimit · fontes habet Sardinia
calidos infirmis medelam prebentes / furibus cecitatem si sacramento dato oculos
aque eius tetigerint ·

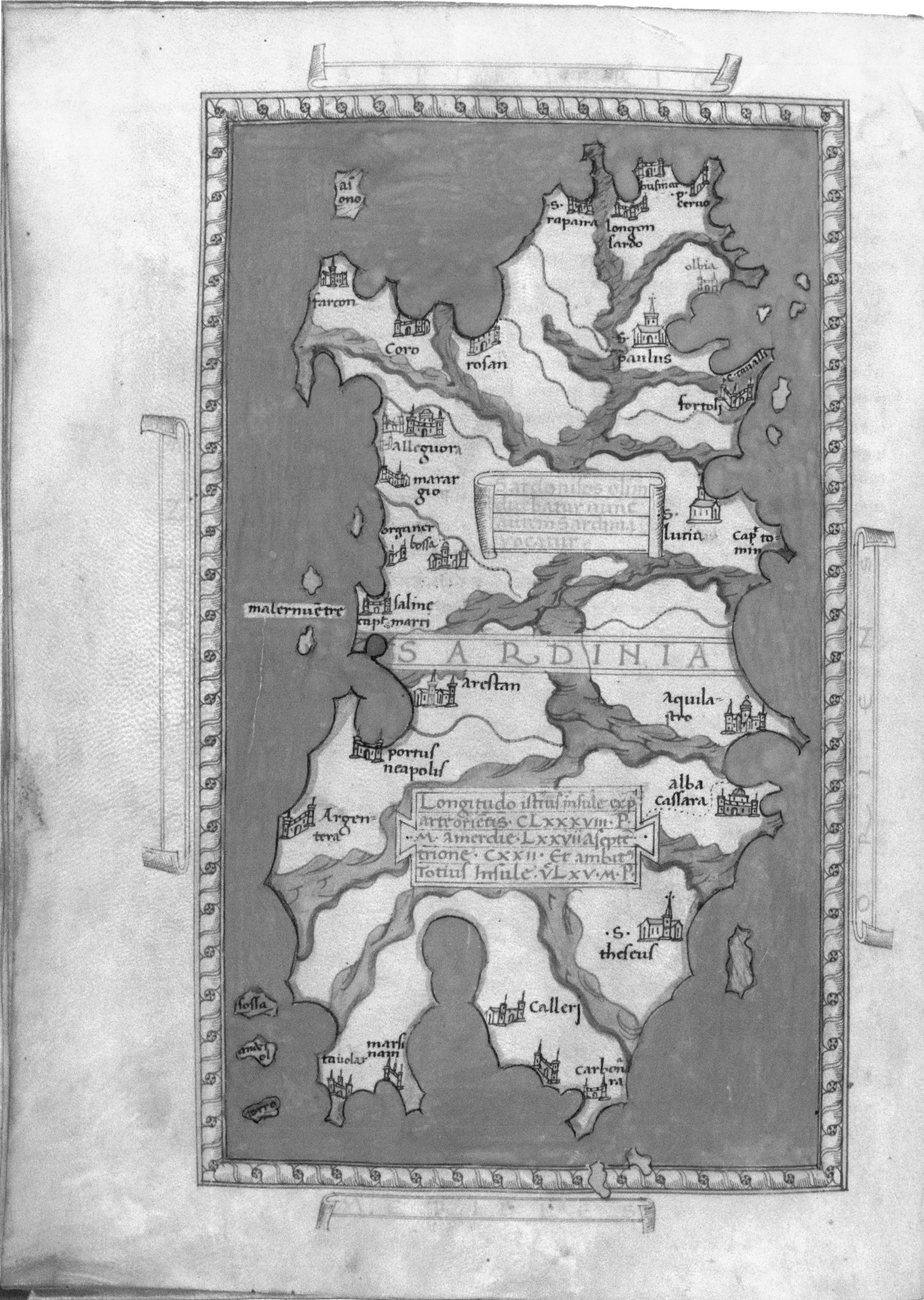
SARDINIA
Longitudo istius insule ex parte orientis CLXXXVIII. M. P.
A meridie LXXVII a septentrione CXXII. Et ambitus totius insule DLXV. M. P.
Sardonisos olim dicebatur nunc autem Sardinia vocatur
Coro
rosan
S. paulus
olbia
fortoli
longon sardo
S. rapaira
arestan
portus neapolis
alba cassara
S. theseus
Callers
carbonara
Argentera
Saline
malernuetre
fossa

SICILIAM ferunt angustijs quondam faucibus italie adhesisse direptamq; uelut a corpore maiore impetu superioris maris
quod toto undarum onere illuc uehitur. Est aut̄ ipsa terra tenuis ac
fragilis & cauernis quibusdam fistulisq; ita penetrabilis: ut uentorum
tota ferme flatibus pateat: necnon & ignibus generandis nutriendisq;
soli ipsius naturali ui. Quippe intrinsecus stratum sulphure & bitumine
traditur: que res facit: ut spiritu cum igne inter interiora luctante frequēter
& compluribus locis: nunc flamās: nunc uaporem, nunc fumum erupt&.
Inde denuq; Aethne mōtis per tot secula durat incendium & acrior p spiram-
ta cauernarum uentus incubuit harenarum moles egeruntur. Proximū italie
promōtorium regium dicitur. Ideo quia grece abruta hoc nomine pronuntiatur. Hec mirum si fabulosa est loci huius antiquitas: in quem res tot
coiere mire. Primum q nusq̄ alias torrens fretum nec solum citato impetu uerum etiam seuo: neq; experientibus modo terribile uerum etiā
procul uisentibus undarum porro in se concurrētium tāta pugna est ut
alias ueluti terga dantes uorticibus mergi ac in imum desidere alias
quasi uictrices in sublime ferri uideas. Hunc hic fremitum feruentis
estus: nūc illic gemitum in uoragine desidentis exaudias. Accedunt ui-
cini & perpetui aethne montis ignes & insularum eolidum uelut ipsis
undis alatur incēdium. Neq; enim in tam angustis terminis aliter durare tot seculis tantus ignis potuiss& nisi & humoris nutrimentis aleretur. Hinc igitur fabule Scyllam & carybdim peperere: hic latratus
auditos, hinc monstri credita simulacra: dum nauigantem magnis uorticibus pelagi desidentis exterriti latrare putant undas quas sorbētis
estus uorago collidit eadem causa etiam aethne montis perpetuos ignes
facit. Nam aquarum ille concursus. Raptum secum spiritum ī imum
fundum trahit atq; ibi suffocatum tamdiu ten& donec p spiramenta
terre diffusus nutrimēta ignis incēdantur. Iam ipsa italie Sicilieq; uicini-
tas iam promontoriorum altitudo ita similis est ut quantum nunc admirationis tantum antiquis terroris dederit credentibus coeuntibus in se
promontorijs ac rursum discedentibus solida intercipi absumiq; nauigia.

5

Neq; hoc ab antiquis in dulcedinem fabule compositum. Sed metu & admiratione transeuntium. Ea est enim procul inspicientibus natura loci ut sinum maris nõ transitum putes quo cum accesseris discedere ac seiungi promontoria que ante iuncta fuerant arbitrare. Sicilie primo trinacrie nomen fuit. Preterea Sicania denominata est. Hec a principio patria Cyclopum fuit. Quibus extinctis Aeolus regnum insule occupauit. Postquem singule ciuitates in tyrannorum impetum concesserunt quorum nulla terra feracior fuit. Isidorus. Sicilia a

Isidorus

Sicano rege Sicania cognominata est, deinde a Siculo Itali fratre. Sicilia pri° autẽ trinacria dicta propter tria acra idest promontoria. Pelorum. Pachinum & Lilybeum. Trinacria enim grecum est quod latine triquadra dicitur quasi in tres quadras diuisa.

112
strogoli
luppari
Saline
wulcanus
regio
silla
messena
melazo
ulisera
mons gibel
patti
tauermena
Caroma
petra de roma
Catanea
Cifalu
Castellum bonum
tosa
termini
colata uoltore
Calasuenetta
Siracusa
Castoiani
chieza
Calata gerone
castellu ueteranu
potentia
Caput passeri
rassacata
terra noua
butera
talicata
Sacca
Cotriga
marsera
Pantalanea

BRitania occeani insula interfuso mari toto orbe diuisa a uocabulo
sue gentis cognominata. hec aduersa galliarum parte ad prospectum
hispanie sita est. Circuitus eius quadragies octies. LXXV. milia. Multa & magna in ea flumina: fontes calidi metallorum larga & uaria copia gagates
lapis ibi plurimus & margarite. Pomponi mella. Britania qualis sit qua-
lesq; progeneret: mox certiora & magis explorata dicentur. Quippe tã diu
clausam aperit ecce principum maximus nec indomitarum modo ante se
uerum ignotarum quoq; gentium uictor propriarum rerum fidem ut
bello affectauit ita triumpho declaraturus portat. Ceterum ut adhuc habuimus: inter septentrionem occidentemq; proiecta grandi angulo rheni hostia
prospicit: deinde obliqua retro latera abstrahit. Altero galliam altero germaniam spectans tamen rursus perpetuo margine directi litoris ab tergore
abducta. Iterum se in diuersos angulos cuneat triquetra & Sicilie maxime
similis. Plana ingens fecunda. Verum ijs que pecora quam homines benignius alant. fert nemora saltus ac pregrandia flumina alternis mõtib;
modo in pelagus modo retro fluentia. & quedam gẽmas margaritasq; generantia. fert populos regesq; populorum sed sunt inculti omnes atq; ut lõgius
a continenti absunt: ita aliarum opum ignari magis tantum pecore ac finibus dites: in corpum ob decorem an quid aliud ultra corpora infecti. Causas
aũt & bella contrahunt ac si frequenter inuicem infestant maxime imperitandi cupidine studioq; ea prolatandi que possident. Dimicant non equitatu modo aut pedite: Verum & bigis & curribus gallice armati couinos
uocant: quorum falcatis axibus utuntur.

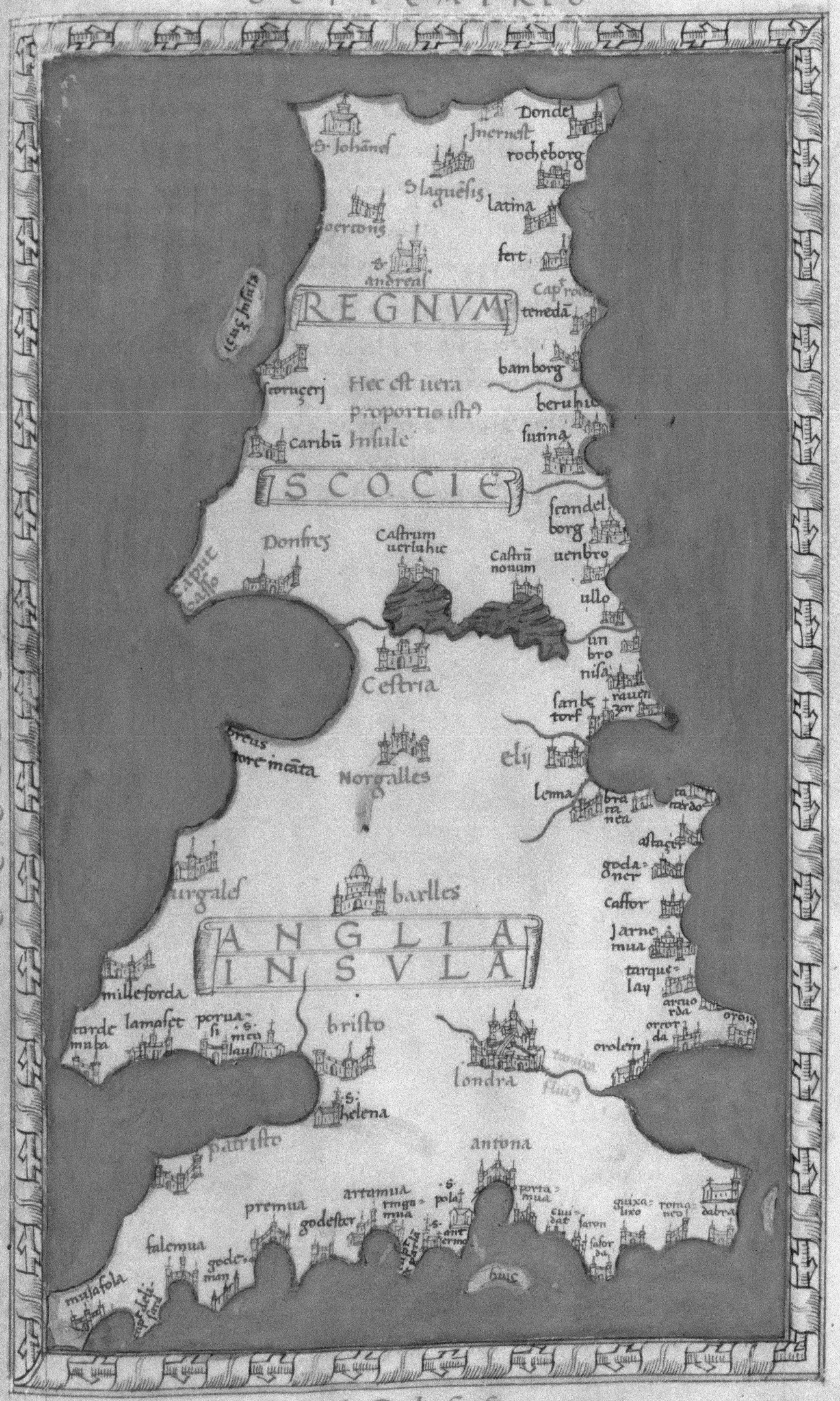
SEPTEMTRIO
Donde
Jnernest
S. Johānes
rocheborg
Slaguesis
latina
fert
S. andreas
REGNUM
temedā
bamborg
Hec est uera
proportio istius
Insule
caribū
SCOCIE
Donfres
Castrum uerluhic
Castrū nouum
uenbro
ullo
Cestria
Norgalles
eliī
lema
castor
barlles
ANGLIA
INSULA
milleforda
bristo
londra
S. helena
patristo
antona
premua
artamua
godester
falemua
OCCIDENS
ORIENS

MERIDIES

Super britaniam hiuernia est pene par spatio sed utrinq; equalis tractu litorum oblonga celi ad maturanda semina iniqui: uerum adeo luxuriosa herbis non letis modo sed etiam dulcibus: ut se exigua parte diei pecora impleant & nisi pabulo prohibeantur diutius pasta dissiliant. Cultores eius inconditi sunt & omnium uirtutum ignari quam alie gentes aliquatenus tamen gnari pietatis admodum expertes.

Scotia eadem & hiuernia proxima britanie insula spatio terrarum angustior sed situ fecundior. Hec ab affrico in boream porrigitur cuius partes priores hiberiam & cantabricum occeanum intendunt Unde & hiuernia dicta. Scotia autem quod ab scotorum gentibus colitur est appellata. Illic nullus anguis: auis rara: apis nulla adeo ut aduectos inde pulueres seu lapillos siquis alibi sparserit inter aluearia examina fauos deserant.

Cristoforo Buondelmonti

Description of the Archipelago and the Cyclades and Other Islands

Latin Transcription

//1r[1]// Christofori Ensenii Florentini Sacerdotis dignissimi Descriptio Arcipelagi et Cicladum aliarumque insularum foeliciter incipit.

Cicladum caeterarumque insularum hinc inde sparsarum enarrationis et picturae libellum aggressus non antiquos scriptores tantum imitatus quaeque ab his describuntur verum est quae hodie in illis sunt antiquae novaeque formae nec non civitates, castra, fontes, nemora, flumina, maria, montes, promontoria, portus atque loci naturam succinte breviterque recensere ac depingere constitui. Quo etiam veriora memorentur non qua auribus percepi sed quae ipse ego in sex annis propriis luminibus post multa discrimina rerum & vidi & tetigi describentur quae nonmodo legentibus gratissima erunt verum etiam navigantibus utillima si didicerint quae petenda quae ve sint e fugienda quae singula quam maxima brevitate percurram et insularum numerum ac nomina explicabo ut facile legentibus iter pateat.[2] Ergo meum inceptum a Corfu dirigatur quae hodie a multis prima grecie versus occiduum est appellata. Deinde Pachisos, Leucata, Ithaca,[3] Chefalonum, Iacinthus, Strophades, Sapientia, Chitarea, Sequilus, Creta, Carpathos, Rodos, Simie, Charistos, Delos, Caria, Astimphalea, Egasa, Sicandros, Policandros, Milo, Siphanos, Serfinos, Termie, Cea, Andros, Caloieros, Tino, Michone, Delos,[4]

//1v// Suda, Paros, Antiparos, Panaia, Nasos, Podia, Raclea, Chero, Nio, Anaphios, Amurgo,[5] Chinera, Levata, Caloieros, Choa, Calamos,[6] Herro, Patmos, Dipsi, Crusie, Icarea, Mandria/Agatusa/Formachui, Samo, Furni, Tenosa, Psara, Chios, Lesbos, Tenedos, Galipolis, Marmora, Calanonimo, Scopuli Caloierorum, Constantinopolis,[7] Stiliminii, Embaros, Mandrachi,[8] Taxo, Mons Sanctus, Santrati, Limen, Dromos, Macri, Schiati & Scopuli, Sanctus Elias, Schiros, Egrippos, Egina, Ciprus, Sicilia, Cursica & Sardinia, Albion sive anglia, Gottia, Norvegia, Suetia, Hiberniaque.

Restat nunc[9] generales monstrare[10] particularitates & provincias circum circa positas cum marium[11] amplitudine[12] & qui in hodiernum dominantur in illis. Dicitur ergo

1. First page has beautiful capital C, floral border down left edge, and two cherubs holding a blank shield at the bottom.
2. S and Dd have different opening paragraphs.
3. Dd + S: Dulichia
4. S: Dilufanos; Dd: Dily
5. S: Buport; Dd: Brupot
6. Dd + S: Claros
7. Dd + S: Polis
8. Dd: Samotrachi
9. Dd: pater. A reference to Cardinal Orsini.
10. S: demonstrare
11. Dd: marine
12. S: plenitudine

Archipelagum mare quasi dominus maris. A Rhodo igitur per lineam rectam usque malium promontorium nunc caput sancti angeli[1] miliaria CCCCL. & a Creta usque Tenedon CV[2] in quibus totum mare concluditur arcipe-

//2r// lagi. Huic Asia Minor adheret in qua ciliciae, pamphiliae, phrygiae, betuliaeque provinciae ampliantur. Sed postquam Turchi[3] eam diu possedere ab eis[4] Turchia nomen accepit. Qui ruentes per civitates sive[5] moeniis, populi sub eis pacifice gubernantur. Ad occiduum postquam mare transitur Hellespontum, Grecia statim plana ampliatur & in omnibus usque ad Andrinopolim fertilissima nimis & a leva tendens versus Tessalonicam provinciam populata satis reperitur ubi civitates locaque delinquimus & ad montes devenimus altos cito ad Euboiam Athenarumque[6] loca pergitur ultro[7] quarum pars maxima turris[8] possidetur. Egeum vero mare volunt antiqui ab egeo rege & patre Thesei dictum. Quod ab Hellesponto incipit & multos abluens sinus usque malleum distenditur promontorium. Chidos[9] enim Grecae Latinae circulus eo quae omnes insulae rotundae[10] inter istos archipelagi scopulos ex cicladibus vocabantur. Peractis igitur generalibus divisionibus huiusmodi descriptionis ad particularitates dictarum insularum revertemur.[11] Ea propter ut cuncta comprehendantur[12] in nigro montes, in albo planities, in viride aquae pandentur[13] manifeste.

Insula haec quae prius ostenditur Cercira vel Corcira a rege olim dicta est quae Corfu nominatur & C mil. circuit. Versus autem meridiem montuosa per totum remanet, quibus montibus arbores valanidarum fructificantur. In Amphipoli vero promontorio oppidum sancti angeli munitissimum erigitur quod a longe nautae prospectant. Ab oriente usque Corfu & ultra ex parte trionis planities amena

//2v// & multis[14] habitata gentibus[15] ampliatur: & in ea olim Cercira urbs deleta cernitur torniamentis[16] columpnisque ampliata. Phalarius mons altissimus ab ea videtur: qui Dodonam silvam in terra conspicit firma. In qua ait Ovidius templum fuisse Dodoneum

1. Dd + S omit: nunc caput sancti angeli
2. 500; Dd + S: D.
3. Dd: Theucri; S: Turci
4. S: iis
5. Dd + S: sine
6. Dd: Thenarum
7. S: ultra
8. Dd Turchis; S: a Turis
9. Dd + S: Cyclos
10. Dd: omits insulae rotundae
11. Dd + S: reference to acrostic, omitted by HMG: "in quibus, dum rubeas ennumerabis ipsarum litteras, nomen mei que tui, et quo in loco, tempore perfeceram opus, manifestabis."
12. Dd + S: comprehendas
13. S: panduntur
14. Dd + S: multarum
15. Dd + S: gentium
16. S: tormentisque

maximum Iovi sacrum: in quo duas de celo columbas descendere solitas & veteribus insidere quercubus: & ex eis postulantibus responsa dare. Tandem ex eis ut aiunt altera transvolavit in Delphos Boetiae civitatem & ibi Appollinis Delphici clarum fecit oraculum. Altera ad amonis Iovis templum in Africa transmigravit. In radicibus autem montis huius scopulus est quem ad similitudinem Ulixis navis[1] fuisse dixere vetusti. Prope vero Leucumam[2] promontorium Cassiopis moenibus erectis etiam a pyrratis olim desolata videtur. Cuius in radicibus planities una cum infecta palude probatur. A latere vero horum moeniorum ecclesia matris domini ab hominibus visitatur multis qui exauditi repatriantur ylares[3].

Ad trionem vero Epirus a rege dicto[4] altissimis incipit montibus in quibus Heleni propinqua patre[5] troiaque a butroto[6] panditur ultro. Virgilius.

Littoraque Epiri legimus portumque[7] subimus.

Caonio & celsam Butroti ascendimus arcem.[8]

Per hanc igitur insulam Titus quintus flamminius ut securus[9] pergeret ad Romanum exercitum bellum cum Philippo Macedoniae rege facturus[10] transitum fecit.

//3r// [Map: East. *Occupies whole page.* Corfu,★[11] Saline, Amphipolis promontorium,★ Mons Amphipolis,★ St. Angelus★ *(city)*, Corcira olim,★ Corfu,★ Falarius mons,★ S. Maria Casiopi,★ Cassiopis. *Island*★: Scopulus Ulixi. *On mainland:* Fanari, Montes magni, S. Basilis, Saline, Provincia Epiri,★ Turris Scuate, Dodona Silva magna valde,★ Butroti vel Butrento,★ Templum Cassi Iovis, Montes magni.]

//3v// Supra Corciram ad orientem Pachiso est insula x milia in qua sine moeniis nulla[12] est paucorum possessa hominum propter turchorum insidias: media ergo ad orientem plana remanet vineis domesticisque arboribus fecunda & portus tutus in ea includitur[13] quae ut aiunt una cum Corchira olim tenebatur insula. Sed propter crebras tempestates Neptuni atque Eoli terra tenax quae inter duarum insularum medio est inventa mare efficitur & Corchira ab illa parte die ac nocte minuitur.

1. S: navem
2. Dd + S: Leucinnam
3. Dd: hylares
4. Dd + S: dictus
5. S: matre; Dd: mare
6. S: nunc
7. S: portuque
8. S: urbem
9. Dd + S: securius
10. Dd + S: facturum
11. Stars (★) indicate places mentioned in the text.
12. Dd + S: villa
13. Dd + S: concluditur

.2. Pachiso olim et nunc. Ambitus totius insulae m. p. 10. [Map: North. *Houses, trees, no toponyms.*]

Transiens nostra ratis ad orientem per centum milaria antiquum olim Leucon montem subimus & iam diu inter ipsum adiacentes colles mare deveniens propter fluxum refluxumque quater in die LXXX milaria insula est effecta. Que inter[1] umbrosas valles fontium irrigua efficitur nimis: quo in medio campus rurium circumdatus est. & cum armentorum multitudine videtur ad orientem vero portus concluditur. & si ad trionem prosequeris alterum tutiorem reperimus qui a montibus silvisque ac fontibus est ornatus. Cumque non diu procedens[2] fons in littore fluentissimus reperitur quo in loco viatores circumstantesque refrigerantur. A leva vero in radicibus montium civitatem vetustissimam deletamque olim videmus: in qua templum Apollinis erat vetustum & in eo loco Eneas discedens a troia arma dimisit Abantis.[3] Virgilius. Mox & Leucate nimbosa[4] cacumina montis & formidatus nautis reperitur[5] Appollo. Huc[6] petimus fessi [et] parvae succedimus urbi.[7] Deinde peractis seculis hanc Octavianus Caesar restauravit deletam civitatem quae Nicopolis appellabatur. Ibique templum Appollinis edificavit postquam Antonium in hunc locum & Cleopatram devicerat. Virgilius "Hic Augustus agens Italos in proelia Caesar." In conspectu vero huius in mari turris est. A qua non longe opidum cum ponte denotatur. Ubi aer in estate infectus spirat. Quibus in locis ampla pandebatur planities. Si autem ad trionem accedens[8] silvam & Ambrachium sinum offendes,[9] ad orientem denique in fide[10] incultae propalantur in quibus olim habitavere patres: nunc tandem propter insidias pyrratarum ad desolationem devenere.[11]

//4r// Leuchate olim, nunc S. Maura. Ambitus totius insulae m. p. 80. [Map: East. Nicopolis,* Fons nobilissima, planities fertilissima, S. Maura opidum,* Leucata,* Panaia. *On mainland:* Ambracius sinus,* Silva magna, S. Nicolaus.]

Ostendimus Leucatam nunc ad Dulichias[12] transimus quae olim Itacha & nunc Valdecompare nominatur altis rupibus circumsepta quae montuosa & inutilis nisi in medio exiguus planus aliquibus arboribus casisque habetur & circumcirca portuosa satis. De oriente ad occiduum XXX & in latitudine III[13] milaria ampliatur, cuius quidem duo extrema

1. Dd: intus
2. S: procedes
3. Dd omits: Abantis
4. Dd: umbrosa
5. Should be aperitur
6. S: hunc
7. Dd omits: Huc...urbi
8. S: accedes
9. Dd: ostendes; S like MN
10. Dd + S: insulae
11. Dd: deveniens
12. Dd + S: Dulichiam
13. Dd: XXV

in duobus aperiuntur cornibus a nautis in nocte periculosis. Fuit enim hinc ut asseruit ille eloquentissimus grecorum Ulyxes qui quasi ad omnia modum inveniebat Penelopem Itaci filiam sumpsit in coniugem & ex ea Telemacum[1] suscepit filium.[2] Tandem rapta Elena a Paride ire ad Troiam conatus[3] est. & se insanum simulavit & veniente Palamede ad Itacam animalia diversi generis iugo coniunxit[4] ad aratrum & salem[5] seminare compertus est. Verum Palamedes astutiam viri suspicatus capto parvulo Telemaco ad explorandam ingenii sui fraudem cum aratro opposuit. Ulixes autem[6] viso filio confestim demovit aratrum: & sic cognitus in expeditionem ire coactus est. Capta

//4v// denique Troia in contione eloquentia sua arma achillis contra aiacem vicit. Postquam igitur a troia recessit & coactus[7] visitare patriam multis quippe agitatus procellis in longissimos errores ac peregrinationes decennio[8] eiectus[9] est. Tandem multa in itinere passus ad hanc devenit insulam. & facto in domo sua cum procis[10] penelopes prelio non[11] multo post tempore vitam finivit.

Effugimus scopulos itace laertia regna.

Et terram altricem sevi execramus ulixis.

.4. ITHACA OLIM NUNC VALDICOMPARE. Habet in longitudine m. p. 30, in latitudo m. p. 3. [Map: North. Valdicompare, Mons Neritos.]

Finis de Itaca, de chrephalonia[12] incipiamus quae olim cephalonum[13] dicta & in montibus tota. Chephalim grece, caput latine quia apparet nautis ab austris venientibus rotunda vel hominis caput vel quia a tempore troianorum usque hodie caput dominii insularum istarum hec fuit & titulus ducatus huius ab ea incohatur. Legi enim in antiquis cronicis Ulyxem ducem fuisse regionis huius & a cephalonia titulum inceptabat[14] quae rotunda & in montibus aspera centum circuit milliaria cuius in medio elatus mons erigitur. Hodie leo sine flumine scaturiginibus aquarum dicitur. In quo multitudo fagorum pinorumque per circuitum insurgunt & quod plus est silvestra non pauca errantia[15] sine potu nusquam

1. S omits: Telemacum
2. S: Filiam
3. S: coactus
4. S: iunxit
5. S: sal
6. Dd: vera
7. Dd + S: conatus
8. S: decennes
9. Dd + S: evectus
10. Dd + S: procatoribus
11. Dd: deinde
12. S: Cephalonia; Dd + S: ducati
13. Dd: cefalonum
14. Dd: interpretabatur
15. Dd: errantes

aqua[1] invenientia ore aperto auram[2] e motibus[3] recipiunt in potum estate illa. Serpentes & enim ibi aspides inveniuntur. Qui calorem sentientes hu-

//5r//manum sine lesione cum eo[4] dormiunt. Ad orientem vero in littore francisci ecclesiam adoramus & ab eo edicificatam quae in orto[5] omnia dulcia producebat. Fuit etiam insula haec quasi ultima quam tempore belli macedonici romani ceperunt in deditionem. Ad occiduum ergo viscardus portus a Roberto viscardo domino apuliae dicto[6] apparet. In qua olim pitilia ubi chilon lacedemonicus philosophus aliquibus annis stetit ut ait epiphanus[7] cipricus & tante extitit[8] auctoritatis[9] tanta vis est ut scribit Cicero quod[10] nulli hominum tribuatur.[11] Cum enim dicit nosce te animam tuam intelligit nec intellexit de membris aut statura quod est facile. Sed intellexit ut cognitos defectus animi reformarerемus & quod actibus nostris nosmet ipsos metiamur nec inertia sinamus corrumpi nobilitatem nostram. Aut opinione tumefacti audacia ridicula corrumpamus.[12] Belisarius denique nepos iustiniani augusti classe sua huc venit & eam a procellis reparavit. Qui audiens italiam a Gotis[13] subiugatam pietate motus sua classe in affricam devenit & Ghotos ab ea trinachriaque expulit. Deinde pervento neapolim quia patefacte porte non fuerunt per annum in obsidione stetit. Qua capta viros mulieres et infantulos & quos in ea repperit igni ferroque defixit.[14] Deinde versus Romam deviens Ghoti fugam arripuere. Contra vero itacam samus[15] est & ad meridiem portus sancti ysideri manifestatur.

Iam medio apparet fluctu nemorosa iacinthus
Dulichiam Samos et Neritos ardua saxis.[16]

//5v// .5. CEFALONIA. Ambitus totius insulae m. p. centum. [Map: North. Cefalonia★ *(above)*. Viscardus portus★ *(NE)*, Pitilia★ (olim), Pilarirus *(on plain)*, Mons,★ S. Giorgi, Elatis

1. Dd + S: aquam
2. Dd: aeram
3. Dd + S: montibus
4. Dd omits: cum eo
5. Dd: mortuo
6. S: dictus
7. S: epiphanius
8. S: exstitit
9. Dd + S add: quae industriae, quod in templo Apolonis litteris aureis haec scribi fecit scilicet: nosce te ipsum! cuius precepti
10. S: quae
11. S: tribuetur
12. Dd: corrumpamur
13. Dd: manifeste; S: iniuste
14. Dd: destruxit
15. The city of Same, or Sami on a bay on the northern side of the island.
16. Virgil, *Aeneid* III.270. Dd + S: omit.

Mons,★ S. Nicolas, S. Franciscus,★ Samo portus★ *(north in bay)*, Portus S. Sideri,★ S. Siderus *(church)*. Trapano: *small island to the south.*]

Ostendimus de chephalonia: nunc de iacintho dicemus. Fuit ergo Iacinthus a quoddam domino vel a flore dicta quia florida & amena dicitur & quia contra corinthiacum sinum sita est. Ex qua in hispaniam ivisse[1] dicitur: qui sangunthum oppidum nobile romanorum amicissimum condiderunt, quod ab hanibale expugnatum deletumque fuit: haec etiam Ierusalem ollim nominata est: quae cum robertus viscardus dux apuliae sepulchrum visitare dispositus. & in somnis revelatum est ipsum ierosolime moriturum. Ille autem[2] chefaloniae deveniens ut dictum est ad hanc applicuit insulam & egrotus in loco ut audivit nomen insulae Ierusalem[3] nuncupari, paucis expiravit diebus. Ad trionem vero[4] planam pascuis ruribusque[5] opulenta apparet. Ad orientem vero portus Nacte[6] dictus. Quo coram in campo lacus picis liquide restat. In quos bos punctus a musca cecidit & statim suffocatus est. Iuxta[7] & enim hunc navis onerata malvagie[8]

//6r//[9] caliginose ventis prosperis cum harena[10] velis tumidis ignari navigationis sine lesione irruit & sic immobilis effecta est. Veronica etiam audiens nomen eius insulae Ierusalem ob devotionem in eam ascendit & ibi ut dicitur sudarium Christi demonstrans & mortem salvatoris dum predicaret ad fidem devote sunt reversi. Ad orientem in ripa ut aiunt vena metallorum reperitur[11] & per totam meridiei plagam inter umbrosas arbores in montibus elevatur: ubi ad occiduum venimus. Pilosus & Sancti Nicolai portus includuntur optimi & salinarum planus prope aperitur.

Ad trionem denique prope medium civitas insurgit quae a terremotis saepe deleta est: ibique ducissa mecum[12] in progenie sepulta iacet. Ambit igitur[13] LX milliaria aere bono atque placabili dilectione omnium habitatium. Virgil. Iam medio apparet fluctu nemorosa iacinthus.

1. Dd: misse
2. Dd: ante
3. Dd: Hyerosolime; S: Hierosalem
4. Dd + S: ergo
5. Dd: roribus
6. Dd: Naet
7. Dd iusta
8. Dd: marvaxie; S: malvasine
9. Dd +S: in nocte
10. Dd + S: in eadem arena
11. Dd: aperitur
12. Dd: ducissa meus
13. S: in super

.6. IANCINTHUS. Ambitus m. p. 60. [Map: North. Portus Nicolai, S Nicolaus *(church in SW)*, S. Nicolaus★ *(north)*, Iacinthus,★ S. Basilius, Lacus pice,★ Nacte portus,★ Jerusalem,★ Pilosus portus★ *(SW)*. *10 names on map, 6 of these in text.*]

Restat nunc[1] in hoc ionio mari ad austrum[2] scopulos[3] demonstrare sanctissimos qui olim obsecratissimi habebantur Plotae dicti unius milliari in circuitu deinde achinnades[4] ab echinnis piscibus in acheloo flumine propinquo. Postea strophades a strophe grece reversio latine interpretatur. In ea igitur fraternitas caloierorum resedit quae cum piscibus & aqua asperam trahit vitam & quia semel a barbiris[5] captivi omnes vediti fuerunt. Moderni colentes ut securam viam dei contemplare possent turrim edificavere in qua vere vitam

//6v// gerunt heremiticam & ex omni progenie plusquam La [quinquaginta] ibi coadunati recreantur. Haec igitur cum parva propinqua tempore phinei regis archadie & a pyrratis habitate fuere. Certum est qui scientes ipsum[6] phineum filios suasu Arpalice eorum noverce cecasse & in huius sceleris ultionem usque in archadiam phineum obsederunt & ad miseriam reduxerunt. Quos Zetus & Chalais arpalices fratres fugaverunt ipsumque phineum a pyrratis liberavere & pyrratas usque ad istas pepulere insulas. Ergo ipsi iuvenes dixerunt Strophades hoc est reversionem inmutavere insulis. Tempore igitur Enee qui a Troia profugus petens italiam cum huc applicuisset suisque comitibus epulantibus, arpie de archadia pulse has insulas colentes pabula aut rapiebant unguibus aut tactu fedissimo polluebant & ab eo ferro expulsi Celeno harum maxima dixit.[7] Ibitus italiam portusque intrare licebit. Sed non ante datam cingetis menibus urbem. Quam vos dira fames vestreque[8] iniuria cedis Ambesas subigat malis absummere mensas.[9] Ergo dicte sunt arpie a voracitate quia ibi pyrraticum congeries & omnes applicantes fedabant avaritia & rapina. Servatum ex undis strophadum me littora primum. Excipiunt strophades graio sic nomine dicte insulae ionio in magno quas dira celeno Arpieque colunt alie phineia postquam clausa domus mensasque metu liquere priores. Tristis haud illis monstrum nec senior[10] ulla. Pestis & ira deum stigiis sese extulit undis. Virginei volucrum vultus fedissima ventris. Proluvies unceque manus & pallida semper ora fame. Nunc autem de malo in bonum hae insulae sunt reverse quod quanto magis olim procul navigantes sistebant: tanto melius nunc affectuose devotis precibus eis adherere festinant in quibus turris cum ecclesia est: & caloieri horis canonicis in ea conveniunt ubi gummus[11] vel prior vitam

1. Dd + S retains: iordane pater. Blank in this MS
2. Dd: haustrum
3. blank, Dd: tibi
4. Dd: Echinade; S: Echinnadae
5. Dd + S: barbaris
6. Dd: dictum
7. Dd: ut in virgilio vatem. *Aeneid* III.209-218.
8. S + Virgil: nostraeque
9. *Aeneid* III.254 ff.
10. Dd: sevior; S: saevior
11. Dd: gumicus: *higoumene*; S: Guminus

sanctorum patrum coram omnibus legendo declarat. Igitur quid sit vita istorum iudica pater: quia certissime asperrima reputatur cum spatium unius habeant miliarii & a terra octingentorum stadiorum elongati. Ibi carnes neglecti sunt & cum piscibus saepe a sole combustis: paneque arido & aqua vitam substentare congaudent ut altissimo immaculatam quilibet suam reddere possit animam.[1]

.7. STROPHADES INSULAE. Ambitus totius insulae m. p. 3. [Map: North. *Shows two islands,* Monasterium Caloierorum,★ *large church on larger island.*]

//7r// Venio inde ad Sapientiam coram modonense civitate: quae parva & infructuosa apparet & dicta est Sapientia, ut navis transeundo sapienter a scopulis ibi occultis se custodiat vel quia ibi mulier greca eum habitaret, futura incantationibus transeuntibus resolvebat. Cuius in medio mons erigitur in quo modonenses a longe velum vigilant & circumstantibus innotescat. Ad orientem vero alique apparent insulae incultae & ab egis habitate: quarum minor tempore amoracti[2] magni turchorum, una biremi [biremis] infidelium in tempestate noctis hic licuit[3] qui subito ecclesiam invasit. Cumque circumsisterent[4] & caloierum psallentem audirent, porta ecclesiae usque[5] inventa est & sic usque mane ibi remanserunt. Luce[6] autem facta insidias christianorum timentes, donec caloiero sua damna restitueret, a litore recedere non valuerunt. Coram ergo insulis dictis due eriguntur civitates modonis prima liquoris bachi abundantissima coronis secunda a liquidem dee palladis coronata: que ambe in provincia moree consistunt. & olim peloponesus dicta a pelope filio tantali ut[7] barlaam homo bellorum & insignis plurimum qui cum apud frigias[8] regnaret bellum habuit adversum Oenomium regem elidis atque pise unde bellum ingens cognovit[9] atque Ipodamia potitus est. Tandem cum apud argos regnasset a suo nomine peloponneses denominavit.

.8. Sapientia .9. Capra .10. S. Venetus. Continens peloponesi. [Map of Peloponnesian coast. *East:* Oliveti per totum, Vineta per totum, Arancia per totum, Modona,★ Corona,★ Caput Galli. *Small islands:* Capra★ and Sapientia,★ *island* S. Venetus *with church. City of Corona on peninsula.*]

//7v// Superfluum enarrare mihi videtur quot istis in partibus apparent scopuli; quia extremum[10] nullum invenimus in eis nominare factum. Ideo de eis taceamus & ad chituriam vel cythaream insulam accedamus quae citri hodie nominatur. Ubi prima

1. Dd: reddere vitam
2. Dd: Amorati; S: Amurati
3. S: applicuit
4. Dd + S: circum consisterent
5. Dd and S: nusquam
6. Dd + S: Lux
7. Dd: ait; S: ut ait
8. Dd: stigias; S: Phrygias
9. Dd + S: commovit
10. Dd + S: strenuum

insularum ampelagi[1] ad occiduum computatur. Quae quasi per totum in montibus insurgit in quibus oppidum citheron aperte videtur. Ubi Venus honorifice celebrata est ex quo & Venus & insula sumpsit nomen. Sculpebatur[2] "enim puella pulcherrima nuda et in mari natans tenens concham marinam in dextera, ornata rosis &[3] columbis circumvolantibus comitata. Vulcano deo ignis rustico turpissimo in coniugium assumpta.[4] Ante eam[5] tres stabant nude[6] iuvencule. Que tres gratie vocabantur quarum due facies ad ipsam conversae erant. Altera[7] vero in contrarium vertebatur."[8] Cui etiam cupido filius suus alatus & cecus assistebat qui sagitta & arcu appollinem sagittabat propter quod diis turbatis[9] ad matris gremium puer timidus fugiebat. Iste planeta est feminae complexionis & ideo in spetiae puellae callida & humida & ideo vulcano, id est in igni dicitur maritata & in mari immersa quia coniuncta calori & humori cupidinem deum amoris peperisse, id est carnis concupiscentiam.[10] Tres puellae, id est tres culpe: avaria[11] ad lucrandum cum actu venereo, carnalitas ad coniugendum actum carnalitatis. Infidelitas quia propter denarium diligere hominem demonstrant. Alatus quia cito accendit & coniugitur, cecus quia non curat ubi diligit. Igitur ex hac insula paris Priami filius Helenam Menelai uxorem non invitam rapuit. Quae ad diem festum iuxta mare situm templum hodie cognitum venerat. ubi cum alter alterum respexisset utriusque forma operam dedit rapinae. Qui cum operam facto dedisset maximum denique excidium consecutum est. A qua rapina omnes grecorum principes in desolationem Troie unanimes fecerunt coniurationes. Cumque illa frustra saepius repetissent subducatu Agamemnonis cum ingenti exercitu post decennium ylionem[12] ceperunt & menelao helena restituta est. cum qua ipse tempestate maris ipse circumactus[13] primo in eqiptum delatus[14] est. Inde in Lacedemonia sunt reversi. Circuit itaque[15] LX milia in qua pauci habitant & circumcirca scopuli videntur cum recentissima aqua scopulorum draconariae dictae.

1. Dd + S: archipelagi
2. B: pingebatur
3. S adds: a
4. PB: assignata
5. PB: quam
6. Dd: mire
7. Dd + S: una
8. Quote from B, p. 28.
9. S: turbatus
10. Dd + S add: quia stella ista excitat concupiscentiam.
11. Dd + S: avaritia
12. Dd: Ylion; S: Ilium
13. Dd: circunacta
14. Dd: delata
15. Dd + S omit: itaque

.11. CITHAREA, NUNC CITRI. Ambitus totius insulae m. p. 60. [Map: North. Citeron oppidum *and* templum★ ubi helena a paridi rapta est. *On small island to NE:* Draconara★.]

Breve de hinc spatium brevem[1] Sichilum enumerare possumus. & x milia circuit in qua oppidum olim erat. Nunc vero cum ab agrestibus sit possessa asinis, nemo hominum in ea habitat. Itaque si supra corium asini agrestis dormies, demones non timebis, epilenticum curabis. Si de corio frontis super se tenebit vel de ungula arsa bibet vel anulum portabit.

//8r// Etiam fumigatione de ea facta parturientem liberat. Si de rasura petre capitis vel maxille febricanti[2] ad bibendum praebes[3] liber erit. Si de sanguine auriculae bibes vel unguentum facies cum suco serpentarie & oleo rosato[4] & unge renes ante accessionem quartane sanus remanebis. Solventur membra contracta sicci humoris & si cum brudo[5] earum carnium abluentur. & femine cum brodio asine & cum adipe ungantur. Etiam in cicatricibus[6] valet & medulla ossium in nervis. Semel turchi huc venietes navis naufragium pertulit: hoc audientes cretici cito ad inferos viam sibi[7] paravere. Etiam navis in tempeste noctis in hanc ruit insulam. In qua naute die octava una in tabulis iam ab eis congestis natantes contra[8] chituriam perierunt: nisi unus illorum qui remanens in scopuli & pastus radicibus arborum atque herbarum circa[9] annum transeuntibus recollectus incolumis evasit.

//8r// .12. SICHILUS. Ambitus totius insulae m. p. 10. [Map: North. *Shows ruined city, labeled:* "Sichilium olim."]

Omnia quamvis quae hic narranda erunt in libro quem de creta composui sint prolixiora hic propter lege[n]tium commodum succincte in tribus partibus insulam clare dividam que est in medio mediterranei[10] maris posita fereque ab omnibus partibus montibus circumdata & undique a ventis agitata. De oriente ad occiduum ducenta & xxx & in latitudine xxxv distare videtur. Ad orientem salmon mons qui ad insulam carpati prospectat; ad occiduum mons oricis[11] elevatur qui ad mallium respicit promontorium. Fuit autem a filio nebrot creto creta dicta: vel quia terra hec ad modum terrae tenacis & albe nomen accepit. habuit enim centum civitates quarum vestigia ad sexagesimum accessi numerorum. In qua saturnus sagax & potens ut dixit filius urani, id est celi & veste, id est terrae erat & ad dei similitudinem se fecit orare. Ipse & enim prius aera signavit & nomen ipsius apposuit. Ignaros arva colere docuit & semina agris imponere atque colligere ordinavit. Ad sui laudem aram & sacra instituit saturniaque appellavit.

1. S omits: brevem, adds: usque
2. Dd: fabricanti; S: febricitanti
3. S: praebebis
4. S: rosae
5. S: brodio
6. Dd: meritricibus
7. Dd + S: eis
8. Dd: versus
9. Dd: cura
10. S: medii terranei
11. Dd + S: Coricis

Vestam sororem suam sacro cupulavit connubio &[1] ea plures susceptos filios scripsere quos aiunt omnes devorasse ne eum de regno expellerent ut invenerat. & iovem servatum uxoris fraude clam in eundem[2] montem nutriendum misit & curetis populis commendatus & in antrum montis yde delatum ne[3] ad vagitum audiretur, cymbala et tympana pulsabant & ad sonum apes mella

//8v// in os eius inferebant[4] vel nutrices de lacte & melle nutriebant. Hic tandem cum adolevisset, bellum habuit cum titanis. Inde patrem regno expulit quia severus erat & carnem humanam docuit imolare, etiam filios proprios. Iupiter igitur ex fuga patris dominus cretensium factus sororem suam Iunonem in coniugem accepit. & glorie avidus in multis locis ad sui nomen templa construxere. Licet multi[5] fuerint iupitres tamen iste cretensis maior omnium fuit quia multa bona & utilia humane vite adinvenit. Mortuo vero corpus iuxta oppidum aulacie[6] posuere quamvis dicatur in celum esse deificatum. Ibi ergo prope montem hodie de suo nomine dictum in radicibus ad trionem ptolemeo demonstrante viam antrum manufactum albatumque parvo ore XL in longitudine & quattuor in latitudine brachiorum reperimus cuius in capita sepulchrum iovis maximi suo epithaphio deleto[7] cognovimus. Extra vero in superficie edificia[8] maxima admodum ampliabantur templi. Cum itaque versus australem plagam vergimur prope mare ad orientem ierapolis cum ingentibus marmorum edificiis est. Mathalia[9] cum musaicis edificiis Finicis[10] nobilissima ruinarum quo in templo grecis sculpebantur litteris. Munda pedem, vela caput & inera.[11] Chissamessolis[12] magnifica erat ubi promontorium cadistum, hodie Spatam. appropinquatur deinde chidonia quae hodie acanta[13] amenissima habetur. In qua metellus contra cretam veniens primo in duobis annis igni ferroque. Insulam totam posuit et vindictam fecit de Marco Antonio qui conflictum in mari & a creticis rome reportabit[14], ut[15] titus livius. Ad Retinam venio, deinde ad canda cum hodie candia & metropolis postquam veneti eam emere & denuo hanc edificavere ad chersonesum venio olim alta meniorum, deindi a doloexopolim[16]

1. Dd + S: ex
2. Dd: ydeum; S: Idaeum.
3. Dd deletes: ut…non
4. Dd: afferebant
5. Dd + S: plures
6. Dd: alavere; S: Arilatiae
7. Dd: delecto
8. Dd + S add: spelunce
9. Dd: in italia
10. Dd: fimicis; S: finitis.
11. Dd + S: intra
12. Dd: Chisamopolis; S: Chisamospolis
13. Dd + S: Achanea
14. Dd +S: deportavit
15. Dd: ait
16. Dd: Clopixopolim; S: Settolopixopolim

hodie histrinam concurro in qua fons octo molendinorum aperitur et iuxta sequendo mare oppida in sumitatibus montium alia reperiuntur[1] quorum in medio sarandapolis civitas olim gigantum erat a qua Sectia derivata est. In fine vero insule ad orientem Salmon mons appellatur[2] omnium altissimus vicinorum. Regredior ergo usque ad occiduum postquam a salmone monte recedimus & per medium insule vergens ad Dicteum properamus montem & in sumitate huius lassiti campus xviii in circuitum milliaria in pascuis fertilissimus[3] habetur. Ad austrum autem ampla elongatur planities Messarea dicta in qua circa medium non parva vestigia amplissime urbis Gorthine olim metropolis apparet, quae Minois regis principalior extiterat, & quantum nostra florentia in habitu[4] manifestatur cum arce[5] magnifica & conductu aquarum descendentium quae totam deinde rigabat[6] urbem in qua duo ad plus milia columpnarum marmorum & idolorum prostrata enumeravi. Ad septrionem autem in monte per miliare ore_strenuo Labirintus ut aiunt reperitur in quo minotaurus a dedalo collocatur & per Theseum fraude fredre[7] sorori in eodem loco interemptus occubuit. Ad occiduum ad. x milliaria mons famosissimus & altissimus apparet ida cuius in radicibus gnosia civitas olim videtur. In quinque ergo collibus sine arboribus mons erigitur iste quorum in medio pars sublimiore est; ubi saturnus ut dicitur templum ad sui laudem stabilivit & ibidem carnem primo sacrificare instituit.[8] Sunt etiam de medio usque summum per totum annum nives. & de Gnosia usque ad apteriapolim XL[9] milliaria & in latitudine xxti quo in spatio multa essent ennaranda auctoritatibus multorum auctorum. Ad occiduum vero ad[10] umbrosas valles de xxti duobus[11] domibus romanorum Constantini tempore huc venerunt habitatum & de gente in gentem diu renovarint arma & cognomen antiquae cognationis usque in hodiernum diem tenuerunt & ad grecum tenuerunt ritum. & primo gortaci latine saturi quingenti numero mellissimi vespasiani trecenti ligni suttiles melle[12] secenti. vlasti papiniani ducenti. Cladi ramuli centum octuagintem. Scordili aglati octingenti Colonni colonnenses triginta. Arculeades Ursini centum remansem. Versus denique angulum huius insulae leucus elevatur mons a quo flumina hic inde descendunt plura & in umbrosis ipsorum vallibus tot & tanti

1. S: aperiuntur
2. Dd + S: propelatur
3. Dd: fortissimus
4. Dd + S: ambitu
5. Dd: arte
6. S: irrigabant
7. S: Phaedrae
8. Dd + S: ordinavit
9. Dd: IIII milliaria et in altitudine II
10. Dd + S: inter
11. Dd + S: XII
12. Dd: mille

//9r// cupressi[1] pululant & crescunt quod incredibile[2] foret ad narrandum & ex eis per universum tabulae mittuntur in anno. Virgilius. Creta iovis magni medio iacet insula ponto. Mons ideus ubi & gentis cunabula nostrae. Centum urbes habitant magnas uberrima regna.

[Map of Crete. East*:* Chersonus, S. Isidro, Termara, Sirapolis eperta,[3] Dimmis Mons,* Girapetra *(ruins),* planum arenosum absque fruttum, Sesia,* Tera mons, Omalo planitie, Istrina,* Lassiti,* Cap Gabello, Mons Altissimus, Pidiata, Belvedere, Chersonesus, Gortina* minoris, turris Regis, S. Georgius. *In center:* Laberintus,* Sepulcrum iovis,* Ida mons iovis famossisima,* Lassa, S. Iohannes, Cadia,* Candia, Mons, Retimo, Nilopotamus, Bonifacio, Acthanea,* Stirapolis, S. Constantinus, Piriotissa, Gnosia.* Leutus y Letolus mons, in eo cipressi infiniti,* Chissamopolis,* Caput Spada.* *Many small islands: from top east, south side:* Cristiana, niso, galdaro, umica, bali, pathmadi, gozo. *North side:* Pori, Diva, Moso, Soron, Sira, Pimolis, Pisinidi, Dia, Odore. *At west, small island with church, no name. In lower border islands:* Capa, Bruse. *Written along river in the middle in faint red ink:* Silva magna oleastrum *(wild olives)*, Mesarea Planus* m. p. 40. *Map:* 44 *names,* 21 *in text.*]

//9v//[4] Narravi de creta nunc ad insulam carpathi[5] venio: carpos enim grece fructus latine & pallene dicta a filio titanis[6] ibi dominante. Ab hac igitur pallas nomen[7] sortita est: ex qua[8] in ea fuit nutrita cum prius vocaretur Minerva, dea sapientiae, & de cerebro iovis nata. quae in similitudine unius domine armate erat sculpta. Caput circumcincte idrie[9] & cassis cum crista, lancea in dextera & in sinistra scutum cristallinum cum monstro gorgone. Vestes triplici colore, iuxta se oliva cum noctua de super. Igitur erat armata quia sapiens est armatus virtutum. Scutum fortitudinis, lance rectitudinis & iustitie, galea sobrietatis & temperantie, iris claritatis & prudentie: oliva pietatis & prudentie[10]: noctua humilitatis & occultantie. Triplicem vestem tres virtutes theoricas:[11] Cristallinum splendorem veritatis. Imago terribilis timor divinus. Gorgona imago mortis vel diaboli. Crista honoris[12] fuit & enim hec patria iapeti: qui duos habuit filios epimetheum & prometheum maximi ingenii & vehementis studii: qui de limo terre hominis formasse simulacrum dicitur.[13] Quo dilecta Minerva prometheum duxit in celum: ut si quid de celestibus vellet ad

1. Dd: Ciparisa
2. S: mirabile
3. Hierapolis?
4. Capital "N" followed by "Narravi."
5. Dd + S: Carpanti
6. S: Titani
7. Dd omits: nomen
8. S: quia
9. Iride; S: hydrae
10. Dd, S + PB: misericordiae
11. S + PB: theologicas
12. Dd: hominis
13. Dd omits: dicitur

sui operis[1] perfectionem posset eligere qui de cursu[2] solis unum ex radiis furatus intra eius pectus animavit simulachrum. Unde a Iove fulminatus, in caucaso monte ligatus iecuri[3] vulturi praebuit perenniter corrodendum. In monte vero caucaso Prometheus studens naturam hominis, a principio terram esse consideravit. Veniens ad aliam naturam comprehendit animam ex celo procedere cui vigorem & celestis origo furasse radium solis, id est sua consolatione[4] ad celestia dirigens. Quod vultur seu Aquila iecur corrodat, nil aliud est: quia viri studentes exteriora inficiunt & interiora consumunt. Fuerunt ergo hic oppida septem quorum tria hodie inter montes habentur. quae circuit LXX[5] milia. & ad orientem Olimbos civitas extat cum portu Tristomos scopuloque sario.[6] Ad occiduum in portu Theatros duo erant oppida in acrotiri, id est puncta videlicet Teneo[7] & Circassas[8] ubi nunc Sanctus Theodorus denominatur & in conspectu Cusso[9] insula.[10] Ad trionem vero iuxta mare olim Fianti civitas ampliata erat: ubi non longe quasi in medio insule Mons Achinata & Oros[11] & Sancti Elie manifestantur ubique. Ad meridionem[12] vero planus estat[13] cuius in capite portus Agata ampliatur; per totam denique tamquam bruti habentur qui laborantes in pice cum lacte substenantur.[14] Unde semel infideles in eam venientes & clam in nocte per insulam lucratum dum irent. Carpathi ergo vigilantes super eos viriliter biremem incendere illi vero redeuntes[15] contristati nimis dimissa[16] praeda, in montibus plusquam centum fame periere.[17]

//10r// .14. SCARPANTHA. Ambitus totius insulae m. p. 70. [Map: North. Fianti* civitas olim magna, *with ruins.* Paleo rostro. Oras mons* *with church.* Olembos,* Tristomos Portus.* *NW:* Portus Theatros.* S. Minias portus. S. Theodorus,* olim Thero,* Arnissus* olim. Theatros portus.* Menetoso. Archinata mons. Goma Mons.*[18] *Off the east coast, island*

1. Dd: corporis
2. S: curru
3. Dd + S: iecur
4. Dd: contemplatione
5. Dd: LII
6. Dd: Fano
7. Dd: Turcho; S: Theutho
8. Dd + S: Archassus
9. S: Casso
10. Dd + S add: est. Venetesque. Dd: Montesque. Corachi oppidum prope montem Gomali apparent in alto.
11. Dd: Anginam & Foros; S: Anachi mara et Oros.
12. Dd + S: trionem
13. S: exstat
14. Dd: sustentantur
15. Dd omits: redeuntes
16. Dd: de amissa
17. Dd omits: fame
18. Dd: Gomali

of Saria.★ Cassos★ *on west. To the south:* Agata portus.★ Pigadia *(drawing of a well).* 17 *names,* 13 *mentioned in text.*]

Venio[1] igitur ad antiquissimam rhodianam civitatem quae receptaculum dominorum minoris asiae & olim grecia[2] quae nunc Turchia est[3] & mercatorum peregrinorumque ex omnibus mundi partibus huc venientium. Dicitur ergo Rhodo grece, rosa latine, quia hic in perfectione magis quam in aliis[4] rose habeantur. Vel dicitur Rhodi a malo punico quia plena hominum olim ita erat & ad modum scuti ampliabatur a Sancto Stephoro[5] usque ad Sanctum Ioannem leprosorum & Sanctum Antonium & Sanctam Gallinicum & ad primum redeundo Sanctum circumdabat. Quo in circuitu turres ducente erant ut in cronica habetur, quarum quaelibet cubitorum quinquaginta erigebatur, quarum in medio colossum ydolum mire magnitudinis cubitorum LXX supereminebat ubi velum a longe LXXX milia manifestabatur. & cacumina totius civitatis ad unum[6] submittebat: quae potentissima nimis multis annis cum egiptiis proelium paravere,[7] tandem ab eis desolata remasit.[8] Aliique volunt propter crebros terremotus[9] collossum atque turres magna hominum cede funditus periisse.[10] Quorum eversiones[11] opiniones multe & diverse predicantur. Ideo nihil audeo & rem tam antiquam ignorare.[12] Scimus tamen tot esse sententias quot capita & quasi homines[13] voluntate potiusquam ratione ferre iudicium. Reperi equidem in quodam greco volumine colossum idolum eneum altitudine cubitorum ut supra qua in medio pectoris speculum amplissimum monstrabat.[14] & ipsum aspicientes[15] naves ab Egyptiis egredietes[16] viderent. Hic igitur & per insulam totam plusquam mille colossi supra columnas inminebant. In super & inumerabilium opus columpnarum insignitum capitibus cerbie & per omnes partes. hinc inde cesaris signo reperimus, una cum urceis cadaverum mortuorum[17] infinitis quorum vestigia usque hodiernum[18] perhibent testimonium. Nunc etiam de novo prope Sanctum Antonium Salvatoremque in vinea quadam quingenta idola omnium manerierum in fovea

1. Dd + S. Should be *Devenio* for acrostic.
2. Dd + S: greciae
3. Dd + S: fuit
4. S adds: partibus
5. Dd + S: Stephano
6. Dd: ymum; S: imum.
7. Dd: peravere; S: paravit
8. S: remansit
9. S: Sed aliqui vero volunt, quod propter crebra terremota
10. S: periere
11. Dd omits: eversiones
12. Dd + S add: mee, mihi conscius affirmare
13. Dd + S: omnes
14. Dd + S: lustrabatur
15. S: respicientes
16. DD + S: egredientes
17. Dd + S: combustorum
18. S adds: diem

//10v// reperta sunt.

Nunc vero ad comparationem antique civitatis modica est: quae ad orientem prospectat & in quattuor divisa remanet. Quarum[1] prima magister hospitalis Sancti Iohannis resedit. Secunda a fratribus dicti ordinis possessa est. Tertia hospitale ipsorum visitatur. Quarta et ultima a mercatoribus una cum grecis habitata est. quae a colosso colocensis scribitur ubique. Est & enim amenissima omnium insularum maris mediterranei & CLIIII[2] circuit milia. Quae iuxta mare a parte ponentis de puncta trionis usque ad austrum plana habetur cum oppidis ruribusque ibi apparentibus multis, quorum olim una civitas Vasilica dicta quae latine imperatrix manifestatur & ad nihilum redacta. Ad austrum vero prosternata oppida diu[3] & rura plura videntur, ubi Polachia Cattania[4] eminent fulcita rusticorum & cultivata satis[5] cum armentorum multitudine. Ad orientem vero prope salo murus immanium lapidum quadratum per montes vallesque, ut aiunt, inceptabat & insulam dividebat & sic indicat[6] dominorum fuisse dominium. Lindum denique munitissimum videmus, in quo sacra Herculi fuere instituta ceterorum ritu diversa quia carnem diis sacrificabant. Cumque non parva sed magnificaque per circuitum desolata videmus liniamenta. Faradum fandum oppida petimus cum Archangelo rure: deinde Rhodum propinquamus ubi tanta est viriditas arborum & amenitas locorum quod est mirabile ad videndum & presertim paradisum a florentinis factum. In medio denique insulae Artamita Mons[7] cum flumine Gadura patescunt. & a leva rus virginis matris Marie Appollona habetur miraculis multis. Ad quintum millia prope civitatem in monte Filerinus[8] est oppidum & domina omnium gratiarum[9] saepe visitata adoratur a multis. Ab hinc igitur leges navalium habuisse videntur originem & natus Appollonius qui de octo partibus orationibus[10] laute[11] tractans: ab eo Priscianus extraxit multa & sibi adactavit.[12] Tullius denique perveniens in hanc urbem eloquentissimos grecorum philosophos reperit & coram eis atque populo orationem preclaram recitavit. Quamobrem a Rhodianis laudabilem[13] acquisivit laudem. Paulus etiam apostolus ad Colocenses epistolam mittit:[14] Coloncenses enim a colosso

1. S adds: in
2. Dd: CLXXXX
3. Dd: duo; S like MN
4. Dd + S: et Aghanea
5. Dd: culturata nimis
6. Dd + S add: duorum
7. Dd: Rinos
8. Dd: Fileimus; S: Filermus
9. Dd: grurum
10. Dd + S: in greco
11. Dd: late
12. Dd + S: adaptavit
13. S adds: que magnam
14. Dd + S: in Asia Minore positi. Et nunc

Rhodiani scribuntur ubique. Quibus[1] & si pluvie sint semel in die sol apparet & iam octo annorum experientiam una cum Varro comprobavi.

//11r// .15. RODOS. [Map: North. Entire page. S. Calfocus *(with windmill)*, S. Nicolas, S. Antonio,* Steffanus,* Leprosarum,* S. Helias,* Triando, Cremasto, Filerno,* Fando,* Archangelo,* S. Nicolaus *(on island to the east).* Farado,* Villa Nova, Arthamiti Mons, * S. Maria Filerno,* Lindo,* Sominii, Salaco, Gadura flum.* Sciama, Vasilica.* Appollona,* Pibechia, Cottania,* Sclipio, Laganea.]

//11v//[2] [Erat Saturni] tempore haec insula Simie dicta a Simeni[3] ibi dominante vel [a Simane grece], latine propinqua, quia iuxta minorem asiam appropinquatur[4] et [comertium cum] vicinis habens vitam cum labore trahebant. Sed postquam a Iove maximo Prometheus Iapeti filius, in hanc vi missus habitantibus multa demonstravit[5] ad vitam conservandum humanam. Qui valens in ingenio hominem ex luto finxit quod[6] audiens Jupiter in simiam eum[7] constituit & ibi vitam finivit. Colentes itaque hanc hodie astuti nimis suis cimbis inter civitates turchorum rhodiorumque victum studiose frequentant. Ad meridiem denique scopuli adherent quibus crebre[8] naves vela deponunt. Castellum igitur prope mare munitissimum est & in montibus aliud desolatum quae xxx mil circuit vino optimo inter saxa eghe ab alto caprizant.

.16. SIMIA OLIM ET NUNC. Ambitus totius insulae m. p. 30. [Map: North. Turchia,* Simie* portus et civitas, S. Nicolaus. *On island to south, church:* S. Paulus.]

//12r//[9] Longe non[10] nimis ab ista supradicta Caristos olim nunc Cal[chis videtur insula, in qua titani re] gnavere, et insulas[11] briareo[12] instituisse divina & pauci omnibus incoluere[13] [temporibus quia arida] nimis & infructuosa remanet : ideo mortales non edificia ponere curaverunt. In ea [igitur ficus hab]entur quorum tanta redundat copia quod naves circumnavigantes loca fecundant[14] . Ad orientem [vero po]rtus ampliatur cuius in sumitate oppidum vetustum munitumque[15] valde videtur : ubi nicolaus sanctus ex itinere fatigatus

1. Dd: quantumque plume; S: quotumcunque
2. Ms torn here and mended with blank parchment. Words in brackets are added from the Düsseldorf ms., fol. 35v.
3. S: Simene
4. S: appropinquat
5. Dd: demiravit
6. Dd + S: Quamobrem
7. S lacks: eum
8. S: crebro
9. Upper right corner blanked out: mended tear. Missing parts in brackets, provided by Düsseldorf ms., f. 36r.
10. Dd omits: non, adds: vero
11. Dd + S: incolas
12. Dd + S add: filio
13. Dd: paucioribus in culture
14. secundant?
15. S: minutum

residens[1] gentibus illis viam rectitudinis demonstravit. Quorum precibus adeo gratiam consecutus est, quod secures & ad fodiendum ferramenta continue laborando in istis aridis lapidosisque montibus non minuerentur.[2] A quo tempore usque in hodiernum illesa salvantur[3] quae ad dotes filiabus computant cariores. Eapropter ecclesiam ad laudem ipsius ditissimam auri[4] argentique constituere quam corde & animo gubernare laborant.

.17. Calchi olim Dic<...>[5] Ambitus totius insulae <...>. [Map: North. Chalcis: *large fortified building in center plus house, trees, church, islands to east.*]

Mostravimus de Calchi, nunc ad Diluphanos[6] olim hodie Piscopia transitum parabo.[7] Diluphanos olim grece latine omnibus apparentibus interpretatur. Piscopia grece ab *epi* quod est supra & scopos, speculator, quasi supra speculatrix quia in montibus valde elevata est & a longe cernitur nimis. De oriente ad occiduum elongatur & xxxv circuit millia. Ad orientem frondifluus elevatur mons, cuius in radicibus duo extant scopuli quorum unus ascina appellatur. Ad trionem vero oppidum Sancti Stephani[8] in quo portus & planus manifestatur. Ad occiduum Zucharola[9] erigitur[10] egestate plenus. In medio quoque alia duo oppida male habitantur quibus potius eghe vagantur quam homines loca valeant custodire.

.18. Diluphanos olim, nunc Piscopia. Insulae totius ambitur m. p. 35. [Map: North. Piscopia,* S. Steffanus,* Zucharola.*]

//12v//[11] [Ostendi situm Piscopie], nunc ad cariam[12] olim nunc Nixaros indicare valeam, cum suo ethneo [monte]. Caribdi grece, <...>[13] latine, nunc nixos grece, insula latine interpretatur. Hic Flaminius consul rediens de partibus orientis & accedens pugnaturus contra gallos auguratus est victoriam obtinet & sic factum in luce resolvit: itaque insula haec semper benivola[14] romanis[15] habita esse. Per hanc etiam transiens Cleopatra cum Antonio & nolentes cives preceptis ipsorum obedire totam insulam delevere. Quae xviii circuit millia & quinque videntur oppida quorum duo principaliora Mandrachi & Paleo Castra apparent. Et Pandenichi, Nichea & Argos sunt in circuitu. Circa medium

1. S: residet
2. Dd: numerentur
3. S: servantur
4. Dd omits: auri
5. MS damaged here.
6. Dd: luffanos
7. Dd: properabo
8. S adds: video
9. Dd: Zucalora; S: Zuccalora
10. Dd: arigitur
11. Upper left corner blanked out. Words in brackets are taken from the Düsseldorf ms., f. 36r.
12. Greek for nut is *karuon*.
13. blank, Dd: nux
14. S: benevola
15. Dd: rationis

mons erigitur altissimus quo in sumitate per subterraneos meatus sulphureus ignis die ac nocte eructat in altum ut in insula Strongili apud Liparum habetur. In discensu[1] vero montis ad iactum lapidis fons calidissimus emanat in unum.[2] & in plano circa lacum profundissimum obscurumque aque descendunt. Ibique colentes quantitatem maximam sulphuris mercatoribus preparant. & quia in tantum viget intensitas caloris de medio usque verticem, nullus est ausus sine sotularibus accedere ligneis. Etiam hic tanta fecunditas ficuum quae in anno naves onerantur parve. Ad trionem in pede montis contigue[3] maris[4] consistit ad quam circumstantes doloribus oppressi accedunt & diu morati in patriam incolumes revertuntur & quia concava, ut presumitur, haec insula habetur saepius tot & tanti terremotus[5] ubique: gignuntur[6] quod forenses ob hoc perterriti locum cito maledicentes derelinquunt & procul accedere gaudet. Colentes vero tale sterminium pro nihilo reputant.[7]

.19. NICAROS. CARIA OLIM, NUNC NISARI. Insulae totius ambitur m. p. XVIII. [Map: North. Balneus sulfureus, Mandrachi,★ Mons altissimus a quo sulfureus ignis semper eructat★ *(shows flames leaping from mountaintop)*, [gira] (paleo) castro, Pandenichi,★ spelunca,★ Nichea,★ Argos.★]

//12v// Nunc ad Stimphaleam[8] olim hodie speluncham[9] meum properabo cursum &, ut ait Plinius, Astimphalea[10] libere civitatis circuitus[11] octuaginta novem milia passuum. & in super Ovidius: hinc Anaphem sibi iungit & astimphalea regna. Promissis Anaphem, regna & Stimphalea bello.[12] cinctaque[13] piscosis astimphalea vadis.[14] In medio autem & tenuissima est & in extremis ampla in quibus plurima castra[15] desolata videntur. Ad trionem Vathi oppidum. Ad meridiem occiduumque civitas apparet Stimphalea dicta. Sunt etiam per insulam antiquitates multorum[16] oppidorum: & hinc inde per circuitum portus[17] optimi concluduntur & desolati iamdiu a pyrratis sine apparatu usque in hodiernum panduntur

1. Dd + S: descensu
2. Dd: nimium; S: in imum
3. S: contigua
4. Dd + S add: spelunca
5. S: terramota
6. Dd: regnant; S: regnunt
7. Dd adds: et in eo non advertere curant; S: curant. This passage also lacking in C.
8. Dd: Stinfaleam; S: Astimphaleam
9. Dd + S: Stampaleam
10. S adds: rectae vel
11. S: circuitu
12. S: bella
13. Dd: contaque
14. *Ars Amat.* II.85
15. S: castella
16. Dd + S: aliquorum
17. S: porti

ubique. Tempore igitur[1] morbosani[2] turchi preventa[3] magna classa[4] istas insulas in totum delevere pyrrate. Igitur usque in hodiernum relicta a cultoribus.[5] Solus nobilis ille Venetus Johannes Quirinus suis viribus eam cepit[6] tempore Concilii Constantie restaurare.[7]

//13r// .20. ASTIMPHALEA. Insulae totius ambitus m. p. 8 <Illeg.>. [Map: North. Saint Clemens, Saint Chaterina, Stimphalea,* S. Iohannes, Vathi,* Vathi *(in water, north)*, Paleo Castro *(2x)*, Saint Benedictus.]

Testantur veteres & maxime Plinius quod haec insula Egasa dicebatur, deinde Filetera a Filete ibi dominante; postea Calista a bonitate humoris terrae: denique Therasia antequam emersisset dicebatur. Si postquam circa medium emersit etiam elapsis temporibus usque in hodiernum Santellini nominavere. Quae fertilis & populata nimis existimabatur & propter Vulcani combustionem medietas in profundum maris est sumersa[8] cuius particulam ad modum lune exustam videmus & Therasia hodie nuncupatur & sic inter unam aliamque partem magnum chaos remansit aquarum. In quo tanta profuditas[9] demonstratur quod nullo modo illustris dux Jacobus harum insularum in mille passibus fundum attingere potuit. & funem nimis ponderantem totaliter in abissum dismisere[10] quae circuit[11] ad modum lune cornute disteditur.[12] Ubi a parte ponentis iuxta mare magnifica ampliabatur civitas. Coloni vero dimissa ruina in monte superbo oppidum edificavere munitum. Cumque ibi cum quadam ianuensium nave polipum[13] sexaginta cubitorum in circuitu videremus & sua ampliates[14] brachia & iter ad[15] petetem cito hoc cernentes navem reliquimus omnes & perterriti prope ripas speculamur ab alto donec cito velum vento prebemus cum salute. Quinque autem[16] galee Venetorum in[17] eis diebus de Baruto revertentes in loco sunt submerse isto quorum[18] quidem naufragium omnes evasere homines. Repperi etiam ut ait Titus Livius quod ad hanc insulam oppugnandam trium iunctarum classium naves

1. S: ergo
2. Dd: morat bassa
3. S: perventa
4. S: classe
5. S omits: Igitur...cultoribus.
6. S: incepit
7. Dd: reparare
8. Dd: subcersa; S: submersa
9. Dd + S: profunditas
10. S: profundum disersere
11. Dd: LXXX Millaria; S: XL; MN omits
12. sic. should be: distenditur
13. Dd: pulpum; S: Phulpum
14. Dd + S: ampliantem
15. Dd: nos a
16. S: etenim
17. Dd: mergit illique; S: meis itaque diebus
18. S: quarum

Romanorum Rhodiorum & Attali regis pervenere omnisque[1] tormentis & machinis onuste ad[2] urbis excidia prebebant videlicet[3] multis oppressionibus ac[4] machinationibus oppressi a Romanis, civitas haec in ruinam et depredationem posita est.

//13v// .21. ET .22. THERASIA NUNC, DUE OLIM UNA FUIT. [Map: North. Therasia,* Mare per totum, Camon, Cristina, Santellini,* olim civitas magna *(ruins)*.]

Cum[5] sic cernimus versus Sicandrum iter arripimus & dicitur Sicandras[6] a multitudine ficuum ibi olim fructificantium. Sica in grece latine ficus interpretatur. Quae montuosa nimis a vetusto tempore usque nunc inculta remansit tum propter Turchorum & pyrratarum insidias tum propter ignaviam rusticorum cohaderentium[7] & portus incommoditatem[8] in qua aselli forte per insulam relicti usque nunc errantes per asperas ripas magno hinc inde capiuntur labore. Volunt igitur quod in hoc loco Meleus[9] quidam vir strenuus tempore Troianorum ad exercitum[10] Grecorum duabus accessit navibus, qui adherens insulae Deli a longe oraculum adoravit & persequens suum iter tempestate facta necatus est. & sic viduate mulieres ex tunc oppidum in exterminium declinavit. Que cum in longissima perseveraret etate in solitudine paucorum, castellum ruraque & infine ad nihilum pervenere.

.23. in numero. SICANDROS OLIM ET NUNC. Ambitus totius insulae m. p. 17. [Map: West. Sicandros *(ruins). Rest of island dotted with trees.*]

//14r// Est sequens insula Policandros dicta ab herba sic nominata ad morbum caducum[11] optima. Vel dicitur a Poli, civitas, & Andros, homines, vel civitas hominum vel virorum. Constat igitur a nomine eam habitatam fuisse cum tam seculis multis a domibus moeniisque sint[12] ad nichilum reducta. Haec[13] xx circuit millia modicis[14] arboribus virentibusque herbis. Evenit autem quod[15] [quidam heremita[16] diu hic deo serviens et in

1. Dd + S: generis
2. S: et
3. S omits; Dd + S: sed postquam.
4. Dd: re-
5. Dd: Dum. Should be Dum for acrostic
6. Dd + S: Sicandros
7. Dd: quo adherentium
8. S: porti minuitatem
9. Dd: Milius
10. S: excidium
11. Dd + S: morbo caduco
12. S: fuit
13. Dd + S: quae
14. Dd: medio
15. Dd adds: quidem...sedet.
16. S: emerita

angusta spelunca sedens,[1]] cum[2] [in]fideles eam igne suffocaverunt. Cumque recessum capere vellent, vox audita est[3] hominem innocentem & mihi propitium necavistis. Ibitis.[4] non impune transire non licet. Cumque hoc explicaret ensem[5] inter culpabiles ruit & sternit improbes.[6] Residuum vero ad patriam remeare[7] dimisit qui devote miraculum narrantes ad fidem christi devenere.

.24. Policandros. Ambitus totius insulae m. p. 20. [Map: North.]

Ferunt[8] quod haec insula Polimio numquam fuit habitata sed cum sit in aliquo nemorosa loco & forme casarum patefacte homines[9] habitasse in ea manifestatur. Sed quid in eo loco vetustum fuerit[10] ab hominibus hoc tempore ignoratur. Verum quod una biremis Turchorum dum hanc appeteret & ad capiendum egas accederent. Eolus boream emissus ab antro cito ratem in saxa latentia torquet & in unum[11] miserabile visu demissa[12] est. Cumque hoc[13] socii perciperent & in longam exclamationem erumperent in xx dierum spatio omnes animam maumeto tradidere. Circuit millia xviii. In qua falcones quolibet anno pullos nutriunt suos.

.25. Polimio olim et nunc. Ambitus totius insulae m. p. 18. Tota deserta <illeg.>. [Map: North. *No place names, ruins.*]

//14v// Legimus equidem[14] multis grecorum annalibus nomen huius insule discordare. & primo Aristoteles Mellidam dicit de quo nomine Plinius ab abundantia mellis in montibus cavernosis concordat. Gorgias Zephiram a vento illo qui in eodem regnat loco. Calimachus mimallida[15] a domina sic dicta. Eraclides Simphim a sibilo quia aque descendentes & cadentes sonitum tamquam sibilum emictant.[16] Hodie vero Milos, quod latine molendinum sonat, quia per omnes contratas illas lapides molendini inveniuntur & fere in aliis[17] &[18] ideo. Milos merito dicta: quae in egeo terminatur & contra malleum

1. From Dd. This line missing from MN
2. Dd: in
3. Dd adds: dicere; S: dicens
4. Dd: nam et
5. S: ensis
6. Dd + S: improbos
7. S: redire
8. Dd: Figunt
9. Dd omits: homines
10. S: fuerat
11. Dd: ymum; S: in imum
12. Dd: demersa
13. Dd: hec
14. blank. Dd + S: mi Jordane pater
15. Dd: Minalida; S: Numalida
16. Dd: sibilum sonus auditur
17. Dd: malii
18. Dd adds: inde

promontorium elevatur altissima. Sardus hic invenitur lapis sepe qui desubter niger in medio candidus & desuper rubeus[1] manifestatur, et castum furentem[2] reddit. Huc rex athenarum ministeus demofontis[3] frater & thesei,[4] de bello troiano revertens, applicuit marisque procellis in austa[5] lacessitus occubuit. Cui usque[6] in hodiernum diem honorabile sepulchrum, epithaphio sculptum, cernitur.[7] Circuit hic milia LXXXX,[8] cuius in medio ad trionem portus nobilissimus aperitur. aquarum medicinalium sulphuris existentium in circuitu. In quo turris & planus apparet domibus aliquibus. Ab ea[9] vero parte quae est inter orientem & trionem civitas elevatur munitissima. In qua evenit mancipii capto tempore, postquam cives hinc inde in laboribus, accedentes castellum dicte invaserunt & dominam[10] loci occiderunt. Hoc autem cum perciperent circumstantes, armis viribusque totis, elapsis diebus, inexpugnabile vicerunt castrum & mancipia ad tartara descenderunt. Cybeles etenim, ut repperi, adorabatur, quae sculpta in[11] pretiosis lapidibus ornata cum corona turrium et galli sequentes & leones currum trahebant: quae claves in manu gestabat. Igitur Cybeles terra dicitur: in curru quia terra in aere[12] pendet; in rotis quia mundus rotatur & volubilis est; leonibus ut ostendatur[13] materna pietas, omnis enim feritas materne subicitur affectioni. Lapidibus pretiosis vestita quia terra est mater omnium lapidum metallorumque. Galli quia eius sacerdotes castrati erant qui & coribantes dicebantur. Turribus coronata quia in terra sunt civitates & castra. Clava[14] quia verno tempore terra aperitur & in[15] hieme clauditur. Ad occiduum oppidum erat Pollona quo coram scopuli insuleque inculte apparent multe & hinc inde sparse per totum.

.26. MELO OLIM NUNC MILO. Ambitus totius insulae m. p. 30.[16] [Map: North. S. Dimitri, Turris episcopi, Pollona,* Apano Castro. *Islands to the north:* Antimilo, Argentera, Thimilo. *Islands to south:* Octema, Sermemilo.]

//15r// Ostendi de Milo, nunc ad insulam Siphani accedamus.[17] Siphanos grece surbo latine cumque per eam accesseris montes & aridam calcabis viam & ab egis comitata. XL circuit

1. Dd repeats: candidus
2. Dd: ferentem
3. Dd: xenophontis
4. Dd + S: filius
5. Dd + S: et nausea
6. Dd: husque
7. Dd + S: condiderunt
8. Dd: LXXX
9. Dd: versus
10. Dd: dominum
11. Dd + S add: curru
12. Dd: quia mare e terra
13. Dd: ondatur
14. Dd: clave; S: claves
15. S omits: in
16. Should be 80 or 90?
17. S: transeamus

millaria. Ad orientem vero in monte prope Sarraglam[1] civitas est de nomine insule dicta. Ad occiduum Schinosi locus aperitur & sinus.[2] & ad meridiem portus concluditur olim cum urbe deruta quae nunc plati iallo nominatur. & in conspectu scopulum[3] chitriani dictum videmus. In medio vero turris erigitur Exambeles dicta a qua fons usque emanat mare. In quo ortus omnium virescit pomorum. Pan etiam deus naturae[4] colebatur ut in sublimiori loco statua deleta[5] demostrat.[6] Sed postquam paulus & reliqui apostolorum verbum divinum per has predicavere contratas, omnia idola ruere. Igitur Pan[7] cornutus & rubicundus superiorem partem mundi indicat, ignem & etherem cum radiis denotamus. Pectus stellatus stelle celi. Septem calami in ore: septem planete. Femora[8] arbores & herbe; pedes caprios[9] animalia denotabantur. Habitant denique hic pauci & miserabiles quorum numerus pars maxima sunt mulieres quae propter[10] defectum virorum usque ad senium vitam vi castam deducunt & quamvis linguam ignorent latinam tamen catolicam fidem non amictunt.[11]

.27. SIPHANI. Insulae totius ambitur m. p. 40. [Map: North. Schinosi,★ Exambeles *(tower)*,★ Seraglia,★ Sifana, fons cum viridaris, paleo castro, Plati Giallo portus.★ *Island to south:* Chitriani.★ 8 *names, all in text but one.*]

Desummo[12] Serphinum quae in montibus tota XL circuit millia & dicitur a serfi grece herba[13] quae ad dolorem renium[14] salutifera hic invenitur vel dicitur a serfino conditore a quo[15] assumpsit nomen. Cumque ad meridiem vergis portus coram scopulo quodam panditur ultro et citro[16] in latum[17] iuxta planum oppidum elevatur. Quod usque in hodiernum a serfino conditore antiquum servat nomen. Ibique circum & per abrupta viarum eghe innumerabiles vagari[18] cernuntur, carnes quarum assate a sole diu in cibum a colonis summitur. laute in qua appollo celebratur[19] in puerili forma, & qui[20] in senili. In

1. S: Serraglam
2. Dd: insignis
3. Dd: sculptum
4. Dd: noster
5. Dd: delecta
6. Dd: demonstrat; S: demonstratur
7. B, 53–55
8. Dd: feminam
9. Dd + S: caprinos
10. S: per
11. Dd: amittunt
12. Dd + S: Resumo
13. S adds: latine
14. Dd + S: renum
15. Dd + S: de eo
16. S: cito
17. Dd + S: altum
18. Dd: regnare
19. S: colebatur
20. Dd: quanquam; S: quidam

capite tripodam auram,[1] in manu pharetra & sagitta cum arcu. In altera cytharam tenebat. In pedibus monstrum serpentinum[2] tribus capitibus scilicet caprino[3] lupino & leonino. Iuxta erat Laurus cum corvo[4] volitante. Appollo sol interpretatur puer in mane, vir in meridie, senex in sero quia pallet. Arcus & sagittas quia radios ad nos mittit.

//15v// Cythara quia mollificat sonos[5] totius celestis melodie. Tripoda propter tria[6] beneficia. Splendorem, calorem & interiorem vigorem quem in cunctis iuvenibus[7] operatur. Monstrum trium capitum. Tempus canis blandientis tempus futurum quia semper per spetiem[8] futurorum homini blanditur. Lupus tempus praeteritum quod moris[9] est lupi capit[10] & fugit. Leo tempus presens quod stat & fugere non dignatur. Laurus quia virgo[11] in estate durat. Nunc ergo pater[12] quid sit in hac insula nisi calamitas certum est cum tempus & vitam tanquam adbruptalem[13] persequentur modum. & quod plus estat die ac nocte magno tremore ne in manus[14] perveniant infidelium; tremuli annos fatigant consumere suos.

.28. SERPHINUS OLIM ET NUNC. Ambitus totius insulae m. p. 40. [Map: North. Serphino civitas,★ *wall with towers, 3 unnamed islands to the east.*]

Est etiam post supradictam Thermia[15] nuncupata insula quae dicitur a Thermo grece latine tepidum, et montuosa valde & XL circuit milliaria. Ad orientem vero sancta elini[16] cernitur cernitur ubi planus extat quo in capite civitas Thermia erigitur, quam Turchi ibi mancipii proditorie[17] in nocte captis civibus desolavere; sed nunc populata est. Ad occiduum autem in ecclesia Sancti Lucae optimi portus civitas olim erat edificiis adornata.[18] In monte vero quasi in medio insulae turris erigitur a qua rivulus aquarum rivat[19] usque salum domesticus[20]

1. Dd + S: auream
2. S: serpentibus
3. S: canino; PB: caninum
4. Dd: corio
5. Dd: sanos
6. Dd: terra
7. B + S: viventibus
8. Dd: spem
9. Dd: mori
10. B: rapit
11. B: viror
12. Dd: patet
13. Dd: Brutalem; S: ad brutalem
14. S: manibus
15. Dd: Fermeniae
16. S: Helena
17. Dd: prodictorie
18. Dd: edomata
19. Dd + S: rigat
20. Dd: salo domestica

& ibi apocreos planus nascitur.[1] & ad meridiem sinus & planus piscopie manifestatur. & planus merta[2] prope terminatur. In vino vero blado[3] sirico[4] carnibusque bene habetur. In qua semel prope civitatem in portu Turchi forte pernoctaverunt & due intempeste noctis eiusdem[5] galearum cretensium ad sunt quo mane facto christiani[6] irruentes in eos ad inferos omnes mandavere.

//16r//.29. THERMIA OLIM ET NUNC. Ambitus totius insulae m. p. 40. [Map: North. *Walled city:* Therma,* S. Elini* *(church)*, portus Sancti Luce,* planities apaneos,* Piscopie sinus,* nobilis fons.]

Nunc ad Ceam transeo; a Ceo titano & terre filio nominata, qui cum extranee ferocitatis superbieque existeret. Ipse cum fratribus suis una contra iovem insurrexerunt. Cum praelium tempore multo invicem fuisset,[7] tandem[8] a dicto iove extra insulam crete sunt expulse[9] & hinc inde facultatibus diminuti. Ea propter iste Ceus maior suorum fratrum[10] ad hanc devenit insulam in qua Latonam at Asteriem[11] virgines pulcherimmas genuit de quibus multa dicendo dimitto.[12] Quae montuosa L. circuit millaria. Ad occiduum portus extat & inter[13] ipsum castellumque planus habetur. In quo silvestria[14] pervagantes & oppidum valide[15] antiquum retinentem[16] olim erat ritum[17] ut qui senio confectus aut infirmatus vitam veneno finiret. Mors eius maximis laudibus extollebatur. Cumque Sextus[18] Pompeius Asiam petens, huc actus tempestatibus applicaret audiretque matronam quandam etate & virtutibus venerandam, ad eam accessit & ut diutius venenum illam non acciperet exorabat. Illa autem lectulo cubans agnatas circumhabens sic verbis Pompeio alloquitur. "Quintum & nonagesimum annum ago & semper fortuna vultum mihi ostendit ilarem & gremium mihi felicem[19] aperuit & ut saepe sit flatu quodam subito mutate fortune

1. Dd + S: noscitur
2. Dd: mercha; S: Merca
3. Dd: bladu
4. Dd + S: serico
5. Dd:earum
6. Dd: adds audacter
7. Dd + S: extiterit
8. Dd + S: in fine
9. S: expulsi
10. Dd: fratribus
11. Dd: Astoriam; S: Asteram
12. S: omitto
13. Dd: intus
14. Dd: silvaria
15. Dd: Iulida
16. S: retinens
17. Dd: ritus
18. Dd: Sistus
19. Dd: facile

calamitosum vite mee exitum posse feliciter[1] experiri. Igitur cum laeta vita sit & ilarior mors erit." & ab omnibus licentiam accipiens diisque vocatis constanter obiit[2] & cito spiritus[3] evolavit. Hic etiam fons invenitur cuius potu[4] faciunt homines hebetes sensu & postquam ad digestionem[5] venerit mens ad pristinam reducitur sanitatem. & quia prope[6] hanc ad occiduum versus tenaron pegastumque[7] sinum[8] atque mirteum mare multi adiacent scopuli insuleque inculte, ideo nomina aliquarum hic ponam sine narratione[9] aliqua. Sira vel Sidra, Macroniso, Albera, Chitisos de qua proculus poeta fuit: qui cum Samiam adamaret gregem[10] multa carmina ad laudem sui nominis compilavit.

//16v//.30. CEA OLIM ET NUNC. Ambitus totius insulae m. p. 40. [Map: East. *City in center, trees.*]

Constat hanc insulam Andros multis nominibus pronuntiari[11] ut philosophi dicunt & primo Mirsius caurum Calimachus antandrom. Alii Lagiam Nonagriam Idrussam a fontibus multis & Plinius Pagrim nominat. Andros dicta est a filio Annei regis haec[12] nobilis & pulchra satis & aquarum copiosissima apparet, humane nature[13] omnia producente. In montibus tota & LXXX circuit millaria. & civitas ad orientem sine portu habitatur & prope eam[14] vero parva insula cum antiquo[15] oppido apparet. Ad quam per pontem lapideum amplis edificiis accedebant. In mare prope litus turris cernitur in qua circumastantes[16] in nocte residebant ut a pyrratis salvi fierent. Dicitur enim filias Annei[17] regis aufugisse de quibus per Ovidium sic fingitur. Bachum eisdem proprietatem[18] attribuisse ut quicquid tangerent in segetem vinum oleumque transformaretur. Quo per Agamemnon cognito cogit eas ut pascerent[19] exercitum quem ad Troiam conducebat. Illae autem fugientes fratrem in manibus Agamemnonis elegit eas tradere. Agamemnon dum vincula parabat, tollens[20] brachia celo a libero patre, poposcerunt auxilium. In columbas verse sunt.[21] Rei

1. Dd: possem faciliter; S: posse faciliter
2. Dd: ebibit; S: venenum ebibit
3. Dd: separatus…a carcere; S: a carcere
4. Dd: potus facit
5. Dd: digniorem
6. Dd: propter
7. Dd: thenarum pegaseum; S: Pegasseum
8. Dd: signum
9. Dd: ratione
10. Dd: grecam
11. Dd: prenuntiari
12. S: quae
13. S: humana natura
14. Dd + S add: ad occiduum
15. Dd: aliquo
16. S: circum adstantes
17. Dd: Armi
18. Dd: per eccatem
19. Dd: parent
20. S: tollentes
21. S adds: Sed in

veritas[1] sic est, quod filie Annei[2] regis in emendis agris magnam habuerunt solertiam adeo ut in magna copia de omnibus habudabant,[3] divites facte sunt. Qua re comperta per Agamenonem in exercitu suo omnia abstulit eisdem & sic de divitibus facte paures.[4] Ad questum & velut columbae luxuriose ad publicum lucrum vivendi dee[5] veneris devenerunt. Quid igitur fuerit in hac insula actum vestia[6] manifestant cum nil aliud invenitur nisi magna ac magnifica sculpta per totum. In super & deum mercurium fuisse videtur alatum[7] virgam in manibus circumseptam[8] serpentibus habentem galerum[9] in capite & gallus coram eo; caput caninum. Alatus quia stella Mercurii citissime[10] facit cursum suum. Somniferam virgam quia propter dulcedinem verborum homo sopit.[11] Caninum caput quia in eloquentia latrando, id est loquendo attrahit homines. In capite galerum cum gallo quia mercator sollicitus est hinc ingredi cum mercantiis & mutat propositum ad sui conformitatem.[12] De hinc etiam ille Terentius poeta comicus carthaginensis fabulam suam incepit qui hominum descripsit mores iuvenumque senumque; & Andriam primam suam comediam intitulavit, qui Pamphilam primo de hinc Elicerium[13] hinc discessisse[14] ponit. Denique Crito homo senex Athenas accedens pacem & gaudium[15] conclusionis fabule adaptavit. Nunc tamen haec regio propter crebras Turchorum insidias ad infimum est reducta, quamvis ad comparationem aliarum haec melius habetur.

//17r//.31. Andros Insula. Ambitu totius insulae m. p. 80. Andros. [Map: North. *Three constructions, including a fortified city on a peninsula to the northeast. Shows island and stone bridge.*]

Inter Chion[16] et Andrum scopulus eminens caloierus dictus, rupibus rapacissimus, solus est. Unde colos[17] grece latine bonus & gherus[18] senex vel bonus senex. Inde caloierus interpretatur per antifrasim qui valde malus & a navigantibus minacissimus omnibus

1. S: sed in rei veritate
2. Dd: Amei
3. Dd: abundabant
4. Dd + S: pauperes
5. Dd: die
6. Dd + S: vestigia
7. Dd + S: allatus
8. Dd: circumspectam
9. Dd: galorum
10. Dd: cicissime
11. Dd: sopitur
12. quia...conformitatem appears to be Buondelmonti's invention. B, p. 32 reads: "sicut mercator et gallum qui evigilat mercatores."
13. Dd: glicerium; S: Glycerium
14. Dd + S: recessisse
15. Dd: gladium
16. Dd: Chirum; S: Chium
17. Dd + S: calos
18. Dd + S: geros

invenitur[1] temporibus. Igitur hinc[2] naves transeuntes saepe[3] nocte submerguntur in eo. In quo in eis[4] diebus una cannuensium[5] navis de pera descendens[6] in hunc periit scopulum. Ea propter naute transeuntes anathematizare saepe convalescunt & digito procul indicantes[7] cito velum vertuntur in altum. Cumque semel turchorum ratis ibi mergeretur ad saltum[8] in scopulis hominum eventum est. Tertia vero die xprianorum[9] [Christianorum] puppis coram affuit eis. Que misericordia mota[10] omnes illos semivivos evasit in altum. Qui post cibum convalescentes in xprianos irruere & navigantes in patriam xprianos tante[11] evasionis causas ad continuam posuere servitutem. Hic est falcones in anno pullos nutriunt infra in meabiles[12] ripas.

.32. CALOIERUS. [Map: n.d. *High rocky cliff.* Schopolus Caloierus.]

//17v// Aristoteles propter aquarum abundantiam Idrusam[13] hanc nominat quod latine aquatica sonat. Demosthenes & Eschinus fuissam[14] dicunt: hodie vero Tino dictam[15] est propter suam rotunditatem ad modum tini derivata & contigua andro. XL circuit millia. quo in spatio duo eriguntur scopuli[16] in qua olim mulier venefica quaedam, cum videret semel hostes appropinquantes ad urbem desolandam, in montem sublimiorem[17] ascensa est & nuda sparsis[18] crinibus ad celum brachia extendens nondum incantationem expleverat quod[19] affricus repentinus ventus contra illos insurgens classem in imum evertit & sic per insulam pars illorum evasit maxima que potita[20] licoribus incantationum & carminum insensati remanserunt quo in loco ad servitutem sunt redacti & cives effecti divites. tempore Alexandri claruere. Postea a romanis in exterminium devenerunt. Evenit autem[21]

1. Dd + S: reperitur
2. S: adhinc
3. S: in
4. Dd + S: meis
5. Dd + S: Ianuensium
6. Dd: discedens
7. Dd: ludicantes
8. Dd + S: salutem
9. Hybrid Greek/Latin term.
10. S adds: super
11. Dd: tandem
12. Dd: innumerabiles; S: immeabiles
13. Dd: ydrusam; S: Hydrusam
14. Dd: friusam; S: -Fuissam. Ophiusa (best guess for "fuissam" and "friusa") is one of the names given for this island (and a number of others). It means "Snake Island." Pliny IV.66.
15. Dd + S: dicta
16. Dd repeats: duo eriguntur scopuli
17. Dd + S: sublimiori
18. Dd: aspersis
19. S: quum
20. Dd: potata
21. Dd + S: et enim

non diu navem ab occidente oneratam equorum huc attigisse magna maris tempestate. Que in ruinam omnium animantium evasione[1] eversa est & per insulam ferentes[2] in maximum devenerunt numerum. in qua circa medium castrum in monte[3] cum plano habetur fertili.[4] Ad orientem denique turris sancti nicolai in mari elevatur & in monte ad occiduum altera erigitur munitissima. Ad trionem vero vallis amena aperitur & ad meridiem olim oppidum colebatur.

.33. TINO. Ambitus totius insulae m. p. 40. [Map: North. Tino civitas, Turris Tiscori, paleo castro,* S. Steffanus, S. Nicholas.* *Tower to the east.*]

Postquam dixi de Tino ad Michonos accedamus olim a rege dicta vel Micos grece longitudo latine vel paululum quia in loco parvo habetur. Fuit olim igitur & splendida[5] nimis ut per edificia testatur quia Delo propinqua & peregrini ut possent plures[6] in anno idolum visitare, hic habitaculum petebant. Cumque semel turchi per insulam ruerent caloierum virum dei adorantem in quadam invenerunt[7] spelunchum[8] & dum strepitum facerent[9] ut ipsum caperent spelunca ruit in imum[10] in quo[11] omnes praeter[12] caloierum periere. Hec etenim una ex Cicladibus dicta & in Egeo Mari sita XXX circuit millia. Quae cum portu & molo antiquissimo ad meridiem. Stephanus Georgius Johannesque Sancti habentur & Sancta Anna ad orientem manifestatur cum Padermo portu. quae arida tota cum eghis multis comprobatur. Virgil. Errantem Micoe celsa giaroque revinxit.[13]

MICHONE[14] OLIM ET NUNC. Ambitus totius insule m. p. 30. [Map: North. S. Giorgius,* S. Steffanus,* Portus S. Johannes,* S. Iohannes,* S. Anna,* Padermo Portus.*]

//18r// Restat nunc insulam indicare deli de qua saepe[15] inter auctores habetur mentio & famosissima in medio cicladum explendebat.[16] Quam olim mobilem vetustas asserit & multis modis vocata fuit. Delos, Asteria, Corona, Midia, Lagia, Cineto, Pirpile[17] & nunc

1. S omits
2. Dd + S: fetantes
3. Dd + S add: pachino
4. Dd: fortius
5. S: exsplendida
6. Dd + S: pluries
7. Dd: invectine
8. Dd + S: speluncha
9. Dd omits: et dum...spelunca; S: faciunt
10. Dd: in qua vix caloierum repierunt
11. S: qua
12. S: nisi
13. *Aeneid* III.76
14. Numbering missing.
15. Dd: semper
16. Dd: splendebat
17. Dd: Afferia, Ligia, Cuneto, Purpile

Sdiles dicta est.[1] De qua poetae taliter finxere iovem latonam cei titanis filiam vitiasse:[2] quo persequente ipsa cunctis regionibus fugabatur. Tandem a sorore asteria iam in insulam transmutata, se littoribus applicante[3] edidit.[4] Qui statim occiso phitone ultus est matris iniurias. Asserunt matri parturienti dianam & appollinem praebuisse officium obstetricis, unde ergo dianam virginem fingunt sub lucine nomine eo quod luci reddat infantes, parturientibus invocari.[5] Diana omnium fere testimonio poetarum iovis et latone fuit filia. Hanc veteres[6] insignem virginitate perpetua voluere. & quoniam[7] spreto omnium consortio venationibus operam dedit. Querebat in silvis cum luna in nocte feras & cum suo frigore concupiscentias venereas expellebat. His[8] igitur ab ea observatis hanc veteres lunam esse credidere & secum lunam iniunxere & circum circa arcum sagittasque a latere posuere & nemorum deam vocavere & circumcirca nymphas locavere[9] tamque ipsorum[10] deam scilicet Oreades,[11] Driades, Naiades, & Nereides quae inter Grecos hodie venerantur & affirmant quamlibet exercere officium suum. Luna ergo mater est humoris habet[12] in silvis in montibus in mari in fontibus humorem multiplicare & in agris herbas & semina procreare. Hec etiam[13] proserpina dicta est.[14] Similiter & appollo diversis nominibus secundum sibi diversas attributas potentias nominatur. Quandoque[15] sol phebus titan & a loco ut delius. Duo igitur numina haec huic insulae[16] mobili tunc erranti. diana per noctem id est luna prius nata est & postea natus appollo id est dies qui solem alluminatur.[17] Delos grece manifestum latine quia post diluvium apparuit in nocte vaporibus lune estuantibus.[18] Postea in die sequenti radiis solaribus ea monstrantibus apparuit manifeste & ideo delos id est manifestatio. cum primo ortigia vocaretur a multitudine perdicum ibi coadunantium Ortix[19] grece

1. Names from Pliny IV.66; Solinus XI.19.
2. Dd + S add: Iunonen, quae cum ex eo gravidam cognovisset, ad eam persequendam fitonem misisse,
3. S: applicans
4. S adds: Apollinem et Dianam uno partu
5. Dd: invocatur
6. Dd: veterem
7. Dd + S: quidam
8. Dd: hic
9. Dd + S: collocaverunt
10. S: ipsarum
11. Dd: Choriades
12. Dd: habitat
13. Dd + S: enim
14. B, 37-39
15. Dd: quinque
16. S adds: tunc
17. Dd + S: per solem illuminatur
18. Dd: extuante; S: aestuante
19. Dd: Ornos

//18v// perdix latine. Cynthius mons ibi est[1] in quo diana nata est & ideo aliquando cyntia dicta est.[2] postea dictus appollo a filio vulcani & minerve qui primus[3] decrescit eo tempore & hora nili fluminis quod mirum est. In hac itaque appollo colebatur in qua de longinquis partibus[4] dona ad eius templum ferebantur una cum virginibus circumstantium regionum. Cumque enim tarquini avunculi bruti rome regnans[5] filii ad hanc insulam appollinis de more sacrificaturi muneribus perexissent. Ipsisque sacrificantibus brutus qui cum eis[6] istrionis accesserat iocabundus scipionem quo aurum ascenderat[7] palam enim venerari numen timebat[8] ipsi deo donasset eis, oraculum interrogantibus. Quisnam post tarquinum regnaturus esset rome? respondit oraculum qui ex eis primum[9] matrem obscularetur. Quo audito brutus quasi casu advolutus in terram eam osculatus est. unde postea[10] Tarquini filiorum & consulatus consequutus est. Ostendit ipsum brutum appollinem de terra comuni omnium matre intellexisse. Brutus enim[11] fugato Tarquino primus consul factus est. Sunt autem insule he due contigue quarum minor delos est. in circuitu IIII millia altera decem. & de trione ad meridiem elongantur ambo. Igitur in delo prope olim templum vestutum in plano preparato[12] columnarum idolum vidimus[13] quod in tanta magnitudine iacet quod nullo modo nos quod[14] mille[15] fuimus, erigere potuimus argumentis rudentum galearum.[16] Sed ad suum pristinum dimisimus locum. In super hinc inde plusquam mille idolorum omni[17] magisterio laudabili videntur prosternata.[18] Altera denique humilibus montibus cultivata erat & per eam habitationes infinite parabantur quarum porte fenestreque versus templum prospectabant. Quorum in medio turris erigitur in qua post desolationem templi cerimoniarumque idolarum coloni recreabant. Virgilius.

1. Dd + S add: quia
2. Dd: dicitur; S: erat
3. Line here in ms, indicating omission? Dd + S add: inventor fuit medicine. In pede etiam montis huius fons est, quae crescit. Also missing in Ms C, Sinner, 189 n.
4. Dd: pertibus
5. Dd + S: regnantis
6. Dd adds: more
7. Dd: ascederat
8. Dd: cernebat
9. Dd: primo
10. Dd + S add: expulsio
11. S: nempe
12. Dd + S: preparatum
13. S: videmus
14. S: qui
15. Dd: quimde
16. Dd adds: ingenio
17. S: omnium
18. Dd: prostrata

Huc feror, hec fessos tuto placidissima[1] portu
Accipit & gressi[2] veneramur appollinis urbem…
Templa dei saxo venerabar structa vetusto.[3]

.35. DELOS OLIM NUNC SDILLOS. Ambitus istis minoris insule m. p. 4. Maior autem in circuitu m. p. 10. .36. Et ambe hec Sdille, nunc diruntur. [Map: North. *Two islands. On west (left):* templum apollinis,* Cintius mons* *and fallen columns. A single tower on the eastern island.*]

//19r// Est ad occasum suda hodie dicta. XL millia in circuitu, quae olim iaro vel ghero[4] latine senex vel sanus interpretatur. In hoc itaque scopulo dux quidam Calaber Sidim dictus pervenit unde[5] magna grecia & civitate Scillaea:[6] qui a manibus suorum aufugerat inimicorum & peractus nimia tempestate iam fessi naute propter obitum eo tempore regis insule[7] in coniugem reginam accepit. Postquam funus sui viri laute[8] eo in loco finierat. Igitur cum iam diu sine prole regnaret, filiam procreavit[9] quam Sudam denominavit a qua insula nomen accepit. Nunc vero ad comparationem preteritorum[10] temporum nihil reputatur quia ordeaceo pane currubis[11] & egharum carnibus vescuntur maximo pirratarum timore. Ergo eorum vita in ansietate ponitur. Quamvis propter prolem & affinitatem & intrinsecum amorem patrie contentur[12] in loco. Est etiam[13] ut videtur ad trionem Capraram[14] scopulus in quo ut aiunt spiritus pervagantur immundi: & dum naves prope transeunt vel in nocte casu morantur tantus strepitus & mugitus[15] vocum erigitur quod celum terraque ruere videtur & vocantes nomina illorum venientium altis vocibus convalescunt.[16]

Virgilius: Errantem michoe celsa giaroque revinxit.[17]

1. S: placidissima
2. Virgil: egressi
3. *Aeneid* III.78–79 and 84.
4. S: Geros
5. S: dum de
6. Dd: Silicea recedat.; S: Scyllacea recedebat.
7. S: Sidim
8. Dd: vel ante
9. Dd: procitavit
10. Dd: predictorum
11. Dd omits; S: carribus (carob)
12. Dd + S: contentantur
13. Dd + S: et enim
14. S: Capraria
15. S: rugitus
16. Dd: cumvalescunt
17. "Wandering (Delos) he joined to Mikonos and lofty Gyaros." *Aeneid* III.76.

.37. SUDA INSULA. Ambitus totius insule m. p. 40. [Map: North. Suda *with a fortified city. To the north is an island:* Caprara.]

Sequitur Paros albissima[1] valde & ex Cicladibus una quae olim Platea ab amplitudine dicta. Deinde Minoa[2] a civitate regis minois edificata multorum edificiorum. Sed Pareante[3] pluti filius quem ibidem & oppidum construxisse aiunt, insulam & oppidum paron a suo nomine nominavit & gignit adeo marmorem candidissimum ut a longe

//19v// videntibus[4] nix[5] existimaretur.[6] & maxime Carpesus Mons sublimior aliis cum scartuginibus[7] aquarum & fluminibus[8] exundatione. Quae LII[9] circuit millaria. Ad occiduum minoa[10] urbs erat coram delphica insula in qua columnarum edifica superant prata[11] cum templo marmoreo immaculato. In super ad radices[12] eiusdem montis oppidum vetustissimum erigitur inmanium structum lapidum. Ad trionem vero civibus paucis paron[13] castrum habetur cum molo atque parvo portu. Quo in loco fons est in quo si album lineum vel corium posueris niger[14] remanebit & ex eo molendina triturant. Coram autem naxos chefalum[15] oppidum in monte habetur cuius ascensus[16] tanta est difficultas[17] quod[18] celum tangere videtur. In quo quidem ex laborioso itinere macilente nimis & rigose[19] anus usque verticem convalescentes sarcinam sine sudore conducunt & ultra LIII[20] annum prolem concipiunt vitalem. Ad orientem portus pyratarum videtur & ibi campus per totum ostenditur[21] maximus. Sunt[22] igitur hec ex alio[23] circumstantes insule a turchis

1. S: insula
2. Dd: minica
3. Dd: parante
4. S: videntes
5. Dd + S: nivem
6. S: esse dicant
7. Dd: scaturigionibus
8. S: fluminum
9. Dd: quelii cerasula. Misreading for: que LII circuit mil.
10. Dd: minda
11. Dd: plata
12. Dd: radicem
13. Dd: parum
14. Dd: nigrum
15. Dd + S: chefalo
16. Dd: assensum; S: ascensu
17. Dd +S: facultas
18. Dd adds: in
19. Dd + S: rugose
20. Dd + S: quinquagessimum
21. Dd + S: extenditur
22. S: denique
23. Dd: denique hee et alie

oppresse nimis & in desolatione saepe redacte & ibi habitantes[1] continuum timorem habent[2] ne in servitutem redigantur.

.38. Paros. Ambitus totius insule m. p. 52. [Map: North. Paros★ *(city)*, fons. Minoa urbs★ *(ruins)*. Chephilo opidum in mare hoc altissimo. Chephilo★ opidum in hoc monte altissimo. Portus pirratarum.★ Carpesus mons.★ *Other buildings shown. All in text.*]

Breve spatium ab hinc antiparos est & quamvis inhabilis[3] sit ab aquilis falconibusque, non est derelicta. Quisve poterit quot folie[4] parantur in anno cum lapides eo tempore non videantur. tanta est congeries avium folerumque & praesertim aliquarum[5] quae dum in loco praedam conducit nisi magna fame arceatur sola non maducat.[6] Duos lapides pretiosos masculinum feminumque in nido suo colligit & reponit. Sine quibus ut ait plinius parere nequit & achaeos[7] ad custodiendum pullos suos a veneno & reptilium morsu reponit. Sed postquam a nido eos expulit praedari instruit. Quos cum viderit iam praedam capere in altum volans ab eorum tutela se subtrahit. & hiemali tempore modicam aviculam capit. Quam inter[8] pedes de nocte tenens propter calaefactionem ferigendo[9] non perimit sed orto sole illesa abire permittit.[10]

.39. Antiparos. Ambitus totius insule m. p. <...> [Map: no direction]

//20r// Inveni equidem ultra[11] antedictam insulam Panaiam quasi ex eadem asperitate & parve habitudinis. A pan grece latine totum & ya[12] sanitas:[13] erat autem in ea ecclesia sola nimis in qua ut imaginatur aliquis heremita residebat & pro suis necessariis ad insulam pari[14] cimba sua navigabat. Nunc certe magna multitudo avium omnibus habitat temporibus[15] & per saxa nuda diebus noctibus transeunt ululando.

1. Dd + S: habitatores
2. Dd + S: tenent
3. S: inhabitabiles
4. Dd: folee, translates as seabirds; from Greek, nests; S adds: per scopulum
5. Dd + S: aquilarum
6. Dd + S: manducat
7. Dd + S: Achates
8. Dd: intus
9. Dd + S: stringendo
10. Dd: praemittit
11. S: ultimam
12. Dd: aia
13. Dd + S add: quasi tota sanitas
14. S: Paros
15. Dd: pro suis temporibus

.40. Panaia Scopolus. Hec insula olim heremitorium nunc deserta est scilicet aquilis et falconibus habitata. [Map: n.d. *Shows church and a tower, high cliffs.*]

Tuta[1] inter cicladarum insulas Naxos habetur cum LXXX millia in circuitu.[2] Plinius igitur primus strongilem grece latine rotundam eam nominat.[3] Ovidus dynisiam[4] a fertilitate vinearum. Alli Siciliam minorem ab abundantia[5] rerum frugumque; quae est principalior insularum istarum. in qua petra nigerrima & durissima dicta smerigdo[6] reperitur. Coram itaque civitate in scopulo fuit olim oppidum Strongile dictum, a quo seculis multis insula sumpsit nomen. quo coram campus iuxta mare vinearum ampliatur magnus;[7] ideo Bacho dedicata fuit. Qui sculptus prope oppidum puer facie muliebri nudo pectore[8] capite cornuto vitibus coronato & in tigribus[9] equitando. Puer quia hebrius tamquam puer sine ratione gubernatur. Muliebrem faciem quia in concupiscentia mulierum per vinum in hebriis generatur. Tigrides quia furibundi. Nudus propter veritatem. Cornutus propter auctoritatem.[10]

Sunt etiam in ea vespes quod si aliquem transfixerint morte morietur. Theseus etiam filius egei regis missus cretam ut occideretur a minotauro ipsum interemit & athenas a turpi servitio liberavit. Ariadnemque & Fedram Minois filias patri surripuit & apud fontem propinquum civitati dum dormiret, Adrianam non merito dereliquit & phedram sibi coniugio copulavit. & quia in multis epistolis legi Theseum in hanc adrianam reliquisse[11] insulam. Deo[12] potius hic hanc pono historiam cum intersit[13] rectius[14] navigationi athenarum quam Chios salva tamen auctoritate Nasonis qui ponit in Chio[15] hoc fuisse factum. Post autem recessum Thesei bachus totius huic insule dux, comprehendens astutiam & iniquam defectionem[16] tanti iuvenis misericordia motus puellam reconciliavit[17] & cognoscens ipsam esse filiam regis cretensium & pasiphe in uxorem accepit & vulcanus ei coronam gemmis splendentibus donavit quam inter sydera collocavit. Etiam cum in hac insula iuppiter

1. Dd: Multa
2. Pliny IV.68. He gives the circumference as 75 miles.
3. S: vocat
4. Dd: Dionisiam
5. Dd: ab abundatione
6. Dd: xmerigio; S: smeriglo
7. Dd: magno
8. Dd: tectore
9. Dd: coronante et equitante
10. B, p. 57.
11. Dd: relinquisse
12. Dd + S: ideo
13. S: iter sit potius vel
14. Dd: comuniter cum iter sit sic rectus
15. Dd: Iovis
16. Dd + S: deceptionem
17. S: circumciliavit

adversus titanos proficisceretur. & in litore sacrificium faceret, aquila in auspitium[1] eius[2] ad volavit quam victor bono omine acceptam sue tutele[3] subiugavit &[4] tempore belli Troianorum[5] Peleus hic dominabatur. Erat enim tunc temporis habitata nimis & tanta multitudo virorum mulierumque extiterat quod nihil in ea incultum videbatur. Nunc autem per ipsam bubunes[6] ululare

//20v// non desistunt[7] & animalia indomita campis vallisque habentur ubique[8] cum coturnicibus una. Hic numerum magnum repperi mulierum quae copula virorum carentes usque ad decrepitam etatem in virginitate resedunt[9] non zelo constantie merite sed ex defectu hominum finem complent virginalem. Vena auri in aliquibus invenitur partibus quam domini defectu artificum[10] intactam dimittunt. Cunque[11] ad occiduum veteri[12] templum magnificum erigebatur in quo statua appollinis consistebat. Ibique prope salinarum panditur locus & turris diruta conterminatur. Infra denique montes vallis fertilissima est, Darmille dicta, cuius in circuitu aperato[13] oppidum erigitur. & monasterium atque castellum austri[14] una in altum[15] dimittemus & per vallem fructiferam usque viridarium flumine parvo[16] ad arenosum descendimus planum qui ad montem Stellidam conterminatur.

Iamque per egeos ibat Laertia fluctus
Puppis & innumere commutant ciclades auras
Iam paros olereasque latent iam raditur alta
Lemnos & a tergo decrescit bachia naxos
Ante oculos crescente Samo iam Delos opacat
Equor &...[17]

.41. NAXOS OLIM NUNC NIXA. Insulae totius ambitur m. p. 80. [Map: East. Mons altissimus, smirigdi lapis,* Monasterium,* Aperato,* vallis et campus fertilis in arboris,* castel austro, *

1. Dd: hospitium; S: auspicium
2. S: ei
3. Dd: tulelle
4. Dd adds: eo
5. S: Troiani
6. Dd + S: bubones
7. Dd: desinunt
8. Dd: usque
9. Dd: residunt; S: resident
10. Dd: ob defectu artificis; S: defectum artificis
11. S: cumque
12. Dd: veteris; S: verteris
13. Dd: a pirrato
14. Dd: humstri.
15. Dd: alterum
16. Dd: fluca iuneparvo
17. Statius, *Achilleid* 1B, ll. 675-80; Dd: many variations here

fons ubi Teseus relinquit Adriana,★[1] campus arenosis plenus vinearum; burgies *(scattered houses)*, saline, Naxos★ *(walled city)*, Mons Stellida★ *(west)*, Strongilo★ *(on island). River:* Anzarus flum.]

//21r// Erant olim ut dicitur he ambe habitate & podia dicte: podia enim grece, latine pedes, quia ad figuram pedum demonstrantur.maior harum habitabilis erat cum munito olim castello. Nunc autem ad[2] barbarorum insidias hanc colentes naxon accessere. Prima VI,[3] secunda IIII millia circuunt.[4]

.42. PODIA PRIMA in circuitu m. p. 6.

.43. PODIA SECUND[A] habet in circuitu m. p. 4. [Map: n.d. *Two islands, the upper with ruins.*]

Raclea & Chero due insule parve & montuose videntur & inculte nimis propter turchorum insidias quae olim ut aiunt erant habitate quia vestigia in aliquibus partibus percipitur.[5] In quibus multa egarum societas reperitur quae vagatur ubique & parve in circuitu consistunt.[6]

.44. RACLEA SIVE NICHEA.

.45. CHERO. [Map: n.d. 2 *islands with trees, no toponyms.*]

Nunc petimus portum fessi[7] insule Nio & dicitur latine[8] grece latine novum vel nios id est navalis quia[9] libenter in tempestate ruentes hunc portum affectuose appetere curavit.[10] XL circuit milliaria. Ad meridiem vero oppidum[11] sublime[12] positum est & vallis a longe parva cum fecundissimo campo aperitur in totum & in partes divisus a colentibus seminatur. In sero ergo postquam ad occasum perventum erit in munitissimum[13] magno labore descendunt[14] castellum, mane autem facto vetulas ad speculandum per insulam ante auroram mittunt & dato ab eis signo porte panduntur in totum & sic vitam transeunt in[15] tremore. Tempore denique meo dum navis pyrratarum in portu carinam prepararet[16] nutu divino aqua maris eam absorbuit que nusquam visa est.[17]

1. Dd: fons in quo relicta fuit Adriana
2. Dd + S: ob
3. Dd: XVI
4. Dd + S: in circuitu remansere
5. S: percipiuntur
6. Dd adds: una octo, et alia sex in circuunt milliaria.
7. Dd: fossi
8. Dd + S: nio
9. Dd: quae
10. S: curant
11. S adds: in
12. Dd: sublimissime
13. Dd: -e
14. Dd + S: ascendunt
15. Dd + S: cum
16. Dd: -ent
17. Dd + S: fuit

//21v//.46. NIO OLIM ET NUNC. Ambitus totius insule m. p. 40. [Map: North. Nio. *Shows fortified castle in center, small church on shore.*]

Rursus[1] trionem anaphios insurgit insula ab ana grece, latine sine & fios serpens, id est sine serpente quia ibi serpentes non reperiuntur; & si certe illuc portarentur subito morerentur[2] & quod plus est ferre[3] tecum de terra huius in[4] circulum illius prepara serpenti de subito moritur. Erat enim olim civitas in capite insule munitissima nimis. Eapropter pyrrate iuxta ripam eius tute naves collocabant. Cunque per tempora hunc exercererit[5] modum cotermini[6] proceres annis plurimis ad hanc desolandum urbem devenere &, facto fine destructionis, castellum in medio insule usque in hodiernum ordinavere diem.

.47. ANAPHIOS. Insulae totius ambitus m. p. 5. [Map: North. Anaphios. *Castle in center, ruins on coast, no names.*]

//22r// Non nulli olim subort[7] hanc denominaverunt[8] insulam & cultivata[9] satis LXXX millia circuit in montibus tota. Quae nunc amurgospolis dicta est. in qua tria oppida: Amurgo, Ialli, & Plati.[10] Ad trionem vero tres portus[11] videntur. Sancta Anna, Calos & Catapla.[12] Ad occiduum montes non ita elevantur velut orientales & ideo[13] Catomerea dicitur quod latine pars inferior sonat. & ad orientem Apanomerea pars superior declaratur. Ad meridiem denique rupes eriguntur terribiles & navibus minacissime.[14] Quia venti percutientes in mare in ripis redundant & sic scylla carybdisque, ita tumescentes[15] quod naves in naufragio[16] saepe pereunt. & ita mirantes viam a longe capiunt & submersiones[17] galee ibi venetorum recordantur.

1. Dd + S: versus
2. S: morirentur
3. Dd + S: fer
4. Dd + S: et
5. Dd + S: exercerent
6. Dd: cumtermini; S: contermini
7. Dd + S: Buport
8. S: nominaverunt
9. Dd: culturata; S: cultiva
10. S inserts: existunt
11. S: porti
12. Modern: Katapola.
13. Dd: idcirco
14. Dd: minantur
15. Dd: cumtumescentes
16. S: naufragium
17. Dd + S: subversionis

.48. AMURGO SIVE AMURGOSPOLIS. Insulae totius ambitus m. p. 80. [Map: North. *To the west:* Catomerea.★ *On the north coast the church of* Santa Anna★. *In center the walled city of* Amurgo★. *To the east:* Apomerea.★ *On the south coast:* monasterium in spelunca.]

Convicinee due sunt insule scilicet Chinera & Levata. In quibus aiunt[1] non habitavere patres, nunc aiunt pervente ad solitudinem inculte remanent propter insidias malorum hominum & saepe a circumstantibus animalia resolute patescent cum asinis agrestibus una.

.49. CHINERA. [Map: North. *Fallen columns (ruins)*]

.50. LEVATA. [Map: North. *Fallen columns (ruins)*]

Monstrabimus nunc Caloierum Scopulum altissimum in medio maris positum ubi Coa[2] insula ad austrum terminatur. & circumspectum[3] in altissimis ripis propter suam eminentiam omnibus convicineis insulis minatur. In quo cacumine ecclesia cum plano paratur. & eo in loco duo caloieri adorabant secure & naviculam rudente parato una[4] ascenderant ut a saevis pyrratis possent eam custodire. & precibus devotis horisque constitutis sine timore die ac nocte valeant exercere & offerre libamina sacrificiaque inmaculta. Cunque diu misterium[5] tale peregissent

//22v// ecce turchus[6] indutus[7] vestibus similibus ipsorum & ait solus in navicula maculata vocibus altis: Viri religiosi amore christi suscipite me miserum quia istis in scopulis dira tempestas navim[8] nostrorum[9] grecorum impegit salo. & nemo nisi ego solus evasit. Illi misericordia moti per funem ascensum hospitem[10] sinonem in altum acceptaverunt. In nocte[11] vero dum[12] intra ecclesiam adorabant porta[13] ab extra proditor firmavit & vocatis sociis absconsis iuxta scopulum servos christi ac superlectiles[14] ipsorum in Turchiam deportavere.

1. S: autem
2. Dd: Cocha, S: Choa
3. Dd: circumsceptum; S: circumseptum
4. Dd: in alto; S: in altum
5. S: ministerium
6. Dd: esse Teucrus; S adds: in nocte
7. Dd: inductus
8. Dd + S: navem
9. Dd: navem nostram; S: navem
10. Dd adds: in
11. S: monte
12. Dd: mora
13. Dd + S: portam
14. Dd + S: supellectiles

.51. SCOPOLUS CALORIORUM. [Map: n.d. *Island with steep cliffs, church on top and pulley with boat suspended.*]

Iamque ad insulam devenimus Choam, quae latine luctus interpretatur quia propter aeris intemperiem[1] pluribus mensibus anni lugetur atque languetur in ea.[2] provincie actice[3] adiacens suburbana dicta est. De oriente ad occiduum XL millia & plana quasi per totum extat. Ad meridiem vero montes cernimus[4] sublimes. in quibus oppida erant Petra, Chevia,[5] atque Pili quod hodie Peripaton dicunt. In superficie vero altioris montis Ditheus dictus munitissimum extiterat castrum. In quo hodie cisterne apparent quam plurime. Cunque ad radices[6] descendimus huius fontem Fandion reperimus. A quo Sfandanus fluvius derivatur. Qui prope Cillippum oppidum olim prorumpit in mare ad trionem. In medio autem vastissimorum camporum duo soli monticuli eriguntur. A quibus fons olim nobilissimis Licastis hodie apodomarius emanat iuxta olim castri oppidum & moldendina vivariaque[7] marmorea manifestant. In quibus tanta est amenitas loci tantus[8] diversorum avium quod non solum terrenis sed etiam diis immortalibus placitum[9] fore[10] dicatur.[11] Ad orientem in littore arangea metropolis est, cuius in medio lacus ampliatur in estate corruptus & ab extra meniorum arangea multa virescunt. & ideo arangea dicta.[12] In qua tot & tanta edificia marmorea & theatra repperi quod est mirabile ad videndum. Extra vero castrum iuxta lacum ad trionem ampla domorum edificia ypocratis eximii medici cum fonte visa sunt propinquo & palude Lambi dicta quae in hieme ampliatur & crescit. In estate vero desiccatur. Fuit igitur iste ypocrates filius Sclepionis & discipulus esculapi phisici secundi & fuit de genere Esculapii primi a quo incepit ars medicine quam ostendit[13] & docuit filiis suis mandans eis quod medicinam extraneis inmo patres ostenderetis[14] vestris filiis ut artis nobilitas semper fixa maneret in eis. & precepit quod in medio habitationis insularum cycladum manerent

1. Dd: ineptem; S: Acrem ineptem
2. Dd adds: quae
3. Dd: antice; S: acticae
4. Dd: ex minus
5. Dd: Chema; S: Chenia
6. S: radicem
7. Dd: vinaria; S: invariaque
8. Dd + S, p. 102: cantus
9. S: placidam
10. S: esse
11. Dd omits: dicatur
12. S: est
13. Dd: ondit
14. Dd: medicinam enim ondens etiam prius medicinam filiis quam extraneis; lacks: inmo...vestris; S: like MN

//23r// propter aeris temperiem[1] vel in montibus Choe considerent in estate. Duxit[2] igitur[3] perfectam apud grecos medicinam. Ipsa enim medicina ut ait Macrobius & Ysidorus ante ypocratem siluerat per quingentos annos a tempore appollinis & ascelepii qui fuerunt[4] inventores & procedendo nunc ad medium insule parvi monticuli videntur inceptare & sic altior ista planities est illius antedicte arangee. Postquam ad meridiem ad Antimacum[5] oppidum cursum[6] habemus usque in fine insule ubi chephalo[7] paratur in altum. Non diu est quod serpens maximus apparuit devorans armenta & territi omnes fugam arripiebant. Tunc vir strenuus pro salute populi duellum inceptat dum inter bestias ruere vellet. Quod cum serpens hoc percepisset[8] equum morsibus illico[9] prostratum[10] occidit. Iuvenis autem acriter pugnans tandem viperam interfecit. Dicitur etiam & affirmatur quod filia ypocratis per insulam viva apparet. Qua loquente tecum[11] & narrante multa infortunium suum infelicem commemorat[12] rogabatque saepe creatorem ut a tanta pena eam dignaretur liberare, & cum plura[13] loqueretur non longe a paternis domibus lamentabilibus vocibus in sex vel in octo annis semel contigisse transformationem hanc ut a multis civibus comprobatur.

Refert etiam Plinius quod Aristeus filius appollinis consilio matris relictis thebis huc venit & in hanc habitavit insulam & subiugavit eam. Fuit enim, ut aiunt, mulieres hic viros occidisse propter eorum inconstantiam: quia semper in proeliis per asiam minorem accedentes curam insule mulieribus dimictebant. Illae equaliter indignate ad innorme[14] suorum virorum pervenere homicidium. Deinde Jason per hanc transiens ad Colcon hodie Curchum[15] accessit coram civitate posita & constructa multis edificiis.[16] Quae usque hodie in armenia minori coram cipro videtur. Est denique hec omnium abundantissima & primo in feminarum ornamento lanificii hic artem inventam affirmant. In super & nativitas memorabilis Philidis poete hic fuit qui imitatus Saphon[17] poetissam rem[18] Bachidis

1. S: in temperiem
2. Dd: duxere; S: dixit
3. S: ergo
4. Dd + S add: primi eius
5. Modern: Andimakhia
6. Dd: circumssum
7. Dd: phefallo
8. Dd: perciperet
9. Dd + S add: terram
10. Dd + S add: in terram
11. Dd: totum diu
12. Dd + S: connumerat
13. Dd: puela
14. S: enorme
15. Dd: circum; S: Turchum
16. S: multarum aedificarum
17. S: Sapphonem
18. Dd adds: in; S like MN

decantavit. Ibique infra ripas altisissimas avis duo ova peperit ex[1] quibus ex uno avis ex altero canis nascitur. & percipiens mater non esse cani similis[2] illico eum occidit & fratri prebet in cibum: & quia insula hec contigua asie minori ibi[3] magne insurgebant civitates fratres Sancti Johannis ut resisterent[4] infidelibus castellum Sancti Petri hedificavere MCCCC.

//23v// .52. CHOA NUNC OLIM LANGO. Ab oriente usque meridiem longitudo m. p. 40. [Map: North. Full page. *On north coast of Asia:* Turchia★ (3x), Continens Minor Asia,★ Continens (2x), Castellum S. Petri.★ *On island:* Palus Lambi,★ S. Foca *(church)*, Arangea,★ fons et domus ypocrates,★ fons farno,★ dictenus mons, Chilippus★ *(ruins)*, Ffandanus flu.★, Peripaton,★ Apodomaris flu,★ castri olim, Andrimachi,★ Chefalo★.]

//f. 24r// Supereminet in montibus valde claros olim insula que hodie calamos dicta est.[5] Calami enim grece latine arundo interpretatur. Quae tendens de[6] trione ad meridiem XL millia circuit. & tanta est montium sublimitas quod si quis in altiori ascenderet cacumine[7] usque chion insulam vel Ephesum urbem vel Palatiam[8] civitatem turchorum certe visum[9] perciperet clarum tunc cum sol inclinat ad occasum. In istis equidem montibus per omnes saltus lanigerie[10] pecudes tondetes odoriferas herbas incolumes accedunt sine luporum timore & flave eghe devastantes arbores in sumitate petrarum patrizare[11] delectant. Ab oriente vero oppidum ab alto vetustum quo in conspectu insula parva elongatur: quae olim illustrissima usque nunc[12] fuisse videtur & quis possit in ea tot explicare numerum antiquitatum & indicare liniamenta marmorum sparsa per totum cum nil in ea aliud percipere valeam.[13] Igitur in sinu quodam oppidum calamos erigitur munitum & ad occiduum in sinu prope flumen salsum vathi olim ampliabatur civitas in qua edificia plura videmus & veniens ad occiduum meridiemque in radice montis vel promontorii portus[14] duo videntur optimi a quibus magna speluncha habetur. & in ea facundissimus[15] non desinit fons emanare & ubique lignum aloe crescit & salutiferum ab omnibus habetur partibus.

1. Dd + S: a
2. S: similem
3. Dd + S: ubi
4. Dd + S: insisterent
5. Dd: dicitur
6. Dd: ad
7. Dd: cacumen
8. S: Palatscha
9. Dd: vissum
10. Dd: languere
11. Reading: pasturizare; S suggests caprizare
12. Dd + S add: edificiorum
13. Dd: valeamus
14. Dd: porti
15. Dd + S: fecundissimus

.53. CALAMOS HODIE OLIM CLAROS DICEBATUR. Ambitus totius insulae m. p. 10. [Map: North. *Fortified city:* Calamos.★ *On east:* Paleo castro. Fons in speluncha.★ *Island to the south:* Capra.]

//24v// Iuxta hanc erro montuosa valde insula marmorea estat quae ad orientem castellum munitissimum habet ubi omnes coloni recreantur in nocte ut secure patescant & ad austrum Lepida portus erat ubi olim civitas eminebat in nocte[1] & planus in radicibus eius ampliatur[2] Si ad occiduum pergis ferado sinus[3] illico panditur. & oppidum Partini[4] dictum olim cernimus desolatum & sic per totum montuosa videtur[5] Quae XVIII millia circuit & ad omnia in suo gradu[6] ipsarum felicissimam[7] nominamus[8] in qua lignum aloe recolitur[9] & mercatoribus venditur in anno.

.54. HERROS OLIM ET NUNC. Insulae totius ambitus m. p. 18. [Map: North. *Fortified castle on northeast peninsula:* Herro.★ *On northwest:* Partini★ olim *(ruins). On southwest:* mons altissimus.★]

Tractavimus de Herro, nunc ad Patmos veniemus[10] in qua Ioannes xpi disciplus ad exilium tempore Domitiani imperatoris missus est. & in portu in angulo quoddam ipse die dominico raptis[11] in spiritu magna atque arcana de presentibus futurisque vidit contemplando & librum apocalipseum[12] scribens nobis multa revelavit. In eodem denique tempore mortuo domitiano in Ephesum hodie alto loco dictum Iohannes magnis honoribus receptus est. Qui dum Christi fidem miraculis magno[13] predicaret multi ex discipulis suis in hanc insulam accesserunt & monasterium non longe a suo oraculo construxuerent in quo quoddam[14] usque in hodiernum a caloieris habitatur. & a turchis nullam habentes molestiam saepe in Turchiam recurrunt ad substentationem vite. Quae montuosa cum humilibus collibus. In ea vene metallorum reperiuntur multe.

1. Dd: monte
2. Dd + S: ampliabatur
3. Dd: seraclo sinus
4. S: Pantini
5. Dd + S: dicitur
6. Dd + S: nisi cogradu
7. Dd + S: ipsam fertilissimam
8. Dd + S: reputamus
9. S: recolligitur
10. S: venimus
11. Dd + S: raptus
12. Dd: apocalipsis; S: Apocalypseos
13. Dd + S: magnis
14. Dd + S: quidem

.55. PATMOS. PATHMOS. Hic Sanctus Iohannes stetit in exilio tempore Domitiani Imperator[is]. [Map: North. Monasterium caloierum S. Johannis.* Hic S. Iohannes fecit apocalipsim.*]

//25r// Computavi de Patmos: nunc ad Dipsim parvam insulam[1] accedemus & igitur Dipsi grece sitis latine quia siccam est & viriditate caret.[2] Ideo Dipsi nominatur quia arida & montuosa & numquam[3] habitaverent patres in qua sinus ab oriente videtur & nunc ab egis asinisque habitate silvestribus apparet.

.56. DIPSI. [Map: North. *Ruined city in center.*]

Ab alia parte huius ad occiduum Crussie insula inter Icaream[4] Patmonque humilibus montibus circumsepta[5] est cuius in circuitu aliqui scopuli apparent & derelicta longo iam tempore ab omnibus[6] quia in medio oppidum desolatum manifeste fuisse videtur: nunc indomite bestie vagari[7] delectantur & dicitur Crussie[8] grece de aurate latine.

.57. CRUSIE. [Map: North. *With small islands to the south. No buildings or names.*]

Refert Varro quod in hac Icarea insula fuit Icarus Cretensis & ideo Icarea dicta creditur. Qui mox offensus fastu tyrranico[9] relicta domo patria[10] bruto consule qui reges urbe exegit, italiam advectus.[11] Est ergo montuosa valde et <blank space> circuit millia (LXXX[12]). Quae[13] de oriente ad occiduum in longitudine velut unius in mare revolute navis dorsum erigitur et in extremis de-

//25v//clinatur. Cumque naute Ephesiatici maris apicem huius insule coniunctam[14] nubibus videret,[15] illico portum procurare festinant quia signum tale ad detrimetum[16] navium transeuntium revertetur. Sunt & in ea[17] inter anfractus & immeabiles ripas apes suis cavernuculis[18] frequentates & ibi mel valde nutrientes. Hic etiam album[19] bachi liquorem

1. Dd: perva; omits: insulam
2. Dd: carescit; S: rarescit
3. Dd: nunc; S like MN
4. Dd: Achaream
5. S: circumsecta
6. Dd + S: hominibus
7. Dd: vagare
8. Dd: Acrussie; S: Crusiae
9. Dd: tirtanico
10. Dd: paterna; S adds: –que
11. Dd: ad victus
12. From Dd. Blank space also in S
13. S: Quo
14. S: iunctam
15. Dd + S: vident
16. Dd + S: detrimentum
17. S: hac
18. Dd: cavernulis
19. S: belli

illi accepto multiplicare faciunt & circumstantibus mittunt. In cuius[1] cacumine duo sunt oppida & ad orientem prope mare videtur in monte turris altissima quae fanari dicta erat. In qua lumen olim procellosis existebat temporibus ut transeuntes salvarentur quia per totam insulam non poteris portum invenire.

.58. HICAREA. Insulae totius ambitus m. p. 80. [Map: North. *Tower,* Fanari,★ *at southeast. Two other castles shown.*]

Dicitur insula hec Mandria quae prope erigitur Dipsi a scopulis circumdata & quamvis olim habitata fuerit.[2] Nunc ad solitudinem pervenit.[3] in qua asini voce sonora silvestres perambulant sine timore una cum egis infinitis.

.59. MANDRIA. Tota deserta. [Map: East. *No names.*]

Insule due parve & nude habitantium ad orientem insurgunt Aghatusa & Pharmacus[4] dicte que coram flumine palatie diu invente fuere: in quibus saepe saepius pyrrate turchorum[5] vagantur donec consulti quam possint[6] viam capere meliorem discedunt.[7] prima in circuitu milliaria XII. Secunda IIII a quibus ad os palatorum intratur & per flumen cito in[8] urbem perventum[9]

//26r// est. quae a palatiis olim magnificis nomen accepit. Ubi lacus in hieme maximus effectus est & tanta copia piscium anguillarumque reperitur[10] in eo quod[11] ubique transferuntur & biremes ab hinc per insulam[12] devastando saepe in manibus fratrum sancti Ioannis Venetorumque deveniunt & ab eis ad infimum deducuntur.

.60. PHARMACUS. Ambitus totius insule m. p. 4. [Map: North. *Shows two deserted islands.*]

.61. AGATUSA. Ambitus totius insulae m. p. 12. [Map: North.]

Non longe a supradictis[13] Samo invenitur insula parum a[14] continenti distans[15] quae tempore deorum gentilium existimabatur in cunctis sacrificiis sublimior: tunc cum societas maxima philosophorum regnabat in ea: quae circumdata altissimis montibus. LXXX milia circuit.

1. Dd + S: quo
2. Dd + S: exstiterit
3. Dd: perventa; S: est perventa
4. Dd: Formacus
5. Dd: Teucrorum
6. Dd: possent
7. Dd lacks: discedunt
8. Dd: citoni
9. S: deventum
10. Dd + S: reperiuntur
11. S: quae
12. S: insulas
13. S inserts: insulis
14. Dd: et
15. Dd lacks: distans

& longa de oriente ad occiduum. ex una atque altera parte portus aquis frigidissimis emanantibus reperimus. Ad meridiem vero in plano iuxta mare magnifica existebat[1] civitas & tanta ruina edificiorum colupnarumque cernitur quod per diem impossibile[2] foret ad narrandum & ibi[3] iunonis maximum amplissimis columpnis ereptum[4] ut dicitur fuisse quia effigies[5] eius prope sculpta erat. Regina cum sceptro & in capite nubes: Iris ex transverso: pavones in pedibus eius lambebant & ideo aves illius dicte. Iuno aer est & soror & uxor iovis, id est[6] ignis, uxor quia sub eo & ab eo calorem accipit & nutrit inferiora: soror quia prope eum est. Virgo quia de aere nihil exit & nihil nascitur. Iris & nimphas[7] quia in aere gignitur & fumi de mare ascendentes cum aere se immiscent[8] & sic neptunus nutritor Iovis, quia sibi alimentum aliquod subministrat.[9] De hac insula Pythagoras natus est, philosophus eximius,[10] qui babiloniam ad perdiscendum siderum motus originemque mundi spectandum profectus est. summa scientia consecutus est. Polycratus ut ait Valerius sevissimus tyrannus in hac fuit insula & fortunatus in omnibus suis factis ad manus orotis persarum[11] venit, qui dictum polycratum in monte maedalense altimissimo suspendit in[12] cruce.[13] In super hic orta sibilla quadam nomine Phemo ex decem una quae postea dicta est samia a loco. Hic etiam Paulus Emilius Romanus vicit regem persae[14] & filium philippi macedonem quo in proelio Xxti hostium milia interemit.[15] Hic etenim Turchi innumerabiles a Tamburlano fugati evaserunt. Aiunt denique quod in medio insulae locus fructificat pomorum & licitum est homini comedere ex eis volens vero[16] cum fructibus eiusdem loci ad socios remeare, a via re[17] deviabit.[18] Si nihil capiet[19] libere via patefacta erit. Igitur per insulam altissimi montes & arbores pomorum videntur quorum unus aote[20] alter medalens. Ad occiduum alii altiores apparent.

1. S: exstabat
2. Dd: possibile
3. Dd + S insert: templum
4. Dd + S: erectum
5. Dd: effigine
6. Dd: vel
7. S: nympha; C like MN
8. Dd + S: miscent
9. Dd: suum ministrat
10. S lacks: eximius
11. Dd: Oruntis; S: Orontis Psaram
12. S adds: in ligno vel
13. Dd: crine
14. Dd: Persem; S: Persim
15. S: intererat; C like MN
16. Dd: ergo
17. Dd + S omit: re
18. S: demeabit
19. Dd: caput; S: portabit
20. Dd: acethe; S: Acte

.62. SAMO OLIM ET NUNC. Insulae totius ambitus m. p. 80. [Map: North. Mons altissimus *(2x)*. Maxima.* Hic fuit civitas. Aote.* Aote mons.* Hoc Veneti fecerunt et propter feras habitare non potuerunt. Medalensi mons.*]

Ad occiduum prope supradictam deserte insulae furni dicuntur: quae nusquam habitate fuere & aride nimis riparum immeabilium circumdate. In quibus saepe naves recursum capiunt. & tute a ventis sine rifrigerio[1] aquarum dulcium magno timore turchorum[2] pyrratarum vigilando pernoctant quarum prima duo, secunda III, tertia X, quartaque quinta quattuor circuit millia. In maiori itaque harum[3] cum e[4] partibus rhodi & versus Chium iter facerem[5] nocte obscurissima nimbosaque nimis demisso carbaso & in portu[6] intrare credentes in scopulis iuxta promontoria ruimus.[7] Heu cecidere manus quia a ripis navem nullo modo separare poteramus:[8] cumque hoc cerneremus in terram descendimus omnes & sic per nimbosam illam pertransivimus[9] noctem, donec ad lucem pervenit dies. Adveniente autem aurora, nusquam vidimus navem quia iam in imum submerserat tota. Sed postquam ad hanc quintum sextumque diem sine phebo vitam transivimus[10] ad aquam quae fuerat[11] in cavernosis lapidibus, saepe perveneramus ubi[12] aliqui nostrum[13] animam deo reddidere. Cumque ad septimum veniret[14] diem & substatiam[15] iam herbarum non invenirem[16] ad vescendum in spileum[17] declinavi, gladioque in petra nomen sculpsi meum. "Hic dira fame presbiter[18] Cristoforus mortuus est." Hoc autem facto socii convolescentes[19] navem convocant transeuntem, quae fuit causa nostre salutis.

1. Dd + S: refrigerio
2. Dd: Teucrorum
3. S: earum
4. Dd: ex; S: a
5. Dd: faceret
6. S: portum
7. Dd: irruimus
8. S: potuimus
9. Dd + S: transivimus
10. Dd + S: trasieramus; C like MN
11. Dd: fumat; S: fuit
12. Dd: unde
13. S: nostrorum
14. S: veniremus
15. Dd + S: substantiam
16. S: inveniremus
17. Dd: speleo; Gk: cave
18. Dd: pre; S omits
19. Dd + S: convalescentes

//27r// .63. FURNIO DICUNTUR. [Map: North. *Shows five islands, each with its circumference marked on it: 2, 4, 10, 3, and 4 miles.*]

Linquimus tum portus desolatasque insulas & ad undas tenose ingressum petimus laeti: ubi cum in ea venimus magno labore antiquitatis[1] inter vepres anfractusque reperimus. In quibus quidem propter nimiam fluctuationem ventorum in nocte luctantium tamquam scintille lapilli corruscant in altum & suavissime voces ventorum interim infra arbusculos in auribus audientium percipiuntur valde. Quae montuosa X millia circuit.

.64. TENOSA. Ambitus totius insulae m.p. 10. [Map: n.d. *Shows ruins.*]

Iuxta Chium ad occiduum Psara[2] dicitur & piscator latine interpretatur. Quo in spatio XII millia opidum insurgebat. & cum ad desolationem deveniret & domestica quamvis[3] plura dimitterent[4] indomita sunt effecta. Coram itaque hac scopuli parantur & sic nipsorum[5] medio portus exstat: in quo biremis Turcorum semel pervenit. Quae &[6] secure propter insidias christianorum in nocte[7] ad aliam secrete partem[8] accessit insule & dum pernoctaret illico boreas emissam[9] ab antro navem submergit in imum. Turchi vero perterriti per insulam ambulantes[10] asinos egasque una silvestres cito capiunt & carnes illarum edentes bestiarum coria plena venti ordinavere ubi ad numerum[11] pervenerunt optatum lignis circumpositis super navigium tale consedere & versus Turchiam prope[12] innumero XL non desistunt navigare. Cum itaque per triduum tandem prope Traciam studiosius devenientes navicula sex hominum eos invasit & eos ad unum occidit.[13]

//27v// .65. PSARA. Insule totius Ambitus m.p. 12. [Map: North. *Ruins in center, no names.*]

Insulam Chion post hanc visitamus quam Plinius Scirosior[14] & Assanso nominavit. deinde Chios dicta est quia[15] lingua sirica mastix latine interpretatur. in egeo sita mari prope minorem asiam XVII[16] millia passuum[17] & centum XXti IIIIor in circuitu eam numeravimus.

1. Dd + S: antiquitates
2. S: greco
3. Dd: quia; S: quam
4. S omits
5. Dd + S: in ipsorum
6. Dd + S: ut
7. Dd + S add: maneret
8. Dd + S add: huius
9. Dd: emissa; S: emissus
10. S: perambulantes
11. Dd: nostrum
12. S: propere
13. Dd + S: ad tartara mandavere; C like MN
14. Dd: Sirosior; S: Syrisior
15. S: quod
16. Dd + S: quattuor. Correct number is five miles.
17. Dd + S: millibus passibus

Dicitur etiam Chios Grece latine Pregnans[1] vel Chion columpna vel Chion canis. In qua Ysiphiles[2] Thoantis filia patrem transmit[3] fingens lemniadibus[4] ipsum occidisse. In hac[5] etiam insula ut ait Ovidius[6] postquam Theseus occidit Minotaurum & aufugiens de Creta & secum deferens duas filas Minois regis, Adrianam non merito dimisit & Phedram sibi coniugio copulavit.

> Protinus egides rapta Minoide Chion[7] vela dedit comitemque suam crudelis in illo litore destituit. Deserte & multa querenti amplexus & opem liber tulit utque Perini[8] sidere clara foret suptam[9] de fronte coronam. inmisit celo: tenus[10] volat illa per auras.

Quae longa de trione ad meridiem in duabus dividitur[11] partibus, harum[12] prima quae ad trionem spectat,[13] apanomerea grece dicitur & latine pars suprema interpretatur. Secunda catomerea grece latine pars infima declaratur. Prima quarum in montibus asperis elevatur[14] et ab arboribus pinorum platanorumque fulcita est. Quibus fontes emanantes[15] per umbrosas valles flumina frigidissima in mare decurrentia moledina triturant.[16] Hinc inde igitur castra opidaque in collibus & planis plura cernuntur. Si[17] volisso cum plano optimo Perparea.[18] Sancta Helena, Menedato,[19] Vicco,[20] Picio[21] & Cardamile cernuntur[22] omnia circum[23] cum Sancto Angelo, Elyaque[24] & olim opidum cum rure homeri dictum enumerantur[25] in parte superiori. Quo in oppido diruto sepulchrum vatis homeri ob nimiam antiquitatem

1. Dd lacks: latine pregnans
2. Dd: Isiffiles; S: Hisifile
3. Dd + S: transmisit
4. Dd: lempniadibus
5. Dd: hanc
6. Ovid, *Metamorphoses* VIII.174–79.
7. Ovid: Diam
8. Dd: Perumi; S: perenni
9. Dd + S: sumptam
10. Ovid + Dd + S: tenues
11. Dd: panditur
12. Dd: hec
13. S: expectat
14. Dd + S: elevata
15. Dd: manantes
16. Dd: trituerant
17. Dd + S: scilicet
18. Dd: proparea; S: Perperea
19. Dd: menaleo; S: Melenato
20. S: Vicho
21. Dd: Pathio; S: Pithio
22. S: cernunt; C like MN
23. Dd adds: Voliso
24. Dd: Elia; S: Helia
25. S: enumerant; C like MN

invenitur deletum sed[1] aliquo autore numquam narratum repperi quid de eo certum sit. Ideo posteris ad inquirendum dimittamus. Ad trionem & fons Nao[2] uberrimus extat ubi promontoria minacissima elevantur in celum & non ab ea parum portus cardamile cum plano flumineque habetur optimus. Deinde ad delphinum alterum cum turre[3] ex[4] flumine optamus pervenire portum. A quo civitas chii paucis millia[5] cum portu tutissimo a ianuensibus sublimatur. Quae olim p[6] super montem expugnabilem diu tutissima viguit. Quo in pede coronatam heremitarum laudamus recte locum. Deinde ex qua causa dimisere cives laria nescio & iuxta mare magnificam preparaverent urbem. Unde ab una alteraque parte campi cum vineis ostenduntur[7] fertilissimi omnium pomorum habiti[8] et infra montes nea moni[9] extat.[10] Igitur a[11] cacomerea[12] nunc narratio[13] nostra erit quae a parte meridiei & per occiduum arbore[14] lentisti in humilibus collibus grumam[15] masticis in solo munito coloni tempore veris mirifice in eadem regione preparant producere laute. & quod mirum est, in apanomerea huiusmodi arbor non invenitur.[16] Cumque ad sanctum[17] devenio georgium[18] & in radicibus eius fontes decurrentes in imum prorumpunt & statim flumen per[19] fertilissimum planum descendit in mare. ubi vero ad dexteram in monte[20] castrum recovera recognoscimus magnum.[21] Ad calamotim[22] plano affectamus

1. Dd + S add: ab
2. Dd omits: nao
3. S: turri
4. Dd + S: et
5. Dd + S: millaribus
6. Dd + S: posita
7. Dd: onduntur
8. Dd: habitis
9. Dd: nea mogni
10. S adds: "monasterium in quo ecclesia mirae structurae consistit, plus quam narrare sufficiam. In quo usque hodie plus quam XXX morantur Calogiri ad serviendum Deo. Ibique est cisterna miro artificio fabricata; in quo monasterio omnes transeuntes refocillantur absque pretio. Ibique prope trionem est ecclesia Coronata Virginis Mariae, devotissima cunctis gentilbus. Atque Sanctus Nicolaus prope per unum mil. cum una pulchra ecclesia manifestatur, cum debito viridario et pulchro fonte. Ab hoc vero loco per duo mi. habetur El Dragolio cum pulchra domo pulcherrimoque viridario et fonte atque pulcherrimis possessionibus. Hinc ad unum milliare reperitus Sanctus Iohannes cum viridario bene arbuto atque turre cum fonte aquam recentissimam emanante." Dd omits this passage.
11. Dd: ad
12. Dd: catomerea
13. S: locutio; C like MN
14. Dd + S: arbores; C like MN
15. Dd: gumam; S: gummam
16. S: arbores non inveniuntur; C like MN
17. Dd: factum
18. S adds: de Sicosi
19. Dd omits: per
20. Dd: montem; S adds: reconverti
21. S adds: ubi maxima perdicum copia reperitur
22. Dd + S: calamoti; Dd adds: cum

pervenire donec caput in masticis & scopolum caloierum dictum a longe salutamus[1] recurro deinde ad pigrim[2] in plano oppidum ubi procul[3] Nastasiam sanctam & amistae[4] portum laudamus[5] a quibus cito in plano oppidoque de nomine dicto pervenimus sane & ultra ad occiduum portum Late duorum scopulorum & Litilimenem sinum cum plano et flumine manifestatur.[6]

//28r// .66. CHIOS. Insulae totius ambitus m. p. 124. [Map: North. Chios. *Full page.* Caput melanesi, S. Helena,* nao fons uberrima,* Cardamile portus, *island* (?strivili), Castrum dirionum, Perparea,* Vico,* Cardamile,* *island* (S. Steffanus), Volisso,* Pirio,* P. Delfini,* Litiminia portus,* hic rus est homeris,* S. Helias in monte altissimo,* S. Angelus,* S. Johannes, hic erat civitas chii olim,* sepulchrum vatis homeri,* S. Maria Neo Moni,* Aghia Mons, late portus,* Per totam istam catomeream* arbores masticis nascuntur et non in Apanomerea* et hii sunt parvi montes, *(city on bay, not labelled, shows walls with towers and 2 jetties projecting into the sea; unnamed towers on either side of the bay)*, Coronati,* S. Georgius,* Amistae,* Amistae portus,* Pigri,* S. Anastasia,* Castrum Recovera,* Calamoti.* 34 *names, 5 not in text.*]

//28v// Ostendimus Chion, nunc Lesbos insula manifestatur. & tantum in navigiis valuit quod maris imperium diceretur habere quae in egeo sita[7] mari & dicta mitilena; quia in hac miletum solis filium patremque[8] pasiphis & biblidis caunique patrem[9] de creta ubi venisset profugum eo quod contra Minoem cognatum suum surrexerat regnasse[10] urbemque miletam construxisse & ab eo[11] sic dicta est. Sed postea litteris transmutatis mitilena civitas dicta fuit. Quam Alceus poeta a quodam tyranno liberavit. Saphos poetissa de hac fuit insula & Theophrastus philosophus. Hic Pompeius in thessalia[12] dimicaturus cum Cesare suam coniugem deposuit.[13] Regnavit etiam hic Nicteus, pater Anthiope, ex qua Iuppiter in spetie satyri Amphionem & Zetum[14] genuit. Usque hic[15] Castor & Pollux, capta Helena

1. S: salutavimus
2. S: Pirgi
3. S: et ad
4. Dd: Amistaem
5. S adds: et turrim
6. Dd adds: E nota quod portus delphini Belofanos vocabatur; Dd: mara festamus; S: manifestamus
7. S adds: est
8. Dd + S: fratremque
9. Dd: fratrem
10. S: ubique
11. S adds: civitas
12. Dd omits: in thessalia
13. S: dimisit
14. S adds: Calaimque
15. Dd: huc

eorum sorore in insula Citharea Paridem Priami[1] filium qui eam ceperat, persequentes &[2] tempestate maxima numquam comparuisse. Dictum est, immortalitatem adeptos, quod dicitur, in signum celeste transmutatos quod hodie gemini commemoramus.[3] Huc Paulus apostolus de Syria veniens tempestate maris, vix[4] ad terram evasit qui predicans fidem xpi anguem maximum occidit & multos convertit. Sunt etiam[5] per omnem[6] circuitum plura castra quorum maior Mitilena videtur. Quae seculis preteritis magna potentissimaque civitas extiterat[7] & per circuitum quatuor & plus millia. Hodie vero ad exiguum est reducta spatium. Caloieros[8] equidem ab hinc deo devotus ruinam civitatis dominique vidit in futurum qui cito civibus desolationem urbis[9] palam locutus est. Quod non credentes dominus suique ac multitudo civium terremotu periere.[10] Evenit enim meis[11] diebus dominum per insulam accedere & cum in quadam pernoctasset[12] domo[13] scorpio manum infixit suam. Cumque famuli clamorem audirent illius per scalam ad eum fuit ascensus[14] & quesita restauratione doloris[15] ita & taliter domus[16] impleta procerum[17] famulorumque quod in ruina est eversa & dominus cum multis insperatam mortem substinuerunt.[18] Ad meridiem magnifice urbis IIIIor columpne eriguntur una cum edificiis multis atque cavernis mira industria[19] edificatis. Ad austrum colpus[20] Geremie descenditur[21] ubi plura oppida usque ad occiduum videntur. Castel Gero,[22] Geremia,[23] Chidonia, Chaloni,[24] Vasilica, Castelpetra, Castelmulgo.[25] Ad trionem Castel Sancti Theodori[26] turris &c. circa

1. Dd: pereidem primum
2. S adds: exorta
3. Dd: connumeramus
4. Dd: iusta
5. Dd + S: etenim
6. S: totum
7. Dd: existebat
8. Dd + S: caloierus
9. Dd: verbis
10. Dd: dominium que suos ac multitudinem civium ex terremotu periete; S inserts "a" before terremotu
11. Dd: in eis; S: itaque
12. Dd: percontasset domum
13. Dd: domum; S: turri
14. S: faciunt ascensum
15. Dd: Solaris; S adds: fuit
16. S: turris
17. Dd: per totum
18. S: sustinuit
19. Dd + S: mire industrie
20. Dd: colfus; S: gulphus Hieremiae
21. Dd: discenditur; S: distenditur
22. Dd: Castellum Cerra; S: Gera
23. S: Hieremiae
24. Dd + S: Caloni
25. Dd: molvio; S: Molino
26. S adds: Castel Angerino, Castel Parrachila et

medium planus est fertilis. Ad orientem occiduumque montes & indomita animalia sunt una cum cipressis fagis pinetisque.[1] Est denique in circuitu portuosa & CXXX circuit millia & scopuli eriguntur & prope Turchiam determinatur.[2]

//29r// In numero 67. LESBOS OLIM SIVE MITILENA NUNC METELINO VOCATUR. ET AMBITUS TOTIUS INSULE M. P. 130. [Map: North. Castel Sancti Teodori,* Castel Mulgo,* montes et silve magne, turris, Vassilica,* Castel Petra,* Paleo Castro (ruins), Geremia,* Caloni,* Cidonea,* Laurisia, Gera,* Mitilena,* Sinus Geremie.* *Island to south:* Petra. *On coast:* Turchia.*]

Desummo[3] nunc insulam Tenedi quae coram introitu stricti Romanie vel Hellesponti posita est & in conspectu antiquissime Troie apparata est in egeo mari. Quae a quodam iuvene sic dicto nominata est qui Athenis infamatus quod suam cognovisset novercam, ob verecundiam ad hanc applicuit insulam & vacuam cultoribus occupavit. Hec tempore Laumedontis & Priami opulentissima fuit & in eius sinu greci paraverunt insidias troianis a quibus Troia deleta fuit. Per hanc bellum atrox inter Venetos & Ianuenses tempore meo fuit quia quilibet ipsorum eam possidere volebat: tandem ex concordia ambarum[4] desolata remansit & sic nullus in ea audet habitare. Sed postquam vi omnia relicta fuere domestica multa

//29v// & animalia indomita devenere. In radicibus vero altioris montis fons est qui ab hora tertia noctis usque sextam solstitio existente tantum exundat in aquis quod flumen maximum videtur.[5] In aliis autem horis nil in ea fuisse comprehendimus aque. Hec etiam plana habetur & circumdata humilibus montibus manifestum est praeter unum[6] quod inter alios sublimatur. In quo tria milia francorum postquam veneti classem turchorum coram gallipoli in mari submerserunt[7] suspensi sunt. Quia ex omni gente in favorem infidelium ibi erant in classe congregati tempore concilii constantie. & hinc inde per planum tot vineta[8] inculta & alia reperiuntur poma quod hodie transeuntibus prebeat[9] refrigerium & sic[10] versus nobilissimam olim aspicis[11] troiam multa fragmenta antiquitatis[12]

1. S adds: manifestantur
2. Dd + S: conterminatur
3. Dd + S: Resumo.
4. Dd + S add: partium
5. Dd: habere; S: esse
6. Dd + S: nisi unus
7. S: summerserant
8. Dd: iumenta; S like MN
9. Dd + S: praebent
10. S: si
11. Dd: aspicit
12. Dd + S: antiquitatum

ipsius vere videbis. A leva vero[1] hellespontum intramus mare ore strenuo in quo introitu dardanellum offendimus. Ubi nunc & olim columpne elevantur multe.[2]

.68. TENEDOS. Ambitus totius insulae m. p. XL. Per totam istam planitiem et per strictum usque Dardanellum puto Troiam fuisse. [Map: East. *On Turkish coast: Fallen columns and domed buildings.*] Dardonello,* Troia.* *On Tenedos:* Fons qui solsticialibus vorat in flumine magnitudino crescit.*]

Dignum[3] fore arbitror[4] postquam huc usque venimus urbem Constantinopolim demostrare[5] ut animus audientium[6] alacer sit ad ea que dicturi sumus cum multa miranda erunt inspecturi.[7] Est ergo hic introitus ad Hellespontum usque strenuo ore[8] strictum Gallipoli dictum & Asia ab Europa dirimitur. In quo

//30r// primo postquam ad dexteram antiquam reliquimus Troiam turrim a leva iuxta mare inveniemus que propinquior asiae fuisse memoravimus[9] & de hinc usque Abidon oppidum parva extat[10] via. Ergo ille rex persarum Xerses in isto loco ponte sub navibus ordinato de Asia in Europiam transitum fecit & ait Demostenes decem centenis milibus militum elatum quattuor milium & ducentarum navium numero,[11] terribilem exigua latentem navicula fugere coegit. Ponit etiam lucius quod cum Philippo rege abidenos oppugnante ad destructionem murorum iam venisset cives ob misercordiam cum superlectilibus[12] recedere volentes.[13] Capitaneus in castellum eos revocavit dicens. Non pepercistis patrie et domibus vestris ideo ad occisionem eritis omnes accepturi: ita quod ipsimet in disterminium[14] mortis irruere[15] & domos omniaque ad ignem miserere.[16] Ultra vero XL millia ex parte europe munitissimum gallipolim oppidum videmus in altum: quod sponte Turchis infidelibus imperator grecie tradidit & filias proprias eis copulavit. Ex qua largitione tanta secuta est & sequitur strages christianorum quod vix homo in sua etate posset nomina scripta captorum occisorumque numerare.[17] Igitur Turchi de montibus armeniae persieque pauperes in hanc

1. Dd + S add: in
2. Dd adds: et per strictum usque dardanellu puto Troia ampliabatur.
3. Dd: ignum
4. Dd lacks: arbitror
5. Dd + S add: paremus
6. Dd + S: legentium
7. S: inspecturis
8. Dd + S add: hodie
9. Dd + S: numeramus
10. Dd + S: restat
11. S: dominio
12. Dd + S: supellectibus
13. Dd: volentibus
14. Dd: destremium
15. Dd: erruerunt; S: irruerent
16. Dd + S: misere
17. Dd + S: ennumerare

venientes minorem asiam dominium ex consensu[1] imperatoris supradicti inceptaverunt. Ex quibus cito provincia novis linguis gentibusque usque in hodiernum diem[2] impleta est. quorum aliqui in bello fuerunt strenuissimi[3] & memorie digniores qui secundum ritum[4] secte[5] eorum laute gubernaverunt regnum & dominia multa vi abstulerunt Christianis. Quorum unus amoratbei[6] merito diceretur.[7] Mulier dum ferculum lactis viro in agro portaret famulus domini nimis[8] epulum mulieris commedit. Que conquesta[9] cito reus[10] coram eo conducitur & abscissus in medio lac cognoscitur & iustitia coram amoracto[11] sublimatur. Abba[12] quidam ornamenta sanctorum ecclesieque sue[13] abstulit & coram amoracto magno gaudio mahometum adoravit. Monaci vero[14] ex quo viam didicerunt abbatis coram eodem imperatore conquesti sunt. Ille igitur dum astutiam atque fraudem abbatis[15] comperit restauratis caloieris coram eo de altissimo monte in imum delapsus est. Subulcus[16] suo aratro[17] vas plenum argenti adinvenit qui cito coram amoracto[18] onerato curru accessit & monetam sibi consignavit. Ille, requisitis senioribus, cuius ymago esset & neminem inveniret. Ait: Subulco[19] vir bone. Hec[20] ymago mea neque meorum antecessorum fuit. Quare iustum non fore factum alienum capere & rectum[21] alicui[22] occupare. Ergo tua[23] est. Vade in pace.

//30v// TURCHIA. [Map of Gallipoli: North. *Full page.* Strictum Galipolis* et Romonie. Moldendina hoc sunt 40 seu plura. Cimiterium Turchorum.... Domus curie ubi dantur Juditiam. Domus armamentorum galearum. platea. *A gallows with someone hanging from it.* Turchia.* Turchia. Turris Lapsaco. A leva tur.* *Two other inscriptions too faint to read, one by a building in the upper right, and one in the sea.*]

1. Dd: concesu
2. Dd + S omit: diem
3. Dd: extremissimi
4. Dd: ritu
5. Dd: sette
6. Dd: Amorat bej; S: Morathbey
7. S: dicitur
8. Dd: minis
9. Dd: cum questa
10. Dd: reum
11. Dd: Amorato; S: Morato
12. Dd + S: abbas
13. S omits: sue
14. Dd: ergo
15. Dd: abbate
16. Dd + S: Bubulcus
17. Dd: arato; S: sub aratro
18. Dd: Amorato; S: Morato
19. Dd + S: Bubulco
20. S: nec
21. Dd: ereptum
22. S: alieni
23. Dd: tuum

//31r// Ad orientem in introitu maris Hellesponti Marmora insula est. & XXX[1] circuit millia & tota montuosa marmorum & arborosa zapinorum reperta est. a qua constantinus Iustinianus & alii imperatores inumerabilia edificia marmorum pro urbe Constantinopoli extraxerunt & in ponte lapideo onerabantur. Ab alio latere oppidum elevatur paucorum habitantium ubi scopuli aliqui prevalent. Dicitur enim mare hoc Hellespontum.[2] Elles[3] ergo Athamantis filia cum Frixo[4] fratre insidias fugientes[5] novercales aureo vecta ariete infortunio suo[6] in undas decidit. Absorta[7] de se nomen dedit undis perpetuum ut quod pontum dicebatur ante, dicentur[8] Hellespontum. Habet igitur mare istud initium ab eritheo[9] ubi aiacis sepulchrum erigitur usque chersonesus[10] et ibi infine europe mergitur.

.70. MARMORA. Insulae totius ambitus m. p. 30. [Map: North. Marmora.★ *Walled city to the south and arched bridge to the north (to nowhere). Text written after map.*]

Navigando igitur per mare supradictum & ad Urbem accederemus ad dexteram colonimon[11] insula videtur[12] in montibus posita[13] nimis & quia olim per omnem greci dominabantur tunc temporis hec erat habitata. Nunc vero ad desolationem redacta & indomita animalia per eam vagantur.

//31v// .71. CALONIMON. [Map: North. *No text. Circular walled city.*]

Ostenduntur prope polim parve insule cum aliquibus scopulis hinc inde positis & quia vicinee urbi Constantine[14] permanent ideo caloieri habent refugium. In quibus magna edificia olim habebantur. & monasteria sparsa per omnem[15] apparent in istis. Ultra has insulas ad orientem erat prope mare civitas olim maxima[16] dicta in qua nihil aliud nisi marmorea edificia prostrata videntur. Quo in loco bubulcus arcam repperit.[17] In qua rex illesus corona sceptro & ense aureato erat. Dum vero nuntiatur domino & ab archa eum

1. Dd: LXXX
2. S adds: mare
3. Dd: eles; S: Helles
4. S: Phrixa
5. S: fugiens
6. Dd: in furtivo
7. Dd interprets this to mean Apsyrtos, the brother of Medea.
8. S: diceretur postea
9. Dd + S add: litore.
10. Dd: Chersonison; S: Chersonesum
11. Dd + S: Calonimon
12. Dd: videmus
13. Dd: insulam...positam
14. Dd: Contantini; S: Constantini
15. S: omnia
16. Dd adds: comidia; S: Comedia (Nicomedia)
17. Dd: repperisse

abstrahere[1] vellent[2] in cinerem illico est reversus. De hinc ad nicheam igitur[3] civitatem & ad bursiam olim & nunc metropolim plana demonstratur via, in qua imperator turchorum suis uxoribus filiabusque resedit quamvis modico tempore in uno moratur loco sed semper cum tentoriis vagantur ubique.

.72. Haec insulae sunt sine nominae.[4] [Map: North. *Five islands with buildings, two without.*]

//32r// Revenio[5] ad lesam nunc[6] Constantinopolim urbem & quamvis insula non sit, postquam huc pervenimus de ea pauca pertractabimus ut ad inditium[7] legentium perveniant.[8] Est aut igitur a Constantino dicta; quae iuncta cum Bisantio eam maxime ampliavit. Post autem seculis labentibus imperatores ecclesiis[9] ornavere & presertim[10] Iustinianus qui leges condidit & sanctam Sophiam edificavit cum palatioque prodomo.[11] Remanet ergo triangulata & X & VIII est in circuitu millia. Primo igitur[12] de angulo Sancti Dimitri usque ad angulum Vlacherne sex millia[13] quo in spatio centum & X eriguntur turres. Ab hinc igitur usque ad cresecam[14] portam quinque millia cum muro & antemurale munitissimo & vallo aquarum surgentium & turres in muro altiori nonginta sex. Dehinc usque iterum ad Sanctum Dimitrium milia VII. & turres centum nonaginta octo. In quibus[15] est campus ab extra & olim portus Vlanga ubi greci LM[16] ut dicitur Francorum plane[17] calcinee frumentato[18] dolose ex invidia vel dolore[19] occiderunt. Quorum ossa innumerabilia usque in hodiernum perhibent testimonium & propinquo huic conescali[20] vel arsana restat. & ultra fuit super menia amplissimum Iustiniani palatium cum ecclesia Enea dicta nobilissima[21]

1. Dd + S: extrahere
2. S: vellet
3. S: itur
4. Skopuli Prinkipi, or Princes' Islands
5. Dd + S: Devenio
6. S omits: nunc
7. Dd: indicium; S: iudicium
8. Dd + S: perveniatur
9. Dd + S add: eam
10. Dd: per certum
11. Dd: podromo
12. Dd omits: igitur
13. S adds: spatium
14. Dd: chriseam; S: Criseam
15. Dd + S add: menibus
16. Dd: La
17. Dd + S: pane
18. Dd: furmentato; S: fermentato
19. Dd + S: timore
20. Dd: condescali; S: condoscali
21. Dd omits: nobilissima

musaicorumque edificiorum atque cum pavimento miro[1] ingenio contexto.[2] Ibique in alto & super[3] mare erat speculum immensurabilis magnitudinis circumspectum a longe nimis & omnia edificia eius marmorea in mari videntur prosternata prope portulum imperatoris dicti. Etiam de immenso palatio usque Sanctam Sophiam erat per miliare via columnarum binarum per quam dominus accedebat, ubi octingentorum clericorum per circuitum domus erat[4] & de totius insule Trinacrie ut dicitur fructum[5] capiebant. Nunc autem sola testudo ecclesiae remanet in ea quia omnia diruta[6] sunt & ad nichilum devenerunt. a qua usque ad pavimentum centum triginta[7] brachia & a pavimento usque planum fundamenti quia tota una cisterna optima[8] aquae ampliatur brachia XXII. In super per ecclesiam sunt de angulo ad angulum centum XXti brachia. Quia[9] de super rotunda & in plano quatrangulata[10] resedit. Quis[11] autem poterit enumerare ornamenta marmorum atque porphirorum cum musaicis liniamentis. Quia,[12] quo latere incipere, vellere[13] evanesco. Extra igitur ecclesiam ad meridiem in platea columna septuaginta cubitorum alta videtur cuius in capite Iustinianus eneus equester habent[14] & pomum cum leva aureum tenens ad orientem cum dextera minatur. & iuxta hanc sex columne marmoree erecte magne videntur seriatim. Ultra vero has ad meridiem Hippodromus distenditur, quod latine equicursus appellatur. In hoc autem spatio nobiles coram iustrabant populo & duella atque[15] tormenta[16] parabantur. VI C LXXXX[17] etiam in longitudine brachiorum & C.XXIIII[18] ampliabatur & super columnas edificatum est in quibus cisterna[19] optime aquae totum supradictum continet spatium. In capite vero Hippodromi XXIIIIor erant[20] altissime columne ubi imperator cum principibus residebat. Ab una autem parte alteraque Hippodromi sedilia gradatim in longitudine erant ipsius marmorea ubi populus sedendo omnem ludum comprehendebat. Per medium denique

1. Dd: mirii; S: miri ingenii
2. Dd: ingenii contesto
3. Dd + S: supra
4. Dd + S: erant
5. S adds: ad vescendum
6. Dd: dirupta
7. Dd + S: CXLIV
8. Dd + S: optimae
9. S: quae
10. Dd + S: quadrangulata
11. Dd: Quisve
12. Dd + S: a
13. Dd + S: vellem
14. Dd + S: habetur
15. Dd: ac
16. Dd + S: torniamenta.
17. Dd: DCLIIIIta; S: DCLXXXX
18. S adds: in latitudine
19. Dd + S add: amplissima
20. Dd: nunerant

dicti cursus in longitudine humilis est murus & primo versus[1] Sanctam Sophiam est ecclesia cum muro magnifico

//32v//[2] innumerabilium fenestrarum adornato ubi domine iuvenculeque cum matronis suos prospeciebant dilectos, ubi in principio dicti muri sumus[3] balneum erigebatur in quo vulnerati ponebantur. Deinde agulia[4] XLIIII cubitorum alta ex uno latere[5] in quatuor eneis taxillis in altum recta cernitur & in pede eius versus sic sonant: "Difficilis quondam dominis parare[6] serenis Iussus & extinctis palmam parare[7] tyrannis. Omnia Theodosio cedunt sobolique perenni. Ter denis sic victus ego domitusque diebus. Iudice sub proclo superas elatus ad auras." Ultra hunc lapidem tres eneos[8] serpentes[9] ex multis lapidibus agulia connexa.[10] LXIII[11] cubitorum erigitur. Ultra denique in fine humilis muri huius quatuor humiles columne marmoree videntur erecte. In quibus imperatrix[12] preeminebat ad festum.[13] Fecit ergo Theodosius omnia ista & alia multa per urbem laudanda. Reperiuntur in super hodie infinite columne quarum quidem quinque videntur maiores[14] & LX cu. pro qualibet elevatur in altum et primo columna[15] Iustiniani dicta. Secunda crucis; quo in loco quatuor erecte porphiree[16] videntur. In quibus quidam equi quatuor enei aureati positi erant & Veneti illos Venetias[17] apostolum Sanctum detulere Marcum columnis remanentibus. Tertia quartaque columnarum qui[18] in medipolis[19] sunt posita in quibus circumcirca acta imperatorum sculpta cognoscuntur. In ecclesia Sanctorum Apostolorum quinta cum angelo eneo & Constantino genuflexo columna est & ecclesia iam diruta amplissimaque omnia sepulchra imperatorum porphirea videntur magnifica una[20] immenso & ibi columna ubi Christus ligatus & flagellatus est. In monasterio Pandocratora[21] est lapis ubi Ioseph revolvit

1. Dd: proversus
2. Marginal notes on this page: Agulia, Tres eneas serpentes, Columna Iustiniani, Columna Crucis
3. Dd: summum; S: summus balneus
4. Dd + S: use very different word order in what follows.
5. Dd: lapido
6. Dd + S: parere
7. Dd + S: portare
8. Dd: ereas
9. Dd + S add: in unum vidimus oris apertis, a quibus, ut dicitur, aqua vinum lac ab eis exibat diebus iustrantium. Ultra etiam in altera
10. Dd: conventa
11. Dd + S: LVIII
12. Dd: imperatoris
13. Dd: effestum
14. S adds: marmorae
15. Dd: pro colunna
16. Dd: purfere
17. Dd: a pre; S: Venetiis; S adds: apud
18. S: quasi
19. Dd + S: medio polis
20. Dd + S: cum constantino
21. Dd: pandocaterum

Christum in sindone. In monasterio Sancti Iohannis de Petra sunt vestimenta Christi & arundo cum spongea lanceaque[1] in unum servata.[2] Sunt denique per urbem innumerabiles ecclesiae atque cisterne mire magnitudinis & industrie fabricate & in ruina posite. Vinea pro qualibet in ea trium vel quatuor vegetum vini crescit. Cisterna Sancti Iohannis de petra, cisterna Pandepopti, Cisterna Pandocratora. Cisterna Apostolorum. Cisterna Maumethi.[3] In qua ita subtili artificio sunt ordinate columne quod est incredibile ad narrandum. & alie multe sicut Santa Sophia quae est principalior aliis & Iustinianus in XV annis illud explicavit opus. Sanctus Georgius de Mangana. Sancta Hereni,[4] Sanctus Lazarus, Chirame,[5] Enea, Petrus & Paulus. Sancti XLta martirum milia[6] & sua cisterna amplissima optime aquae[7] cuius finem inventi nequaquam dicitur posse. Anastasis. Perile Sanctos.[8] Sanctus Iohannes de Studio. Sanctus Andreas. Vlacherna &c. In qua tanta copia ubique edificata remanent ipsarum ecclesiarum & ut[9] pulchrior altera quod longum esset enarrare. Sunt etiam per civitatem pauci imperatores[10] & inimici latinorum qui numquam secretam[11] pacem cum eis obtinebunt. & si promittent non observabunt. Fuit etiam hec urbs pulcherrima valde & aula sapientie honestatisque. Nunc vero ad ignorantiam duritiamque vetuste opinionis perventi. Peccato gule adheserunt & in tantum delati propter copiam piscium carniumque quod quarta pars ipsius ad morbum inciderunt[12] lepre. & doctrinam Iohannis Chrysostomi[13] aliorumque sanctorum patrum dimisere. Ad trionem per unum miliare Pera Ianuensium pulcherrima civitas est. quae per sinum ab urbe separatur. Sunt & enim ab isto loco usque mare pontum seu Eusinum XVIII millia. Ad trionem ore strenuissimo cum periculo intrantium hodie navium. Cum quibus postquam de urbe narravimus[14] ad egeum mare ad insulam Stimlimini[15] revertemur.[16]

[*Marginal notations:* Agulia, Tres eneas serpentes, Columna Iustiniani, Columna Crucis.]

//33r// Tracia sive Grecia (2x). [Map: North. *Full page.* Galatha nunc Pera★ *(windmill)*, S. Dominicus, arsana.★ *Caption in water:* ab ista porta usque ad portam Sancti Dimitri★

1. Dd adds: ferrum lancee, de spinis corone et de pilas barbe
2. Dd + S: conservata
3. Dd: Mahometi; S: Mahumeti
4. Dd: Erigni
5. Dd: Theramas; S: Chiramas
6. Dd + S omit: milia
7. Dd + S: in qua, ut dicitur, nullum invenere finem
8. Dd: Perileftos; S: Periulestos
9. Dd + S: una
10. Dd + S: habitatores
11. Dd: securam
12. Dd: incidunt
13. Dd + S: Damasceni
14. Dd: nantuimus
15. Dd + S: Stalimni
16. Dd adds: prope Peram ad Eonem per milliare sunt gemine colunne vero est recessus Navium et ibi capsiam cum thesauro non penitentium in annum cum uxore accepta et hec vero

6 m.p. et centum et decim turres. CONSTANTINOPOLIS. *City walls with many towers, double wall to the west. On west:* Angulus★ et Porta Vlacherne,★ Porta Sancti Iohanes, Porta Chamidi. Angulus et Porta Crescea★ ab angulo iste usque ad angulum Vlacherne 4 m. passuum et 96 turres. usque ad angulum Sancti Dimitri.★ 7 m. passus et turres centum nonaginta octo. *Inside the walls from north:* S. Andreas, hic Constantinus genuflexu,★ Palatium Imperatoris,★ Sancta Marta, S. Iohannes de petra sive para,★[1] S. Salvatorem, *(2 columns):* Columpna Crucis★ and hic Justinianus in equo,★ S. Sophia,★ Hippodromos,★ S. Dimitrius, S. Giorgius de Mangana,★ S. Lazarus,★ Domus Papae, Sancti Apostoli,★ S. Andreas *(again)*, S. Johannes de Studio,★ Porta antiquissima et pulchra, Perileftos, Domus Constantini, *another inscription SE:* Portam olim palatii imperatoris.★ *On the shore:* Turchia (3x). *On east:* Angulus et Portus S. Dimitri.★ *Offshore:* Receptaculum dictum Conticali.★]

//33v// Erat hec insula Lemnos dicta, nunc vero Stalimini[2] denominatur. In egeo mari sita & plana tota, centum circuit millia. Limmi[3] in greci, lacus latine. Ad quam propter eius bassitudinem periculosum est accedere. Cum in ea sinus & portus sint optima[4] & plura oppida habitantur in ea. Legitur etiam in hac insula[5] Venerem concubuisse cum Marte eiusque adulterium solem Vulcano suo coniugi prodidisse. Quos ambos Vulcanus adamatinis catenis ligavit eosque aliis diis turpiter accubantes ostendit. Mulieres autem Lemniadis[6] adulterium Veneris damnantes ipsam tanquam indignam pretermictendam,[7] his odorem hircinum[8] misit unde omnes mulieres instigatione[9] Veneris omnes viros occiderunt. Sola vero Isiphile.[10] Quorum princeps Iason cum Isiphile concubuit Oeneum Thoantemque filios procreavit. Ubi autem Lemniades Ysiphilem servasse[11] comperiere eam interficere voluerunt. Illa vero fugiens a praedonibus capta[12] Licurgo regi argolico[13] in nutricem vendita est.[14] Ex hac etiam insula Minii traxerunt originem, unde a pelasgi[15] expulsi a Spartanis recepti sunt. Qui cum imperium civitatis[16] mutatis vestibus uxorum in carcere inclinatis tectisque capitibus in signum calamitatis relictis

1. .ad.
2. Dd: Stalimni
3. Dd: Limni
4. Dd + S: porti sint optimi
5. Dd: hanc insulam
6. Dd: Limniades
7. S adds: dixerunt
8. S adds: Venus indignata
9. Dd: rusticatione
10. Dd + S add: toantis filia, patri pepercit clam ceteras. Quae regina a mulieribus facta est. Argonaute, colcos euntes, hanc invaserunt. S adds: insulam
11. Blank. Dd + S add: patrem
12. Dd + S add: et
13. Dd: argolici
14. Dd: vendiderunt etc.
15. Dd + S: Pelasgis
16. Dd + S add: usurpare tentarent, in carceribus missi et a Spartanis ad mortem damnati. Viri igitur

uxoribus[1] evaserunt. Hic Thias[2] filius Bachi rex fuit. Que abundantissima in frumento habetur.

.75. LEMNOS OLIM, NUNC STALIMINI. Insulae totius ambitus m p. 100. [Map: North. Ephesithia, Paleo castro *(ruins: ancient Hephaestia)*, Sala, Coziro. *Three deeply cut gulfs on the south, one on the north.*]

//34r// Versus trionem embarus est grece quod ambra latine sonat. In egeo sita mari & montuosa nimis. Pauci habentur[3] in ea. Quae XXX circuit milia & inpuncta hellesponti oris prospectat. Ubi iam civitas imperfecta ab Agortanis[4] apparet[5] & insula hec ab imperio grecie possessa est.

.76. EMBARUS. Ambitus totius insulae m. p. 30. [Map: North. *Shows one city:* Embro.]

Restat nunc ut de Mandrachi aliqua dicamus quae clausura pedum[6] latine nominatur & habitata satis in cultura in melleque & in egis splendida habetur a qua in sinu maliaco[7] intramus, ubi civitas enni[8] habitatur cum acheloo[9] flumine propinquo.

.77. MANDRACHI. [Map: North. *No names. One tower with wall.*]

Sequitur etiam taxo insula quod promicto latine sonat prope monte sanctum hodie dictum quae XL circuit millia & habitata valde. Tria in ea oppida enumeravi pulchra cum fertilitate maxima quae coram acheloi[10] fluminis famosissima[11] adiacet.[12]

.78. TAXO. Ambitus totius insulae m.p. 40. [Map: North. *Three cities shown, no names.*]

//34v// Invenimus post dictam insulam montem athos olim & quamvis nunc[13] sit tempore Xersis regis persarum a continenti mons iste divisus erat.[14] nunc cum terra firma coniunctus est & Mons Sanctus nominatur. Prope salonicensem[15] civitatem in

1. Dd + S add: ex carceribus
2. Dd: Toas; S: Thoas
3. Dd: habitant
4. Dd: agonitanis; S : Agortanis
5. S adds: incepta
6. Dd: peccudum; S: pecudum
7. S: Miliaco
8. Dd: ennei istorum Gateluxii; S: Emi
9. Dd: atheleo
10. Dd: achilei
11. Dd + S: famosissimi
12. Dd adds: et tunc a gateluxiis dominata.
13. Dd + S add: continens
14. Dd: est
15. Dd: Thesalonicensem

provincia tracie altissimus valde & ibi propinquus cuius in sumitate acroaon[1] opidum[2] erat. longior quam in aliis terris etas habitantium extendebatur. Et in circuitu montis ad plus CXXIII[3] milia videtur habere. Quo in loco tot & tanta monasteria sunt caloierorum Sancti Basilii, Chrysostromi, Nazanzeni & praeteritorum[4] monacorum quod difficile foret ad narrandum. Surgunt igitur in tempestate noctis silentio[5] postquam signum primum lingee[6] campane rauca voce dederat secundum grecorum consuetudinem et ad ecclesiam accedentes, matutinale divinum[7] offitium. Cumque hoc finitum est ad suas redeunt casas & quicquid a suo mittitur priore separatim[8] cum pace commedunt. Sunt & aliqua horum monasteria quae ad comunem caloierorum trahunt vitam. Aliqua ad alium asperiorem modum vivendi vitam ordinavere. Quia in sabbato de monte atque solitudine omnes in cellulis redeuntes & in officio divino die dominico usque meridiem orantes ad refectorium accedunt. & completo pradio[9] pars ipsorum pane[10] leguminibusque in heremo preparatur[11] introire. & ibi suspiciens celum ac stellas tota mente suspirans & patriam cogitans eternam de exilii sui loco protinus ad orationem humilem os suum[12] convertit & vibrare[13] iam sole[14] exorto ad diurnas dei laudes pio letus ore prorumpit.[15] Ipse sibi comes, ipse sibi famulatur nec metuit solus esse dum[16] secum est. Celum spectare, non aurum, terram amat calcare & benedictio[17] cum gratiarum actione saepe est in ore suo. Scit vite hominum pauca sufficere & summas verasque divitias nil optare. Sumumque imperium nil timere, letum agit atque tranquillum evum, placidas noctes, occisos[18] dies & secura convivia. It[19] liber sedet[20] intrepidus, nullas struit aut cavet insidias. Angelorum aula conviviis odor colorque[21] optimus. Iudex morum testisque[22] modestie: mensa[23] pacifica,

1. Dd: acrohaom; S: Achroano
2. Dd: ollim; S adds: olim
3. Dd: CXXV; S: CXXIV
4. Dd: predictorum
5. Dd: scilentium
6. Dd: lignee; S: ligneae
7. Dd + S add: cantant
8. Dd: separatum
9. Dd + S: prandio
10. Dd: perane
11. S: paratur
12. S: secum
13. Dd + S: ubi iubare
14. Dd + S: solis
15. S: praerumpit
16. Dd: deus
17. Dd: beneficiorum
18. Dd: occiosos; S: otiosos
19. Dd: Ita
20. Dd: cedet
21. Dd: calor
22. Dd: testesque
23. S adds: -que

luxus ac tumultus nescia, gule domitrix, et voluptas feda[1] exulat & regina sobrietas regnat. Cubile castum & quietum conscientia paradisus est preparatus. Multi itaque in huiusmodi monte talem sponte elegere[2] vitam quae in tantum trahit eos ad contemplationem quod si maceries lapidum contra rueret eos, nullo modo timerent atque caput vel oculos torquerent ad videndum. Aliqui etiam in monasteriis cum silentio tribus in ebdomoda[3] cibum capere vicibus[4] sunt assueti. In quibus pro quolibet centum caloieros comunis vite. & in aliquibus quingentos enumerabis. Igitur monasteria de decem usque XXXta multa videntur vite communi. Hic autem apes ficus oliva in amenissimis vallibus virescunt & sedentes in[5] fusum in lana revolvit. Iste canistrum viminibus plicat[6] & omnes alternatim, horis stabilitis deum laudare conantur & pax in eis regnat sempiterna.

//35r// MONS SANCTUS. Ambitus eius m p. 123. [Map: North. Monasterium Vatopedi calogeri,[7] Monasterium Lavra calogeri.[8] Aote mons. *Other churches, unnamed, and a walled enclosure. Outside frame to west:* Thessaloniki.*]

Non longe ab insula Lemni Sanstrati parva insula & montuosa in eo[9] mari quam turchi[10] desolaverunt in qua animalia indomita ambulantia[11] cunctis habitant temporibus & oppidum sine meniis fuisse videtur. XV circuit millia.

.80. SANSTRATI. Ambitus totius insulae m. p. 15. [Map: North. Samitraca. *Shows wall with two towers.*]

//35v// In hoc igitur[12] mari egeo Limen insula in monte apparet. Non magna valde sed pulcra olim extiterat que parum habitata. XL circuit millia & Limen dicta a limite quia naves a tessalonica civitate venientes recto tramite per istam transire student ut navigatio[13] securius habeatur.

.81. LIMEN. Ambitus totius insulae m. p. 40. [Map: North. *A walled city:* Limen.]

Sequitur insula Dromos dicta latine cursus, quia naves de oriente ad occiduum navigantes ab ista signum capiunt. & saepe cives transeuntibus in nocte signum demonstrant ut tutius navigetur. Fertilis & XXX circuit millia.

1. Dd: fida; S: foeda
2. S: eligere
3. Dd: hidomada
4. Dd: visibus
5. Dd + S add: in cenobiis aliqui pannos texunt, aliqui sotularia struunt, aliqui retia nectunt, in manu ille
6. Dd adds: ille camala fihi plegit; S: no
7. Dd adds: 500
8. Dd adds: 800
9. Dd: egeo; S: Aegaeo
10. Dd: Theucri
11. S: ambulantes
12. S: ergo
13. Dd: navigando

.82. DROMOS. Ambitus totius insulae m p. 30. [Map: North. *Walled city.*]

//36r// Macri seu Calchis olim in egeo mari insula dicta est in qua pauci habentur.[1] Ad hanc autem Poemidas prefectus classis anthiochi pervenit insidias[2] Romane classi & sic devictus remansit in totum. Quae circuit XL[3] millia.[4]

.83. MACRI. Ambitus totius insulae m. p. 40 <illeg.>. [Map: North. Macri, *wall with three towers.*]

Capimus alias duas convicineas insulas[5] quae Schiati & Scopuli dictae erant. In egeo mari quarum prima[6] XXXII, secunda XXII millia.[7] Harum quidam olim dominus magne erat industrie & astutie nimis. Qui semel cum ad insulam euboiam navigasset ad predandum[8] & in terram omnes descendissent, cives clam invasere biremes. & sic pyrrate ad occisionem omnes pervenerunt.[9]

.84. SCOPOLI. Ambitus totius insulae m. p. 32.

.85. SCHIATI. Ambitus totius insulae m. p. 22. [Map: North. *Two islands, each with a single walled building with towers.*]

//36v// Consurgit coram dictis insulis Scopulus sanctus Elyas dictus quod sublimior aliis ubique minatur. In cuius cacumine ecclesia parva insurgebat et ibi caloierus serviens deo ad solem dum dormiret, aguila credens ipsum esse brutum in eum descendit & cum rapacibus ungulis oculos evulsit suos. Ille infinitum dolens & deum affectanter[10] rogans, ad eum Elyas venit omnibus videntibus sociis qui oculos suos restauravit.[11]

.86. SCOPULUS SANCTI HELYE. Scopulus sancti helye dictus in medio mari altissimus. [Map *(sidebar)*: n.d. *Island is a tall cliff, with a small church on top.*]

Consequitur Schiros insula, quae longa de trione ad meridiem de egeo mari. LXXX circuit millia. Portuosa nimis & Pegaseum[12] prospicit sinum. Quae nemorosa satis in montibus tota. Tethis Achyllis mater Carpathii vatis vaticinio monita periturum filium si ad bellum iret

1. Dd: habitentur; S: habitant
2. S: insidians
3. Dd: XXX
4. Dd + S add: rubea hic littera mille important.
5. Dd + S add: supradictae
6. S: prior
7. S: XXII and XII
8. Dd: depredandum
9. S adds: Haec litera rubea centum
10. Dd: affectuose
11. S: haec littera rubea centum important.
12. Dd: Pegesshum

Troianum ipsum Achillem in habitu femineo in hac insula apud licomedem[1] regem ascendit.[2] Hicque[3] a Deidamia regis filia dilectus & cognitus[4] & eam non invitam[5] clam sororibus aliis oppressit & ex ea filium habuit. Protinus aggreditur regem atque ibi testibus aris, "hanc tibi," ait, "nostri germanam, rector, Achillis. Nonne vides ut torva genas equandamque[6] fratri?" Tradimus arma humeris arcumque animosa[7] petebat...etc. & quia nemorosa atque aspera, tot & tanta animalia multarum generum silvestria[8] quod est mirum. Quia pauci sunt habitatores & in circuitu magna consistit. Ea propter Turchi saepe eam visitant sine habitantium timore. In qua quatuor erant oppida habitata & nunc duo extant.[9]

.87. Schiros. Insule totius ambitus m. p. 80. [Map: East. Schiros. *Two walled cities shown.*]

//37r// Coram ducatu athenarum ad trionem Euboia olim nunc Egrippum[10] quae contigua continenti quia pons in medio elongatur cum turri[11] munitissima. Sub qua tam impetus aquarum habetur bis in die quod mirabile sagitta velocissima permeatur[12] cum profunditate nimia. In capite pontis Egripos civitas ampliatur & fertilis in partibus reputatur istis: quam Naupalus[13] possidebat & pro vindicta filii sui Palamedis qui in castris[14] grecorum proditorie occisus[15] est Ulixis astutia cepit omnem greciam circuire[16] & regias intrare grecorum principum[17] & ibi suasione[18] coniuges eorum in adulterium cum quibuscumque poterant exortabat:[19] & sic ad vindictam filii arbitratus est. Qui multi principes in reversione ab amatoribus uxorum suarum[20] occisi sunt. Ultra hoc Nauplus in Caphareum conscendit montem & nocte accensa face[21] greci de Troia redeuntes ad evadedam[22] tempestatem ad ignem in portu salubrem credentes intrare in letiferos scopulos perierunt & sic vindictam

1. Dd: Nicomedem
2. Dd + S: abscondit
3. Dd + S add: solum
4. Dd + S add: est
5. Dd: invictam
6. Dd: equidemque; S: aequandaque
7. S: ominosa
8. Dd: manierum silvaria; S: manierum silvestria
9. S: restant. Rubea littera centum importat.
10. S: Egrippos; Dd + S add: nominatur
11. Dd + S: turre
12. Dd: permitatur
13. Dd + S: Nauplus
14. S adds: principum
15. S: excisus
16. Dd: cicurem
17. S omits: regias...principum
18. Dd + S: suasionibus
19. S: exortabatur
20. Dd: illorum
21. fasce? facie?
22. Dd + S: evadendam

cepit de morte filii Palamedis. In hac etiam insula Orpheus poeta vetustissimus claruit. Qui dixit esse unum deum verum & magnum qui cuncta[1] gubernat. & quod ante ipsum nihil sit genitum[2] & ab ipso sint cuncta[3] generata. Gorgias etiam philosophus de hac fuit insula & magister Socratis qui in[4] matris feretro natus dum ferebatur ad sepulchrum, subito vagitus infantis auditus est & fuit primus inventor retorice & complevit centum annos nec unquam a suo studio opere cessavit. Fuit etiam Neptunus pater Naupli huius insule dominus. Quae longa de oriente ad occiduum C milia & CCC in circuitu. Ad trionem Caphareus habetur mons ubi Aulis insula est. In qua Ephigenia, Agamenonis filia, erat sacrificanda numini diane[5] propter cervi mortem & contra Troianos prosperos haberent ventos. Sed miseratione numinis Ephigenia sublata cervam superpositam sacrificavit. Ad meridiem civitas est posita & a longobardis[6] usque nunc habitata qui diu huc[7] venere & hodie a Turchis[8] possidetur.[9]

[*Marginal notations:* Nauplus, Palamedes, Orpheus, Gorgias magister Socratis, Neptunus, Aulus insula, Ephigenia.]

//37v// .88. EUBOEA★ OLIM SIVE EGRIPPUS★ NUNC AUT NEGROPONTUS. Ambitus totius insule m. p. 300 et longitudo ab orientem ad occidentum m. p. 100. [Map: North. Full page. Otheo. Caphareus★ promontorium, Egrippus★ *(city)* olim, nunc Nigroponte. *Walled cities, bridge★ to mainland.* DUCATUS ATHENARUM.★ *Island:* Aulis.★ *On mainland:* Thebe, Athene. *On isthmus:* Ex milia. *Below:* Morea, Peloponesus.]

//38r// Egina mox sequitur in conspectu athenarum parva quidem ac deserta insula. In cuius medio relliquie oppidi apparent cum parva adiacente planitie. Cetera montem silve collesque occupant. Ubi etiam caput sancti georgii adoratur.

.89. EGINA ULTIMA IN OPERA NOSTRA ET CICLADI INSULARUM SIVE ARCHIPELAGI. [Map: North. *Two islands, the larger with a walled town labelled Egina.*][10]

Cyprus insula[11] a civitate Cypro, quae in ea, est nomen accepit. Ipsa est & Paphos Veneri consecrata in Carpathio mari vicina austro. Famosa quondam divitiis & maxime eris, ibi

1. S: omnia
2. Dd: sumptum
3. S omits: cuncta, adds: et creata
4. Dd omits: in
5. Dd + S add: irate
6. S : Lombardis
7. S: hic
8. Dd + S: Venetis
9. S adds: Haec littera rubea centum importat.
10. Other manuscripts have this text for Aegina: "Christus a chrismate dicitur, ergo a Christo christiani vocamur, quia chrismate ungimur. Et Graeci neque chrisma neque oleum sanctum habent, nisi quod, baptizato puero in sindone munde eum involvunt, et cum saleque oleo patrini circumdando frontem perungunt. Sit itaque finis a modo, postquam insulas totius Archipelagi in IV. peregi annis, timoreque anxietate nimia, et ad Aeginam hanc insulam, ubi caput Sti Georgii adoratur in conspectu urbi Athenis, venimus. Et hic navicula nostrae imbecillae navigationis portum futurae recreationis cum salute accepit.
11. In margin: Isidorus. From Isidore, *Etymologiae* XIV.vi.14.

enim prima huius metalli inventio & utilitas fuit. Luciflori. Aderat[1] fatum insularum. Igitur & cipros recepta sine bello. Insulam veteribus divitiis abundantem & ob hoc Veneri sacram Ptholemeus regebat. &[2] divitiarum tanta erat fama nec falso ut victor gentium populus & donare regna consuetus Publio Claudio tribuno[3] duce socii virique[4] regi confiscatione mandaverit & ille quidem ad rei famam veneno fata precepit. Ceterum Portius Cato Cyprias opes liburnis per tyberinum hostium[5] invexit quae res latius erarium populi romani quam ullus triumphus implevit. Tortellus. Cyprus[6] insula est in Carpathio mari sita porrectaque inter Ciliciam & Syriam inter alias orbis insulas. Famosissima veterum divitiis abundans luxui plurimum dedita ob quod Veneri sacram esse dicunt.

[*Marginal notations:* Isidorus, Luciflorius, Tortellus]

//38v// CIPRI INSULA.[7] [Map: North. *From the west (promontory):* S. Befamo, *(promontory)* St. Giorgius, Galmixa, *(promontory)* Cornaquiti, Limina, Cermis, Lapidus flum, Lapidus, Nicosia *(large city with towers and walls)*, Calmixa, Macarium, Aphrodisia, Carpasia, Olimpus, Caput Sancti Andree. *Moving south:* Salaminia, Famagosta, Podios fl., Arsinoe Altera, Adena. *To the west:* Saline, Caporicisso, Quito, Maxito, Beritium, Limiso, Galmie, Piscopia, Caput Lemco, Paphus Nova, Baffa, Paphus, Drepanum, Drepanum prom., Athamos, Arsinoe, Acamos prom. *In the center:* Olimpus Mons, Mons Sanctae Crucis. *Islands:* Carpasie *(NW)*, Clides *(E)*. *It has no interior names. None of these are mentioned in the text.*]

In Ligustico mari est Corsica:[8] quam Greci Cirnon appellavere sed Tusco proprior[9]; a septentrione in meridiem proiecta, longa p. CL. m., lata maiore ex parte L in circuitu CCC.m. XXV; abest a Vadis Volateranis LXII m.p. Civitates habet XXXII & coloniam marianam a Mario deductam, Aleriam a dictatore Silla.[10] Citra est Oglosa,[11] intra vero LX m. p. a Corsica planaria[12] a spetie dicta; equali[13] freto ideoque navigiis fallax. Amplior Urgo ac Capraria quam Greci Aegilion dixere. Item Igilium & Diannium: quam Artemisiam ambe contra Cosanum litus & Barpana, Menaria, Columbaria, Nevaria,[14] Ilva cum ferri

1. In margin: Luciflori. Lucius Annaeus Florus, *Epitome of Roman History* [extracted from Livy], ed. and trans. Edward S. Foster (Cambridge, MA: Loeb Classical Library, 1984).
2. Loeb: Sed
3. Loeb inserts: plebis
4. Loeb: vivique
5. Loeb: ostium
6. In margin: Tortellus.
7. Other manuscripts of HMG, including Florence and London, have an expanded text on Cyprus, including Strabo XIV.6.
8. See Pliny III.vi.80–83.
9. Pliny: propior
10. Pliny: Sulla
11. Pliny: Oglasa
12. Pliny: Planasia
13. Pliny: aequalis
14. Pliny: Venaria

metallis. Circuitus C. m. p. a Populonia X; a Grecis Etalia[1] dicta; ab ea Planasia XXVIII ab his ultra Tiberina hostia in Antiano Scura[2] mox Palmaria,

//39r// Snivenia[3] adversum Formias Pontia. In Puteolano autem sinu Pandetoria[4] procida[5] non ab Enee nutrice, sed quia profusa ab enaria erat, Enarie, a statione navium Enee, homero Inarime dicta, Grece[6] Pythicusa non a simiarum multitudine ut aliqui existimavere sed a figulinis[7] doliorum. Inter Pausilipum & Neapolim, Megaris mox a Surento VIII m. distans.[8] Tiberii principis arte[9] nobiles Capree circuitu XL[10] m.p., Leucothea extra quem[11] conspectum, pelagus Affricani[12] atttingens. Sardinia minus VIII m. p. a Corsice extremis, etiam[13] eas artantibus insulis parvis que Cunicularie appellantur. Itemque Pintonis[14] & Fosse a quibus fretum ipsum Taphros nominatur.[15] Isidorus dicit.[16] Corsice insule exordium incole ligures deberunt appellantes eam ex nomine ducis. Nam quedam Corsa nomine Ligus mulier, cum taurum ex grege, quem prope litora regebat, transnatare solitum atque per intervallum corpore aucto remeare videret, cupiens scire incognita sibi pabula, taurum[17] ceteris digredientem usque ad insulam navigio persecuta[18] est. Cuius ingressu[19] insule fertilitatem cognoscentes, Ligures ratibus ibi profecti sunt, eamque nomine mulieris auctoris & ducis appellaverunt. Hec autem insula Grece Cyrne dicitur a Cirno Herculis filio habitata. De qua Virgilius,[20] "Cyrneas taxos." Dividitur autem a Sardinia XX milium freto, cincta Ligustici equoris sinu ad prospectum Italie. Est autem multis promontoriis angulosa, gignens letissima pabula & lapidem quem cacociten Greci vocant.

//39v// CIRNON OLIM NUNC CORSICA APPELLATUR. Longitudo a septentrione in meridiem CL m. passum, latitudo vero L. In circuitu CCCXXV. [Map: North. Full page. *Island off northern coast:* Caprara.★ *From north down east side:* Capo Corso, Sisthe, Brando, Cosa f., Bastia,

1. Pliny: Aethalia
2. Pliny: Astura
3. Pliny: Sinonia
4. Pliny: Pandeteria
5. Pliny: Prochyta
6. Pliny omits: Grecie
7. Pliny: figlinis
8. Pliny: distantes
9. Pliny: arce
10. Pliny: XI
11. Pliny: extraque
12. Pliny: Africum
13. Pliny: etiamnum angustias
14. Pliny: Phintonis
15. Pliny III.vi.83.
16. *Etymologiae* XIV.vi.41-42.
17. Isidore: a
18. Isidore: prosecuta
19. Isidore: regressu
20. *Eclogues* IX.30.

Tegoli, Belgede, Foriani, Beppiglia, Borgo, Lotriana, Porrano, Venzolasta, Lovesthovada, Ibigano, Corti, Omessa, Lorastello, Tavagnia, Cafarroni, Lampeta, Meriani, Aleria,* Golo fluminis, ampoq mare<?>, Anzanti, Petrellarata, Orezza, Alto flum., Campoloro, Matre, Atriani fl., Altiani, Porto Faone, *(river)* Rotamus fl., Iera flu., Lugo, Port Cepria, Porto Vechio, Amansa, Amasi fl., Bonifatia. *From north down west side:* S. Columbanus, Cintora, Borreto, Canari, Nonza, Ferinola, Elgualdo, Tardeta. *Promontory to west:* Ostritine, Balagaro, Lespilonthe, Loro, P. di Nebio, Nebia fl. *Inland:* Speloncata, Palastra, S. Antolino, Calvi, Belgode. *Far west:* Roniela, Monti, Zinalite, Cirasa fl, Larie, Saoni, Aiasso, Lorca fl, Cinarcha, Vazzo, Istria. *South end:* Boregin, Pitana fl, P. Polo, P. Elese, Monaco. 78 *names.*]

//40r// Sardinia[1] ab oriente patens CLXXXVIII m.p., ab occidente CLXXV, a meridie LXXVII, a septentrione CXXII,[2] circuitu DLXV. Ab est ab Africa Catalitaon[3] promontorio CC a Gadibus XIIII. Inde habet a Gorditano promontorio duas insulas quae vocantur Herculis a Sulcensi Canosmiam[4] a Caralitano Ficariam. Quidam haud procul ab ea & Belliridas[5] pontum[6] & Calode[7] & quam vocant Baralitta.[8] Celeberrimi in ea populorum Ilienses, Salari,[9] Corsi oppidorum XVIII, Suliritani,[10] Valentini, Neapolitani, Nirenses,[11] Caleritani[12] civium Ro. & Norenses. Colonia autem una quae vocatur ad turrim Libisonis. Sardiniam ipsam Timeus Sandaliotim appellavit ab effigie solee. Mirsiluriem[13] Ichivisam[14] a similitudine vestigii. Contra Prestanum[15] sinum Leuchasia est a sirene ibi sepulta appellata. Contra Veliam Pontia & Isacia utreque uno nomine Oenotrides in argumentum possesse ab Oenotriis Italie; contra Vibonem parve quae vocantur Ithaesie[16] Ulyxis specula.

Isidorus ait:[17] Sardis[18] Hercule procreatus cum magna multitudine a Libia profectus Sardinam occupavit & ex suo vocabulo insule nomen dedit. Hec in Affrico mari facie vestigii humani in orientem quamvis in occidentem latior proeminet, ferme paribus lateribus quae in meridiem & septentrionem vertunt. Ex quo ante comercium a navigantibus

1. Pliny III.vi.84–85
2. Pliny: CXXV
3. Pliny: Caralitano
4. Pliny: Enosim
5. Pliny: Berelida
6. Pliny: ponunt
7. Pliny: Callodem
8. Pliny: Heras Lutra
9. Pliny: Balari
10. Pliny: Sulcitani
11. Pliny: Vitenses
12. Pliny: Caralitani
13. Pliny: Myrsilus
14. Pliny: Ichnusam
15. Pliny: Paestanum
16. Pliny: Ithacesiae
17. *Etymologiae* XIV.vi.39.
18. Isidore: Sardus

grecorum "Ichnos" appellata est. Terra patet in longitudine milia CXL, in latitudine XL. In ea neque serpens gignitur neque lupus sed solifuga tantum, animal exiguum hominibus pernitiosum. Venenum quoque ibi non nascitur, nisi herba per scriptores plurimos & poetas memorata, apiastro similis, quae hominibus rictus contrahit & quasi ridentes interimit. Fontes habet Sardinia calidos, infirmis medelam prebentes, furibus cecitatem, si sacramento dato oculos aque[1] eius tetigerint.

//40v// SARDINIA. Sardonisus olim dicebatur, nunc autem Sardinia vocatur. Longitudo istius insule ex parte orientis CLXXXVIII p.m. A merdie[2] LXXVII a septentrione CXXII et ambitus totius insule V/CLXV m.p. [Map:[3] North. *North:* Busmar, Longonsardo, S. Repaira, Olbia. *Northwest: Island of* Jascono. Farcon, Coro, Rosan, S. Paulus, C. Cavalli, Fortoli, Alleguora, Marargio, S. Lucia,[4] Cap. Tomin, Orgoner, Bossa. Island: Malernventre. Saline, C. Marri. Arestan, Aquilastro, Portus Neapolis,[5] Alba Cassara, Argentera, S. Theseus, Tavolar, Marsinam, Callerj, Carbonara. *Islands to southwest:* Sossa, Anadiol?, Forro.]

//41r// Siciliam[6] ferunt angustiis[7] quondam faucibus Italie adhesisse direptamque velut a corpore maiore impetu superioris[8] maris quod toto undarum onere illuc vehitur. Est autem ipsa terra tenuis ac fragilis & cavernis quibusdam fistulisque ita penetrabilis, ut ventorum tota ferme flatibus pateat. Necnon & ignibus generandis nutriendisque soli ipsius naturali vi.[9] Quippe intrinsecus stratum sulphure & bitumine traditur, quae res facit ut spiritu cum igne inter[10] interiora luctante frequenter et compluribus locis, nunc flammas nunc vaporem nunc fumum eruptet.[11] Inde denique Aethne montis per tot secula durat incendium &[12] acrior per spiramenta cavernarum ventus incubuit harenarum moles egeruntur. Proximum italie promontorium regium dicitur. Ideo quia grece abruta[13] hoc nomine pronumptiatur.[14] Nec mirum si fabulosa est loci huius antiquitas: in quem res tot coiere mire. Primum quod nusquam alias torrens fretum nec solum citato impetu verum etiam saevo: neque experientibus modo terribile,[15] verum etiam procul visentibus.

1. Isidore: aquis
2. Sic.
3. Almost no connection between text and map.
4. Or S. Luna? There is a S. Lucia on the coast.
5. Mussolinia?
6. From M. Junianus Justinus (fl. third c. CE), *Epitome of Historiae Philippicae et Totius Mundi Origines ut Terrae Situs,* of Pompeius Trogus (late first c. BCE). IV.I. Transcription 1886 at: www.thelatinlibrary.com/justin. Translation at: www.tertullian.org/fathers/justinus_03.
7. Justinus: angustis
8. Justinus: superi
9. Justinus: naturalis materia
10. Justinus: in terra
11. Justinus: eructat
12. Justinus: ubi
13. Justinus: abrupta
14. Justinus: pronuntiatur
15. Justinus omits: saevo…terribile

Undarum porro in se concurrentium tanta pugna est ut alias veluti terga dantes vorticibus mergi ac[1] in imum desidere, alias quasi victrices in sublime ferri videas. Nunc hic fremitum ferventis estus. Nunc illic gemitum in voragine[2] dissidentis[3] exaudias. Accedunt vicini & perpetui Aethne montis ignes & insularum eolidum velut ipsis undis alatur incendium. Neque enim in tam angustis terminis aliter durare tot seculis tantus ignis potuisset, nisi & humoris nutrimentis aleretur. Hinc igitur fabule Scyllam &Carybdim peperere. Hic[4] latratus auditos,[5] hinc monstri credita simulacra, dum navigantem[6] magnis vorticibus[7] pelagi desidentis exterriti latrare putant undas, quas sorbentis estus vorago collidit. Eadem causa etiam Aethne montis perpetuos ignes facit. Nam aquarum ille concursus raptum secum spiritum in imum fundum trahit atque ibi suffocatum tamdiu tenet, donec per spiramenta terre diffusus nutrimenta ignis incendantur.[8] Iam ipsa italie Sicilieque vicinitas, iam promontoriorum altitudo ita[9] similis est, ut quantum nunc admirationis tantum antiquis terroris dederit, credentibus, coeuntibus in se promontoriis ac rursum discedentibus solida intercipi absumique navigia.

//41v// Nec[10] hoc ab antiquis in dulcedinem fabule compositum, sed metu & admiratione transeuntium. Ea est enim procul inspicientibus natura loci, ut sinum maris, non transitum putes, quo cum accesseris discedere ac seiungi promontoria quae ante iuncta fuerant arbitrare.[11] Sicilie primo Trinacrie nomen fuit. Preterea[12] Sicania denominata[13] est. Hec a principio patria Cyclopum fuit, quibus extinctis Aelolus[14] regnum insule occupavit. Postquem singule civitates in tyrannorum impetum[15] concesserunt quorum nulla terra feracior fuit. Isidorus.[16] Sicilia a Sicano rege Sicania cognominata est, deinde a Siculo Itali fratre. Sicilia prius autem Trinacria dicta propter tria acra, id est promontoria: Pelorum, Pachinum, et Lilybeum. Trinacria enim grecum est, quod latine triquadra[17] dicitur, quasi in tres quadras divisa.

1. Justinus omits: vorticibus mergi ac
2. Justinus: voraginem
3. Justinus: desidentis
4. Justinus: hinc
5. Justinus: auditus
6. Justinus: navigantes
7. Justinus: verticibus
8. Justinus: incendat
9. Justinus adds: ipsa
10. Justinus: necque
11. Justinus: arbitrere
12. Justinus: postea
13. Justinus: cognominata
14. Justinus: Cocalus
15. Justinus: imperium
16. Isidore, *Etymologiae* XIV.vi.32.
17. Isidore: triquetra

//41v–42r// [Map of Sicily:[1] North. *West side (islands):* Marem, Falignano, Elienza. *Northern coastal cities from west:* Caput Galli, Marsardinio, S. Giorgius, Castellummare, Palermo, Solanto, Himera fl., Termine, Monalus fl., Tosa, Cifalu, Cicla fl., Petra de Roma, Caroma, Timetus fl., Caput Norlandi, Patri, Elicon fl., Ulifera, Melazo, Marti, Messena, Fanale del Farro. *Interior from west:* Monte Real, Pulici, Coriglione, Castellum Bonum, Castellum Veterani, Petralia Lasotana, Colata Voltore, Castoiami, Chieza, Calavenerta, Calata Gerone, Nicosia, Petralia Lasonurana *(repeat)*, Minio, Aterno, Dandozo, Mons Gibel, S. Nicolaus de Arena, Mons Peloro, *fiery sign for* Etna *but no name*, Palaoma. *West coast:* Trapani, Batis fluvius, Scodero. *Along south coast from west:* Marsera, Cotrigo, Sacca, Ispa fl., Cavo Bianco, Talicata, Hymer fluvius, Butera, Terranova, Rassacata, Isporus fl., Isoiciri?, Caput Passeri. *East coast:* S. Alexia, Laschaletta, Tauermena, Jati, Lamota, Catanea, Parenno, Panthacus fluis, S. Maria, Labesca, Lantine, Lagesta, Siracusa, Alabus fl., Potentia, Ortus flu. *Islands to north:* Alicur, Felicur, Saline, Lippari, Wulcanus, Strongoli. *Island to south:* Pantalanea. *Northeast:* Caribi, Silla. Italia, Regio.]

//42v// Britania occeani insula interfuso mari toto orbe divisa a vocabulo sue gentis cognominata. Hec adversa Galliarum parte ad prospectum hispanie sita est. Circuitus eius quadragies occies[2] LXXV milia. Multa et magna in ea flumina, fontes calidi, metallorum larga & varia copia gagates lapis ibi plurimus & margarite. Pomponi Mella. Britania qualis sit qualesque progeneret, mox certiora & magis explorata dicentur. Quippe tamdiu clausam aperit, ecce principum maximus nec indomitarum modo ante se verum ignotarum quoque gentium victor propriarum rerum fidem ut bello affectavit ita triumpho declaraturus portat.[3] Ceterum ut adhuc habuimus: inter septentrionem occidentemque proiecta grandi angulo rheni hostia prospicit: deinde obliqua retro latera abstrahit. Altero Galliam altero germaniam spectans tamen rursus perpetuo margine directi litoris ab tergore abducta. Iterum se in diversos angulos cuneat triquetra & Sicilie maxime similis. Plana ingens fecunda. Verum iis que pecora quam homines benignius alant. Fert nemora saltus ac pregrandia flumina alterius montibus[4] modo in pelagus modo retro fluentia. & quaedam gemmas margaritasque generantia. fert populos regesque populorum sed sunt inculti omnes atque ut longius a continenti absunt, ita aliarum opum ignari magis tantum pecore ac finibus dites, in cortum[5] ob decorem an quid aliud ultra[6] corpora infecti. Causas autem[7] & bella contrahunt ac si frequenter invicem. Infestant maxime imperitandi cupidine studioque ea prolatandi que possident. Dimicant non equitatu modo aut pedite verum & bigis & curribus gallice armati covinos vocant quorum falcatis axibus utuntur.

1. None of these names are in the text.
2. Isidore, *Etymologiae* XIV.6.2: octies
3. Pomponius Mela III.49–52.
4. Pomponius Mela: motibus
5. Pomponius Mela: incertum
6. Pomponius Mela: *vitro* (woad).
7. Pomponius Mela adds: bellorum

//43r// REGNUM SCOCIE, ANGLIA INSULA. Hec est vera proportio istius insule. [Map: North. *Island on northwest:* icuç insula. *Island to south:* huic. *From north down eastern side:* Donde, Inernest, Rocheborg, S. Laguensis, Latina, Fert, Caput Rodi, Tenedam, Bamborg, Beruhic, Sutina, Scandelborg, Venbro, Ullo, Unbro, Nisa, San Betorf, Ravenzor, Elii, Lenna, Bracanea, Ca Toerdo, Astaçer, Godaner, Cassor, Jarnemua, Tarquelay, Arcuorda, Orois, Orrorda, Orolein. *Southeast, east to west:* Dabra, Romaneo, Guixalixo, Saforda, Saron, Civibat, Portamua, Antona, S. Pola, S. Anterino, Caput Parlan, Ringumua, Artamua, Godester, Premua, Godeman, Falemua, Caput Delisard, Musafola. *Down west side:* S. Johannes, Oercons, S. Andreas, Scoruçeri, Caribun, Caput Basso, Donfres, Castrum Verluhic, Castrum Novum, Cestria, Breus Tore Incanta, Norgalles, Urgales, Barlles, Milleforda, Cardemuba, Lamaset, Porvasi, S. Nicolaus, Bristo, S. Helena, Patristo, Londra, Tamixa Flum.]

//43v// Super britaniam Hivernia[1] est. Paene par spatio sed utrinque equalis tractu litorum oblonga; celi ad maturanda semina iniqui verum adeo luxuriosa herbis non laetis modo sed etiam dulcibus ut se exigua parte diei pecora impleant, & nisi pabulo prohibeantur, diutius pasta dissiliant. Cultores eius inconditi sunt & omnium virtutum ignari quamvis alie gentes aliquatenus tamen gnari pietatis admodum expertes.[2]

Scotia eadem[3] et Hivernia proxima britanie insula, spatio terrarum angustior sed situ fecundior. Hec ab affrico in boream porrigitur cuius partes priores hiberiam et cantibricum occeanum intendunt. Unde est Hivernia dicta. Scotia autem quod ab scotorum gentibus colitur est appellata. Illic nullus anguis, avis rara, apis nulla, adeo ut advectos inde pulveres seu lapillos si quis alibi sparserit inter alvearia examina favos deserant.[4]

1. Pomponius Mela: Iuverna
2. Pomponius Mela III.53.
3. Isidore: idem
4. Isidore, *Etymologiae* XIV.6.6–7.

English Translation

//1r// THE DESCRIPTION OF THE ARCHIPELAGO AND THE CYCLADES AND OTHER ISLANDS BY CHRISTOPHER ENSENIUS, A MOST DISTINGUISHED FLORENTINE CLERIC, AUSPICIOUSLY BEGINS:

I have herewith undertaken to write a little book of text and pictures of the Cyclades and the other scattered islands, not merely copying the ancient writers by whom they were described, but setting forth both the ancient appearances and those they have today, not only cities, castles, springs, groves of trees, rivers, seas, mountains, promontories, ports and towns, but I also survey and depict the nature of each place clearly and briefly.

So that more accurate facts might be placed in memory, I will describe not what I have learned by hearsay but what I have seen in the past six years with my own eyes after much reflection, which will be very pleasing not only to readers but also most useful to sailors, once they know what places they might be seeking and the point from which they are departing. With the greatest brevity I will run through the number and names of the islands one by one and will explain them so that an easy road lies open for readers.

I take my beginning from Corfu, which today is called by many the beginning of Greece toward the West. Next Paxos, Levkas, Ithaki, Chefalonum, Zakynthos (Zante), Strophades, Sapienza, Cytharea (Kithera), Sikili (Antikythera), Crete, Karpathos, Rhodes, Syme, Chalke, Tilos, Nisyros, Astypalaia, Thira (Santorini), Sikinos, Folegandros,[1] Melos, Siphnos, Seriphos, Thermia (Kithnos), Kea, Andros, Caloieros, Tinos, Mykonos, Delos,

//1v// Syros, Paros, Antiparos, Dhespotika, Naxos, Podia, Iraklia, Keros, Ios, Anafi, Amorgos, Kinaros, Levitha, Caloieros,[2] Kos, Kalymnos, Leros, Patmos, Crusia, Arkoi, Ikaria, Thimena, Agathonsisi, Pharmakonision,[3] Samos, Fourni, Donousa, Psara, Chios, Lesbos, Tenedos, Gallipolis, Marmora, Calanonimo, Scopuli Caloierorum,[4] Constantinople, Lemnos, Imbroz, Samothrace, Thasos, Holy Mountain (Mt. Athos), Agios Efstratios, Kyria Panagia, Alonnisos, Peristera, Skiathos and Skopelos, Sanctus Elias, Skyros, Negroponte (Euboea), Aegina,[5] Cyprus, Sicily, Corsica & Sardinia, Albion or England, Gotland, Norway, Sweden, and Ireland.

//2r// Now it remains to show both generally and in detail the surrounding provinces with the width of the seas and what is outstanding in them nowadays, for it is said that

1. Buondelmonti omits Polimio from this list, but it can be found following Policandros in the text.
2. Caloieros: not identified.
3. Many of these small islands are difficult to identify. The names of these three are derived from Düsseldorf 2:69–73.
4. Scopuli Caloierorum, a generic name which could apply to any number of rocky islets in the Aegean Sea.
5. From this point on, additions to Buondelmonti's list. Despite his promise, this manuscript does not treat "Gottia, Norvegia and Suetia."

Archipelago means "the ruler of the sea." A straight line from Rhodes to the promontory of Malea, now the Cape Sant'Angeli, is 450 miles and from Crete to Tenedos, 500 miles, in which is contained the whole sea of the archipelago. [1]

Adjacent to this sea is Asia Minor in which the provinces of Cilicia, Pamphilia, Phrygia and Betulia lie, but after the Turks possessed it for a long time, it took the name Turkey from them. At one time the Turks rampaged through the defenseless cities, but now the people are governed peacefully under them. To the west after the Hellespont is crossed by the sea, Greece immediately stretches out as a plain, as far as Andrianopolis, and most fertile in everything. From the left reaching toward the province of Thessalonica, one finds it well populated, at which point we leave cities and towns behind and at once arrive at high mountains, and finally come to Euboea and the towns of the Athenians, beyond which a major part is possessed by the Turks.[2]

The ancients thought the Aegean Sea was named after King Aegeus, alleged to be the father of Theseus. It begins at the Hellespont and washes an undulating coastline as far as Cape Malea extends. *Cyclos*[3] in Greek means circle, *circulus*, in Latin, and here all the islands lying like a wheel among the reefs of the archipelago, are called the Cyclades. The general divisions of this description having been completed, we descend to the particulars of the aforesaid islands.[4] So that everything may be understood, the mountains are clearly drawn in black, the plains in white, and the waters are shown in green.

The island shown first is Cercira or Corcira, named after a king, which is now called Corfu and is 100 miles in circumference. Toward the south it is mountainous throughout. In these mountains are chestnut trees[5] bearing fruit. On the promontory of Amphipolis is the well fortified city of Sant'Angeli, which sailors can see from afar.

From the east to Corfu and to the farthest point north is a pleasant plain inhabited by many people. And in it the destroyed former city of Cercira is seen, full of sculptures and

1. Probably Italian nautical miles, which were not a standard measure in the Middle Ages. Tony Campbell reviewed various equivalents and settled on 1250 m. or 1372 yards. Modern distances are 340 miles from Rhodes to Cape Malea, and 375 miles from Crete to Tenedos. "Portolan Charts from the late 13th Century to 1500," *Cartography in Prehistoric, Ancient, and Medieval Europe and the Mediterranean, History of Cartography,* J.B. Harley and David Woodward, eds., (Chicago: University of Chicago Press, 1987), 1:389.
2. Reading *Turchi* for *turris* as in other mss. "Turchis," Düsseldorf MS G.13, fol. 28v; Sinner, "Turcis," 53.
3. Reading *Cyclos* for *Chidos*, as in Düsseldorf, fol. 28v.; Sinner, 53.
4. At this point, in other manuscripts, there is a reference to the acrostic, made up of the first letters of each entry: CRISTOFORO BONDELMONT DE FLORENCIA HUNC MISIT CARDINALI JORDANO DE URSINUS MCCCCXX. Our manuscript lacks this passage: "When you see the initial red letters of the descriptive passages, you will find my name and yours and the place and time in which I completed this work.".
5. Sinner, 143, says this is Quercus aegylops, or a variety of oak.

columns. The very lofty Mt. Phalarius, which looks toward the forest of Dodona on the mainland, can be seen from here.

In this place Ovid says there was Dodona, a temple sacred to Zeus. Here two doves used to come down from heaven to perch in the ancient oak trees and there to give answers to petitioners. Then, as they say, one of them flew away to Delphi, a city in Boeotia, and there created the famous oracle of the Delphic Apollo. The other removed to the temple of Jupiter Ammon in Africa.[1]

At the base of this mountain is a rock which was said by the ancients to be a likeness of the ship of Ulysses. Near the Lefkas promontory can be seen Cassiope with its mighty walls, long ago destroyed by pirates. At its base is a plain with a noxious swamp. At the side of these fortifications a church of the mother of our Lord is visited by many men, who having had their prayers heard, return home consoled. To the north Epirus begins, named after a king, with very high mountains in which Troy, now Butroto, was founded by Helenus who came from Troy by sea.

"We cruise along the shores of Epirus
And enter the Chaonian port and ascend
to the lofty city of Buthrotum."[2]

Titus Quinctus Flaminius, made a passage through this island in order to rejoin the Roman army safely, when he was about to make war with Philip, king of Macedonia.[3]

//3r// Corfu, formerly Corcira. [Map: *East on top, but should be south. Clockwise: South, West, North.*[4] Salt works. Mt. Amphipolis. Promontory of Amphipolis. Angelokastro. Mt. Falarius, S. Maria Casopi. Kassiopi, Promontory of Lefkas. *Island:* Ulysses's rock. *On mainland:* Fanari, great mountains. St. Basilis. Salt works. Province of Epirus. Scuate Tower. Dodona, very great forest, Butroti or Butrinto, temple of Jupiter Cassius].

//3v// Beyond Corcira to the east is the island of Paxos (Pachisos), 10 miles in circumference, on which there is an unfortified town inhabited by few men on account of the incursions of the Turks. In the middle on the east side there is a plain fertile in vines and fruit trees. It has a secure harbor. They say the island was formerly one with Corcira, but on account of the fierce tempests of Neptune and Aeolus, the solid ground which was found between the two islands was taken by the sea and Corcyra is diminished on that side by day and by night.

1. This story cannot be found in Ovid.
2. *Aeneid* III.292–293.
3. Philip V, 198 BCE. Second Macedonian War, Livy XXXII.9.
4. These cardinal directions in Latin are around the frame of succeeding maps. From this point on only the top direction will be noted.

.2. PAXOS FORMERLY AND NOW. The circumference of the whole island is 10 miles. [Map: North. *Houses, trees, no toponyms.*]

Our boat crosses to the east for 100 miles, and we come to the ancient mountain once known as Leucon, and now, because of the ebb and flow of the sea four times a day between it and the adjoining hill, it has become an island 80 miles in circumference, where among shady valleys it is well watered by springs. In its center is a plain surrounded by farmsteads and a multitude of grazing herds. The eastern end is terminated with a port.

And to the north, we found another, safer harbor which is graced with mountains, forests and springs. And after going a little ways a most abundantly flowing spring is found on the shore, where travelers and local people are refreshed.

To the left at the base of the mountains we see a most ancient city long destroyed, in which there was a venerable temple of Apollo, and in this place Aeneas, fleeing from Troy, left the armor of Abas.[1]

> 'Soon there appears the cloud-capped headland of Leucata,
> And Apollo's temple on the promontory, which sailors hold in dread.
> Being weary, we put in to land and walked up to the little city."[2]

Later, years having gone by, Octavius Caesar restored this ruined city which was called Nicopolis. In this place, after he had conquered Antony and Cleopatra, he rebuilt the temple of Apollo.

Virgil: Here Augustus Caesar is leading the Italians into battle.[3]

In view of the city is a tower on the seacoast. Not far from there one can see a town with a bridge.

Here the air in the summer breathes contagion. In these places all around stretches a plain. Or if one goes to the north you come upon a forest and the Ambracian Gulf. To the east are seen uninhabited islands[4] in which our forefathers once lived: now on account of the treacherous ambushes of the pirates, they have become desolate.

//4r// .3. LEFKAS, LEUCATE FORMERLY, NOW ST. MAURA. The circumference of the whole island is 80 miles. [Map: East. Nicopolis, very famous spring, very fertile plain. S. Maura *(town)*,.Leucata. Panaia. *On the mainland:* Ambracian Gulf, great forest, S. Nicolaus *(church)*.]

We have shown you Lefkas, now we pass on to Dulichias which was once called Ithaca and now is Valdecompare, surrounded by high cliffs, mountainous and unproductive except for a small plain in the center which has a few trees and houses, and abounding

1. Virgil, *Aeneid* III.286–288.
2. *Aeneid* III.274–275.
3. *Aeneid* VIII.678. Refers to an image on the temple.
4. Reading *insule* for *in fide*.

in sufficient harbors all around. It extends from east to west 30 miles and is three miles wide. The two ends are spread out like two horns, very dangerous to sailors at night. It was here that the most eloquent of the Greeks, Ulysses, who almost always found a way, took Penelope, daughter of Ithacus and married her and got from her a son, Telemachus.

Later Helen, having been seized by Paris, was forced to go to Troy. Ulysses pretended to be insane. When Palamedes came to Ithaca, Ulysses put animals of different kinds in harness to the plow and was discovered sowing salt. Palamedes, suspicious of the cleverness of the man, seized little Telemachus for the purpose of exposing the subterfuge of his cleverness, and put the child in front of the plow. Ulysses, at the sight of his son, at once dropped the plow; and thus, unmasked, was forced to go on the expedition.

//4v// After Troy was captured, by his eloquence in the assembly Ulysses won the arms of Achilles against Ajax. Later he departed from Troy and, anxious to seek his fatherland, was forced by many storms into very long wanderings and pilgrimages. He was away for ten years. At length, having suffered much on the journey, he came to this island, and, having fought a battle in his own house with the suitors of Penelope, he ended his life not long after.

> "We evaded the rocks of Ithaca, Laertes' kingdom,
> And cursed the land which had given birth to savage Ulysses."[1]

.4. Ithaca formerly, now Valdicompare. It is 30 miles long and 3 miles wide. [Map North. Valdicompare. Mt. Neritos.]

So much for Ithaca. Let us begin with Chephalonia, which used to be called Cephalonus and is completely mountainous. *Chephalim* in Greek is head, *caput*, in Latin, since it looks round or like a man's head to sailors coming from the south; or because, from the time of the Trojans up until today, it has been the capital of the ruler of these islands, and the ducal title was derived from it.

I have read in ancient chronicles that the Lord Ulysses was from this region and took his title from Chephalonia. This island, round and rugged with mountains, is 100 miles in circumference in the midst of which rises Mt. Elatus, today known as Leo,[2] without a single river or any springs of water. Around the edge a large number of beech trees and pines grow, and what is more, a wilderness. Many wanderers without something to drink, never finding water, must take in the breeze from the mountains with an open mouth to drink in the summer heat.[3] In the summer serpents and asps are found here, which, sensing

1. Virgil, *Aeneid* III.272–273.
2. Now Mt. Ainos.
3. This story comes from Pseudo-Aristotle, *De mirabilium auditu,* in which the wanderers were goats, not humans. See *Complete Works of Aristotle,* Jonathan Barnes, ed. (Princeton: Princeton University Press, 1984), 2:1273.

//5r// human warmth, sleep with one without harm.

To the east on the shore we worship at the Church of St. Francis, built by him, which produced in its garden all delicious things. This island was the last, or almost the last, which the Romans seized in surrender at the time of the Macedonian War. To the west is Port Viscard,[1] named after Robert Guiscard, lord of Apulia.

Here was once Pitilia, where the Lacedaemonian philosopher Chilon[2] lived for some years, according to Epiphanius the Cypriote, and he was of such great authority[3] and strength that Cicero wrote that he needed to defer to no one among men. For when he wrote, "Know thyself," he meant know your soul and not your body or its parts, which are easy to understand. He understood that we should reform the failings known to be in our soul, because we ourselves should be judged by our actions, and should not end up corrupting our noble nature with inactivity. We must not be corrupted by swollen self-importance or ridiculous pride.

Later Belisarius, the protégé[4] of Emperor Justinian, came here with his fleet and sought refuge from violent storms. He, hearing that Italy was overthrown by the Goths, and moved by pity, went with his fleet to Africa and expelled the Goths from there and from Sicily.[5] Then, having reached Naples, since the gates were not opened to him, he besieged it for a year. Having captured the city, he put iron shackles on the men, women and children he found there and threw them into the fire. Then, returning to Rome, he seized the fleeing Goths. Across from Ithaca is Samus[6] and to the south the port of St. Isidore appears.

> "Now appears forested Iacinthus in the midst of the waves
> And then Dulichiam, Samos and Neritos with its steep, stony cliffs."[7]

//5v// .5. Cefalonia. The circumference of the entire island is 100 miles. [Map: North. Port Fiskardo, formerly Pitilia. Pilarirus, mountain. S. George. S. Nicolas. Cefalonia. Mt. Aino. St. Francis. Port Sami. Port Isidore. S. Siderus. Trapano *(small island to the south)*.]

We have described Chephalonia; now let us speak of Iacinthus.[8] Iacinthus was named either from some lord or from a flower (hyacinth), as it is said to be flowery and pleasant;

1. Fiskardo Bay. Chephalonia was conquered by the Romans in 189 BCE, during the Macedonian Wars. The siege of Same lasted four months.
2. Chilon, one of the Seven Sages, sixth century BCE.
3. DD + S add: "and diligence that in the temple of Apollo he caused these words to be written in golden letters, that is: 'Know Thyself,' which precept"
4. Buondelmonti uses the term *nepos*, or nephew.
5. 535 CE.
6. The city of Same, or Sami.
7. Virgil, *Aeneid* III.270.
8. Zakynthos

it is located across from the Gulf of Corinth. It is said that colonists went from here to Spain, where they founded Saguntum, a noble town most friendly to the Romans, which was destroyed fighting against Hannibal.[1]

This island was once called Jerusalem. When Robert Guiscard, duke of Apulia, was on his way to visit the Holy Sepulchre, it was revealed to him in a dream that he would die in Jerusalem. Arriving at Chefalonia, he then landed on this island. Having become ill here, and hearing that the island was called Jerusalem, he expired in a few days.[2]

To the north appears a plain rich with flocks and country estates. To the east there is a port called Nactis, before which lies a lake of liquid pitch. Here a cow bitten by a fly fell into the lake and was immediately suffocated.[3]

Near here one dark night a ship laden with malmsey,

//6r// driven by fair winds and full sails, rushed onto the sandbank with no injury and thus became stuck. Veronica, hearing that the name of this island was Jerusalem, came to it out of devotion, and there, as they say, displaying the head-cloth of Christ, she preached the death of the Savior, and many devout souls were converted to the faith.

To the east on the coast is said to be a vein of metals and it rises up into the mountains across the whole district among groves of trees which are shady at mid-day. Then we come to the west which ends with Pilosus and the port of St. Nicolas, most excellent, and nearby is a plain with saltworks.

Finally to the north near the middle of the island rises a city which has often been destroyed by earthquakes.[4] There my duchess lies entombed along with members of the family.[5] Iacinthus is sixty miles in circumference with good air and pleasant delight for all living there.

Virgil: "Now in the midst of the waves appears forested Iacinthus."[6]

1. 219–218 BCE. Livy XXI.7–15.
2. Robert Guiscard, Norman duke of Apulia, Calabria and Sicily, who rampaged around the eastern Mediterranean, presenting a serious threat to the Byzantine Empire. He died in 1085 of an epidemic disease, perhaps typhoid. This event is usually stated to have taken place on the neighboring island of Cephalonia.
3. Pitch wells, referred to by Herodotus IV.195, used for waterproofing ships.
4. This island has frequently been devastated by earthquakes, most recently in 1953.
5. Maddalena Buondelmonti, great-aunt of our author. Married to Leonardo Tocco, count of Cephalonia and duke of Lefkas, she died in 1401. Like many Florentines, Buondelmonti had numerous family contacts throughout the islands.
6. *Aeneid* III.270.

.6. IANCITHUS. Circumference of the whole island 60 miles. [Map: North. *From top:* S. Nicolaus *(church)*, Iacinthos, Jerusalem, Lake of pitch. Port Nacte. S. Basilius. Port S. Nicolai. St. Nicolaus *(church)*. Port Pilosus.]

It now remains to describe the most sacred rocky islets found in the Ionian Sea to the south, formerly called holy Plotae, the perimeter of each of which does not exceed one mile. They were then called Achinnades from the sea urchins near the river Achelous. Later they were called STROPHADES from the Greek *strophe*, translated into Latin as *reversio*, turning back.

A brotherhood of monks resided here, who followed a strict regime of fish and water until they were all made captive by Barbary pirates and sold. The present inhabitants, so that they might contemplate the secure path to God, built a tower in which they might live the eremetical life.

//6v// The community there has recovered to include more than fifty with all their associates.[1]

It has been established that this island along with a small one nearby was inhabited by pirates in the time of Phineas, king of Arcadia.[2] Knowledgeable people say that Phineus himself blinded his sons, persuaded by Arpalice, their stepmother, and in revenge for this wickedness, pirates besieged Phineas in Arcadia and reduced him to misery. But Zetus and Chalais, brothers of Arpalice, set them to flight and freed Phineas, driving the pirates as far as these islands. Therefore they called the young men the Strophades, that is, they returned to these islands, without having achieved their goal.[3]

In the time of Aeneas, who, having fled from Troy and seeking Italy, he arrived here and was feasting with his comrades. The Harpies, expelled from Arcadia and inhabiting these islands, seized the food with their claws and sullied it with their foul touch. They were driven out by him with iron weapons. Celeno, their leader, spoke:

> "To Italy you will go, and you will be allowed to enter its harbors,
> but not granted a city until you surround it with walls;
> a fearful hunger will drive you to devour your tables
> which will punish you for your sin in striking us."[4]

Therefore they are called Harpies for their voracity, and there a band of pirates used to despoil those sailing by with avarice and rapine.

1. There still is a community of monks on one of the islands.
2. Phineus's kingdom is usually described as being in eastern Thrace, or, according to Apollonius of Rhodes, in Bithynia. The connection with the Strophades appears to come from Virgil, see the quotation below.
3. Phineus is usually represented as being tortured by the Harpies. The "pirates" appear to be Buondelmonti's invention. Arpalice, the wicked stepmother, has a name suspiciously close to Harpy. The name, Strophades, or turning, has been interpreted in various ways. Graves, 150.3, says they were called this because sailors could expect the wind to turn as they neared the islands.
4. *Aeneid* III.254 ff.

"Saved from the waves, I first found haven on the shores of the Strophades
in the wide Ionian Sea. They have been called by the name Strophades in Greek,
where the ferocious Celeno and other Harpies dwell,
since the palace of Phineas was closed against them
and in fear of their pursuers they abandoned the tables
where they had previously fed. There is no more savage monster than the Harpies;
no stroke of divine wrath was ever more cruel,
and no wickeder demon ever rose from the waters of the Styx.
They are birds with girls' faces, and a disgusting outflow from their bellies.
Their hands have talons and their faces are always pallid with hunger."[1]

Now these islands have turned from evil to good. Once they were waylaying sailors; now how much better that they lovingly speed them to draw near with earnest prayers. Here there is a tower with a church, and the monks gather in it for the canonical hours, where the hégoumène, or prior, reading the life of the holy fathers, explains it to all.

Judge, oh Father,[2] what the life of these men is. Their strict regimen is well known, conducted within the space of one square mile and removed from the mainland by 80 stades. There they reject meat and rejoice to sustain life with sun-dried fish, dry bread, and water so that each might render his soul pure to the Almighty.

.7. Strophades Islands. Circumference of the whole island is 3 miles. [Map: North. monastery of monks, *church on the larger island*.]

//7r// I arrive at Sapientia across from the city of Modon[3]. The island is small and unproductive, and is called Sapientia because a passing ship would wisely protect itself from the hidden shoals there, or because a Greek woman lived there who, by means of incantations, disclosed future events to passers-by. In the midst of it rises a mountain on which the people of Modon watch for a distant sail from afar off, and warn all the surrounding regions.

To the east are uncultivated islands inhabited by goats. On the smaller of these in the time of Murad the Great of the Turks,[4] a bireme of infidels landed there one stormy night and immediately attacked the church. When they had surrounded it and heard the monks singing, the door of the church was nowhere to be found, and so they stayed there until dawn. Dawn having broken and, fearing an ambush from the Christians, they could not depart from the shore until they had repaired the damage done to the monastery.

1. *Aeneid* III.209–218.
2. One of the few references to Cardinal Orsini in this manuscript.
3. Modern: Methóni.
4. Reading for Amoratus. Murad I, r. 1362–89, referred to as Moratus Bey in Venetian accounts. He attacked this area in 1387. Setton, *Crusades* 3:245 n.

Facing these islands are two cities. First is Modon, rich in the liquor of Bacchus, and the second is Corona,[1] crowned by the liquid (olive oil) of Pallas. Both are in the province of Morea.

This was once called the Peloponnesus after Pelops, the son of Tantalus, who was, as Barlaam[2] says, a man of battles and many distinctions, who, when he ruled the Phrygian kingdoms, made war against Oenomius, the king of Elis and Pisa. He started this great war and was overpowered by Hippodamia.[3] Finally, since he had ruled Argos, he called it Peloponnesus after his own name.

.8. Sapientia .9. Capra [Map: East. Peloponnesian land, olives everywhere, vines everywhere, oranges everywhere. *Island with church:* St. Venetus. Corona, Modon (Methóni). Cape Galli. *Islands:* Cabrera (Schiza). Sapientia].

//7v// It seems superfluous to me to tell how many small rocky islets there are in these parts, for we found no outstanding deed in them to relate. So we shall be silent about them and go on to the island of Chituria or Cytharea,[4] which today is called Citri. It is the first of the islands of the archipelago to the west. The island is completely mountainous in which the town of Citheron is clearly seen.

Here Venus is celebrated with honor and from this both Venus and the island take their name. She was sculpted[5] as a beautiful nude girl, swimming in the sea and holding a marine conch shell in her right hand, adorned with roses and accompanied by doves flying around her. She was taken in marriage by Vulcan, the base and rustic god of fire. Before her stand three naked girls, which are called the Three Graces, two of whom turn their faces toward her, and the other turns away.

Also standing with her is her son Cupid, winged and blind, who with bow and arrow shot at Apollo on account of which, the gods were disturbed, and the timid boy fled to his mother's lap. The planet Venus is of a feminine complexion, and, like a girl, it is warm and humid. Married to Vulcan, who is said to be fiery, and, immersed in the sea, which is composed of heat and humidity, she gave birth to Cupid, the god of love, that is, the desire of the flesh.

The Three Graces symbolize three sins: avarice, in profiting from a sexual act; carnality, in binding together in a carnal act; infidelity, since they teach a man to take pleasure for

1. Koróni.
2. Barlaam (1290–1348), Greek monk from Calabria who taught Greek in Florence. Cited as a source by Boccaccio for information on Greek mythology in *Genealogiae deorum gentilium*.
3. Hippodamia, daughter of Oenomius. Pelops won her in a chariot race.
4. Modern: Kithira.
5. The following lines are taken from Pierre Bersuire, 2, except he says she is painted, not sculpted.

money. Cupid is winged because he flames up quickly and joins in sexual union, and blindfolded since he does not care where he takes his pleasure.

From this island Paris, son of Priam, seized Helen, the not unwilling wife of Menelaus. On a festival day she had come to the temple--still known today-- situated near the sea. When they had gazed at one another, the beauty of both gave impetus to the crime. When this deed had been accomplished, great destruction followed.

Because of this abduction, all the princes of the Greeks swore unanimously to destroy Troy. And after they had repeated these oaths very often in vain, they captured Troy after 10 years with a huge army led by Agamemnon, and Helen was restored to Menelaus. He, diverted by a storm at sea, was first carried into Egypt. Then they returned to Lacedaemon.

The island is sixty miles around with few inhabitants, and around about many rocky reefs are seen, one with a stream of very fresh water of the name of Dragon Spring.

.11. Cytharea now Citri. Circumference of the whole island 60 miles. [Map: North. Town of Citheron, temple where Helen was seized by Paris. *Island to the northeast:* Arencanara.]

In this small space we can briefly describe Sichilus.[1] It is ten miles in circumference. There once was a town, but since it has now been taken over by wild asses, no human being lives on it. If you were to sleep on the hide of a wild ass, you would not fear demons. One can cure an epilepsy, if one will hold the skin of an ass's brow over oneself, or drink a potion of the ashes of the hooves, //8r.// or wear a ring (made from them). The smoke made from the ashes will ease the pangs of a woman in labor. If you give the scraping of a stone found in the head or jaw to a feverish person to drink, it will relieve him. If you drink or make a salve of the blood from the ear, mixed with the juice of snakeweed and oil of roses, and smear it on the loins before the onset of quartan fever, you will remain healthy. Crippled limbs of a dry humor will be relaxed if they are washed with a broth from ass's flesh and are rubbed with the broth and fat of a female ass. The marrow of the bones is good for wounds and nerves.

Once the Turks, coming here, suffered a shipwreck. Hearing this, the Cretans quickly made ready a road to the underworld for them.

And also a ship in a tempest at night crashed into the island. The sailors on it, swimming, crowded onto planks. They perished on the eighth day opposite Kithera, except one of those who stayed on the rock, and, eating the roots of trees and herbs, was saved by passers-by about a year later, and escaped unharmed.

1. Antikythera

.12. Antikytherea, formerly Sichilius. Circumference of the whole island, 10 miles [Map: North].

//8r// Since everything which will be related here was told at greater length in the book which I wrote about Crete,[1] here for easy reading I briefly and clearly divide the island into three parts. It is located nearly in the middle of the Mediterranean, is surrounded on all sides by mountains, and everywhere buffeted by winds.

From east to west it appears to measure 230 (miles) and is 35 miles wide. To the east is Mt. Salmon, which looks toward the island of Carpathia; to the west rises Mt. Corycis,[2] which looks toward Cape Malea. Crete was named after Cretus, son of Nebroth (Nimrod), or because of its soil of clinging, white clay (*creta* in Latin). It had 100 cities, of which I have seen the remnants of sixty.

Here lived Saturn, wise and powerful, said to be the son of Uranus, that is, heaven, and Vesta (Hesta), that is, the earth. He caused himself to be prayed to as an image of god. He was the first to coin bronze money and to put his name on it. He taught the ignorant people to cultivate the land and to sow seed in the fields, and he ordered them to gather the harvest. He set up an altar for his worship, instituted holy rites and gave his name to the Saturnalia.

He took his sister, Vesta, in holy marriage and from her it is written that he had many children, all of whom, they say, he devoured, lest they expel him from the kingdom. To save Jove (Jupiter) Saturn's wife sent him by a ruse secretly to Mt. Ida[3] to be nursed. Entrusted to the people of the Kouretes, he was hidden in a cave of Mt. Ida. So that his crying might not be heard, they beat upon cymbals and drums, and at the sound bees put honey

//8v// in his mouth, and his nurses nourished him on milk and honey.

When he had grown up, he made war on the Titans. Then he drove his father from the kingdom since he was a harsh ruler and had taught the people to sacrifice human flesh, even his own children. Therefore, Jupiter, after the flight of his father, was made lord of the Cretans and took his sister Juno in marriage. Eager for glory, he constructed temples in his name in many places.

There are many gods called Jupiter, but this Cretan one was greater than them all, since he introduced many things good and useful to human life. At his death they placed his body near the town of Aulacia[4] although it is said that he was deified in heaven.[5]

1. Buondelmonti had written a book about his travels in Crete in 1415. See the critical edition by Marie-Anne van Spitael, *Descriptio Insule Crete* (Hierakleion: Syllogos politistikes anaptyxeos Herakleiou, 1981).
2. Corycus for manuscript's Oricis, Pliny IV.59.
3. Reading *Idaeum* for *eundem*.
4. Variants of this name: Alavere, Avlakra, Arilatiae.
5. The tomb of Jove is a traditional site in Crete, dating back to antiquity. Callimachus denounces

Near the mountain known today by his name, at its base to the north, from the evidence of Ptolemy,[1] we found a man-made cave of white stone with a small opening 40 cubits long and 4 wide, at the head of which we recognized the tomb of mighty Jove with its damaged epitaph. Outside, widely scattered on the ground, were the great buildings of a temple.

When we turn to the south coast near the sea to the east there is Hierapolis with its huge buildings of marble, and Mathalia with mosaic decorations, and Fenicis, most noble city, now in ruins.[2] Here, on the temple, are carved in Greek letters: "Wash your feet, veil your head, and enter."

Here was magnificent Kissamopolis where one approaches the promontory Cadistus, today Cape Spata. Then comes Chidonia (Echidonia), which today is Acanta (Chanea), a most pleasant place. In this place Metellus attacked Crete for two years with fire and sword, seized the whole island and got revenge for Mark Antony, who had fought at sea.

Creticus[3] returned the island to Rome, as Titus Livius says.[4] I come to Retina, then to Canda, now Candia, the metropolis, after the Venetians acquired it and rebuilt it. Next I arrive at Chersonesus, formerly with high walls. Then I go to Doloexopolis,[5] today Histrina, in which there is a spring which drives eight mills. Nearby along the seacoast there are other towns on the tops of the mountains, in the midst of which is the city of Sarandapolis, once a city of giants, from which Sectia is derived.

At the east end of the island is Mt. Salmon, higher than all of its neighbors. Retracing my steps to the west, after we have left Mt. Salmon and passing through the middle of the island, we arrive at Mt. Dicteus, and on its summit is the plain of Lassitus, 18 miles in circumference, most rich in pastures.

To the south stretches the broad plain called Messarea in which near the center appear the not inconsiderable remains of the great city of Gortina, once the capital, which was the chief city of King Minos and seems as great as our own city of Florence in size. With great skill and arrangement of downward flowing waters they watered the whole city, in which I counted more than a thousand fallen marble columns and idols.

---

the idea in his "Hymn to Zeus," saying that all Cretans are liars. Early Christian apologists jumped upon this idea, pointing out that their god rose from the dead, while Jupiter is still in his tomb. Origen, *Against Celsus.*

1. This mountain is not in Ptolemy, but Elautherae may be his version of the above: III.xv (Crete).

2. Matalia and Fenix or Phoenix appear on Ptolemy's tenth map of Europe.

3. Honorary title for Metellus.

4. Refers to a lost book of Livy's history. Metellus's conquest of Crete took place in 69 BCE. The Marcus Antonius mentioned here, father of the more famous Mark Antony, had failed in his attempts to wipe out piracy based on Crete, and died around 71 BCE.

5. Leiden: *Dolopexopolis*; Dd: *Clopixopolim*; van Spitael: *Olopixopolis*.

About a mile to the north on the mountain is found the narrow opening of the Labyrinth, in which, they say, the Minotaur was confined by Daedalus and slain by Theseus, by means of a trick by the sister of Phaedra.[1] The slaughtered beast lies buried in the same place. Ten miles to the west appears the most renowned and lofty Mt. Ida, at the base of which once the city of Knossos was seen.

This mountain has five peaks and no trees. In the midst of it is the lofty part where, it is said, Saturn founded a temple for his worship, and there first instituted the sacrifice of flesh. From halfway up as far as the summit the snows lie all year round. From Knossos as far as the city of Aptera is an area 40 miles by 20 miles, a space in which many things have been related by the authority of many authors.[2]

To the west to the shady valleys is the dwelling place of twelve families of Romans, who came here in the time of Constantine,[3] and from generation to generation have renewed their coats of arms and kept the name of their forefathers up to the present day. They follow the Greek rite. First there are the *Gortaci*, in Latin *Saturi*, 500 in number; then the *Mellissimi* or *Vespasiani*, 300; *Ligni* or *Suttiles*, 1,600; *Vlasti* or *Papiani*, 200; *Cladi* or *Ramuli*, 180; *Scordilli* or *Aglati*, 800; *Coloni* or *Colonnenses*, 30; *Arculeades* or *Ursini*, 100 remaining.

Finally in the far corner of this island rises Mt. Leucas from which many rivers descend and in its shady valleys

//9r// so many huge cypress trees sprout up and grow that it is incredible to tell. Planks made from them are exported throughout the world every year.

Virgil:

> An island rises in mid-sea, Crete, great Jove's land,
> where first Mount Ida rears, the cradle of our people.
> The Cretans live in 100 spacious cities, rich domains.[4]

Crete. [Map: *East*: Chersonesus, St. Sideros. *Down the north coast (left):* Termara, Sectia, Istrina, Chersonesus, S. Giorgius, Candia, Heraklion, Milopotono, Rethymnon, Bonifacio, Chanea. *Down the south coast (right):* Hierapolis, Girapetra, Cape Gabello, very high mountain, Belvedere, Tower of the King, Lassa, S. Iohannes, Piriotissa, S. Constantinus, Levka, White Mountains. In this place are an infinite number of

1. That is, Ariadne.
2. Apteriopolis or Stimpolis. Among the authors is probably Ovid, *Metamorphoses* VIII, which recounts the stories of King Minos, the Labyrinth and Theseus.
3. This MS says 22, but other manuscripts say 12 families; in any case only eight are named here. Van Spitael says that Buondelmonti has pushed the origins of these families too far back. They were actually settled in Crete by the Byzantine Emperor, Alexis Comnenus, in 1182.
4. Virgil, *Aeneid* III.126–128, Fagles translation.

cypresses. Kissamou, Cape Spada. *Interior from east (top):* Mt. Dikti sandy plain without fruit, Mt. Tera, Omalo Planitie, Lassiti, Pidiata, Gortina Minoris, *in red, faded:* Gortyn, Labyrinth, tomb of Jove, Mt. Ida, famous mountain of Jove, plain of Messarea, *in faded red ink:* 40 miles, mountain, great forest of wild olives, *in faded red ink:* Knossos, Stirapolis. *Many small islands: from top (east), south side:* Cristiana, Niso, Galdaro, Umica, Ballo, Paximadhia, Gozo. *North side:* Pori, Diva, Moso, Soron, Psira, Pimolis, Pismidi, Dhia, Odoro. *Two islands in border at west:* Capa, Bruse. *Northwest, small island with church, no name.*[1]]

//9v// I have spoken of Crete; now I come to the island of CARPATHIA, from *karpos* in Greek, which is *fructus*, or fruit in Latin, and Pallene from the son of the Titan who ruled there. From this the name of Pallas was derived, since she who was first called Minerva was nursed here, and, born from the head of Jove, she was the goddess of wisdom.

She has been sculpted in the image of an armed woman. Her head is encircled by a rainbow[2] and [she has] a helmet with a crest, a lance in her right hand and in her left a golden shield with a monstrous Gorgon's head. Her vestments are of three colors, and near her is an olive tree with an owl perched on it. So she is armed as the wise man is armed with virtue, [and bears] a shield of bravery, a lance of rectitude and justice, a helmet of sobriety and temperance, and the rainbow of clarity and prudence, the olive tree of piety and prudence,[3] the owl of humility and secrecy.

The tricolored vestments are the three contemplative virtues: the golden shield the splendor of truth; the terrible image, fear of the divine; the image of the Gorgon, of death or the devil; the crest, of honor.

This was the fatherland of Iapetus, who had two sons, Epimetheus and Prometheus, the latter endowed with great intelligence and eagerness for learning. It is said that he made the likeness of a man from mud. Minerva was delighted with him and took Prometheus into heaven so that he could choose what he wanted of heavenly things for the perfection of his handiwork. There he stole a ray of the sun, and, planting it in its bosom, gave life to his creation. Then, thundered at by Jove, he (Prometheus) was tied up on Mt. Caucasus, and gave his liver to be perpetually gnawed upon by a vulture. There on Mt. Caucasus Prometheus, studying the nature of man from his beginning, considered him to be of the earth. Turning to his other nature, he understood that the soul came from heaven, its celestial origin stolen in the ray of the sun, directing him toward celestial things for his consolation. The vulture or eagle that eats his liver is nothing other than this: that studious men stain their outer selves as they are burned up with interior passions.

1. Map has 40 names, 18 in text. 18 islands, none in text.
2. Reading *iride* for *idrie*: see below. Bersuire, 40–41.
3. Other manuscripts use *misericordia*, mercy.

Here there are seven towns of which today three are found among the mountains. The island is 70 miles in circumference and to the east the city of Olimbos stands out, with its port Tristomos and the island Sario. To the west near the port of Theatros are two towns on the heights of the promontory, Teneo and Circassus, which is now called St. Theodore, and in view is the island Cusso.

To the north near the sea there once lay the city of Fiantus. Not far, almost in the middle of the island, Mt. Achinaea and Oros and the mountain of St. Elias can be seen on all sides. To the south there is a plain at the head of which Port Agata lies. Finally throughout the island the population is brutish, and working in pitch, they subsist on milk.

Once the infidels, coming secretly by night, went through the island seeking treasure. The Carpathians on guard bravely burnt their boat. The infidels, returned, distressed at having missed so much booty, and more than a hundred perished of hunger in the mountains.

//10r// .14. SCARPANTHA. Circumference of the whole island 70 miles. [Map. *From upper right corner:* city of Fiantus formerly great, Paleo Rostro, Mt. Olympus. Port Agatha. Mt. Archimata, Port S. Tristomos, Mt. Oros Mons *(with church).* Port S. Minias. S. Theodorus, Arnissus formerly. Port Theatros, formerly Thera. Menetes. Mt. Goma. Pigadia *with well;* now Karpathos. *Off the east coast:* island of Saria. Kasos, *island to the west.* 18 *names,* 13 *of these in text.*]

So I come to the most ancient city of RHODES, a refuge for the lords of Asia Minor and former Greek lands, now part of Turkey, and of merchants and pilgrims from all parts of the world who come here. It is said that *Rhodo* in Greek is *rosa* in Latin, since here roses flourish in greater perfection than in other places. Or, it is named from the Punic apple or pomegranate, since it once was full of men[1] (as a pomegranate is of seeds). It lies in the shape of a shield, going around from St. Stephen as far as St. John of the Lepers, and St. Antony and St. Gallinicus, returning to the first saint. There are 200 towers around it, as it says in the chronicle, each of which rises 50 cubits.

In the midst there stood a giant idol of amazing size, 70 cubits, which a ship could see from 80 miles away. And the highest point of the whole city was lower than this. Rhodes, most powerful for many years, did battle with the Egyptians. Eventually it was destroyed by them. Others think it was on account of frequent earthquakes that the Colossus and the towers perished, shaken to the foundations, and a great number of people also died. Many diverse and contrary opinions of these matters are offered. I dare not speak, being ignorant of such ancient history. For we know that there are as many judgments as there are heads, as men make judgments according to their desire rather than reason. However, I have found in a certain Greek book that the Colossus was a bronze idol with a height

1. As a pomegranate is of seeds.

of [70] cubits and in the middle of its chest it displayed a great mirror.[1] Ships departing from Egypt and looking toward it could see it.

Here and throughout the whole island are more than 1000 colossi mounted on columns. There are in all parts innumerable columns decorated with the heads of deer. Here we also found a coin with the image of Caesar, as well as an infinite number of burial urns, the remains that they hold being lost to modern memory. Again near St. Antony and St. Savior in the vineyards 500 idols of all types were found in a pit.[2]

//10v// Now the city is small in comparison to the ancient city. It faces east and is divided into four parts. In the first of these resides the Master of the Hospital of St. John.[3] The second is possessed by the brothers of the aforesaid order, the third by those who would visit the hospital, and the fourth and last is inhabited by merchants, along with the Greeks. The city is everywhere called Colocensis from the colossus.

This island is the most pleasant of all the islands of the Mediterranean Sea. It is 154 miles around. Near the sea from the western part of the northernmost part, as far as the south, there is a plain with towns and many country estates. One city, formerly called Vasilica, which in Latin is *imperatrix* (empress), is found here, reduced to ruins.

To the south lie two notable towns and many country estates, where Apolakia and Kattavia are most eminent, sustained by agriculture and well cultivated with a multitude of cattle. To the east near the sea there was once a wall of immense squared stones, running over mountains and valleys, which divided the island. This shows that it was ruled by two lords.

Finally we see well-fortified Lindos, in which religious rituals different from the rite elsewhere were dedicated to Hercules, since they sacrificed human flesh to the gods.[4] Then we see the deserted remains of Faradum, not small but magnificent in extent. We find towns such as Fandum and the village Archangelo. Then we draw near to Rhodes, where there is such lush greenery of trees and enchanting places that it is wonderful to see, particularly "Paradise" made by the Florentines.[5]

1. The Colossus was erected in 302 BCE and destroyed by an earthquake in 227 BCE.
2. Bessi suggests that these were votive statuettes for the near-by shrine of Demeter. "Cristoforo Buondelmonti: Greek Antiquities in Florentine Humanism," *Historical Review* 9 (2012): 63–76, esp. 73.
3. The Hospital, Knights of St. John of the Hospital, founded in 1048, was one of the military orders who fought in the Crusades. After the Christians were expelled from the Holy Land, the Knights set up their headquarters first on Cyprus, then in 1306 on Rhodes, where they remained until 1523 when the island was conquered by the Turks.
4. This practice is greatly expanded upon by Silvestri, along with moral reflections. He takes his information from Lactantius, *Institutes* 1.21,31.
5. Paradisi, a town on the west coast.

Finally in the middle of the island lies Mt. Artamita with the river Gadura and to the left the village Appollona with its many miracles of the Virgin Mother Mary. About five miles from the city on Mt. Filerinus is a town and the much-visited Lady of all Graces, who is worshipped by many.

From here the laws of the sea appear to have had their origin, and Appollonius[1] was born, who wrote elegantly "On the 8 Parts of Orations," from which Priscian extracted many things and took them for his own use. Finally Tullius [Cicero], arriving in this city, found the most eloquent philosophers of the Greeks, and before them and the people he made a famous speech.[2] For this reason he received extravagant praise from the Rhodians. Paul the Apostle sent his epistle to the "Colossians," for they were called Colossians from the Colossus of Rhodes.[3] If it rains, still every day the sun appears, and now I have over the past eight years confirmed the experience of Varro.

//11r// Rhodes. Circumference of the whole island <…> miles.[4] [Map: North. *Top:* S. Calfocus *(with windmill)*. S. Nicolas. S. Antonio. S. Steffanus. St. John of the Lepers. *Down east coast (right):* S. Helias. Aphandou. Archangelos. Nicolaus *(on island in the east)*, Farado. Lindo. Gadura *(river)*. Asklipeion. *Down west coast (left):* Triando. Kremasti. Philerimos *(mountain and monastery)*. S. Maria Filerno. Villa Nova. Sominii. Vasilica. Pibechia. Lachania. *Center:* Mt. Akramytis *(monastery)*. Salaco. Sciama. Appollona. S. Gerama monastery.[5] Kattavia.]

//11v//[6] In the days of [Saturn] this island [had been] named Simia after the Simeni who ruled there,[7] or [from the Greek *Simane*, in Latin *propinqua* (near)], since it was close to Asia Minor, and [trading with] its neighbors, they obtained a living from their labor. But later Prometheus, the son of Iapetus, sent here by the great Jove, demonstrated many things to the inhabitants, useful for preserving human life. He, being powerful in ingenuity, made a man from mud. When Jupiter heard this, he turned him into a monkey and there he ended his days.[8]

1. Karl von Bayer, ed., *Cristoforo Buondelmonti Liber Insularum Archipelagi* (Düsseldorf MS), 62 n. 27. This is Appollonius Dyskolos, second century BCE, who wrote a number of works on Greek syntax, of which four survive.
2. Cicero went to Rhodes in 50 BCE; the speech is lost.
3. The Epistle to the Colossians was actually written to the residents of Colossae, a city in Phrygia.
4. Parchment damaged here.
5. Perhaps Domina Gratiarum, Our Lady of Graces.
6. The manuscript is torn and mended with blank parchment here. The words in brackets are added from the Düsseldorf MS, fol. 35v.
7. *Simane:* derivation from modern Greek. Gerola, "L'etimologie dei nomi," 1161.
8. I have seen no other version of this story. Possibly inspired by the similarity of the word "simian.'

The inhabitants today are very resourceful. They travel in their boats between the cities of the Turks and those of the Rhodians, busily seeking their sustenance. To the south there are reefs at which ships frequently lower their sails. There is a well-fortified castle near the sea and another abandoned in the mountains. The island is thirty miles in circumference, with excellent wine. The goats frolic in the high places, among the rocks.[1]

.16. Simia formerly and now. Circumference of the entire island, 30 miles. [Map: North. Turkey, Simia port and city, S. Nicolaus. *On island to the south:* S. Paulus *(church).*]

//12r//[2] Not very far from the island named above, another island is seen, once Caristos, now Calchis, in which the Titans reigned. The inhabitants established divine rites to their son, Briareus. The inhabitants are few because of the weather, and, since the island is very arid and unproductive, they have not troubled to erect buildings. Here there are figs in such abundance that they enrich the ships sailing past these places.

To the east lies a harbor at whose summit is seen an ancient, well-fortified town. Here, weary from his travels, St. Nicholas rested and showed the path of virtue to those people. By their prayers he has granted such grace, that, laboring continuously to dig with iron tools in these dry and rocky mountains, they are not diminished. From that time to this the mines have been maintained, and they reckon them to be rich dowries for their daughters. Because of this, they have built a church to the honor of St. Nicholas,[3] very rich in gold and silver, which they take more pains to manage than they do their heart and soul.

.17. Calchis, formerly Dicteus. Circumference of the entire island <illeg.> [Map: North. Chalcis. *Large fortified building in center plus house, trees, church, islands to east.*]

We have shown Calchis, now I am going to cross to what was once Diluphanos, today Piscopia. Diluphanos[4] is Greek, which translates into Latin as *omnibus apparentibus* or "with all appearing." Piscopia is Greek from *epi,* which is above, and *scopos*, which is a look-out, as a high vantage point, since it is raised high with mountains and can be seen from a very long way off. It is elongated from east to west, and is 35 miles around.

To the east rises Mt. Frondifluus, at the base of which are two rocky islands, one of which is called Ascina. To the north is the town of S. Stephen in which a bridge and a plain are seen. To the west rises Zucharola, a miserable place. In the middle also are two other towns are poorly inhabited. There are more goats wandering about than there are men able to guard the places.

1. See Legrand, 186, variant; Barsanti, 139. In the Greek ms the wine is said to be so good because the vines are fertilized by the goats.
2. Upper-right corner blanked out: mended tear. Words in brackets from Düsseldorf MS, fol. 36r.
3. The Church of St. Nicholas is still there.
4. Tilos

.18. Diluphanos formerly, now Piscopia. Circumference of the entire island 35 miles. [Map: North. Piscopia, S. Steffanus. Zucharola.]

//12v//[1] [I have shown the situation of Piscopia], now I am able to point out what was once Caria, now Nixaros, with its Mt. Etna. *Caribdi* in Greek[2] is *nux* (nut) in Latin, and *nixos* in Greek is translated *insula*, island, in Latin. Here the consul Flaminius was returning from the east and arrived ready to fight the Gauls. It was prophesied that he would obtain a victory, and this in fact came to light.[3] So this island always had favorable feelings toward the Romans.

Through this place Cleopatra was passing with Antony, and as the citizens were unwilling to obey their orders, they destroyed the whole island.[4] The island is 18 miles around and five towns are seen of which the two principal ones are Mandrachi and Paleo Castra. And Pandenichi, Nichea and Argos are on the coast.

Around the middle of the island rises a very high mountain, which on the summit, belches forth sulphurous fires from subterranean channels day and night, just like the island of Strongilus in the Liparian Islands. On the downward slope of the mountain, about a stone's throw, a hot spring pours forth in flames, and the waters descend to the plain around a very deep and dark lake. Here the inhabitants provide a very great quantity of sulphur to merchants.

And such an intense heat prevails from the middle to the top of the mountain, no one dares to come near without wooden shoes. There is such an abundance of figs that each year small ships can be loaded with them. To the north at the foot of the mountain near the sea stands a cave to which come the local people when suffering from pain, and, after staying for a while, they return home, healed. The caves, it is presumed, are here because the island has so many and such great earthquakes. When the earthquakes burst forth, the terrified people of the market place, cursing, quickly abandon the place and are glad to get a long way off. The inhabitants, however, think that this shaking is nothing.

1. Upper-left corner blanked out. Words in brackets are added from Düsseldorf MS, f. 36r.
2. The Greek words for nut is *karuon*.
3. Titus Quinctius Flaminius was elected consul in 198 BCE. He was the triumphant general in the Second Macedonian War, and hailed as the liberator of Greece from the Macedonians. The campaign against the Gauls, or Galatians, took place soon after, but he was not the general. Plutarch, "Flaminius," *Parallel Lives;* Livy XXXIII.
4. Cleopatra and Antony were sailing around the Aegean before the Battle of Actium in 31 BCE, but I can find no other reference to the destruction of Nisyros (Caria).

.19. Caria formerly, now Nixaros Circumference of the entire island, 18 miles. [Map: North. Sulphur bath, Mandrachi, very high mountain from which a sulphurous flame always erupts, gira castro, Pandenichi, *(cave),* Nichea, Argos.]

Now I hasten my course to Stimphalea, formerly, today Spelunca, or, as Pliny says, "Astimphalea, a free state 89 miles around."[1] In addition Ovid writes,

"[Minos] joined to his cause both Anaphe and Astypalea, Anaphe
by promises and Stimphalea by threat of war."[2] and
"Astimphalea lies here, surrounded by the fish-filled sea."[3]

It is very narrow in the middle and wide at the ends, where many ruined fortresses are to be seen. To the north is the town of Vathi. To the southwest appears the city called Stimphalea. There are throughout the island the ruins of many ancient towns. Around the coast are many excellent harbors, now long made desolate by pirates. They lie everywhere, without walls, not rebuilt up to our day. In the days of Morbasson,[4] the Turks, pirates with a great fleet came to these islands, and destroyed them completely. Until recently it was abandoned by the inhabitants, but the noble Venetian Giovanni Quirini[5] with his men took it over in the time of the Council of Constance in order to restore it.

//13r// .20. Astimphalea. Circumference of the entire island 89 miles. [Map: North. S. Clemens. S. Chaterina. Stimphalea. S. Iohannes. Vathi. Vathi. *In water, north:* Paleo Castro *(2x).* S. Benedictus.]

The ancients, especially Pliny, assert that this island was called Egasa,[6] then Filetera from Filete who was ruling there, later Callista from the goodness of its land, and finally it was called Therasia before it had risen to the surface. Later it rose in the middle and then, some time having gone by up until today, it was named Santorini (Santellini). The island, fertile and well-populated, was highly esteemed. On account of a volcanic eruption, the middle of it was submerged in the depths of the sea, and we see its burnt up remains in the shape of the moon. Today it is called Therasia. Between one part and the other, larger part is an unfathomable abyss of water, which is of such a great depth that in no way could the illustrious Duke Giacomo[7] of these islands touch the bottom, when he

1. Pliny IV.12.71: Astypalaea.
2. Ovid, *Metamorphoses* VII.461f.
3. Ovid, *Ars Amatoria* II.85.
4. Omarbeg Morbasson, self-styled Prince of Achaia, laid waste this island in 1341. Miller, *Latins in the Levant*, 589.
5. Giovanni Quirini repopulated the island in 1413. Miller, *Latins in the Levant*, 606. The Quirini family of Venice ruled the island from 1207 to 1522, when it was taken by the Turks.
6. Pliny IV.12.70 supplies a number of names for this island, but Egasa is not one of them.
7. Giacomo I, duke of the Archipelago, d. 1418. Miller, *Latins in the Levant,* 601.

lowered a heavy rope one mile long into the abyss. In circumference it extends[1] between the horns of the moon. At the western part near the sea a magnificent city spreads out. Its inhabitants abandoned it in ruins and built a fortified city on a high mountain.

While we were there on a Genoese ship, we saw an octopus, with its arms spread out 60 cubits wide, reaching toward us. Seeing this we all left the ship at once, and, terrified, watched near the banks from above until we might sail away with a saving wind. In my days five Venetian galleys, returning from Beirut, were sunk in this place, with all their men escaping the shipwreck. I have found that Titus Livy says, that to this island at war arrived ships from three united fleets — the Romans, the Rhodians and King Attalus[2] — laden with war machines supplied for the destruction of the city. With much violence and the use of siege machines the city was overcome by the Romans, and laid waste.[3]

//13v// .21. and .22. Therasia two, which was formerly one. [Map: North. Therasia. Sea throughout. Santellini, formerly a great city *(ruins)*. *Islands:* Camon. Cristina.]

When[4] we had seen this, we took our way toward Sicandros. It is called Sicandrus from the multitude of figs and other fruit trees formerly there. *Sica* in Greek is *ficus,* or fig, in Latin. It is very mountainous, and from ancient times up until now, it has remained uncultivated: first from the treacheries of the Turks and the pirates, then from the idleness of the peasants, and the inconvenience of the port. Here wild asses left behind by chance wander throughout the island along the rugged banks, and are captured only with great difficulty.

It is said that in this place Meleus,[5] a certain strong man in the time of the Trojans, brought two ships to the Greek force. Drawing near to the island of Delos, he worshipped the oracle for a long time, and, when he was going on his way, a tempest came up and he was killed. Thus the women became widows and from that time on the town declined into ruin. When it had remained deserted for a very long time with few inhabitants, the town and the villages in the end came to nothing.

1. Sinner, 78, suggests that the gap is 40 miles. The transcribers of the Düsseldorf MS read 80 miles. These are exaggerated; the distance is closer to 10 miles.
2. Attalus, king of Pergamum, r. 241–197 BCE. In 201–199 Pergamum and Rhodes, allied with the Romans, conducted several sieges of island cities, though Livy does not mention Santorini. The assault on Oreus, in Euboea, is described in terms similar to those here. Livy XXXI.46.
3. Second Macedonian War, could not find this incident in Livy.
4. Here Henricus writes *cum* instead of *dum*, which would be part of the original acrostic spelling out Buondelmonti's name.
5. Not identified.

.23. Sicandros, formerly and now. Circumference of the entire island 17 miles. [Map: West. Sicandros. *Ruins. Rest of island dotted with trees.*]

//14r// The next island, called Policandros, is named for a plant which is very efficacious for the falling sickness.[1] Or it is called from *Poli*, a city, and *Andros*, men, city of people or men. For under this name it was inhabited for many centuries with houses and walls, but now is reduced to nothing. It is 20 miles in circumference with small trees and green grasses.

It happened once that [a hermit lived here in a narrow cave, serving God for a long time.][2] Here infidels came and suffocated him with fire. And when they wanted to leave, a voice was heard saying, "You have killed an innocent man, who was dear to me. You will go, but you will not be able to leave without a penalty." When he said this, he thrust his sword amongst the guilty ones, and overthrew those evil-doers. The rest he sent home, who, telling reverently of the miracle, converted to the Christian faith.

.24. Policandros completely deserted. Circumference of the entire island 20 miles. [Map: North.]

They say that this island, Polimio, was never inhabited but since in a wooded area there lie the foundations of buildings, it appears that men had lived here in the past. But whatever there was a long time ago in that place, now it is not known by men. It happened that a Turkish bireme approached this place and the crew set about to capture wild goats. Aeolus, having raised the north wind from his cave, swiftly turned the boat onto hidden rocks and—miserable to behold—it sank into the deep. And when the company on shore saw this, they broke into a long lament, and in the space of twenty days, all had given their souls to Muhammad. It is eighteen miles around. Here falcons raise their chicks each year.

.25. Polimio formerly and now. Circumference of the entire island 18 miles. [Map: North. Completely deserted. *No place names, ruins.*]

//14v// Certainly, we read[3] that the name of this island varies in the many annals of the Greeks. First, Aristotle calls it Mellida, with which name Pliny agrees, from the abundance of honey in its cavernous mountains.[4] Gorgias calls it Zephira[5] from the wind which prevails in that place. Callimachus calls it Mimallis, named thus after its queen. Heraclides calls it Siphim from the whispering sound which its falling waters emit. Today it is Melos, which is Latin for mill, since throughout millstones are found gathered together and

1. This is the medicinal herb polion or Teucrium polium, commonly called the felty germander.
2. This line is missing from the manuscript. Text supplied from Düsseldorf MS, fol. 38r.
3. A blank in the manuscript at this point is filled in other mss with *mi Jordane pater.*
4. Pliny IV.12.70.
5. Zephira, the name of one of the island's towns.

hardly anywhere else. Thus it is rightly called Milos. It is bounded by the Aegean Sea and its highest point faces toward Cape Malea.

The stone, *sardus*, is often found here, which appears black below, white in the middle and red above. It renders its wearers chaste.[1]

Here Menestheus, king of the Athenians, brother of Demofontis and Theseus, returning from the Trojan War, landed, and having been worn out by tempests at sea,[2] he died. An honorable tomb carved with an inscription to him may be seen to this day.

This island is 90 miles around. In the middle to the north a very famous harbor appears, and around it are medicinal waters of sulphur. Here appears a tower and a plain with several houses. In the northeast rises a well-fortified city, in which it once happened that the slaves, being fired up, seized a time when the citizens were away on business, stormed the castle and killed the queen of the place. When the bystanders saw what had happened, they reconquered the supposedly invincible castle with arms and troops in a siege lasting many days, and they sent the slaves to perdition.

Cybele, as I have discovered, was worshipped here. Her figure was carved and adorned with precious stones, and with a crown of towers. Lions drew her chariot, followed by roosters. She carried keys in her hand. Cybele is said to be the earth. As with the chariot, the earth hangs in the air. The wheels represent the fact that the universe turns and is changeable. Her maternal pity is shown in the lions, for all ferocity is tamed by maternal love. She is dressed in precious stones, because the earth is the mother of all stones and metals. The roosters represent her priests who were eunuchs called Corybantes. She is crowned with towers as the earth is with cities and fortresses. The key is here because in the springtime the earth is opened, and in winter it is closed.[3]

To the west is the town of Pollona, across from which reefs and uncultivated islands lie scattered about.

.26. Melos formerly, now Milo. Circumference of the entire island 30 miles.[4] [Map: North. S. Dimitrius, bishop's tower. Pollona. Apano Castro. 3 *islands to the north:* Antimilo. Argentera. Thimilo. *Islands to the south:* Octema. Sermemilo.]

//15r// I have described Melos, now let us approach the island of Siphanos. It is *Siphanos*[5] in Greek, *Surbo* in Latin.[6] You will find mountains throughout, and a dry road with

1. Reading *ferentes* for *furentes* [Düsseldorf]. The stone is carnelian, a variety of chalcedony..
2. *Iliad* II.552. No mention of Demofontis or Theseus here. Other manuscripts assert that he died of seasickness.
3. This imagery comes from Bersuire, 47.
4. Should be 80 or 90.
5. Modern Siphnos.
6. Meaning of this word is not clear.

limestone, overrun by goats. It is 40 miles in circumference. To the east on a mountain near Serragla is the city called by the name of the island [Sifana]. To the west the site of Schinos appears and a gulf. And to the south was once a port with a ruined city which is now called Platigiallo,[1] and we can see in the distance an island by the name of Chitriani. In the middle arises a tower, called Exambeles, from which a spring flows to the sea. Here a garden flourishes with all sorts of fruit trees.

Pan, the god of nature, was worshipped here, as a ruined statue, set on a high place, shows. But after Paul and the rest of the apostles preached the divine word in these parts, they destroyed all the idols. Pan, horned and ruddy, indicates the upper part of the world, and we understand fire and aether from these rays.[2] His breast is adorned with the stars of heaven. Seven reeds in his mouth are the seven planets. His thighs are trees and plants. His goat feet denote his animal nature.

A few miserable folk live here, most of whom are women who, because of a lack of men, live chaste into their old age. Although they are ignorant of the Latin language, they do not abandon the Catholic faith.[3]

.27. Siphanos. Circumference of the entire island 40 miles. [Map: North. Schinosi. Exambeles *(tower)*. Seraglia. Sifana, spring with gardens, old fortress. Port Plati Giallo. *Island to south:* Kitriani. 8 *names, all in text but one.*]

I now go on to Serphino, which is completely mountainous. It is forty miles around and is called Serfi in Greek from an herb, which is found here and is good for kidney disease, or it is named from the founder, Serfino, from whom it takes its name. On the southern edge a port opens up opposite an island. Then above it near a broad plain a town rises. Even today it preserves the ancient name of Serfino, its founder. And there by steeply ascending roads are seen innumerable stray goats, whose flesh, roasted for a long time by the sun and then moistened is consumed as food by the inhabitants.

Here Apollo was worshipped grandly in the form of a child and an old man. On his head he wears a golden tripod, and in his hand are a quiver and arrows with a bow. In his other hand he held a cythera. At his feet is a monstrous serpent with three heads, that is, a dog,[4] a wolf, and a lion. Nearby was a laurel tree with a crow in flight. Apollo is to be understood as the sun, a boy in the morning, a man at mid-day, and an old man in the evening when he fades. The bow sends its arrows to us as rays of light.

//15v// The cythera softens all sounds with a celestial melody. The golden tripod is in three parts because of three benefits. It causes the light, the warmth, and the internal

1. Modern Plati Yialós.
2. Symbolism for Pan can be found in Isidore, *Etymologies* viii.11.81–83. See also Bersuire, fol. xxb.
3. Reading *amittunt*, instead of *amictunt*.
4. Reading *canino* for *caprino* (goat); the dog is referred to a few lines further on. Bersuire, Prologue, fol. vb.

vigor which is in all young people.[1] The monster with three heads is time. The fawning dog is the future, because it always flatters men through their hope[2] for things to come. The wolf is time past because, in the manner of a wolf, it seizes its prey and flees. The lion represents the present time which stands fast and does not deign to flee. The laurel is because it remains green all summer.[3] Now therefore, father,[4] what can there be in this island except calamity, when it is clear that they spend their time and life in such a harsh way. What is more, they are by day and by night in a great tremor of fear lest they fall into the hand of the infidels. Such fears wear out and consume their years.

.28. Serphino formerly and now.[5] Circumference of the entire island 40 miles. [Map: North. City of Serphino *(wall with towers)*, 3 *unnamed islands to the east*.]

After the island described above is an island named Thermia,[6] which is so called from *thermo* in Greek, *tepidum*, warm, in Latin. It is very mountainous and is 40 miles in circumference. To the east is found [the church] of St. Irene[7] where the plain is, at the head of which the city of Thermia is erected. The Turks, through the treachery of a slave, destroyed this city in the night, having taken the citizens captive. But now it is [re]populated.

To the west at the church of St. Luke is a city with an excellent port, formerly adorned with buildings. On a mountain almost in the middle of the island stands a tower from which flows a stream of waters as far as the sea, and there begins the Plain Apocreos.[8] To the south the gulf and Plain of Piscopia is seen and the Plain of Merta is nearby. It is rich in wine, grain, silk and grazing animals. Here, near the city, the Turks by chance came into port to spend the night. During a stormy night two Cretan galleys arrived. In the morning the Christians, rushing upon the Turks, sent them all to hell.

//16r// .29. Thermia formerly and now. Circumference of the entire island 40 miles. [Map: North. Therma. S. Elini *(church)*. Port Sancti Luce. Plain of Apaneos. Gulf of Piscopia. Great spring.]

Now I cross over to Cea, named for Ceus [Coeus], a Titan and son of the earth, who lived with extravagant ferocity and pride. He with his brothers rose up against Jupiter. When the battle between them had lasted a long time, they were expelled by Jove from

1. *Iuventibus*, other mss read *viventibus:* all living things.
2. Reading *spem* instead of *spetiem*.
3. Reading *viror* for *virgo* or *virga*, which has inspired some inventive translations. Bersuire, 23.
4. One of the rare remaining references to Cardinal Orsini in this manuscript.
5. Modern Seriphos.
6. Kynthos
7. Today a village, Agia Irini, is in this location. In Bordone's book this church is called St. Clivi. Sinner opts for St. Helena.
8. Apaneos on map.

the island of Crete, and thus were their powers diminished. On account of this Ceus, the elder of the brothers, arrived in this island, where he fathered Latona[1] and Asteria, most beautiful maidens, about whom much has been said, so I desist. It is mountainous and 50 miles in circumference. To the west there is a port and plain between it and a castle.

Here wild beasts roam free and there is the town of Ioulis,[2] which had an ancient ritual in which those made ill by old age ended their life by poison. Such death was celebrated with the highest praises. When Sextus Pompey, on his way to Asia, landed here, driven by storms, he heard about a certain matron, venerated for her age and virtues.[3] He came to her and urged her at length not to take the poison. She, lying on her bed with her kinswomen around her, spoke these words to Pompey, "I am in my ninety-fifth year, and fortune has always shown me a smiling face and has opened its kindly heart to me. Since often by a breath, a sudden change of fortune might make my life calamitous, I will be able to make my departure joyfully. Thus since my life has been happy, death will be happier," and, accepting permission from all and, having called constantly upon the gods, she died and her spirit quickly flew away.

A spring is found here which makes men who drink of it, dull of sense. After it is digested, the mind is restored to its original state of health. Near here to the west toward the Tainaron and Pagasaean Gulf and the Myrtoan Sea[4] there are many reefs and uncultivated islands. I shall place here the names of others without additional narration: Sira or Hydra, Makronissi Albera, Chitisos, from which came the poet Proculus. He fell deeply in love with a Greek woman named Samia and composed many songs in praise of her name.[5]

//16v// .30. CEA FORMERLY AND NOW. Circumference of the entire island 50 miles. [Map: East. *Unnamed city in center, trees. No place-names.*]

It is agreed that this island ANDROS is called by many names, as the philosophers say, first Myrsilus, that it is Cauros, and Callimachus called it Antandron. Others have called it Lagia, Nonagria, and Idrussa, from its many springs, and Pliny called it Pagrim.[6] Andros is named from the son of King Anius.[7] It is very beautiful and noted for its plentiful waters,

1. Greek: Leto.
2. Reading *Ioulida* for *valide*. Ioulis is the ancient and modern name of the town.
3. Sextus Pompey, son of Pompey the Great, died in 37 BCE in Asia Minor, pursued by Octavian. The story of Pompey and the old woman comes from Quintus Valerius Antias, first century BCE, *Annales*. It also appears in Montaigne, "A Custom of the Island of Cea," *Essays* 2.3 (New York: Modern Library, 1946), 303.
4. Pliny IV.65: the Myrtoan Sea. Gulf of Taenaron, Pagasicus Sinus (Pliny IV.72).
5. Reading *graecam* instead of *gregem*. Sinner, 86. Neither the island nor the poet can be identified.
6. Pliny IV.65: "Myrsilius tells us that Andros was once called Cauros and later Antandros; Callimachus says it had the name of Lasia, others call it Nonagria or Hydrusa or Epagris. Its circuit measures 93 miles." He refers to it as Andrus.
7. Ovid, *Metamorphoses* XIII.643–649.

and it appears to produce all things needed for human life. It is totally mountainous and 80 miles in circumference. A city to the east is inhabited but has no port, and near it a small island appears with an ancient town. To get to it the inhabitants cross by a stone bridge, magnificently constructed. On the sea near the shore a tower is seen where people in the area took refuge at night to be safe from pirates.

It is said that the daughters of King Anius fled here,[1] and Ovid tells a story about them. Bacchus endowed them with the peculiar gift that whatever they touched would be turned to grain, wine and oil. When Agamemnon learned this, he forced them to supply the army which he was leading to Troy. They fled to their brother, who betrayed them into the hands of Agamemnon. While Agamemnon was preparing their chains, they, stretching their arms to heaven, sought aid from Father Liber, and were changed into doves. The truth of the matter is that the daughters of King Anius had great skill in improving their fields, and so they produced a great plenty from all of them and became rich. Having discovered this, Agamemnon seized everything from them for his army, and thus, from their riches, they were made poor.[2] They became luxury-loving doves, earning their living from the public by the trade of the goddess Venus.

Of what used to be in this island, remnants[3] are seen, for nothing is found here but huge and magnificent sculptures everywhere. Especially noteworthy is a sculpture of the god Mercury,[4] a winged staff surrounded by serpents in his hands, having a cap on his head, with a rooster and the head of a dog before him. He is winged, since the star of Mercury makes its course most swiftly. [He carries] a sleep-inducing wand because a man is put to sleep[5] by the sweetness of words. The dog's head is because in eloquence by barking or speaking he attracts men. The cap with the rooster on his head is because a merchant is eager to enter here with his goods, and he changes his proposal to suit himself.[6]

The Carthaginian comic poet Terence began his tale in Andros, which described the customs of men young and old, and he entitled his first comedy, "The Girl from Andros."

1. Ovid, *Metamorphoses* XIII, story of the daughters of King Anius, ll. 650 ff. This story also appears in Silvestri, #41.
2. Reading *pauperes* for *paures*. Sinner, 87.
3. Reading *vestigia* for *vestia*. Sinner, 87.
4. Second century "Hermes of Andros" is to be found in the town museum, but it has none of the attributes described here. For more on this depiction of Hermes, see Barsanti, 157–59.
5. Reading *sopitur* for *sopit*. Sinner, 87.
6. Bersuire's version has the rooster in front of him, not on his head, and the dog beside him is Argus, "whose head is full of eyes." The last part of this sentence ("because the merchant is eager . . .") appears to be Buondlemonti's invention. Bersuire writes, "sicut mercator et gallum qui evigilat mercatores," or thus he is a merchant and the rooster is the one who wakes up merchants. (Prologue, fol. VIIr). Bersuire also describes Mercury as a thief.

It puts Pamphilus first with Glycerium and then separates them. Finally Crito, an old man, arriving at Athens, brought peace and joy in the conclusion of the story.

Now this region is reduced very low on account of the frequent incursions of the Turks, although in comparison to some others, it is better off.

//17r// .31. Andros Island. Circumference of the entire island 80 miles. [Map: North. Andros. *Three unnamed constructions, including a fortified city on a peninsula to the northeast. Shows island and stone bridge.*]

Between Cea and Andros, isolated, with rocky shores, stands an island called Scopulus Caloieros. It is *kalos*[1] from Greek, *bonus*, good, in Latin, and *gherus*, old, or good old man. Thus Caloieros can be understood as an antiphrasis, for it is very evil, and found to be most menacing to sailors at all times. Ships passing here by night are often sunk on it. Here in my days a Genoese[2] ship coming from Pera, wrecked on this reef. On account of this ship, sailors passing often gather their strength to curse it and, pointing a finger from a great way off,[3] they swiftly raise their sails high. When, likewise, a Turkish ship sank here, it happened that the men got out to safety[4] on the rocks. On the third day a Christian ship appeared before them. Moved by pity, the ship took them all, half-dead, on board. After some food and recovering their strength, they attacked the Christians, and sailing to their own country, placed the Christians, the cause of their escape, into perpetual slavery. Here falcons raise their chicks each year among the inaccessible cliffs.

.32. Caloierus. [Map, no direction. *High rocky cliff.* Scopolus Caloierus.]

//17v// Aristotle calls this island Hydrussa, which in Latin is *aquatica*, watery, on account of the abundance of springs.[5] Demosthenes and Aeschines called it Ophiusa.[6] Today it is called Tinos on account of its round shape, which is like a *tinus*.[7] It is near Andros and is 40 miles in circumference. In this island are two high cliffs from which long ago a sorceress saw enemies approaching to destroy the city. She climbed onto the higher

1. Reading *kalos* for *colos*. Sinner, 88.
2. Reading *Ianuensium* for *Cannuensium*, Sinner, 88.
3. Nautae...digito...indicantes: Latin idiom for " throw up one's hands" in submission.
4. Reading *salutem* for *saltum*, Sinner, 88.
5. Pliny iv.66. Aristotle is said to have written a constitution for Tinos, *Politia Tinion*, which does not survive.
6. Demosthenes (384–322 bce) and Aeschines (390–314), both Athenians, were rivals during the wars with Philip ii of Macedon. Ophiusa (best guess for *fuissam* and *friusa*) is one of the names given for this island (and a number of others). It means "Snake Island." Pliny iv.66.
7. A round jar or balloting urn. Gerola points this out as one of Buondelmonti's mistaken etymologies. Tino in Greek means "oyster," but Buondelmonti's "casual homophony" associates it with a similar sounding Latin word. "Le etymologie dei nomi luoghi," *Atti del Reale Istituto Veneto in Scienze, Lettere ed Arti* 92 (1932/33): 1158.

mountain and, naked, with her hair spread out, and extending her arms to heaven, made an incantation so that Affricus, a sudden wind rising against them, should capsize the ship into the depths. The greater part of those on board escaped onto the island, but they were rendered unconscious from drinking poisonous liquor, and from her incantation and song. In this place they became slaves, and the citizens were made rich.

In the time of Alexander the island was famous. Later everyone was driven out by the Romans. It happened not long ago that a ship from the west bearing a cargo of horses struck here, driven by a great storm at sea. The horses escaped, all souls being lost, and breeding[1] throughout the island, became very numerous. In the middle is a fortress on a mountain with a fertile plain. To the east rises the tower of S. Nicholas in the sea, and on a mountain to the west arises another strongly fortified tower. A pleasant valley opens to the north, and to the south is a town formerly inhabited.

.33. Tinos. Circumference of the entire island 40 miles. [Map: North. City of Tino. Tower of Tiscori. Old fort. S. Steffanus. S. Nicholas. *Tower to the east.*]

I have spoken of Tinos, let us now go to Mykonos, named for a king, or from *mikos* in Greek, which means length, *longitudo* in Latin, or very small, *paululum*, since it is contained in a small space. It was once very grand as is evident from the remains of buildings. As Delos is nearby, many pilgrims, in order to visit the idol every year, sought a place to stay here. Once when the Turks attacked the island, they found a monk, a man of God, worshipping in a cave. While they were making a great noise trying to seize him, the cave fell in a landslide in which all but the monk perished. This island is called one of the Cyclades, located in the Aegean Sea, and is 30 miles around. There is a port with an old jetty to the south. Here are churches of Saints George, Stephen and John, and one of St. Anne in the east near the port of Pandermo.[2] It is acknowledged that the whole island is arid, with many goats.

Virgil: "(Delos), wandering, was bound to Mykonos and lofty Gyaros."[3]

//18r// .34. Michone formerly and now. Circumference of the whole island 30 miles. [Map: North. S. Giorgius. S. Steffanus. Michona. Port S. John. S. John. S. Anne. Port of Padermo *(2x). All in text.*]

It now remains to show the island of Delos, of which mention is often made among authors, and it shone out most famous in the midst of the Cyclades. Antiquity declares it was once mobile and it has been called by many names: Delos, Asteria (star), Corona, Midia (Chlamydia – cloak), Lagia (hare), Cineto (dog), Pirpile (fiery)[4] and now Sdiles. It was here, the poets say, that Jupiter raped Latona, the daughter of the Titan, Ceus. [Juno, when she

1. Reading *foetantes* for *ferentes*, Sinner, 89.
2. Modern: Panormos.
3. "Errantem Micone celsa giaroque revinxit." *Aeneid* III.76.
4. Names from Pliny IV.66; Solinus XI.19.

had learned that Latona was pregnant by him, sent Python in pursuit of her.][1] Pursued by Python, Latona fled through all the surrounding regions, and was at last removed to this island by her sister Asteria. Arriving at its shores, she gave birth.[2] By the killing of Python, he (Apollo) avenged the injuries of the mother. They say that Diana performed the office of midwife for their mother when she gave birth to Apollo, and therefore Diana, a virgin, is called on by women in childbirth under the name Lucina, because she delivers infants to the light. Diana, by the testimony of almost all the poets, was the daughter of Jove and Latona. The ancient sources agreed that she was noteworthy for her perpetual virginity. Having disdained marriage with anyone, she devoted herself to hunting. She sought wild beasts in the woods at night by moonlight and with her coldness she drove out amorous desires. Having observed these things about her, ancient authorities believed her to be the moon and associated the moon with her. They placed a bow and arrows at her side, and called her the goddess of the forests. The nymphs gathered around her, and she was their goddess: Oreades, Dryads, Naiads, and Nereids, who are venerated among the Greeks to this day, who affirm that they still carry out their duties. The moon is the mother of water, and she causes water to flow in the woods, mountains, sea, and springs and to create plants and seeds in the fields.[3] She is also called Proserpina.

Likewise Apollo is given various names according to the diverse powers attributed to him, sometimes he is the sun, or Phoebus or Titan, or from this place as the Delian. The two, in motion and wandering, then became gods of this island. Diana or the moon was born first by night, and he, born later, was Apollo or day, which is illuminated by the sun.[4] Delos in Greek is *manifestum* or "manifest" in Latin, because, after the Flood, it appeared in the night from the heaving vapors of the moon.[5] Later on the following day, it appeared openly, shown by the sun's rays, and so it was Delos, or manifest. First it was called Ortigia from the multitude of quails gathered there — *ortix* in Greek,

//18v// *perdix* in Latin. There is a Mt. Cynthius there, on which Diana was born, and so she was sometimes called Cynthia. Later it is said that Apollo took his name [from the son of Vulcan and Minerva who was the first inventor of medicine. At the foot of this mountain is a spring which rises and][6] falls at the same time and hour as the river Nile, which is amazing.

In this place Apollo was worshipped and here gifts were brought to his temple from distant places, along with young maidens from the surrounding regions.

1. These lines are missing from this manuscript. I have taken them from the Düsseldorf ms, fol. 41v.
2. This phrase added by Sinner, 90.
3. Bersuire, Prologue, fol. ixa.
4. Reading "per solem illuminatur" for "solem alluminator." Sinner, 91.
5. Isidore, *Etymologiae* xiv.vi.21.
6. These lines are missing in this manuscript, and there is a mark at this point indicating an omission. Added from Düsseldorf MS fol. 42r.

In the reign of Tarquin, the uncle of Brutus, at Rome, his sons came to this island of Apollo with gifts to be offered according to custom. While they were sacrificing, he (Brutus), who had come with him, dressed as a comic actor, brought a staff in which there was gold and had given it to the god, as if he feared to worship the god openly. While the others were interrogating the oracle: "Who would rule in Rome after Tarquin?" the oracle responded: "Whoever is first among them to kiss his mother." Hearing this, Brutus, as if by accident, fell on the ground and kissed it. Later after the (expulsion) of Tarquin's sons, he became consul. It showed Apollo that Brutus understood the earth to be the mother of all. Tarquin having fled, Brutus was made the first consul.[1]

There are actually two adjoining islands, of which Delos is the smaller. The circumference of it is four miles, the other is ten miles. Both are elongated from north to south.

We saw nearby in Delos an ancient temple on leveled ground and a statue on columns which lay at such great length that in no way, even had there been a thousand of us, could we have set it back up, using the mechanisms of the ropes of the ships. So we left it in its original location. Around here are seen more than a thousand statues thrown down, all made with wonderful skill.

The other island had been cultivated with low mountains, and throughout were provided innumerable habitations whose doors and windows faced the temple. In the midst of these arises a tower, which the inhabitants restored, after the destruction of the temple, the ceremonies, and the idols.

Virgil:

> I am brought here, and the island welcomes our weary band into its safe harbor.
> Disembarking, we pay homage to the city of Apollo…
> I venerated the temples of the god, built of ancient stone.[2]

.35. Delos, formerly, now Sdilos. Circumference of the smaller island 4 miles, the larger is 10 miles around, .36. and both of these Sdille are now destroyed. [Map: North. *On west (left):* temple of Apollo and Mt. Cynthia. *Fallen columns. A single tower on the eastern island.*]

//19r// To the west is Suda,[3] its modern name, 40 miles in circumference. It was formerly Iaro or Ghero, interpreted in Latin, *senex* or *sanus*, old man or healthy. To this island the duke of Calabria, Sidim by name, came from Magna Graecia, the city of Scillaea.[4] He was fleeing from the hands of his enemies, with exhausted sailors, driven by a very great

1. This story is told at the end of Livy I.56, except the event takes place at Delphi, not Delos. The scipio is a staff, which was hollowed out and filled with gold, so that Brutus could make his offering secretly. Lucius Junius Brutus became consul in 509 BCE after the expulsion of the last of the Tarquins.
2. *Aeneid* III.78–79 and 84.
3. Syros
4. Scylaceum, now Squillace, southern Italy.

tempest. On account of the death at this time of the king of the island, he took the queen as his wife, after the splendid funeral of her husband. He remained in this place for the rest of his life. After he had reigned for a long time without an heir, he had a daughter, whom he named Suda, and from her the island took its name.

Now truly in comparison with times past, the island is known for nothing but barley bread, which they eat with carob and goats' flesh, and are in great fear of pirates. So their life is full of anxiety. However, on account of their children, their relatives, and an inborn love of their native country, they are content to stay in this place. There is also, as can be seen to the north, an island, Caprara (Goat Island), in which, as they say, evil spirits roam, and when ships pass near by or tie up here by chance in the night, there is such a roaring and groaning of voices that heaven and earth ring, calling the names of the arriving sailors in loud voices.[1]

Virgil: "Wandering (Delos) he joined to Mikonos and lofty Giaros."[2]

.37. Suda Island. Circumference of the entire island 40 miles. [Map: North. *Island:* Caprara.]

Gleaming white Paros follows, one of the Cyclades, which was formerly called Platea from its great size. Then it was called Minoa, from the city of King Minos, with its many edifices. But Pareante, the son of Plutus, they say, had constructed the town, and he gave island and town his own name, Paron.[3] It produces pure, white marble, and those seeing it from a distance

//19v// would think it is snow. Mt. Carpesus[4] is higher than the others, with gushing springs of water and flowing rivers. It is 52 miles in circumference.

To the west is the city Minoa facing the island of Delos, in which buildings with columns crown the meadows with a pure marble temple. Above, at the base of the mountain arises a very old town built of immense stones. To the north is the castle of Paron with few citizens, which has a jetty and a small port. In this place is a spring in which, if you place white linen or leather, it will come back black. Mills thresh grain by the spring. Facing Naxos is the town of Chefalum on a mountain, the ascent of which is of such difficulty that it seems to touch the sky. On this laborious journey very skinny and wrinkled old women and even sick people go without effort as far as the top, carrying their bundles. The women conceive healthy children beyond their fifty-third year.

To the east is seen a port used by pirates and there a great plain extends throughout. The islands around Paros are greatly oppressed by the Turks, and are often reduced to ruin. The inhabitants are constantly afraid lest they be reduced to slavery.

1. MS adds *convalescunt.*
2. *Aeneid* III.76.
3. Son of Plutus, who was the son of the Titan Iasion. Isidore, *Etymologiae* XIV.6.29. Modern town of Parikia.
4. Mt. Carpesus, now Mt. Profitis Ilias.

.38. Paros. Circumference of the entire island 52 miles. [Map: North. Paros *(city)*. Spring. Minoa city. The town Chefilo is high above the sea on this very high mountain. Port for pirates. Mt. Carpesus.]

A short distance away from here is Antiparos, and although it is uninhabitable, there are eagles and falcons, and so it is not derelict. Who could know how many seabirds' nests are prepared each year at one time among the rocks? Such a gathering of birds and birds' nests has never been seen and especially of eagles, who hunt their prey while in this place; unless forced by great hunger, the eagle does not eat alone. It collects and deposits two precious stones in its nest, one masculine and one feminine. Without these, Pliny says,[1] it would not be able to produce chicks. It deposits these agates to protect its chicks from venom and snake bite. But later it drives the chicks out of the nest and teaches them to hunt. When it sees them seize their prey, flying on high, they will remove them from their care. In winter it (the eagle) seizes a small bird, and holds it close between its feet all night, because of the heat. It does not die, but at sunrise the eagle allows it to fly away unharmed.

.39. Antiparos. Circumference of the entire island <illeg> miles. [Map: n.d.]

//20r// I found beyond the previous island Panaia, little inhabited because of its barrenness. It is called from *pan* (Greek), or *totum* in Latin, and *ya* or *sanitas* (health).[2] There is one isolated church in which it is said that a hermit used to dwell. For his needs he sailed to the island of Paros in his canoe. Now in these days a huge multitude of all kinds of birds lives here, and they fly among the bare cliffs, crying out, by day and night.

.40. Panaia. Scopolus. [Map: n.d. This island was once a hermitage, now deserted; that is, it is inhabited by eagles and falcons.]

Secure among the islands of the Cyclades is Naxos, 80 miles in circumference. Pliny first names it *Strongile* in Greek, *rotunda*, or round, in Latin.[3] Ovid calls it Dionysia from the richness of its vineyards. Others call it Little Sicily from the abundance of fruits and other things. It is the chief of these islands.[4] Here are found the very black and hard stones called emery.[5] Across from the city on an island was once a town called Strongile, from which the island took its name for many centuries.

Across from this a great plain of vineyards stretches out by the sea. Because of this, the island was dedicated to Bacchus. A sculpture near the town shows him as a boy with a

1. Pliny x.iv, describes the "eagle stone," aëtites or gagiten, placed in the nest.
2. *Ya*, sometimes written *aia* has baffled editors. Sinner suggests that the island is named Panagia and the word should be the Greek *Hygeia* or health.
3. Pliny iv.68. He gives the circumference as 75 miles.
4. I.e., headquarters of the duke of Naxos or duke of the Archipelago.
5. Reading *smirigium* (medieval Latin) or *smyris* (Greek) for the scribe's *smerigdo* or emerald. Emery is still mined here.

woman's face, a bare chest and a horned head crowned with vines, and riding on tigers. He is a boy because a drunken boy conducts himself without reason; he has a woman's face because desire of women is generated by wine in those who drink; on tigers because they are wild; naked in reference to the truth; horned[1] because of authority.

There are also some wasps here that, if they bit someone, he would die.

Theseus, the son of King Aegeus, was sent to Crete to be killed by the Minotaur. Theseus killed him instead and liberated Athens from base servitude. He took Ariadne and Phaedra, daughters of Minos, and at a spring near the city, while she was sleeping, he abandoned Ariadne undeservedly, and married Phaedra. Since I have read in many places that Theseus left Ariadne on this island, I am placing this story here instead of Chios, since it would lie more correctly on the sailing route of the Athenians, saving the authority of Naso[2] who claims that this deed was done in Chios.[3] After the departure of Theseus, Bacchus, ruler of this entire island, learning of this sly and evil defection, and moved by pity for such a young thing, revived the girl. Knowing her to be the daughter of the Cretan king and Pasiphae, he took her as his wife. Vulcan gave her a crown, shining with gems, which he placed among the stars.

When Jupiter set forth against the Titans, he made a sacrifice on this island upon the shore. An eagle came flying as his auspice, which he accepted as a good omen. He was the victor and subjected (his enemies) to his guardianship.

In the time of the Trojan War Peleus was ruling here. At this time the island was inhabited by so many men and women that no spot remained uncultivated. Now owls never cease to wail throughout,

//20v// and there are wild animals in the fields and valleys everywhere together with quails.

Here I found a great number of women who, lacking a relationship with men, remain as virgins into old age; not from the zeal of virtuous conviction, but from a lack of men, they die as virgins.

A vein of gold is found in all parts which, from the lack of a proprietor, they leave untouched by artifice. To the west a magnificent old temple was erected in which stood a statue of Apollo. There, nearby, lies a place with salt works, and it ends with a ruined tower.

Within the mountains, finally, is a most fertile valley, called Darmile, in the confines of which is erected a town, Aperato.[4] We pass on the heights a monastery along with the

1. Bersuire, Prologue, Fol. XXI, although he says "horned because of pride."
2. Ovid, *Metamorphoses* VIII.172–82. Ovid uses the name "Dio" for Chios.
3. This observation demonstrates Buondelmonti's grasp of geography; Naxos is indeed on the sailing route to Athens, while Chios is too far to the north.
4. Aparatou still exists, a village on the slopes of the mountain.

castle of Auster,[1] and we descend through a fruitful valley as far as a garden with a small river to the sandy plain, which ends at Mt. Stellida.

> Statius: But now the Laertian bark was threading the winding ways of the Aegean, while the breezes changed, one for another, the countless Cyclades. Already Paros and Olearos are hid, now they skirt lofty Lemnos and behind them Bacchic Naxos is lost to view, while Samos grows before them; now Delos darkens the deep.[2]

.41. Naxos once, now Nixa. Circumference of the entire island 80 miles. [Map: East. Very high mountain. Emery stone. Monastery. Apeiranthos. Valley and fertile field with trees. Apaliros Kastro. Spring where Theseus abandoned Adriana. Sandy field full of vines. Town *(scattered houses)*, saltworks, Naxos *(walled city)*, Mt. Stellida *(west)*, Strongilo *(on island)*. River Anzarus].

//21r// Both of these islands were formerly inhabited it is said, and called Podia. For *podia* in Greek, means *pedes* (feet) in Latin, since they appear in the shape of two feet. The larger of these was inhabited with a fortified castle. Now on account of[3] barbarian incursions the people have gone to Naxos. The first is six miles, the second four miles, around.

.42. Podia Koufonissi.[4] The first is 6 miles around. [Map: n.d.]

.43. Kata Koufonissi. The second Podia is 4 miles around. [Map: n.d.]

Raclea and Chero are two small islands. They appear mountainous and are uncultivated on account of the incursions of the Turks. They say that they were formerly inhabited, since ruins can be seen in all parts. Now a great herd of goats, which wander everywhere, is found here. They are both small in circumference.

.44. Raclea or Nichea. [Map: n.d.]

.45. Chero. [Map: n.d. *No toponyms.*]

Now, weary, we seek the port of the island of Nio. It is called Nio[5] in Greek, in Latin *Novum*, (new), or *Nios* or *Navalis* (naval), since it has kindly and freely provided this port for sailors dashed down in a storm. It is forty miles around. To the south a town is placed on high and not far away a small valley appears with a most fertile plain, sown throughout and divided into parts by its inhabitants. In the evening after sunset they will go to a strongly

1. Auster, variously rendered by translators as *Oustro* (LeGrand) and *Humstri* (Dd).
2. J.H. Mozley, trans. (Cambridge MA: Harvard University Press, 1928). Very peculiar itinerary here.
3. Reading *ob* for *ad*, Sinner, 98; Dd, 35.
4. Best guess: a pair of islands close by those that follow.
5. Ios

fortified castle which they ascend[1] with great effort. In the morning before dawn they send the old women out to look all through the island and, having been given a signal, the gates are opened wide, and thus they pass their lives in fear. Finally, in my time, while a pirate ship was in port, repairing its keel, by divine will the waters of the sea washed over it, and it was seen no more.

//21v// .46. Nio formerly and presently. Circumference of the entire island 40 miles. [Map: North.]

Turning to the north[2] the island of Anaphios rises up, from *ana* in Greek, sine in Latin (without), and *ophios*, *serpens* (serpent),[3] or without serpents, since serpents are not found there. And truly if they are brought there, they die immediately. And, what's more, if you carry with you some dirt from this island and put it in a circle around a serpent, it dies at once.

There was once a well-fortified city at the end of the island. On account of this, pirates gathered all their ships in safety next to its shore. When for some time they had carried on in this fashion, the chiefs of the neighboring region, taking many weapons, abandoned the city. In the end they destroyed it, and built a fortress in the middle of the island where it is to this day.

.47. Anaphios. Circumference of the entire island 5 miles. [Map: North.]

//22r// Many have called this island Buport.[4] It is well cultivated and is 80 miles around, completely mountainous. It is now called Amurgos polis. There are three cities: Amurgos, Ialli, and Plati. To the north appear three ports: S. Anne, Calos and Catapla.[5] The mountains to the west are not so high as those to the east, and so it is called Catomerea, which in Latin means *pars inferior,* or lower part. To the east is Apanomerea, *pars superior,* or upper part. At the south are terrible cliffs, most menacing to ships, since piercing winds in the sea pound against the rocks, just like Scylla and Charybdis.[6] So swollen are the waves that ships often perish here in wrecks. So ships, seeing this, go a long way out of their way, and the sinking of Venetian galleys are recorded there.

1. Reading *ascendunt* for *descendunt.*
2. Reading *versus* for *rursus*, Sinner, 99; Dd, 35.
3. Reading *ophios* for *fios.*
4. Reading *Buport* for *Subort.* Sinner, 100; Dd, 36.
5. Modern Katapola.
6. Ernle Bradford, who sailed throughout these islands, remarks on the "suck and swallow of the swell under the island's venomous cliffs." *Companion Guide to the Greek Islands* (London: Collins, 1975), 158

.48. Amurgos or Amurgospolis. Circumference of the entire island 80 miles. [Map: North. Catomerea. S. Anna *(church)*. Amurgos. Apomerea. Monastery in a cave].

There are two neighboring islands, namely Chinera and Levata. In these islands they say not even our forefathers lived. Now they, completely uncultivated, remain in solitude, due to the attacks of evil men, and frequently animals are found running loose in all parts along with wild asses.

.49. Chinera and .50. Levata. [Map: North. *Ruins*.]

Now we will describe an island of monks, placed very high in the middle of the sea, where the island of Coa (Lango) terminates to the south. On account of its eminence, looking around at its towering banks, it seems to menace all the neighboring islands. On the top there is a church in a flat area. In this place two monks worshipped in safety and, having made a little boat, they raised it with a rope in order to keep it safe from savage pirates. They were able to practice their devout prayers and regular hours without fear day and night, and to offer up their pure libations and sacrifices. And when they had pursued this ritual for a long time,

//22v// look! a Turk, dressed in clothes like theirs, called out with loud shouts that he was alone in a damaged boat: "Holy men! For the love of Christ take me up, poor me, for a dreadful storm has cast our boat upon the rocks in the Greek Sea, and no one escaped but myself alone." The monks, moved by pity, took in their guest, this Sinon,[1] raising him up by the ascending rope. That night, while they were worshipping in the church, the traitor shut the door from the outside and called his comrades, hidden near the island. They carried these servants of Christ and all their belongings away into Turkey.

.51. Scopolus Caloriorum. [Map: n.d. *Steep cliffs, church on top and pulley with boat suspended. Dodecanese Islands.*]

Now we come to the island of Kos, which in Latin is translated as *luctus*, (mourning); this is because of the intemperance of its air, which "weeps" and languishes for many months of the year. The adjoining province of Actica[2] is called Suburbana. From east to west is 40 miles and a plain extends through almost all the island. To the south we see very high mountains in which are the towns of Petra, Chevia, and Pili, which today they call Peripaton. On the top of the higher mountain called Dicteus is a strongly fortified castle, in which today there are many cisterns. When we descend to the base (of the mountain) we find the spring of Fandion from which the river Fandanus flows. Here formerly the town of Cilippus thrust forth into the sea to the north. In the midst of the very vast plains, two little mountains arise. From them a most noble spring, once called Licastis, today Apodomarius, emanates. Nearby were once castles, a town, mills, game preserves,

1. Sinon, the man who convinced the Trojans to take the wooden horse into the city.
2. Sinner, 200 n., suggests Attica.

and marble statues. In this delightful place the songs[1] of a variety of birds are said to be pleasing not only to earthly beings but also to the immortal gods.

To the east on the coast is the great city of Arangea, which lies in the midst of a lake, foul in summer, and outside the walls grow many orange trees,[2] and so it is called Arangea. Here are found so many great marble buildings and theaters that it is amazing to see. Outside the fortress near the lake to the north are seen a large group of the buildings of Hippocrates, the great doctor, with a spring nearby (the Ascalepion), and a swamp called Lambi which is larger in the winter as the water rises. In the summer it dries up. This Hippocrates was the son of Aesculapius and a student of the physician Aesculapius II, and he was of the family of Aesculapius I, from whom the art of medicine got its start, the art which he demonstrated and taught to his sons, commanding them: "you should, as fathers, demonstrate medicine to outsiders certainly and to your sons, that the nobility of this art will always remain firmly established in them."[3] He taught them that they should live in the middle of the Cyclades Islands

//23r// on account of the temperate air, or in summer they should settle in the mountains of Kos. Among the Greeks he led the way to the perfection of medicine. Medicine itself before Hippocrates, as Macrobius and Isidore say, languished for 500 years from the time of Apollo and Aesculapius, who were its inventors.

Proceeding now to the middle of the island, small hillocks are seen, and thus this plain is higher than that of the aforesaid Arangea. Then to the south we take our course to the town of Antimachum as far as the end of the island where Chefalo is at hand. Not long ago a huge serpent[4] appeared, devouring the cattle, and everyone, terrified, took flight. Then a brave man undertook single combat for the salvation of the people. When the serpent went to rampage among the herds and had spied him, it killed his

1. Reading *cantus* for *tantus*, Sinner, 102; Dd, 37.
2. *Arangea*, medieval Latin taken from the Persian.
3. This rather confused version of part of the oath appears in various forms in other manuscripts. The critical part of the oath reads: "I will teach this art if anyone who desires to learn without fee or covenant and without delusion or intemperance and...to my sons and to the sons of him who taught me." The teaching of the art to outsiders is unique to CB and is probably a mistake. *Oath of Hippocrates,* trans. W.H.S. Jones, Loeb Classical Library (New York: Putnam, 1929), 298–301. Hippocrates is connected with the island of Kos in Isidore, *Etymologies* IV.3.2. and XIV.6.18. He is mentioned in passing in Macrobius, *Saturnalia* I.20.4 and VII.5.19. Isidore: Apollo is said to be the author and founder of the art of medicine, according to the Greeks. Aesculapius, his son, developed it still further in honor and scope. But after Aesculapius died from a lightning bolt, medical care was forbidden, and the art declined with its author. It remained hidden for nearly 500 years until the times of Artaxerxes, the king of Persia. Then Hippocrates restored it to the light. He was born of the family of Aesculapius in Kos and died in 357 BCE.
4. Perhaps a dragon.

horse, lying prostrate, by biting it. The young man, however, fighting fiercely, finally killed the viper.

It is said and confirmed that the daughter of Hippocrates appears alive in the island.[1] Speaking with you and telling many tales of her misfortunes, she remembers her unhappiness and asks her creator that someone be worthy to free her from such great punishment. It is said that this appearance, with wailing cries, occurs every six to eight years, and that she has spoken to many, not far from her paternal home. This is confirmed by many citizens.

Pliny reports that Aristeus, the son of Apollo, having on the advice of his mother left Thebes, came here and lived on this island and ruled over it.[2] They say that the women here killed their husbands on account of their infidelity. These men, always going off to battles in Asia Minor, left the care of the island to their wives. The women, outraged, resorted to the appalling murder of their husbands.

Then Jason, passing through here on his way to Colchis, now Turkey,[3] went on to that city, and put up many buildings. Even today this city can be seen in Lesser Armenia, facing Cyprus.[4]

Finally this island is most abundant in everything, and they affirm that here the art was first invented of weaving ornamented woolen clothing for women.[5] In addition, here was the birth of the famous poet Philetas who, imitating the great poet Sappho, sang in praise of Bacchus.[6]

Among the towering cliffs a bird once laid two eggs and from one of them was born a bird and from the other a dog. The mother perceiving that the dog was not like the other, killed it, and fed it to his brother. Since this island is contiguous to Asia Minor, great cities have arisen. The Knights of St. John constructed the Castle of St. Peter in 1400 to defend against the infidels.[7]

//23v// .52. CHOA ONCE, NOW LANGO. From east to south is length is 40 miles. [Map: Full page. North. *On north coast of Asia:* Turkey *(3x).* Asia Minor *(2x).* Castle of St. Peter.

1. Mandeville also tells a version of this story, in which the daughter of Hippocrates turns into a dragon. *Travels,* 53-54.
2. Aristeus: son of Apollo and Cyrene, Graves, *Greek Mythology,* 21.1 and 82.
3. Reading *Turchum* for *Curchum*, Sinner, 102.
4. "Horrendus error!" Sinner, 204, n. Colchis is on the east coast of the Black Sea.
5. The famous Coae vestes, to which this might be an indirect reference, were women's garments of transparent silk. The line about wool-working comes from Isidore, *Etymologies* XIV.6.18.
6. Philetas, poet, lived in the third century BCE. His spring can still be visited, as can the ruins of the temple complex of Aesculapius.
7. See Anthony Luttrell for a discussion of the building of this castle and its appearance on maps in the Buondelmonti tradition. "The Later History of the Maussolleion and its Utilization in the Hospitaller Castle at Bodrum," *Jutland Archaeological Society Publications* 15.2 (1986): 189–94.

On island: Swamp of Lambus. S. Foca. Arangea. Spring and house of Hippocrates. Spring of Ferno. Mt. Dicteus. Chilippus *(ruins)*. Ffandanus River. Peripaton. Apodomaris River. Former castle. Andrimachi, Chefalo.]

//24r// The island, formerly known as Claros, today called CALAMOS, is high and mountainous. *Calami* [reeds] in Greek is *arundo* in Latin. Stretching from north to south it is 40 miles around, and the height of its mountains is so great that if anyone climbs to the highest peak, he can have a clear view, when the sun is in the west, as far as the island of Chios or the city of Ephesus or Palatia, the Turkish city.[1] In these mountains indeed through all the fields the fleecy sheep come, trampling on aromatic herbs, safe with no fear of wolves. The yellow goats, destroying the trees, delight in capering[2] on the summit of the crags.

To the east is an ancient town situated in a high place where a small island lies in view. This was once very illustrious as can be seen even now, for who can recount the great number of antiquities in it and point out the scattered remains of marbles everywhere, when [now] I can see nothing surviving of the city. On the bay the fortified town of Calamos is erected, and on the west of the bay near the river Salsum the city of Vathi was once laid out. Here we saw many buildings.

Coming to the west and south at the base of the mountain or promontory appear two excellent ports. Here there is a large cave and in it is a very powerful spring which never ceases to flow. Everywhere aloe wood grows, which is thought by all to be very good for one's health.

.53. CALAMOS TODAY, FORMERLY IT WAS CALLED CLAROS. Circumference of the entire island, 10 miles. [Map: North. Calamos. Old fortress. Spring in a cave. *Island to the south:* Capra.].

//24v// Next to Calamos stands HERRO,[3] a very mountainous, marble island that has to the east a well-fortified castle, where the inhabitants take refuge at night in order to be safe. To the south was the port of Lepida, where once a city stood high on the mountain,[4] and a plain expands at its base. As you go to the west, there the bay of Ferado that spreads out. The town once called Partini,[5] we see deserted. Everywhere it appears mountainous. It is 18 miles in circumference, and among all the islands of this type, we call it most fortunate of them all. Here aloe wood is gathered and sold by merchants every year.

1. Miletus.
2. Reading *caprizare* for *patrizare*. Sinner, 104.
3. Leros
4. Reading *in monte* for *in nocte*.
5. Partini: modern Partheni.

.54. Herro formerly and now. Circumference of the entire island 18 miles. [Map: North. Herro. Partini formerly. Very high mountain.]

We have passed from Herro, now we come to Patmos, on which John, a disciple of Christ, was sent into exile in the time of the Emperor Domitian.[1] In a quiet corner of the port city on a certain Sunday, he was seized[2] by the spirit and while in contemplation saw great hidden things of the present and future. Writing the book of the Apocalypse, he revealed many things to us. Finally, when Domitian died, John went to Ephesus, today called Alto Luogo,[3] and was received with great honors. Here, while he preached the faith of Christ with great miracles, many of his disciples came to this island [Patmos] and constructed a monastery[4] not far from where he received his vision. Still today it is inhabited by monks. They are unmolested by the Turks, and often go to Turkey to procure their material sustenance. It is mountainous with low hills, and in it are found many veins of metals.

.55. Patmos. Here Saint John stayed in exile in the time of the Emperor Domitian. [Map: North. Monastery of the monks of St. John. Here St. John wrote the Apocalypse.]

//25r// I have reported on Patmos, now let us go on to Dipsi, a small island. *Dipsi* in Greek means *sitis*, thirst, in Latin, because it is dry and lacking in greenery. So it is called Dipsi as it is arid and mountainous, and even our ancestors never lived there. A gulf is seen from the east, and now it appears to be inhabited by goats and wild asses.[5]

.56. Dipsi.[6] [Map: North.]

From the other side of this island to the west is Crusie, an island between Icarea and Patmos. It is surrounded by low mountains, and around it are some small rocky islets. For a long time it has been deserted by all. In the middle an abandoned town can be seen. Now wild beasts wander there at their pleasure. It is called Crusia in Greek which is *aurata*, golden, in Latin.

.57. Crusie. [Map: North. *No buildings or toponyms.*]

Varro reports that on this island of Icarea lived Icarus, the Cretan, and so it is believed to be called Icarea. Icarus, who was quickly offended by the haughtiness of the tyrant,

1. Reigned 81–96 CE.
2. Reading *raptus* for *raptis*, Sinner, 105. Domitian, r. 81–96.
3. The medieval name of Ephesus. The medieval town was situated on a mountain above the old city.
4. The Monastery of St. John was founded in the eleventh century.
5. An example of an island on which Buondelmonti did not land.
6. Düsseldorf suggests this is Arki or the Arkoi islands, but these lie to the north of Lipsi, not between Patmos and Ikaria.

left his native land, when Brutus was consul, who drove the kings out of the city, and conquered Italy. This island is very mountainous and [80][1] miles in circumference. From east to west it rises up like a sinking ship, turning around in the sea, and at the end

//25v// it slopes downward. When ships from the sea of Ephesus see the peak of this island in the clouds, they hurry to find a safe harbor, since such a sign is feared as a bad omen for passing ships. There are in this island in the clefts of inaccessible cliffs, bees, which frequent the caverns there and make good honey. Here, with the honey. they make quantities of white wine and send it to their neighbors. On the highest point of the island are two towns. In the east on a mountain near the sea is seen a very high tower called Fanari.[2] Formerly there was a light so that travelers would be aided in stormy weather, since on the whole island there is no good port to be found.

.58. Hicarea. Circumference of the entire island 80 miles. [Map: North. Fanari.]

This island is called Mandria,[3] which arises near Dipsi. It is surrounded by reefs and, although it was formerly inhabited, now it has come to solitude. Here asses, with their resounding bray, wander the forests without fear, along with an infinite number of goats.

.59. Mandria. Completely deserted. [Map: East.]

Two small islands, bare of inhabitants, rise to the east, called Agatusa and Pharmacus. Along the river palaces[4] have been found. Here very often Turkish pirates come roaming; and then, looking for a better route, they depart. The first is 12 miles in circumference, the second, four. From these to the mouth of the Palaces River one enters and, going by river, quickly arrives at the city,

//26r// which took its name from the formerly magnificent palaces. There is a lake there which reaches its greatest extent in the winter, and such a quantity of fish and eels is found in it that they are shipped everywhere. Biremes from here, spreading destruction throughout the islands,[5] often fall into the hands of the Knights of St. John and the Venetians and are sent by them to the bottom of the sea.

.60. Pharmacus. Circumference of the entire island 4 miles. [Map: North.]

.61. Agatusa. Circumference of the entire island 12 miles. [Map: North.]

//26r// Not far from the above mentioned islands is found the island of Samos, a little ways from the continent [of Asia]. In the days of the pagan gods it was esteemed very

1. Blank in the MS. Dd, p. 41; Legrand, p. 225.
2. There is still a tower, Fano (third century CE), at this location.
3. Thymena: A suggestion in Düsseldorf, 71.
4. Impressive ruins still to be seen here. *Blue Guide to the Aegean Islands*, 429.
5. With Sinner, p. 108, reading *insulas* for *insula*.

highly for its sacrificial ceremonies. Then a great society of philosophers reigned in it. It is surrounded by very high mountains, is 80 miles around and longer from east to west. On one side we found a port with running springs of very cold water.

To the south on a plain near the sea was a magnificent city, and such a great ruin of buildings and columns can be seen that it is impossible to describe in a single day. A huge temple of Juno with enormous columns was erected, and nearby, it is said, her statue was carved. She was shown as a queen with a scepter, with clouds and a rainbow around her head. Peacocks groveled at her feet, and they are said to be her birds. Juno is the air and the sister and wife of Jove or fire. She is the wife because she receives heat under him and from him and feeds the lesser ones. She is his sister because she is nearest to him.[1] She is a virgin because nothing comes from air and nothing is born from it. The rainbow and the nymphs are produced in air and by the foam of the sea, rising through the air, they are united with it. Thus Neptune was the nurse of Jove, since he served him with food.

On this island Pythagorus was born, a most outstanding philosopher, who traveled to Babylonia to learn the motion of the stars and to study the origin of the world. The highest knowledge was pursued by him. Polycrates,[2] as Valerius says, was a most harsh tyrant in this island and fortunate in all his deeds until he fell into the hands of the Persian Oroetes, who hung the aforesaid Polycratus on a cross on Maedalense, the highest mountain.

Furthermore the Sybil named Phemo lived here, one of ten, and she is called Samia from this place. Here also Lucius Emilius Paulus, a Roman, conquered King Perseus, the son of Philip [V] of Macedon, in which battle he killed 20,000 of the enemy.[3] Innumerable Turks also came here, fleeing from Tamerlane.[4] They say that in the middle of the island there is a wealth

//26v// of fruit, and a man can eat as many as he wishes, if he will deviate from the road to feed the fruits of this place to his comrades. If he takes nothing away, the road remains open. Throughout the island can be seen fruit trees and very high mountains, one of which is named Aothe, another Medalens,[5] and to the west other, higher mountains appear.

1. "Juno is the air," Macrobius, *Commentary on the Dream of Scipio* I.17. Most of this text can be found in Bersuire, Prologue, Fol. xb, though it is somewhat garbled here.
2. Polycrates, tyrant of Samos, d.522 BCE. The story of his end appears in Herodotus III.120–125, although his murder and crucifixion took place in Magnesia, not Samos. Quintus Valerius Antias, first century BCE, was a Roman historian. Only fragments of his *Annales* survive.
3. Reading *Perseum* for *Persae*. This battle ended the Third Macedonian War, 168 BCE, but took place at Pydna on the coast. Perseus fled to Samothrace (not Samos) and was eventually captured. Livy XLIV.42.
4. Tamerlane, c.1402.
5. These mountains appear on the map. Today they go by the names of Kerkis and Ampelos.

.62. SAMOS FORMERLY AND NOW. The circumference of the whole island is 80 miles. [Map: North. Very high mountain *(twice)*. This was a very great city. The Venetians made this *(a tower)*, and on account of the wild animals they could not live in it. Aote. Mt. Aote. Mt. Medalens.]

To the west near the island just described are the deserted islands called FOURNIO, which never were inhabited and are very arid and surrounded by impassable cliffs.[1] On these islands ships often seek shelter, safe from the winds, and they pass the night without the refreshment of sweet water and on the watch on account of their great fear of the Turkish pirates. Of these islands the first is two, the second three, the third ten, and the fourth and fifth four miles in circumference. To the largest of these, I made a journey from the area of Rhodes to Chios during a dark and stormy night. We lowered our sail, believing we were entering port, and we crashed upon the reefs near the promontory. Alas, what misfortune befell us![2] When we realized that we could in no way detach the ship from the rocks, everyone went on shore, and thus we spent that stormy night until daybreak. When dawn came, we could not see our ship at all, since the whole thing had sunk into the sea. But after we had passed the fifth and sixth days of this life without the sun, and only the water which was in the hollows of the rocks, some of us were ready to render our souls to God. When the seventh day had come and I could find no nourishing plant to eat, I went down into a cave and carved my name on a rock with my sword: "Here Cristoforo, the priest, died of mortal hunger." When I had done this, my companions, reviving,[3] hailed a passing ship, and this was the cause of our salvation.

//27r// .63. FURNIO IT IS CALLED. [Map: North. *Map shows five islands, each with its circumference marked on it:* 2, 4, 10, 3, *and* 4 *miles.*]

Then we left behind the port and the deserted islands, and, rejoicing, sought through the waves the entrance to TENOSA.[4] Here, when we arrived, we found with great labor antique ruins among the brambles and twisting paths. Among these on account of the great fluctuation of the contending winds in the night little sparkling gems shone on high, and the voices of the winds among the little trees seemed very sweet to our listening ears. The island is mountainous and ten miles in circumference.

.64. TENOSA. The circumference of the entire island is 10 miles. [Map: East.]

Near Chios to the west is PSARA, or *piscator*, "fisherman," in Latin. In this area of twelve miles a town rises up, but since it became deserted, they have let loose many domestic animals there, who have gone wild. In front of this appear some small islands in the midst of which is a harbor. Here, once, a Turkish galley arrived. To be secure against the attacks

1. This island group is now advertised as a "quiet retreat" for tourists: *MapEasy's Guide Map to the Greek Isles* (Wainscott, NY: MapEasy, 1999).
2. "Heu cecidere manus!" The translation is Legrand's.
3. Reading *convalescentes* for *convolescentes*, Sinner and Dd.
4. The Düsseldorf editors suggest this identity, II, 72. It is 15 km. east of Naxos.

of the Christians, they came secretly to another part of the island, and while they were passing the night, the north wind, roaring out of its cave, sank their ship. The frightened Turks, wandering through the island, quickly seized the wild asses as well as the goats, and, eating their flesh, they arranged the hides of the beasts in the wind (to dry). When they had gotten the desired number, they placed wooden boards around them to make them into a ship, and they, nearly forty in number, did not delay to set sail for Turkey. When after three days, arriving eagerly near Thrace, a little ship with six men attacked them and killed them to the last man.

//27v// .65. PSARA. Circumference of the entire island 12 miles. [Map: North.]

After this we visit the island of CHIOS, which Pliny called Scirosior and Assanso.[1] Then it was called Chios because in the Syrian language it is translated as *mastic* in Latin. It is located in the Aegean Sea seventeen miles[2] from Asia Minor and is 124 miles in circumference — we have measured it. It is called Chios in Greek, *pregnans* in Latin, or Chion *(column)* or Chion *(dog)*.[3] Here Hypsipile, daughter of Thoas, sent her father, pretending to the Lemnian women that he had been killed. In this island, as Ovid says, after Theseus killed the Minotaur and was fleeing from Crete, taking with him the two daughters of King Minos, he abandoned Ariadne without cause and took Phaedra as his wife.

> "Straightaway the son of Aegeus, taking Minos' daughter, spread his sails for Dia;[4] and on that shore he cruelly abandoned his companion. To her, deserted and bewailing bitterly, Bacchus brought love and help. And that she might shine among the deathless stars, he sent the crown she wore up to the skies. Through the thin air it flew."[5]

The island lengthwise from north to south is divided into two parts, of which the first looks toward the north, and is called *Apanomerea* in Greek and *pars suprema* (upper part) in Latin. The second is *Catomerea* in Greek, in Latin *pars infima*, or lower part. The first of these rises in the rugged mountains and is guarded by pine and plane trees. From these emanate springs which form very cold rivers, running through shady valleys into the sea, and turning the mills. Here many fortresses and towns are seen on the hills and in the plain. That is to say, Volisso with an excellent plain, Perperea, S. Helena, Menedato, Vicco, Picio,

1. Pliny V.136, does not give these names but instead writes Aethalia, Chia, Macris and Pityusa as alternative names. Scirosio, reminiscent of the more modern name of Scio.
2. Other manuscripts (e.g., Düsseldorf) say four miles, which is correct.
3. Here Buondelmonti has confused the Greek Chi with Kappa, thus creating a false etymology (dog, column). Gerola, 1164.
4. Or Naxos. Buondelmonti gives the name of Chio instead.
5. Ovid, *Metamorphoses* VIII.174–179. Frank Justus Miller, trans. (Cambridge, MA: Harvard University Press, 1916).

and Cardamile[1] are all seen, and, counted in the upper part, along with S. Angelo and S. Elias, is a town formerly called the estate of Homer.[2] In this ruined town is found a sepulchre of the prophet Homer, ravaged by time, but from no author have I received a report so that one might be certain of it. So let us leave it to posterity to be investigated.

To the north is Nao, an abundant spring where towering promontories reach to the sky. Not far from it is the excellent port of Cardamile, with a plain and a river. Then we choose to go to Delphinum,[3] another port with a tower and a river. From here in a few miles is the city of Chios, where a very secure harbor was built by the Genoese.[4] This city flourished securely for a long time, placed on an impregnable[5] mountain. At the foot of the mountain, we rightly praise the monastery of the Crown.[6] Then, for what reason I do not know, the citizens removed their households and built a magnificent city near the sea. From one part to another the most fertile plains appear, endowed with vines of all kinds of fruit, and below the mountains is Neo Moni.[7]

Now our story shall go to Catomerea which from the southern part through the west among the low hills the inhabitants work skillfully in the prepared ground to produce the gum[8] of mastic from the lentisk trees in the spring time. It is amazing that in Apanomerea a tree of this type is not found.

When I arrive at Mt. S. George, there at the base of the mountain springs burst forth, running together and forming a river, which descends through a most fertile plain into the sea. Here to the right of the mountain we recognize Recovera, a great castle. We move on to Calamoti with its plain, said to be the head of mastic production, and there

1. Volissos and Kardhamila are modern names. Mendato on the map is Caput Melanese. Turner: Melanios, Viki, Pitous (Pirgi).
2. The Stone of Homer here is still a tourist attraction. *Blue Guide,* 644.
3. Delphinum: Delphion: an antique foundation.
4. Chios remained under the Giustianini, a Genoese family, 1344–1566.
5. Reading inexpugnabilem for expugnabilem.
6. The Monastery of the Crown of the Virgin Mary, established in the eleventh century, with a wonder-working icon.
7. At this point in some manuscripts, such as those transcribed by Sinner, is a lengthy addition on this famous monastery and surrounding churches. It reads: "A monastery in which there is a marvelously constructed church, more than I can describe. Here, up to now, dwell more than thirty monks, serving God. Here is a marvelously designed cistern. In this monastery all travelers can rest without charge. To the north is the church of the Crown of the Virgin Mary, most holy to all surrounding people. Only a mile nearby is the church of St. Nicolas with an orchard and a beautiful spring. Two miles from this place is El Dragolio with a very beautiful garden, a spring, and magnificent domains. One mile further is found St. John's with a well forested garden, a tower, and a spring flowing with fresh water." See H.L. Turner, "Chios and Christopher Buondelmonti's *Liber Insularum,*" *Deltion* (1987): 47–72.
8. Reading *gumman* for *grumam.*

is an island of monks that we hail from afar. Then I return to Pigri, a town in the plain, where we praise St. Anastasia, and the port of Amista,[1] from which we advance quickly and safely into a plain and town of the same name, and beyond to the west at the port of Late with two islands and the Gulf of Litilimenem, where a plain and a river appear.[2]

//28r// .66. Chios. Circumference of the entire island 124 miles. [Map: North. Full page. Cape Melanesi. S. Helena. Abundant spring. Port Cardamile. *Island* (Strivili?). Diriorum Castle. Perparea. Vico. Cardamile. S. Steven. Volisso. Pirio. P. Delfini, Port Litimitia. This is the estate of Homer. S. Elias on a very high mountain. S. Angelus, S. John. Here was the old city of Chios. Sepulcher of the prophet Homer. S. Maria Neo Moni, Holy Mountain. Port Late. Throughout the whole of Catomerea the mastic trees grow, and not in Apanomerea, and these are small mountains. *City of Chios on bay, not labelled, shows walls with towers and 2 jetties projecting into the sea.* Coronati, S. George, Amistae, Port Amistae. Pigri, S. Anastasia, Recovera Castle. Calamoti.]

//28v// We have described Chios, now the island of Lesbos appears. It had such a powerful fleet that it was said to have an empire of the sea. It is located in the Aegean Sea, and called Mytilene because Miletus, the son of the sun, and brother of Pasiphae and the father of Byblis and Caunus,[3] came here, having fled from Crete where he had revolted against his kinsman Minos. He built and reigned over the city of Mileta and it was named after him. But later, the letters having been transposed, the city was called Mitilene. Alcaeus the poet liberated the city from a certain tyrant.[4] Sappho the poetess was from this island as was Theophrastus the philosopher.[5] Here Pompey, about to do battle with Caesar in Thessaly, left his wife.[6] Here reigned Nycteus, the father of Anthiope, from whom Jupiter, in the form of a satyr, fathered Amphion and Zethus. Castor and Pollux, after their sister Helen had been captured on the island of Cytharea, came this far in pursuit of Paris, the son of Priam, who had seized her. They were never able to find her because of a great tempest. Overtaken by death and transformed into a constellation, they are remembered today as the Gemini. The Apostle Paul, coming from Syria during a storm at sea, barely escaped

1. Modern Mista or Mesta.
2. Modern Lithin. Turner (1987), p. 67. It is her view that this acount of Chios was greatly modified by a local scribe in 1456 to improve on CB's version (p. 56). This version of the text is most similar to those of Paris MSS fonds Lat. NA 76 and 4823. Dd adds: And note that the port of Delphinus is called Belofanos.
3. Confusion with the city of Miletus on the Asian coast. Byblis and Caunus, twin children of Miletus, immortalized by Ovid, *Metamorphoses* IX, 450–665.
4. Pittacus, d. 569 BCE. One of the Seven Sages, he was reputed to be a wise leader and retired voluntarily in 596. There is no indication that the poet, Alcaeus, had anything to do with his overthrow.
5. Theophrastus, d. 287 BCE. A pupil of Plato, head of the Academy for thirty-five years.
6. Cornelia, wife of Pompey the Great, before the battle of Pharsalus against Julius Caesar, 48 BCE.

to land here. Preaching the Christian faith, he killed a great serpent and converted many people.[1]

There are throughout the island many fortified towns of which Mytilene appears the greatest. This city was in past centuries a great and very powerful one, and was four or more miles in circumference. Today it is reduced to a very small space. A pious monk here foresaw the destruction of the city and its ruler. He often spoke openly to the citizens about the destruction of the city, but the lord and his followers and many of the citizens, not believing him, perished in an earthquake.

It happened in my day that a lord came through the island, and while sleeping in a certain house, a scorpion bit into his hand. When his servants heard him shouting, (they) got up to him by a ladder, seeking alleviation for his pain. The house was full of so many noblemen and servants that it collapsed into rubble and the lord along with many other people met an unexpected death.

To the south four columns are still standing of a magnificent city together with many buildings and subterranean vaults constructed with marvelous industry. To the south is the Gulf of Gera, where many towns are seen toward the west: Castle Gero, Kerameia, Chidonia, Chaloni, Vassilica, Castel Petra, Castel Mulgo. To the north is the Castle of St. Theodore,[2] a tower, and around the center is a fertile plain. To the east and west are mountains and wild beasts together with cypresses, beech trees and pines. And with many harbors and islands, it is 130 miles around. It borders on Turkey.

//29r// .67. LESBOS FORMERLY OR MYTILENE, IS NOW CALLED METELLINO, AND THE CIRCUMFERENCE OF THE ENTIRE ISLAND IS 130 MILES and is number 67. [Map: North. Castle of St. Theodore, Castel Mulgo. Mountains and a great forest. Tower. Vassilica. Castel Petra. Paleo Castro. Geremia. Kalloni. Neai Kidoniai. Laurisca, Gera, Mitilena, Gulf of Geremie. *Island to south:* Petra. Pyrrha. *The orientation of the map appears incorrect. Though the Turkish coast is rightly shown on the east, the island of Lesbos should be given a quarter turn clockwise.*]

We now select the island of TENEDOS, which is placed in front of the narrow passage to Romania or the Hellespont, and appears in the Aegean Sea in sight of ancient Troy. Its name is said to come from a certain young man[3] who was infamous among the Athenians because he had had sexual relations with his stepmother. Because of his shame he came to this uninhabited island and populated it with farmers. In the time of Laomedon and Priam, the island was very wealthy, and in its gulf the Greeks made ready their plots against the Trojans, by which Troy was destroyed.

1. Paul came to Mytilene on his second voyage in 53 CE: Acts 20:15. The storm at sea and the killing of the viper took place on Malta, Acts 27–28.
2. Sinner, 116, adds Castle Angerino, Castle Parrachila.
3. The young man's name was Thene or Tenes. Some versions suggest that he was slandered. Isidore, *Etymologies* XIV.6.23.

During the horrible war between the Venetians and the Genoese in my time, each wished to possess the island for itself. Eventually by mutual agreement[1] it remains deserted, and so no one dares to live on it, except for many domestic animals who, left behind,

//29v// have become wild beasts.

At the base of a high mountain there is a spring which flows from the third hour of the night until the sixth hour during the summer solstice with so much water that a great river appears. At all other hours, we understand that there is no water in it.

Here there is a plain surrounded by low mountains, except for one that appears higher than the others. Here 3000 Franks (Europeans) were hanged after the Venetians sank the Turkish fleet in the sea near Gallipoli.[2] This was because among all the people gathered in the fleet were some in alliance with the infidels. This was at the time of the Council of Constance.[3]

Throughout the plain are untended vines and other fruit trees which today provide refreshment to passersby. If you look toward Troy, once so famous, you will see many fragments of its antiquity. To the left, let us enter the Hellespont in the entrance by a narrow strait, and we come upon the Dardanelles, where now and formerly many columns remain standing.

.68. Tenedos.[4] Circumference of the entire island 40 miles. [Map: East. Dardonello. Through all of this plain and through the strait as far as the Dardanelles, I believe was Troy. *On Tenedos:* Spring that rises during the solstice and pours into a great river].

After this I judge it suitable (to wait), until we come to show the city of Constantinople, that the spirit of our listeners will be eager for those things which we are about to describe, where there will be many wonders to be seen. So here is the entrance to the Hellespont as far as its narrow mouth, which is called the strait of Gallipoli. Asia is here divided from Europe.

//30r// First after we have left ancient Troy to the right, we find a tower on the left near the sea, which we have remembered to be nearer to Asia. From here as far as the town of Abydos the way is short. Xerxes, king of the Persians, made his passage from Asia to Europe in this place having constructed a bridge on top of boats.[5] Demosthenes says that there were more than one million soldiers, and 4,200 ships in number, yet a short time after, that terrible man was forced to flee hidden in one small boat.

1. Fourth Genoese War, 1381, Peace of Turin.
2. 1416.
3. 1414–18. Those hanged were Christian mercenaries, serving in the Turkish fleet. Another reference to the Council of Constance is in the account of Astymphalia.
4. Now part of Turkey: Bozca Ada.
5. 480 BCE. Reading *super* for *sub*.

Livy[1] says that when the people of Abydos were being besieged by King Philip,[2] he was about to destroy their walls. They in their misery wished to retreat with their goods. The captain of the fortress called them back, saying, "You have not spared your country and your homes, for you will all be led to your death." And so they not only rushed to their death, but consigned their houses and all their possessions to the flames.[3]

Beyond we see the walled city of Gallipoli on high more than 40 miles from any part of Europe. The Greek emperor willingly betrayed it to the Turkish infidels and married his own daughters to them.[4] From this largesse followed so many disasters for the Christians that a man could hardly in the course of a lifetime count or write all the names of those captured and killed.

The Turks were poor folk from the mountains of Armenia and Persia, who, coming into Asia Minor, began their rule by the consent of the aforementioned emperor. From these people a province of new languages and peoples was swiftly established and endures to this day. Among them some were mighty in battle, and very worthy to be remembered who governed the kingdom well and splendidly accounting to the manner of their sect, and who have taken many kingdoms from the Christians by their strength. One of these, Murad, is spoken of with honor.[5] A woman was once taking a basin of milk to her husband in the field, when a servant of Murad took her food and ate it. The crime was quickly discovered, and he was led before the sultan and cut in half. The milk (pouring out of his body) was recognized, and justice was done before Murad. A certain abbot stole ornaments of the saints and of his church. He went to Murad with great joy and worshipped Muhammad. The monks from there found out where the abbot had gone, and made their complaint before the same emperor. When he discovered the clever fraud of the abbot, the treasures were restored to the monks standing before him, and the abbot was thrown down into the depths of the sea from the highest mountain. A plowman[6] with his plow came upon a jar of silver coins. He loaded it into his cart, took it to Murad, and gave him the money. Murad asked the older men there whose image was on the coins, and nobody knew. He said, "Plowman, you are a good man. This image is not mine, nor is it of my ancestors. Because

1. Reading *Livius* for *Lucius*.
2. Philip V, r. 220–170 BCE.
3. This truly horrifying story of the siege of Abydos is told at greater length by Livy XXXI.16–18. The date is 200 BCE.
4. John V Cantacuzenus (1347–54) pursued a policy of appeasement of the Turks, and gave his daughter in marriage to Emir Orhan. In 1354 Gallipoli was taken by the Turks. In 1373 John Paleologus became a vassal of the sultan.
5. Murad I (r. 1360–89). These are typical of the "wise ruler" tales of the Middle Ages, some of Arabic origin.
6. Reading *Bubulcus* (plowman) for *Subulcus* (swineherd).

it does not seem just to take something made by another, or right to seize something from someone else, it is yours. Go in peace."

//30v// Gallipoli [Map: North. Full page. Here there 40 mills or more. Cemetery of the Turks. Well. Building of the court where justice is done. Building of armed galleys. Plaza. *A gallows with someone hanging from it.* Turkey *(2x).* Tower of Lapsaco. Strait of Gallipoli and Romania. Aleva tur [Aleva Tower *on the left. Two other inscriptions too faint to read, one in upper right*[1] *and one in the sea.*]

//31r// To the east at the entrance of the sea of Hellespont is the island of Marmora. It is 30 miles around and is reported to be entirely mountainous with marble and forested with pines. From here Constantine, Justinian, and other emperors took away marble for innumerable edifices for the city of Constantinople, and they were loaded onto a stone bridge. On the other side there is a town with few inhabitants, and some islands. This sea, the Hellespont, is named for Helle, daughter of Athamas, who, with her brother Phrixus, fleeing the treacheries of their stepmother, rode on a golden ram. To her misfortune she fell into the waves. Swallowed up in these waters, she gave her name forever to the sea that used to be called Pontus before it was called Hellespont. This sea has its beginning from the Erythraean shore, where the sepulcher of Ajax is, as far as the Chersonese, and there, at the end, it is merged into Europe.

.70. Marmora. Circumference of the whole island 30 miles. [Map: North.]

Sailing through the above-mentioned sea, as we approach the City, the island of Calonimon is seen on the right. It is very mountainous and when, long ago, the Greeks ruled all through here, it was inhabited. Now it is reduced to desolation and wild animals roam through it.

//31v// .71. Calonimon. [Map: North.]

Little islands [Scopuli Prinkipi] are found near the City with others placed here and there. Since they are near the city of Constantine, monks have taken refuge in them and there used to be huge buildings. Monasteries appear scattered among them everywhere. Beyond these islands to the east near the sea was a great city[2] in which nothing now is seen but ruined marble buildings. In this place a plowman found a chest with the preserved body of a king with a crown, scepter and golden sword. When he told the lord (of his find), and they wanted to take the body out, it immediately dissolved into ashes. From here to the city of Nicea and Brusa,[3] the former and present capital, is a straight road. Here the emperor resides with his wives and daughters, although he used to stay in one place for only a short time, always wandering everywhere with his tents.

1. Dd, fol. 64r shows a building labelled as "Imarat" (public soup kitchen).
2. Nicomedia. MN omits the name, but Sinner, 120, has *Comedia.*
3. Brusa, captured by the Turks in 1326 and made their capital.

.72. These islands are without names. [Map: n.d. *Five islands (Princes' Islands) with buildings, two without.*]

//32r// I come again to the ruined city of CONSTANTINOPLE. Although it is not an island, after we arrived here, we found a few things in it that might attract the attention of our readers. It was named by Constantine and, uniting it with Byzantium, he greatly enlarged it. In the course of centuries the emperors adorned it with churches. particularly Justinian, who established the laws and built Hagia Sophia with a palace and a race track. It is triangular and is 18 miles in circumference.

Beginning from the corner by St. Dmitri as far as the corner of the Vlacherna [the wall] is six miles, in which space are erected 110 towers. From here to the Golden Gate it is five miles, fortified with a wall and an ante wall and a moat of running water, with 96 towers on the higher wall. From here back to St. Dmitri is is 7 miles and there are 198 towers. There is a field here outside the former Vlanga Gate where the Greeks, it is said, moved by envy or by their own suffering, deceitfully killed 50,000 Franks with bread made of quicklime mixed with wheat. Their innumerable bones give testimony to this event to this day.[1]

Nearby is Coriescali[2] or Arsana.[3] Further on above these walls is the enormous palace of Justinian with the most noble church called Enea,[4] with mosaics and buildings and a wonderfully and ingeniously constructed pavement. There, high up and above the sea, was a huge reflecting mirror of immeasurable size, visible from very far away. All these marble buildings near the little gate of the emperor are now thrown down into the sea.

From the great palace to Hagia Sophia there was a mile-long road of double columns through which the emperor advanced. Here around the outside was the dwelling of 800 churchmen, and it is said they they consumed the revenue of the entire island of Sicily. Now only the dome of the church remains, since all the rest was destroyed and has been reduced to nothing.

1. The Vlacherna or Blacherna is in the northwest corner; the Golden Gate is in the southwest, and St. Dmitri at the east. The walls, mostly built in the fifth century, are 18 miles in circumference. The heaps of bones at the Vlanga Gate were noted by other fifteenth-century travelers, each of whom had his own theory about them. Majeska suggests that they might have been victims of a purge of the Franks in 1261 by Emperor Michael VIII. The story of the poisoned bread comes from the Second Crusade, but took place on the coast of Asia Minor. George P. Majeska, *Russian Travelers in Constantinople in the Fourteenth and Fifteenth Centuries* (Washington, DC: Dumbarton Oaks, 1984), 269–70.
2. The Byzantine harbor of Kontoscalion.
3. *Arsena*, the shipyard (medieval Latin).
4. Nea Ekklesia (New Church), built by Basil I, the Macedonian (867–86). Later the elision of the article and the new name led it to be identified with the Nine Orders of Angels. It is now destroyed. Majeska, 247–48.

From the vault to the ground it is 134 brachia,[1] and from the pavement to the level of the foundation is 22 brachia, where there is an excellent cistern full of water. Above in the church it is 120 brachia from one corner to the other. The church is round above and quadrangular at the base. Who could count the decorations of marbles and porphyry with the mosaic ornamentation? I am reluctant to decide at which point I wish to begin.

Outside the church to the south of the square is a column 70 cubits high at the top of which is an equestrian statue of Justinian in bronze. Holding a golden apple in his left hand, he makes a menacing gesture to the east with his right. And nearby appear six great marble columns in a row. Beyond these to the south lies the Hippodrome, which in Latin is the *equicursus* (horse race track). In this area the nobles jousted before the people, and conducted duels and tournaments.[2] It was 690 brachia long and 124 wide and was constructed on columns, and a cistern of the best water occupies the entire space beneath it. At the top of the Hippodrome were 24 very high columns where the emperor sat with the princes. From one part to another the marble seats of the Hippodrome were graduated in length, and the people might see the entire sport from their seats.

Through the middle of the course along its length is a low wall, and toward Hagia Sophia is a church with a magnificent wall, adorned with innumerable windows, where the ladies and young girls enjoyed the spectacles with their governesses. At the end of this wall was erected a very fine bath in which the wounded were placed.

Then there is an obelisk 44 cubits high, standing on four bronze cubes and on its base are the following verses:

> "Once it was difficult to conquer me,
> but I was ordered to obey the fortunate masters
> and to bear the palm of victory over the dead tyrants.
> All things give way to Theodosius[3] and to his descendants forever.
> In three times ten days I was conquered and tamed.
> Under the judge Proclus I was raised to the heavens above."[4]

Beyond this stone monument are three bronze serpents. Nearby among many stones is erected another obelisk of 63 cubits.[5] Finally at the end of the low wall appear four small

1. Brachium = cubit, 18–20 inches. Buondelmonti estimates the height of the dome at 200 feet. The modern figure is 180 feet.
2. Reading *torniamenta* for *tormenta*, Sinner, 122.
3. Theodosius I, r. 378–95. Proclus was his praetor, responsible for raising the fallen (Egyptian) obelisk.
4. The obelisk is speaking.
5. Sinner, 123, adds: "We saw (the serpents) with open mouths from which on holidays flowed water, wine, and milk." This was a victory monument erected at Delphi by the Athenians after the Battle of Plataea, 479 BCE. Constantine brought it to Constantinople. The bronze column remains, but two of the snakes' heads disappeared in the sixteenth century. The remaining one is now in the Archaeological Museum.

upright marble columns, on which the empress presided at the festival. Theodosius made all these and many other laudable things in the city.

Today moreover there are found an infinite number of columns of which five marble ones can be seen, and the first is called the column of Justinian. The second is that of the cross. In that place appear four upright columns of porphyry on which had been placed four horses of gilded bronze. The Venetians took these to Venice to the church of San Marco, along with the remaining columns. The third and fourth of the columns, which were placed in the middle of the city, were known to have carved around them the deeds of the emperors.

In the church of the Holy Apostles[1] is a fifth column with a bronze angel and Constantine kneeling. The church is now in ruins and all the immense porphyry sepulchers of the emperors can be seen. There is found the column where Christ was bound and beaten. In the monastery of Pantocrator[2] is the stone where Joseph of Arimathea wound Christ into his shroud. At the monastery of St. John of Petra are the vestments of Christ and the reed with the sponge and the lance[3] preserved together.

Finally there are throughout the city

//32v// innumerable churches and cisterns of amazing size and construction all in ruins. There are some vineyards which produce three or four casks of wine. There is the cistern of St. John of Petra, the cistern of Pantepopti,[4] the cistern of the Pandocrator, the cistern of the Apostles, and the cistern of Muhammad, in which the columns are arranged with such subtle artifice that it is incredible to relate.[5]

And there are many other churches of which Hagia Sophia is greater than the others, and Justinian produced that work in 15 years. They are: St. George of Mangana,[6] St. Irene,[7] St. Lazarus, Kyria Hemas,[8] Enea, Peter and Paul,[9] the 40 Holy Martyrs[10] and its

1. The Church of the Holy Apostles was built by Justinian. It was torn down in the fifteenth century to make room for a mosque, Fatih Cami.
2. Church of St. Savior, Pandocrator (All Powerful), built in the eleventh century. After the Turkish conquest it became first a madrassah, then a mosque, Zeyrek Cami.
3. Other MSS add:" the iron of the lance and the crown of thorns and hairs of his beard." Dd, 51.
4. Under the monastery of Christ Pandepoptes, Christ the All-Seeing. The twelfth-century church survives as the mosque of Eski Imaret.
5. This is the cistern of 1000 Columns, now an upscale shopping mall.
6. Built in the eleventh century. Destroyed at the time of the conquest.
7. Holy Peace. The oldest church in Constantinople, it was restored after an earthquake in the eighth century. It is now a museum, located on the grounds of the Topkapi Palace.
8. Or, Our Lady. Düsseldorf, I:68.
9. Built by Justinian, as described by Procopius. Destroyed.
10. The text reads forty thousand martyrs, surely an exaggeration. This chapel, honoring the martyrs of Sebaste, Roman soldiers who converted to Christianity and were martyred in 320, was part of the church of the Chora, built by Justinian.

huge cistern with the finest water, which is so great that its depth, it is said, cannot be found, Anastasis, Peribleptos[1] Sanctos, St. John of the Studion,[2] St. Andrew,[3] Blacherna,[4] etc. There is such a great quantity of these churches standing, each more beautiful than the other, that it would take a long time to tell.

There are throughout the city few inhabitants[5] and they are enemies of the Latins, who never obtain a secure peace[6] with them. If they promise something, they do not keep their promises. This most beautiful city was once a shrine of wisdom and honor. Now it has fallen to ignorance and rigidity in its ancient opinions. They cling to the sin of gluttony, and on account of the great plenty of fish and meat available, a quarter of the population fall prey to the disease of leprosy. They have abandoned the doctrine of John Chrysostom and the other holy fathers.

One mile to the north is Pera, the most beautiful city of the Genoese, which is separated from the city by a gulf. From this place to the Pontus or Euxine Sea is 18 miles. To the north is an entrance by a narrow strait which is a danger to ships entering it today. Now we have talked about the city, we return to the Aegean Sea and to the island of Stalimini.[7]

[Marginal notations: Obelisk, 3 bronze serpents, Column of Justinian, Column of the Cross.]

//33r// Thrace or Greece. [Map: North. Thrace or Greece (2x). *Two columns, unlabelled, marking the entrance to the Black Sea.* Galata now Pera. *Windmill,* St. Dominic. Arsenal. From this gate as far as the Gate of St. Demetrius it is 6 miles and there are 110 towers. Constantinople. *On west:* Corner and Gate of Blacherne, Gate of Saint John, Chamidi Gate. Corner and Golden Gate. From this corner to the corner of Blacherna it is 4 miles and there are 96 towers. As far as the corner of St. Demetrius it is 7 miles and there are 198 towers. *Inside the walls from north:* St. Andrew. Here is Constantine kneeling. Palace of the Emperor, St. Martha. St. John of Petra or Para. St. Salvator.[8] 2 *columns.* Column of the Cross, *(and)* here is Justinian on a horse. Hagia Sophia, Hippodrome. St. Demetrius. St. George of Mangana. St. Lazarus. Palace of the Patriarch. Palace of Constantine. Holy Apostles. St. Andrew. St. John of the Studion. Most

1. Reading *Peribleptos Sanctos* for *Perile Sanctos.* This was a church dedicated to Theotokos, the Mother of God. Now destroyed. The Armenian Church of St. George was built on the site.
2. Built 463, it became a mosque after the conquest. It was seriously damaged by an earthquake in 1894, and is now a ruin.
3. St. Andreas in Krisei, built in the sixth century. It became a mosque in the sixteenth century
4. St. Mary Blacherna, built in the ninth century, was destroyed accidentally in a fire in 1434.
5. Reading *habitatores* for *imperatores*: Sinner, Dd.
6. Reading *securam pacem* for *secretam pacem.*
7. Dd, fol. 53v adds: "One mile to the east of Pera are twin columns where ships pass through, and there is a chest with a treasure for anyone who has taken a wife and does not regret it after one year. And this is true."
8. This is the church of Pantokrator. S. Salvatorem is added in a different hand.

ancient and beautiful gate.[1] Perileftos. Gate of the former palace of the emperor. Turkey *(3x)*. Harbor called Contiscali. *On east:* Corner and Gate of St. Demetrius.]

//33v// This island was called Lemnos, but now is referred to as Stalimini. It is situated in the Aegean Sea, is all flat, and is 100 miles around. *Limni* in Greek is *lacus* (lake) in Latin. On account of the great depth (of this lake) it is dangerous to approach.[2] Since there are in the island excellent gulfs and harbors, there are many towns full of people. One reads that on this island Venus lay with Mars, and the sun revealed her adultery to her husband, Vulcan. Vulcan bound the two of them with iron chains and displayed the lovers in their shame to the other gods. The women of Lemnos condemned the adultery of Venus and neglected her as unworthy, and so she afflicted them with the rank smell of a goat.[3] Whence all the women at the instigation of Venus killed all their husbands. Only Hypsipile, [daughter of Thoas, secretly saved her father from the others. She was made queen of the women.

The Argonauts, returning from Colchis, invaded the island. Jason, the prince among them, lay with Hypsipile and[4]] produced two sons, Oeneus and Thoas. When the Lemnian women realized that Hypsipile had saved [her father], they wished to kill her. She, fleeing, was captured by pirates and sold to Lykurgos, king of Argos, for a nursemaid.

The Minyans derived their origin from this island. Having been expelled by the Pelasgians, they were received by the Spartans. The men escaped by changing clothes with their wives and, going with their heads bent and veiled as a sign of mourning, they left their wives behind in prison. Here Thoas, son of Bacchus, was king. It is very fruitful in grain.

.75. Lemnos once, now Stalimini. Circumference of the entire island 100 miles. [Map: North. Ephesithia, Paleo Castro. Sala, Coziro.]

//34r// Toward the north is Embaros in Greek, which is Ambra, *amber* in Latin. It is located in the Aegean Sea and is very mountainous. Few people live there. It is 30 miles in circumference and looks toward the opening of the mouth of the Hellespont. There is a city left unfinished by the Argonauts.[5] The island was part of the Greek empire.

1. A gate from the walls built by Constantine.
2. Perhaps Lymni Alyki, the salt lake.
3. This MS leaves out the detail that their husbands refused to have sex with them, because of the foul odor.
4. The lines in brackets are from the Düsseldorf MS, II, 53; Sinner, 125–26; omitted in the Minnesota MS Hypsipile's father was king, so she succeeded to the position after his presumed death. When they tried to seize control of the city, they were sent to prison and condemned to death by the Spartans.
5. "Agortanis." Legrand suggests "Argonauts." Or perhaps the name comes from a suburb of Venice, Agora or Agoram, according to Sinner, 246.

.76. Embaros.[1] Circumference of the entire island 30 miles. [Map: North. Embro.]

Now let us say something of Mandraki,[2] which is called *clausura pecudum* (cattle corral) in Latin. It is well inhabited and flourishes in the production of honey and goats. From here we enter into the Gulf of Maliakos, where the city of Aenos is, near the river Achelous.[3]

.77. Mandrachi. [Map: North.]

The island Thasos follows, which means *promitto*, promise, in Latin. It is near what is called the Holy Mountain today, and is 40 miles around and well populated. I have counted three beautiful towns in it. It is most fertile. It lies across from the very famous river Achelous.

.78. Taxos. Circumference of the entire island 40 miles. [Map: No orientation. Taxo.]

//34v// After the aforesaid island [Taxos] we find Mt. Athos, as it was once known. Now it is part of the continent, although at the time of Xerxes, king of the Persians, this mountain was divided from the continent. Now it is connected to the mainland and is called the Holy Mountain. It is very lofty and is near the city of Salonika in the province of Thrace, and there, near the summit, was the town of Acroan.[4] The lives of its inhabitants were longer than those of other lands.[5] The circumference of the mountain appears to be more than 123 miles.

In this place there are so many and such great monasteries of monks — St. Basil, Chrysostom, Gregory of Nazianus and others passed over because it would be difficult to tell them all. The monks arise in the silence of the dark night, according to the Greek rite, after a wooden clapper[6] with its harsh sound has first given the signal. Going to the church, they sing the divine office for Matins. When this is ended, they return to their huts and eat separately in peace whatever they are sent by their prior.

There are some monasteries among these where they follow the communal life of monks, and others with a different mode of life who follow a harsher rule. On Saturday on the mountain all resort in solitude to their cells, chanting the divine office for Sunday until noon when they go to the refectory. Their meal having been finished, some of them

1. Now part of Turkey: Gökçeada.
2. Samothrace
3. Other MSS add that the city is governed by the Gattilusi, a Genoese family who took over the rule of the island in the mid-fifteenth century. Düsseldorf, 2:54 There is some confusion here: the river Acheloos is in Thessaly.
4. The name of this town, variously rendered, is cited in the past tense by Pliny iv.37 as "Acrathon," and della Dora refers to it as a "mythical city." Della Dora, Veronica, *Imago Mundi* 60.2 (2008): 151.
5. Pliny iv.38, refers to the inhabitants as "Macrobii," long-lived. In vii.27 he attributes their longevity to their practice of eating snakes.
6. This is called the sematron and is still used on the mountain today.

prepare to enter into their hermitages with bread and vegetables. There, each one, looking up at heaven and sighing to the stars with his whole mind, thinks of his eternal homeland here in the place of his exile, and his lips constantly turn to humble prayer. When the sun rises in its radiance, rejoicing, he bursts forth with pious lips to the daily praises of God. Each is his own companion, he acts as his own servant, nor does he fear to be alone while (God) is with him. He loves to look at heaven, not gold, and to walk on the earth, a blessing often in his mouth along with the giving of thanks. He knows that little suffices for the life of men and chooses not riches but the highest truths. He does not fear a ruler's power, and he works toward a happy and tranquil eternity, with placid nights, carefree[1] days, and peaceful companions. Each stays free and fearless, neither plotting nor fearing treacheries. (He dwells in) a palace of angels, of celestial odor and color, with his companions. The judge of morals is witness of his modesty: a peaceful mind, ignorant of luxury or conflict. He banishes the power of gluttony and sordid lust, and the queen of sobriety reigns. A chaste and quiet bed and a [clear] conscience is a preparation for Paradise. Many have chosen such a life freely on this mountain, which draws them so far into contemplation that if a great stone wall were to fall around them, they would in no way be afraid or even turn their head or eyes to see it. Others in the monasteries are accustomed to take food in silence three times a week. Here there are 100 monks of the common life, and of the others you will count 500. From ten to thirty monasteries seem to be of the common life.

Here also bees, figs, and olives grow in pleasant valleys. While seated in their cells, some monks in turn weave cloth, [others make shoes, or nets; that one spins wool on a spindle][2] this one weaves a basket of willow twigs. At the fixed hour they proceed to praise God, and eternal peace reigns among them.

//35r//Mons Sanctus [Holy Mountain]. Its circumference 123 miles. [Map: North. Monastery of Vatopedi Calogeri. Monastery of Lavra Calogeri.[3] Mt. Aote. *Outside frame to west:* Thessaloniki.]

Not far from the island of Lemnos in the sea is the small and mountainous island of Sanstrati. The Turks laid it waste and wild animals live in it, wandering in all weathers. A town without walls can be be seen there. It is 15 miles around.

.80. Sanstrati. Circumference of the entire island, 15 miles. [Map: North. Samitraca.]

//35v// In the Aegean Sea the island of Limen appears as a mountain. It is not very large but once was beautiful, though little inhabited. It is 40 miles around and called Limen from *limite*, passage, since ships coming from the city of Salonika sought to cross in a direct line by it so that they might have safer passage.

1. Reading *otiosos* for *occisos*, Sinner, 128.
2. Text in brackets appears in other mss. Düsseldorf, 55, Sinner, 129.
3. These two monasteries still exist.

.81. Limen. Circumference of the entire island, 40 miles. [Map: North. Limen.]

The island Dromos follows, called in Latin *cursus* (passage or journey), since ships sailing from east to west take their bearing from it. Often the citizens light a beacon in the night for passers-by so that it might be navigated more safely. It is fertile and 30 miles in circumference.

.82. Dromos. Circumference of the entire island, 30 miles. [Map: North. Dromos.]

//36r// Macri or formerly Calchis is the name of an island in the Aegean Sea on which few live. To this island Poemidas,[1] the admiral of the fleet of Antiochus, experienced the attacks of the Roman fleet, and thus was conquered. The island remained untouched. It is 40 miles around.[2]

.83. Macri. Circumference of the entire island, 40 miles. [Map: North. Macri.]

We take up two other neighboring islands which are called Schiati and Scopoli. They are in the Aegean Sea. The first is 32, the second 22 miles around.[3] Indeed formerly the ruler of these islands was of great industry and cleverness. Once when he had sailed to the island of Euboea to pillage it, and everyone had landed, the citizens of the island secretly entered the ships and thus put all of the pirates to death.

.84. Scopoli. Circumference of the whole island, 3 miles. [Map: North.]

.85. Schiati. Circumference of the whole island, 22 <illeg>. [Map: North.]

//36v// The island called S. Elias rises near the aforesaid islands, and, because it appears more lofty, it seems to loom over the others in the area. On its summit is a small church. There a monk, serving God, was sleeping in the sun, when an eagle, believing him to be an animal, descended upon him and tore out his eyes with his sharp claws. The monk in agony was calling passionately on God, and St. Elias came to him and restored his eyes, with many of his companions as witnesses.

1. The island of Macri is just off the peninsula of Myonnesus on the Turkish coast between Teos and Samos. Here in 190 BCE Antiochus III and his fleet, commanded by Polyxenidas, were defeated by the Romans in the battle of Myonnesus (Livy XXXVII.28–30). Since the island described here is grouped with other islands on the coast of Euboea, it appears to be a different island. The Düsseldorf editors (p. 72) suggest Peristera. Buondelmonti may have derived this misinformation from Silvestri (Macris or Calvis, #544). Of this passage in Buondelmonti, Sinner remarked "manifestus error" (p. 251 n.). Neither Peristera nor Macri are as large as 40 miles in circumference.
2. In some MSS a note follows that the red letter stands for "M" (1000); "C" in four subsequent entries, and "X" in the last two. These make up the date (MCCCCXX) of Buondelmonti's acrostic. Not in MN.
3. Sinner, 130, has 22 and 12 miles respectively. According to modern measurements, Skopelos is the larger of the two, 47 square miles, as opposed to 30 square miles for Schiati (Sciathos).

.86. Scopulus. The island of S. Elias is very lofty and in the middle of the sea. [Map: n.d.]

The island of Skyros is next, which is long from north to south, and is in the Aegean Sea. It is 80 miles in circumference, has many harbors, and looks toward the Gulf of Pegaseus. It is heavily wooded and mountainous throughout.

Thetis, the mother of Achilles, was warned by the prophecy of a Carpathian soothsayer that her son would perish if he went to the Trojan War. She hid him[1] in a woman's dress on this island at the court of King Lycomedes. Here also he was loved by Deidamia, the daughter of the king, and though he thought that she was not unwilling, he ravished her secretly from her other sisters, and had a son (Neoptolemus) from her.

At once (Thetis) approached the king and there with the altars as witnesses she said, "I present, oh king, the sister of our Achilles. Do you not see that she is proud with eyes like her brother? She has begged us to give her mighty weapons and a bow for her shoulder," etc.[2]

Since the island is forested and wild, there are so many wild beasts of many kinds that it is amazing. Since there are few inhabitants and the island is large, the Turks often visit it without fear of the inhabitants. There were four inhabited towns in this island, and now two remain.

.87. Schiros. The total circumference of the island is 80 miles. [Map: East. Schiros.]

//37r// Across from the duchy of Athens to the north is Euboea[3] formerly, now Egrippum, which is touching the continent, as a bridge stretches in the middle with a fortified tower. Beneath the bridge is such a great rush of the waters twice a day that it is astonishing. Like a speeding arrow it shoots through with a very great depth. At the head of the bridge the city of Egripos[4] spreads out, and it is reputed to be fertile in these parts. Nauplios possessed this island, and in revenge for his son Palamedes, who was killed treacherously in the Greek camps by the wiles of Ulysses, he undertook to voyage around all of Greece, to enter the palaces of the Greek princes, and by his persuasion he urged their wives to commit adultery with whomever they could.[5] He decided to do this in revenge for his son. Many princes were killed on their return by the lovers of their wives. In addition to this Nauplios climbed Mt. Caphareus at night, having lit a torch. The Greeks, returning from Troy, evading a storm, and believing they were entering safety in port because of the fire signal, perished on the deadly reefs. And thus he got revenge for the death of his son Palamedes.

1. Reading *abscondit* for *ascendit*, Sinner, 131.
2. Statius, *Achilleid* 1.350–353.
3. Negroponte
4. Egripos, Euripos, Evripos: usually the name of the strait. Today this is the city of Chalcis.
5. According to Graves, he told them that their husbands would be bringing home Trojan concubines. #162, o-t.

In this island shone Orpheus, the most ancient poet. He said there is one true and great god who governs all things, because before him there was nothing born, and from him were all things created. The philosopher and teacher of Socrates, Gorgias, was from this island. He was born in his mother's coffin. She was being carried to her tomb, when all at once the wail of the infant was heard. He was the first inventor of rhetoric and he lived one hundred years, and never did he cease from activity in his work. Here Neptune, the father of Nauplios, was the lord of this island.

It is 100 miles long from east to west and is 300 miles in circumference. To the north is Mt. Caphareus where the island of Aulis is. Here Iphigenia, the daughter of Agamemnon, was about to be sacrificed to the goddess Diana, [angry][1] on account of the killing of her deer, so that they would have favorable winds to sail against the Trojans. But because of the pity of the goddess for Iphigenia's suffering, she sacrificed a deer in her place.

To the south there is a city still inhabited by the Lombards who came here a long time ago. Today it is possessed by the Turks.[2]

[Marginal notations: Nauplus, Palamedes, Orpheus, Gorgias magister Socratis, Neptunus, Island of Aulis. Ephigenia.]

//37v//.88. Formerly Euboea, formerly or Egrippus or now it is called Negroponte. Circumference of the whole island 300 miles, and its length from east to west is 100 miles. [Map: North. Full page. Otheo. Promontory of Caphareus, Mt. Triferreus. Egrippus *(city)* formerly, now Negroponte. Duchy of Athens. Island of Aulis. *On mainland:* Thebes, Athens. *On isthmus:* Ex milia.[3] *Below:* Morea, Peloponnesus.]

//38r// Aegina soon follows in view of Athens, a small, indeed deserted island. In the middle the remains of a town appear, with an adjacent plain. The remaining parts of the island are made of a mountain of forests and hills. Here the head of St. George is worshipped.

[Marginal notations: Isidore. Luciflorus. Tortellus.]

.89. The island of Aegina, the last in our work of the islands of the Cyclades or the Archipelago. [Map: North.]

[Christ is the name for the chrism or anointing, and Christians are named after Christ. The Greeks have neither chrism nor holy oil, except that when a child is baptized, they wrap it in a clean cloth and annoint its forehead with salt and oil, given by the godfather.[4] So to make an end, now that I have traveled through the entire Archipelago for four years,

1. MN omits *irate*, added from Sinner, p. 133.
2. The Turks conquered Euboea in 1470 from the Venetians, which gives a possible terminus post quem for this MS
3. The Hexamilian Wall built on the Isthmus of Corinth by the Romans.
4. Other manuscripts have this text for Aegina beginning, "Christus a chrismate dicitur," providing an "x" for the date of the acrostic. This section concludes with a personal note, missing from MN.

in great fear and anxiety, we have come to the island of Aegina, where the head of St. George is worshipped, in sight of the city of Athens. And this little boat of our humble journey has safely reached the port of future rest.

I, Christopher, have sent you a gift,[1] reverend Father, first in affection for you, so this information, Giordano, will show you everything about the Cyclades islands. Now, after I have examined it in parts for a long time, I wish to send you this second, more wordy description, so that, when you are at leisure, you may often raise your spirits by turning to this book.[2]]

> //38v// Isidore:[3] Cyprus took its name from the city of Cyprus, which is in it. It is in the Carpathian Sea, near the south and is holy to Venus of Paphos. It is famous for its wealth and especially for copper, for there was the first discovery and use of the metal.
>
> Luciflorus: The fate of the Islands was sealed,[4] and so Cyprus too was taken without any fighting. Ptolemy ruled the island which was rich in ancient wealth and therefore dedicated to Venus. The fame of its riches was so great, nor was this untrue, that the people (Romans) who were accustomed to triumph over other nations and make gifts of kingdoms, ordered Publius Claudius, the tribune of the people, to confiscate the property of the king, their ally and still living. Ptolemy, on hearing this, anticipated fate by taking poison. Then Portius Cato brought the wealth of Cyprus in Liburnian galleys to the mouth of the Tiber. This action filled the treasury of the Roman people more effectively than any triumph.[5]

1. "Ensenium," apparently the origin of the error of giving this as a name for Buondelmonti.
2. Sinner, 133–34. Here ends Cristoforo Buondelmonti's *Descriptio Archipelagi,* completed in the 1420s. The following section includes maps and descriptive texts added by Henricus Germanus Martellus. The five additional islands are Cyprus, Corsica, Sardinia, Sicily and Britain. The maps are highly detailed and quite accurate for their day. Henricus has drawn them from sea charts (Britain, Sardinia), but his maps of Cyprus, Corsica and Sicily are based on other, richer sources. Corsica, for example, is represented by a map made by Giovanni de Campo Fulgaso, or his son Giano, each of whom in turn ruled Corsica for Genoa. The texts are excerpts from antique authors such as Pomponius Mela (first century), Isidore of Seville (seventh century), Lucius Annaeus Florus (second century), Pliny (first century), Justinus (third century). The sole exception is Giovanni Tortelli (1400–1466) of Florence, who composed a gazeteer, *De orthographia,* showing word derivation from Greek and Latin. His entry on Cyprus, copied here, is based on Isidore.
3. Isidore, *Etymologiae* XIV.vi.14.
4. HMG enters his text *in medias res.* Luciflorus: Lucius Annaeus Florus (fl. 2nd c.), *Epitome of Roman History* I.44, trans. E.S. Forster (Cambridge, MA: Loeb Classical Library, 1929). Based on Livy. "Islands": a reference to Balearics, whose conquest was described in the previous chapter.
5. 58 BCE. This is M. Portius Cato, the Younger. The ruler of Cyprus was the brother of the Pharoah Ptolemy XII Auletes, who ruled in Egypt. The notorious Publius Claudius Pulcher was reputed to have a personal hatred for him, which inspired this campaign.

Tortellus:[1] Cyprus is an island located in the Carpathian Sea and placed between Cilicia and Syria among other surrounding islands. Abounding in riches, it was most famous among the ancients for luxury, and because of this they say it was dedicated as holy to Venus.

Island of Cyprus.[2] [Map: North. *From the west (promontory):* S. Befamo.* *(promontory)* S. Giorgius.* Galmixa, (promontory) Kormakiti.* Limina, Lapidus River. Lapithos. Cermis. Nicosia *(large city with towers and walls)*. Almixa, Macarium, Aphrodisia, Carpasia,* Olimpus, Cape S. Andrew.* *Moving south:* Salaminia, Famagosta.* Podios River. Arsinoe Altera. Adena.* *To the west:* Saline.* Capocorisso. Quito.* Maxito.* Beritium. Limassol.* Galmie.* Episocopi.* Cavo Blanco.* Paphus Nova. Baffa.* Paphus. Trapano.* Drepanum Promontory. Athamos, Arsinoe, Acamos Promontory. *In the center:* Mt. Olimpus, Mt. Holy Cross. *Islands:* Carpasie *(NW)*. Kleides *(E)*.]

//39r// In the Ligurian Sea, more specifically the Tuscan Sea, is the island of Corsica, which the Greeks called Cirnos. Its length from north to south is 150 miles and 50 miles wide for the most part. In circumference it is 325 miles. It is 62 miles from the shoals of Volateranis. It has 32 cities and the Marian colony founded by Marius, and the Alerian [colony] founded by the dictator Sulla. Nearer is Oglosa and within that is Planaria, 60 miles from Corsica, called so because it appears level with the sea and so is dangerous to ships. Urgo, which is larger, and Capraria, which the Greeks called Aegilion, and also Igilio and Diannio, which is Artemisia, are both opposite the coast at Cosano, and Barpana, Menaria, Columbaria, Venaria, Elba with its iron mines, an island 100 miles around and 10 miles from Populonium, called by the Greeks Etalia. The distance between Elba and Planasia is 28 miles. From these beyond the mouth of the Tiber near Antianum is Astura, then Palmaria, Sinonia and opposite to Formiae and the Ponza islands. In the Gulf of Pozzuoli are Pandetoria, Procida, called not after Aeneas's nurse but because it was formed from soil deposited by the current from the Aenaria. Aenaria was named from having given anchorage to the fleet of Aeneas, but it was called Inarime[3] in Greek by Homer, and Pythicusa, named not from a multitude of monkeys, as some thought, but from its pottery factories. Between Posilippo and Naples is Megaria; then 8 miles from Sorrento, Capri known for the noble works of Emperor Tiberius, which is 40 miles in circumference. Leucothea, beyond which, touching the sea of the Africans, is Sardinia, less than 8 miles from the end of Corsica, the distance made more narrow by the small islands

1. Giovanni Tortelli, *De orthographia* (Venice: Hermanus Lichtenstein, 1484), II, "Cyprus" (no pagination).

2. The starred names appear on the sea charts of Cyprus analyzed by Tony Campbell. All are found on the coasts as the charts have no interior names. None of the places on the map are found in the text.

3. Modern Ischia.

called the Cunicularia (Rabbit Warren). In the same way are the islands of Phintonis and Fossa, from which comes the Greek name of the strait, Taphros.[1]

> Isidore says:[2] The Ligurian inhabitants of the island of Corsica took their name from the name of the founder. For a certain Corsa by name, a Ligurian woman, had a bull in her herd which she was leading by the shore, and it used to swim across. After a while it reappeared, with a plumper body, and she, desiring to know for herself where this unknown nourishment was coming from, followed the bull in a ship, leaving the others behind. From this journey, the Ligurians, realizing the fertility of the island, went there in their boats, and they named it after this woman, their leader and founder.

This island was also called Cirnos, from Cirnon a son of Hercules who lived there. Virgil mentions "the yew trees of Corsica."[3] It is divided from Sardinia by a strait of 20 miles, girded by a gulf of the Ligurian Sea, looking toward Italy. It is a narrow island with many promontories, rich in grain and a stone which the Greeks call *catochiten*.[4]

//39v// CIRNOS FORMERLY, NOW CALLED CORSICA. Length from north to south 150 miles, width 50. 325 miles in circumference. [Map: North. Full Page. *Island off northern coast:* Caprara.★ *From north down the east side:* Capo Corso.★ Sisco. Brando, Bastia. Tegoli. Belgodere. Furiani. Biguglia. Borgo. Lotriana. Porrano. Vescovada. Venzolasca. Ibigano. Lorastello. Tavagnano. Cafarroni, Lampeta. Aleria.★ Mariana. Corti. Golo River. Omessa, Ampomare(?). Anzanti. Petrellarata. Orezza. Alto River. Campoloro. Matre. Altiani. Favone. Rotumus River. Iera River. Lugo.★ S. Columbanus. Cintora.★ Borretoli. Canari. Nonza. Ferinola. Elgualdo. Tardeta. *Promontory to west:* Ostritine. Balagne. Lespilonthe. Loro. Nebio.★ P. di Nebio *(inland)*. Speloncata. Palastra. S. Antolino. *Far west:* Calvi.★ Rocruela. Belgode. Monti.★ Zinalite.★ Cirasa River. Larie.★ Sagone. Ajaccio. Lorca River. Cinarcha.★ Vazzo. Istria. *South end:* Boregin. Pitana River. Porta Polo.★ Porta Elexe.★ Monacia].[5]

1. Pliny, *Natural History* III.80–83. Note that most of these names are islands or places on the Italian coast, not on Corsica.
2. Isidore, *Etymologiae* XIV.vi.41–42.
3. Virgil, *Eclogues* IX.30, "Cyrneas taxos."
4. "An unknown stone" (Lewis & Short, *A Latin Dictionary*); Solinus, *Collectanea Rerum Memorabilium,* 3.4–5 gives a longer description, describing the stone as very sticky.
5. The only names from Pliny's text that appear on the map are Meriani and Aleria, the Roman colonies. Many of the places on Henricus's map were more important in the 15th century than at present. For example Nonza, now a town of 137 inhabitants, was once a Catalan stronghold, whose tower still stands. The charts have 13-18 place names for Corsica, while Henricus's map has 78. Not all places can be identified. For the source of this map, see introduction, p. 8. Sea charts: G. Benincasa, Milan, Biblioteca Ambrosiana, S.P. 35 (1469); P. Roselli, Minneapolis, University of Minnesota Library, Nautical Chart (1466).

//40r// Sardinia.[1] The east coast is 188 miles long, the west 175, the south 77, and the north 122. Its circumference is 565 miles; and at Cape Carbonara its distance from Africa is 200 miles and from Cadiz 1400. It has two islands off Cape Falcone called the Islands of Hercules, one off Sulcensi called Enosim and one off Cape Carbonara called Ficaria. Near it they say is Berelida, Calodes and the one called the Baralitta.[2] The best known peoples in Sardinia are the Ilienses, the Balari, and the Corsi, who occupy 18 towns, the Sulcitani, Valentini, Neapolitani, Vitenses, Caralitani [who have Roman citizenship] and the Norenses. One colony is called At Libiso's Tower. Sardinia itself was called Sandaliotis by Timaeus, from its likeness to the sole of a shoe, and by Myrsilus,[3] Ichnusa, from its resemblance to a footprint. Opposite to the Bay of Paestum is Leuchasia, called after the Siren buried there. Opposite Velia are Pontia and Isacia, both included under one name as the Oenotrides, in support of the idea that Italy was once possessed by the Oenotri. Opposite to Vibo are the small islands called Ithacaesiae from the Watchtower of Ulysses.

> Isidore:[4] Sardus, the son of Hercules, left Libya with a great multitude and occupied Sardinia. From him the island got its name. Here in the African Sea on the east it is the shape of a human footprint, while it projects more on the west, with almost equal sides on the south and north. From this, before the age of trade it was called Ichnos by Greek sailors. The land lies 140 miles long and 40 miles wide. Here grows neither serpent, nor wolf, but only the "solifuga," a tiny animal which is poisonous to man.[5] No poisonous thing grows here, except the herb memorialized by many writers and poets, similar to "false parsley," which contracts the mouths of men into a rictus, and one dies as if laughing.[6] Sardinia has hot springs, which bring healing to the sick, and blindness to thieves, if, having given a false oath, they touch their eyes with the water.[7]

//40v// Sardonisus, once called, now it is called Sardinia. The length of this island from the east side is 187 miles. Along the south 77, on the north 122, and the circumference of the entire island is 565. [Map: North. Full page. *From the north:* Busmar.★ P. Cervo.★ Capo Longosardo. S. Reparata.★ Olbia. *Northwest:* Island of Asinara]. Capo Falcone. Coro. Rossa.★ Palau. Capo Coda Cavalli. Fortoli. Alghero. Marargio. S. Lucia.★ Capo Comino.★ Orgoner.

1. Transcription of Pliny iii.84 includes many misspellings and other errors.
2. Heras Lutra: the Baths of Hera.
3. Historian from Lesbos.
4. Isidore, *Etymologiae* xiv.vi.39.
5. *Solifuga* or *solipuga*, described by Solinus as a type of spider. Solinus, *Collectanea Rerum Memorabilium* iv.3.
6. Solinus iv.4, calls this "herba Sardonia." Writers and poets include M. Aurelius Olympias Nemesianus, *Eclogae* iv.53; and Q. Serenus Sammonicus, *Liber medicinalis* xxiii.431. It is in the crowfoot family. The rictus is the source of the expression, "sardonic grin."
7. Isidore has condensed Solinus's account (iv.6–7), which describes the testing of the thief. Solinus also says that the water will drive out the venom of the solifuga's bite.

Bossa. *Island:* Mal di Ventre.* Saline.* Capo S. Martiri.* Oristano. Ogliastra.* Mussolinia.* Alba Cassara. Argentera.* S. Theseus. Tavolar.* Marsinam. Cagliari. Carbonara.* *Islands to southwest:* Sossa, Anadiol?, Forro.[1]]

//41r// Sicily. They say that Sicily was once joined to Italy by narrow straits and was torn away from the larger body by the violence of the Upper Sea,[2] which is carried there by the entire force of its waters.[3] The soil itself is light and frangible, and so perforated with caverns and grottos, that the whole land lies open to blasts of the winds. Not only that but the composition of the soil is such that it is open to fires thus generated and nourished. To be sure, there is said to be an interior layer of sulphur and bitumen, which is why, that when air contends with fire in the subterranean region, the earth frequently and in many places bursts forth, now with flames, now vapor, now smoke. Hence it is that the fire of Mt. Aetna has lasted through so many ages. And when an unusually strong wind passes in through the openings of the cavities, heaps of sand are cast up.

The nearest promontory of Italy is called Rhegium, or *Abrupta*[4] because in Greek, things broken off are known by that name. Nor is it strange that antiquity should have been full of fables concerning these parts, in which so many extraordinary things are found together. The sea, in the first place, is nowhere so violent, pouring in with a force not only swift but savage, terrible to those who experience it, but also to those who merely witness it from afar. So fierce is the conflict of the waves as they meet, that you may see some of them turning their backs, being submerged in the whirlpools, and sunk into the very depths, while others, as if victorious, are carried on high. Sometimes in one part you may hear the roaring of the sea as it boils up, then groaning as it sinks into the whirlpools. Nearby are the perpetual fires of Mt. Aetna and of the Aeolian Islands, where the fire burns, flying on the waves. Nor indeed could so much fire have endured in such narrow bounds for so many ages unless it were supported by nourishment from the water. Hence fables produced Scylla and Charybdis; hearing barking noises, they believed to see the form of a monster, as the sailors, terrified by the great whirlpools of the sea, thought that the waves of the sea which swallowed everything up were barking. The same cause makes the fires of Mt. Aetna perpetual, for the collision of the waters forces into the

1. There is almost no connection between text and map. Those marked with * appear on contemporary sea charts: Paris, BNF, Cartes et Plans, Ré. Ge AA 566, Mecia de Viladestes (1413); Milan, Biblioteca Ambrosiana, S. P. 35, G. Benincasa (1469), reproduced in Pujades. Unlike Corsica, with its many names, Henricus's map of Sardinia is more like the charts with fewer, and no internal names. 34 names on this map, 14 on the charts.
2. Tyrrhenian Sea.
3. This passage is taken from Justinus (fl. third century CE), *Epitome of the Philippic History of Pompeius Trogus* IV.1 (late first century BCE), J.C. Yardley, trans. (Atlanta, GA: Scholars Press, 1994). The Latin version can be found at www.thelatinlibrary.com /justin. (Accessed September 2017.)
4. Modern: Abruzzi.

depths a portion of air and then keeps it confined till, being diffused through the pores of the earth, it kindles the matter which nourishes the fire. In addition the nearness itself of Italy and Sicily, with the heights of their respective promontories, which are so similar, gave as much terror to the ancients as it does to us today, believing that entire ships were intercepted and destroyed by the promontories closing together and opening.

//41v// Nor was this invented by the ancients to make a pleasing story, but came from the fear and wonder of those passing by. Such is the appearance of these coasts to those looking at them from a distance that you would take the gulf as a bay in the sea, not a strait, and, as you come nearer, you would think that the promontories, which were before united, now have separated.

The name of Sicily was at first Trinacria. Later it was called Sicania. From the beginning it was the homeland of the Cyclopes and when they were gone, Aeolis[1] took over the governance of the island. Later the cities fell one by one to the attack of tyrants, of whom no land had more ferocious.

> Isidore:[2] Sicily was named from the king Sicanus, then from Siculus, the brother of Italus. Sicily first was called Trinacria on account of its three points or promontories: Pelorum, Pachinum, and Lilybeum.[3] For *trinacria* in Greek is triangular in Latin, as if divided into three parts.

//41v – 42r// Sicily. [Map: North. Across two folios.[4] *West side (fol. 41v). Islands:* Marettimo.* Favignano.* Egadi. *North coastal cities from west (left):* Cape Galli.* Marsala.* S. Giorgius, Palermo.* Trapani, Batis River.* Scodero. *East side (fol. 42r)*: Castellammare. Solunto.* Himera River. Tusa. Termine.* Monalus River. Cefalu.* Cicla River. Petra de Roma. Caroma. Timetus River. Capo D'Orlando.* Patti.* Elicon River. Ulifera. Milazzo. Marti, Messina.* Punto Faro. *Interior from west (left):* Monreale. Pulici. Corleone. Castelbuono. Castel Vetrano. Petralia Soprano. Colata Voltore. Castoiami. Chieza. Calavenerta. Caltagirone. Nicosia. Petralia Lasonurana *(repeat).* Minio. Aterno. Randazzo. Mt. Gibel. Nicolosi. *Fiery sign for Mt. Aetna but no name.* Monti Peloritani. Palagonia. *Along south coast from west (left to right):* Mazara.* Cotriga. Sciacca. Ispa River. Cavo Bianco.* Talicata. Hymer River. Butera.* Gela.*[5] Ragusa.* Isporus River. Isoiciri? Capo Passeri.* *East coast (right):* Capo Sant'Alessio. Scaletta Zanclea. Taormina. Jati. Lamota. Catania.* Parenno. Pantagia River. S. Maria. Labesca. Lentini.* Augusto.* Siracusa.* Anapo River. Potentia. Ortus River. *Islands to*

1. Justin: Cocalus, traditionally king of the Sicanians in the time of Daedalus.
2. Isidore, *Etymologiae* XIV.vi.32.
3. These are now Pelorum or Punta Faro (NE), Pacino (SE) and Lilybeum or Cape Boeo (W).
4. Starred places are found on contemporary sea charts, such as London, British Library, MS Add. 18454 (G. Benincasa, 1463); Pujades A 33. There are 89 names on Henricus's map. The sea chart has 48 names, all islands or coastal cities, some of which are not on Henricus's map.
5. Was Terranova. Restored to its ancient name in 1927.

north: Alicudi. Filicudi.* Saline.* Lipari.* Vulcano.* Stromboli.* *Island to south:* Pantelleria.* *Northeast:* Charbydis. Scylla. Italia, Reggio.]

//42v// Britain is an island of the Ocean, separated by the Ocean, which flows between it and the rest of the world. It is called by the name of one of its tribes. It is located opposite part of Gaul and looks toward Hispania. It is 4,875 miles in circumference. There are many large rivers in it, hot springs, a large and varied supply of metals, and many jet stones and pearls.[1]

> Pomponius Mela:[2] As to what sort of a place Britain is and what kind of people it produces, now more accurate information can be stated. The reason is that — behold — the greatest of princes (Claudius)[3] is opening this long closed place and as conqueror of peoples unknown and unconquered before, he is about to declare a triumph. He bears the evidence of the spoils of what he has accomplished in battle.
>
> Moreover, just as we have thought until now, Britain projects between the north and west in a wide angle and looks toward the mouths of the Rhine. It then draws its sides back at an oblique angle, facing Gaul on one side and Germany on the other with a continuous line of straight shore on its rear side. Again it wedges itself into different angles, being triangular, very much like Great Sicily. A huge plain, it is fertile in those things which feed sheep more generously than men.
>
> It bears groves, meadows and very great rivers, flowing with alternate currents sometimes toward the sea and sometimes back again, some of these producing gems and pearls. It supports kings and their subjects, but all are uncivilized, and the farther they are from the sea, the more ignorant they are of any other kind of wealth than cattle and land, in which they are rich. The skin of their bodies are dyed with woad,[4] whether for decoration or for some other reason.
>
> They foment wars and causes of wars frequently among themselves. They fight, either due to a desire for empire or a wish to expand that which they already possess. They make war not only on horseback and on foot, but they also employ two-horse chariots and carts they call covini, armed in the Gallic fashion with their axles equipped with scythes.[5]

1. Isidore, *Etynologiae* xiv.6.2.
2. Pomponius Mela, *De Chorographia Libri Tres* iii.49–52.
3. Claudius (r.41–54) invaded Britain in 43 ce and celebrated his triumph in 44. For the debate of the identity of the emperor, see Piergiorgio Perroni, "Introduction," *Pomponii Melae, De Chorographia* (Rome: Edizioni di Storia e Letteratura, 1984), 16–22.
4. Reading *vitro* for *ultra* Mela.
5. Translation somewhat altered from F. E. Romer, *Pomponius Mela: Description of the World* (Ann Arbor: University of Michigan Press, 1998), 115–16.

//43r// Island of England. Kingdom of Scotland. This is the true proportion of this island. [Map: North. Full page.[1] *From north down eastern side:* Dundee.* Inverness. Roxburgh.* S. Laguensis, Latina.* Firth.* Cape Rodi. Tenedam. Bamborg. Berwick.* Sutina.* Scarborough.* Venbro.* Hull. Humber.* Nisa.* S. Betorf.* Ravenzor.* Ely.* Lynn.* Brancaster.* Cape Tardo. Astaçer. Godaner.* Caister.* Yarmouth.* Tarquelay. Ardorda.* Orois. Orford. Orolein.* London.* Thames River. Dover.* *(SE point).* Romney.* Winchelsea.* Seaford. Saron. Civibat.* Portsmouth.* Southampton.* Poole.* S. Anterino.* Cape Portland.* Ringumua. Dartmouth.* Godester.* Plymouth.* Godeman. Falmouth.* Lizard Point.* Mousehole.* *Down west side:* Perth: city of S. John.[2] Oercons. S. Andrews. Scoruçeri. Caribun. Cape Basso. Dumfries. Castrum Verluhic. Newcastle. Chester. Breus. Tore Incanta *(enchanted tower).* North Wales.* Urgales.* Barlles, Milford Haven.* Cardigan[?] Lamaset.* Porvasi. S. Nicolaus.* Bristol.* S. Helena. Patristo. *Island on northwest:* Icuç[3] Insula. *Island to south:* Wight.*]

> //43v// Beyond Britain is Hibernia. It is almost equal in area but it is oblong with extended coastlines. Its skies are hostile to ripening seeds, but the island is so rich with grass, not only abundant but sweet, that the flocks graze only a small part of each day. Unless they are kept out of the pasture, they will burst from feeding too long. Its cultivators are undisciplined and ignorant of all the virtues more than other nations, although they are somewhat acquainted with piety.[4]
>
> Scotia likewise and Hibernia are near the island of Britain, smaller in area but more fertile in their situation. (Hibernia) extends from south to north, the first parts of which reach to the Hiberian and Cantabrian Ocean, hence it is called Hibernia. Scotland also gets its name from the Scottish people by whom it is inhabited. Here there are no snakes, birds are rare, and there are no bees. If dust or pebbles from here are carried away and one scatters them among the beehives, the bees will desert their honeycombs in a swarm.[5]

1. If the same or a similar name appears on the Benincasa sea chart of 1467 (London, British Library, MS Add. 11547; Pujades A 38) it is starred. The Italianized version of British names, including the use of the Venetian cedilla, show the origins of this map in the Italian sea chart. Total: 80 names (41 on sea chart).
2. Both St. Andrews and Perth are situated on the west rather than the east side of Scotland on the map.
3. Uist?
4. Pomponius Mela III.53. My translation of the last sentence differs from Romer, who reads *gnari* as *ignari.*
5. Isidore, *Etymologiae* XIV.6.6. There is no map for Ireland in this manuscript, though there is one in the London MS

BIBLIOGRAPHY

MANUSCRIPTS

Ann Arbor, Michigan. University of Michigan Library. MS 162. Bondelmonti. *De Insulis Cycladis.*

Baltimore, Maryland. Walters Art Gallery. MS 309. *Liber insularum arcipelagi.*

Chantilly, France. Musée Condé, MS 698. Henricus Martellus Germanus, *Insularium Illustratum.*

Florence, Italy. Biblioteca Medicaea Laurenziana, MS XXIX.25. Henricus Martellus Germanus. *Insularium Illustratum.* At: http://teca.bmlonline.it/TecaRicerca/index.jsp. SearchPlut.29.25.

Florence, Italy. Biblioteca Nazionale Centrale, MS Magliabechiano XIII.16. C. Ptolomei *Cosmographia.*

Greenwich, England. National Maritime Museum, Caird Library. MS P.13. Cristoforo Buondelmonti. *Liber Insularum.* At: Collections.rmg.co.uk/collections/objects/541531. html. Images only.

—. MS P.20. Cristoforo Buondelmonti. *Liber Insularum.*

Holkham Hall, Norfolk. Library of the Earl of Leicester. MS 1429. Cristoforo Buondelmonti, *Liber Insularum Archipelagi.*

Leiden, The Netherlands. University Library. MS Voss. lat. F.23. Henricus Martellus Germanus, *Insularium Illustratum.*

London, England. The British Library. MS Add 15760. *Insularium Illustratum Henrici Martelli Germani.*

—. MS Arundel 93. Buondelmonti, fols. 129r.-159v.

—. MS Cotton Titus B.VIII. Buondelmonti, fols. 245-248v. In English.

—. MS Cotton Vespasian A.XIII. Buondelmonti, *Liber Insularum.*

—. Sloane MS 3843. Bondelmonti, *Liber Insularum Archipelagi.*

Minneapolis, Minnesota. University of Minnesota Library. James Ford Bell Collection. MS 1475_fMa. Henricus Martellus Germanus. *Liber Insularum of Christoforo Buondelmonti.*

—. Zuane Pizzigano, 1424. Nautical Chart.

—. Petrus Rosselli, 1466. Nautical Chart (Majorca).

—. Albino de Canepa, 1489. Nautical Chart (Venice).

New Haven, CT. Yale University. Planisphere of Henricus Martellus Germanus.

—. Anon. Sea chart, 1425. Yale *49 cea/1425.

—. Franciscus Beccharius, 1403. MS 1980.158.

—. Jorge de Aguiar, sea chart, 1492. *30 cea/1492.

Paris, France. Bibliothèque Nationale de France, MS lat, 4824. Christoforus de Buondelmontibus, *Liber Insularum Arcipelagi*. At: http://gallica.bnf.fr/ark:/12148/btv1b90725 50g. r=Res+Ge+FF.

Primary Sources

Berchorius, Petrus. *De formis figurisque deorum*. J. Engels, ed. Utrecht: Rijksuniversiteit, 1960.

Bersuire, Pierre (Berchorius, Petrus). "*Reductorium Morale,* Book XIV." James Joseph Foster, ed. Durham, NC: Duke University, M.A. Thesis, 1967.

Boccaccio, Giovanni. *Genealogie deorum gentilium libri*. Vincenzo Romano, ed. 2 vols. Bari: Laterza, 1951.

Bordone, Benedetto. *Libro di Benedetto Bordone*. Giovanni Battista de Cesare, ed. Facsimile of 1528 edition. Rome: Bulzone, 1988.

Buondelmonti, Cristoforo. *Description de les îles de l'Archipel grecque par Christophe Buondelmonti*. Émile Legrand, ed. Paris, 1897. Reprint, Amsterdam: Philo Press, 1974.

—. *Descriptio Insule Crete et Liber Insularum, Cap. XI: Creta*. Marie-Anne von Spitael, ed. Heraklion: Syllogos politistikes anaptyxeos Herakleiou, 1981.

—. *Liber Insularum Archipelagi: Universitäts- und Landesbiliothek Düsseldorf MS. G. 13, Faksimile*. Imgard Siebert, Max Plassmann, Arne Effenberger, Fabian Rijkers, ed. and trans. 2 vols. Wiesbaden: Reichert, 2005.

Clavijo, Ruy Gonzalez de. *Embajada a Tamorlán*. Versión en español actual de Francisco López Estrada. Madrid: Editorial Castalia, 2004.

Florus, Lucius Annaeus. *Epitome of Roman History*. Edward S. Forster, trans. Cambridge, MA: Loeb Classical Library, 1984.

Fulgentius, Fabius Planciades. *The Mythologies*. Leslie G. Whitbread, ed. and trans. Columbus: Ohio State University Press, 1971.

Isidore. *Etymologiarum sive Originum: Libri XX*. W. M. Lindsay, ed. 2 vols. Oxford: Clarendon Press, 1911.

Justin. *Epitome of the Philippic History of Pompeius Trogus*. J.C. Yardley, trans. Atlanta, GA: Scholars Press, 1994. Latin version at: www.thelatinlibrary.com/justin.

Livy. *Ab Urbe Condita*. B.O. Foster, trans. Loeb Classical Library. 14 vols. Cambridge, MA: Harvard University Press, 1988.

Majeska, George P. *Russian Travelers to Constantinople in the Fourteenth and Fifteenth Centuries*. Washington, DC: Dumbarton Oaks, 1984.

Ovid. *Metamorposes*. Frank Justus Miller and G.P. Goold, trans. Cambridge, MA: Loeb Classical Library, 1977.

Pliny. *Natural History*. H. Rackham, trans. Loeb Classical Library. Cambridge, MA: Harvard University Press, 1942.

Pomponius Mela. *De Chorographia: Libri Tres.* Piergiorgio Parroni, ed. Rome: Storia e Letteratura, 1984.

Pomponius Mela. *Description of the World.* F.E. Romer, trans. Ann Arbor: University of Michigan Press, 1998.

Porcacchi, Thomaso. *L'isole più famose del mondo.* Venice: G. Angelieri, 1590.

Reis, Piri. *Kitab-I Bahriye.* 4 vols. Istanbul: The Historical Research Foundation, 1988.

Silvestri, Domenico. *De insulis et proprietatibus earum.* José Manuel Montsdeoca Medina, trans. and ed. as *Los isolarios de la época del humanismo.* Santa Cruz de Tenerife: Universidad de la Laguna, 2004. ftp://tesis.bbtk.ull.es/ccssyhum/cs103.pdf.

Sinner, G.R.L. *Christoph. Bondelmontii, Florentinii, Librum Insularum Archipelagi.* Leipzig and Berlin: G. Reimer, 1824.

Solinus, C. Julius. *Collectanea Rerum Memorabilium.* Theodor Mommsen, ed. Berlin: Frideric Nicolas, 1864.

Tafur, Pero. *Travels and Adventures,* 1435–1439. Malcolm Letts, ed. and trans. London: George Routledge & Sons, 1926.

Tortelli, Giovanni. *Commentariorum grammaticorum de orthographia dictionum e graecis tractarum prooemium incipit ac sanctissimum patrem Nicolaum Quintum pontificem Maximum.* Venice: Hermanus Lichenstein of Cologne, 1484.

Vergil. *Eclogues, Georgics, Aeneid.* H. Rushton Faircloth, trans. Loeb Classical Library. 2 vols. Cambridge, MA: Harvard University Press, 1974.

Secondary Works

Allen, W. Sidney. "Kalóyeros: An Atlantis in Microcosm?" *Imago Mundi* 29 (1977): 54–71.

Almagià, Roberto. "I mappamondi di Enrico Martello e alcuni concetti geografici di Cristoforo Colombo." *Bibliofilia* 42 (1940): 288–311.

—. *Planisferi, carte nautiche e affini dal secoli XIV al XVII esistenti nella Biblioteca Apostolica Vaticana. Monumenta cartografica Vaticana* I. Vatican City: Biblioteca Apostolica Vaticana, 1944.

Ascari, M.C. "La Cartografia nautica della Corsica." *Archivio Storico di Corsica* 16.2. (1940): 121–46; 17.2 (1941): 1–31.

Banfi, Florio. "Two Italian Maps of the Balkan Peninsula." *Imago Mundi* 11 (1954): 17–34.

Barsanti, C. "Costantinopoli e l'Egeo nei primi decenni del XV secolo: La testimonianza di Cristoforo Buondelmonti." *Rivista dell'Istituto Nazionale d'Archeologia e Storia dell'Arte,* Ser. 3.56 (2001): 83–254.

Bessi, Benedetta. "Greek Antiquities in Florentine Humanism." *The Historical Review* 9 (2012): 63–76.

Böninger, Lorenz. *Die Deutsche Einwandering nach Florenz im Spätmittelalter.* Leiden: Brill, 2006.

Bouloux, Nathalie. "L'Insularium Illustratum d'Henricus Martellus." *The Historical Review* 9 (2012): 77–94.

Bradford, Ernle. *The Companion Guide to the Greek Islands.* London: Collins, 1975.

Campbell, Tony. "Cyprus and the Medieval Portolan Charts." Kyriakai Spoudai 48 (1986): 47–66.

Campbell, Tony. *The Earliest Printed Maps,* 1472–1500. London: The British Library, 1987.

Campana, A. "Da Codici del Buondelmonti." *Silloge Bizantina in onore di Silvio Giuseppe Mercati, Studi Bizantini e Neoellenici* IX. Rome: Associazione Nazionale per gli Studi Bizantini, 1957, 30–52.

Caraci, Ilana C. "The Cartographic Works of Henricus Martellus and the 'Pre-discovery' of America." *Rivista Geografica italiana* 83 (1976): 271–80.

Cassi, Laura, and Adele Dei "Le Esplorazioni Vicine: Geografia e Letteratura negli Isolari." *Rivista Geographia Italiana* 100 (1993): 205–69.

Cronier, Marie, and Patrick Gautier-Dalché. "A Map of Cyprus in Two Fourteeenth-Century Byzantine Manuscripts." *Imago Mundi* 69.2 (2017): 176–87.

Dalrymple, William. *From the Holy Mountain: A Journey Among Christians of the Middle East.* New York: Henry Holt 1998.

Della Dora, Veronica. *Imagining Mount Athos: Visions of a Holy Place from Homer to World War II.* Charlottesville: University of Virginia Press, 2011.

—. "Mapping a Holy Quasi-Island: Mount Athos in Early Renaissance *Isolarii.*" *Imago Mundi* 60.2 (2008): 139–65.

De la Mare, Albinia. "A List of Books from the Florentine Braccio Martelli." In *Tributes to Jonathan J.A. Alexander: The Making and Meaning of Medieval and Renaissance Manuscripts.* Susan L'Engle and G.B. Guest, ed. London: Harvey Miller, 2006, 33–68.

Durrell, Lawrence. *The Greek Islands.* NY: Viking, 1978.

—. *Reflections on a Marine Venus.* London: Faber & Faber, 1969.

Gautier Dalché, Patrick. *La Géographie de Ptolémée en Occident (IVe- XVIe Siècle).* Turnhout: Brepols, 2009.

Gentile, Sebastiano, ed. *Firenze e la scoperta dell'America.* Florence: Leo Olschki, 1992.

Gerola, Berengario. "Le Etimologie dei nomi di luogo in Cristoforo Buondelmonti." *Atti dei Reale Istituto Veneto di Scienze, Lettere ed Arti* 92 (1932-33): 1129–74.

Gerola, Giuseppe. "Le vedute di Costantinopoli di Cristoforo Buondelmonti." *Studi Bizantini e neoellenici* 3 (1931): 249–79.

Graves, Robert. *The Greek Myths.* 2 vols. New York: George Braziller, 1957.

Grimal, Pierre. *The Dictionary of Classical* Mythology. A.R. Maxwell-Hyslop, trans. Oxford: Blackwell, 1985.

Hage, Rushika F. "The Island Book of Henricus Martellus." *The Portolan* 56 (Spring 2003): 7–23.

Harvey, P.D.A. "Local and Regional Cartography in Medieval Europe." *History of Cartography* 1. David Woodward and J. B. Harley, eds. Chicago: University Press, 1987, 482–84.

Harvey, P.D.A. *Medieval Maps*. London: British Library, 1991.

Inalcik, Halil. *The Survey of Istanbul, 1455: The Text, English Translation, Analysis of the Text, Documents*. Istanbul: Topkapi, 2012.

Lawrence, D.H. *Sea and Sardinia*. Mara Kalnins, ed. Cambridge: University Press, 1997.

Leduc, François-Xavier, "Les insulaires (isolarii): Les îles décrites et illustrées." *Couleurs de la Terre*, ed. Monique Pelletier. Paris: Seuil/BNF, 1998, 56–61.

Leroi, Armand Marie. *The Lagoon: How Aristotle Invented Science*. New York: Viking, 2014.

Longrigg, James. *Greek Medicine: From the Heroic to the Hellenistic Age. A Source Book*. London: Duckworth, 1998.

Luttrell, Anthony. "The Later History of the Maussolleion and its Utilization in the Hospitaller Castle at Bodrun," *Jutland Archaeological Society Publications* 15.2 (1986): 114–214.

Luzzati Laganà, Francesca. "Sur les mers grecques: un voyageur florentin du XVe siécle, Cristoforo Buondelmonti." *Médiévales* 12 (1987): 67–77.

Manners, Ian R. "Constructing the Image of a City: The Representation of Constantinople in Christopher Bondelmonti's *Liber Insularum Archipelagi*." *Annals of American Geographers* 87.1 (1997): 72–102.

McGilchrist, Nigel. *Blue Guide: Greece, The Aegean Islands*. London: Somerset Books, 2010.

Meyier, K.A. de. *Codices Vossiani Latini*. Leiden: University of Leiden, 1973, 1:47–49.

—. "La Tradition Manuscrit du Liber Archipelagi Insularum á l Bibliothèque Nationale de Paris." *Scriptorium* 29 (1975): 69–76.

—. "Un Manuscrit du 'Liber Insularum Archipelagi' de Christophe Buondelmonti a Leyde." *Scriptorium* 25 (1971): 300–303.

Milanese, Marica. "Il *De insulis et earum proprietatibus* di Domenico Silvestri (1385-1406)." *Geographia Antiqua* 2 (1993): 133–46.

Miller, William. *The Latins in the Levant: A History of Frankish Greece (1204-1566)*. Cambridge: Speculum Historiale, 1908; repr. 1964.

Millingen, Alexander van. *Byzantine Churches of Constantinople*. London: Macmillan, 1912. Reprint, London: Variorum, 1974.

Nicholson, Helen. *The Knights Hospitaller*. Woodbridge: Boydell, 2001.

Norwich, John Julius. *Mt. Athos*. New York: Harper, 1966.

Oliver, Revilo P. "Giovanni Tortelli." *Studies Presented to David Moore Robinson*. G.E. Mylonas, ed. St. Louis, MO: Washington University Press, 1953, 2:1257–71.

Pujades i Bataller, Ramon J. *Les cartes portolanes: la representació medieval d'una mar solcada.* Barcelona: Institut Cartogràfic de Catalunya, 2007.

Ragone, Giuseppe. "Il *Liber Insularum Archipelagi* di Christoforo dei Buondelmonti: Filologia del Testo, Filologia dell'Immagine." *Humanisme et Culture Géographique à l'Époque du Concile de Constance autour de Guillaume Fillastre.* Didier Marcotte, ed. Turnhout, Belgium: Brepols, 2002, 177–217.

Ridyard, Susan J., ed. *The Medieval Crusade.* Woodbridge, Suffolk: Boydell, 2004.

Riley-Smith, Jonathan. "The Structures of the Orders of the Temple and the Hospital in c. 1291." In Ridyard, 125–44.

Ross, Alan. *The Bandit of the Billiard Table: A Journey Through Sardinia.* London: Collins Harvill, 1989.

Rossiter, Stuart. *Blue Guide Greece.* 4th ed. London: Ernest Benn, 1981.

Schiro, Giuseppe. *Chronica Toccorum Cephalleniensium (Cronaca de Tocco di Cefalonia).* Rome: Accademia de Lincei, 1975.

Thomov, Thomas. "New Information about Christoforo Buondelmonti's Drawings of Constantinople." *Byzantion* 66 (1996): 431–53.

Tolias, George. "*Isolarii:* Fifteenth to Seventeenth Century" *History of Cartography* 3. David Woodward, ed. Chicago: University of Chicago Press, 2007, 263–84.

Turner, Hilary Louise. "Chios and Christopher Buondelmonti's Liber Insularum." *Deltion* 30 (1987): 47–72.

—. "Christopher Buondelmonti and the Isolario." *Terrae Incognitae* 19 (1987): 11–28.

—. "Christopher Buondelmonti." *Géographie du Monde au Moyen Âge et á la Renaissance.* Monique Pelletier, ed. Paris: Éditions du Comité des Travaux Historiques et Scientifiques, 1989, 207–16.

Urness, Carol. *Portolan Charts.* Minneapolis, MN: James Ford Bell Library, 1999.

Vagnon, Emmanuelle. *Cartographie et Représentations de l'Orient Méditerreanéen en Occident (du Milieu du XIIIe à la fin du XVe siècle).* Turnhout, Belgium: Brepols, 2013.

Van Duzer, Chet. *The Yale Martellus Map (1491): Multispectral Imaging, Sources and Influence.* New York: Springer, forthcoming.

Weiss, Robert. "Cristoforo Buondelmonti." *Dizionario Biografico degli Italiani* 15 (1960): 198–200.

—. "Un umanista antiquario: Cristoforo Buondelmonti." *Lettere Italiane* 16.2 (April-June 1964): 105–16.

Whitbread, Leslie. *Fulgentius, the Mythographer.* Columbus: Ohio State University Press, 1971.

INDEX

This index is keyed to the pages of the English translation. These page references are set in Roman type. *References to the original manuscript folios — either recto* (**r**) *or verso* (**v**) *— are set in* **boldface**. *The places Buondelmonti visited had a long history both before and after him. Many of the place names in this index therefore have many variations from ancient Greek, Byzantine, ancient and medieval Latin, Renaissance Italian and modern usage. These are indicated either in parentheses or by cross-references ("See" or "See also"). Modern names, if different from the text, are indicated by* SMALL CAPS. *Places unidentified are marked with a star (*★*). We have also distinguished among the many references to saints and their place names: "Saint" refers to the historical persons, "St." to a church named after them, and "S." to a place name.*

A

X

Y

Z

Production of this Book Was Completed on
November 30, 2017 at Italica Press
New York, New York. It Was Set in
Bembo, Bembo Expert &
Columbus Ornaments.

CPSIA information can be obtained
at www.ICGtesting.com
Printed in the USA
LVHW01*0202070318
568929LV00016B/42/P